John Wilson

Select Ayres And Dialogues For One, Two, And Three Voyces

To The Theorbo-Lute Or Basse-Viol.

John Wilson

Select Ayres And Dialogues For One, Two, And Three Yoyces
To The Theorbo-Lute Or Basse-Viol.

ISBN/EAN: 9783744651462

Printed in Europe, USA, Canada, Australia, Japan

Cover: Foto ©Thomas Meinert / pixelio.de

More available books at **www.hansebooks.com**

SELECT
AYRES
AND
DIALOGUES

For One, Two, and Three Voyces;

TO THE

THEORBO-LUTE or *BASSE-VIOL.*

Compoſed by
- *John Wilſon*
- *Charles Colman* } Doctors in Muſick.
- *Henry Lawes*
- *William Lawes*
- *Nicholas Laneare*
- *William Webb* } Gentlemen and Servants to his late Majeſty in his Publick and Private Muſick.

And other Excellent Maſters of Muſick.

LONDON,

Printed by *W. Godbid* for *John Playford*, and are to be ſold at his Shop in the *Inner Temple*, neer the Church dore. 1 6 5 9.

GENTLEMEN,

This Book hath found such generall welcome, that the Impression is all bought off, and I am called upon for more; which hath caused me to Reprint it, but with very large Additions: I have not given you all my store, but with good Advice Selected only such Ayres and Dialogues as are known to be Excellent, as well as now most in Request; and those so familiar and easie, as are usefull to the Teacher, and commodious for the Scholar, especially such as live Remote from London. The Musick is of Three Varieties, and is therefore printed distinct: First, those for One Voyce, next for Two, and then those for Three: The whole contains One hundred twenty foure choice Songs, and all (except very few) of late Compositions, In the setting forth of which, my care, pains, and charge hath not been small, by procuring true and exact Coppies, and dayly attending the oversight of the Presse, as no prejudice might redound either to the Authors or Buyer: And herein I resolve to meet with those Mistakers, who have taken up a new (but very fond) opinion, That Musick cannot as truely be Printed as Prick'd, (and which is more ridiculous) that no Choice Ayres or Songs are permitted by Authors to come in print, though 'tis well known that the best Musicall Compositions, either of our owne or Strangers, have been and are tendered to the World by the Printers hand; To convince the former, and to testifie my Gratitude to those Excellent Masters, from whose owne hands I received most of these Compositions; doe I say thus much, that this my present Endevor and care in the true and exact publishing this Book will redound to Publick Benefit, and the Authors Reputation, as well as my owne Advantage; which may give yet further Incouragement to

A Faithfull Servant to all Lovers of Musick;

JOHN PLAYFORD.

An Alphabetical Table of the Ayres and Dialogues in this Book.

A
About the sweet bag of a Bee   3
As I walkt forth one Summers day   13
Amor merere ched'amor merere   15
Amidst the Mirtles as I walkt   19
A Willow Garland thou didst send   19
A Lover once I did espy   25
Ambitious Love farewell   32
Ask me why I send you here   50

B
Bring back my Comfort   6
Bid me but live, and I will live   30
Bright Aurelia I do owe   30
By all the Glories willingly I go   45
Beauty and Love once fell at odds   55
Brightest, since your pittying eye   64

C
Come Lovers all to me   2
Catch me a Star that's falling   11
Come noble Nymphs do not hide   14
Come from the Dungeon to the Throne   26
Come my Sweet while every strain   26
Come Cloris leave thy wandring   31
Change Platonicks, change for shame   34
Come Adonis come away   37
Come lovely Phillis since it thy will is   51
Cloris farewell I now must go   51
Cloris false love made Clora weep   52
Come O come, I brook no stay   55
Conbelse gella de cretezza   67

D
Dear leave thy home and come   23
Do'st see how unregarded now   63

F
Fuggi Fuggi da lieti amanti   15
Fain would I Cloris ere I dy   39
Fain would I Cloris whom my heart   47
Faith be no longer coy   56
From hunger and cold   64

G
Go and bestride the southern wind   44
Go little winged Archer and convey   50

H
He that will love must be my Scholar   8
He that loves a Rosie cheek   23
How long shall I a Martyr be   40

How cool and temp'rate am I grown   42
How am I chang'd from what I was   58
How happy ar't thou and I   58

I
In vain fair Cloris you design   9
If the quick spirit of your eye   18
I love thee for thy ficklenesse   22
I do confesse thou art smooth and fair   24
I prethee turn that face away   29
I can love for an houre   37
I am confirm'd a woman can   38
In faith I cannot keep my sheep   42
I wish no more thou shouldst love me   48
I love a Lass but cannot show it   55
I will not trust thy tempting Graces   56

L
Like Hermit poore in pensive place   1
Love I must tell thee Ile no longer   12
Ladies you that seem so nice and cold   20
Let longing Lovers sit and pine   21
Ladies fly from Loves smooth Tales   31
Lay that sullen Garland by thee   33
Little love serves my turn   35
Let not thy Beuty make thee proud   54

M
Mistake me not, I am as cold as hot   10
Mans life is but vain, for 'tis   62

N
No more blind Boy, for see my heart   7
No, no, Fair Heretick   46
No, no, I never was in love   65

O
Of thee kind Boy I ask no Red or White   43

P
Phyllis why should we delay   17

S
She that that loves me for my selfe   2
Stay, stay, O stay, that heart I vow   5
See see, how carelesse men are grown of late   36
Silly heart forbear, those are murdering eyes   57
Since love hath in thine and mine eye   59

T
Take, O take those lips away   1
'Tis not i'th power for all thy scorn   10
Thou art not fair for all thy Red   16
Take heed fair Cloris how you tame   21

Tel

An *Alphabetical Table* of the *Ayres* and *Dialogues*.

Tell me not I my time mispend	22	**W**	
To love thee without flattery	28	*Wake my* Adonis, *do not dye*	4
Tell me ye wandering Spirits of the Ayre	41	*Why dearest should you weep*	6
Tell not I dy, or that I live by thee	49	*Why should thou swear I am forsworn*	16
Tell me no more her eyes are like	57	*Whilst I listen to thy voyce* Cloris	25
Tis wine that inspires	65	*Wer't thou yet fairer then thou art*	27
V		*What means this strangeness now of late*	48
Victorious Beauty though your eys	20	*When* Cælia *I intend to flatter you*	58
Victoria, Victoria il micoræ	66		

The TABLE of the Second Part of this Book, being *Dialogues* for *Two Voyces*.

I *Prethee keep my Sheep for me*	*A Dialogue between* Phyllis *and* Clorillo *by M*.Lanear	68
Dear Sylvia *let thy* Thirsis *know*	*A Dialogue between* Sylvia *and* Thirsis	70
Did you not once Lucinda *vow*	*A Dialogue between a* Shepherd *&* Lucinda *by* D.Colman	72
Come my Daphne *come away*	*A Dialogue between* Daphne *and* Strephon	74
Forbear fond Swain I cannot love	*A Dialogue between a* Shepherd *and* Shepherdess	75
Tell me Shepherd dost thou love	*A Dialogue between a Shepherd and a Nymph*	77
Shepheard in faith I cannot stay	*A Dialogue between* Strephon *and* Phyllis	78
Vulcan, *o* Vulcan *my Love*	*A Dialogue between* Venus *and* Vulcan	79
Charon, *o Gentle* Charon	*A Dialogue between* Charon *and* Philomel	80
Thirsis *kind Swain come near*	*A Dialogue between* Thirsis *and* Damon	82

A TABLE of the GLEES and *Songs* for *Two Voyces*.

TO Bacchus *we to* Bacchus *sing*	*Fly Boys, fly Boy to the Cellars bottom*	90
Bring out the cold Chine	*See, see the Bright Light shine*	110
He that a Tinker, a Tinker will be	*Turn* Amarillis *to thy Swain*	112

Pages: 84, 86, 88

The TABLE of the Third Part of this Book, being *Songs* or *Ballads* for *Three Voyces*.

I *Wish no more thou shouldst love me*	91	*O my* Clarissa *thou cruel fair*	100
Though I am young and cannot tell	92	*Gather your Rose Buds*	101
Come Cloris *hie we to the Bowers*	93	*Fear not Dear Love that I reveal*	102
When Troy *Town for ten years*	94	*Fine young Folly though you were*	103
From the fair Lavinian *shoar*	95	*Sing fair* Clorinda *whilst you may*	104
Where the Bees suck there suck I	96	*Smiths are good fellows*	106
When love with unconfined wings	97	*Musick thou Queen of souls*	108
Do not fear to put thy feet	98	*Now we are met lets merry be*	114
In the merry Month of May	99		

ADVERTISEMENT.

Courteous Sirs,

Because I mean to deal very openly, and cover nothing (though never so small) I must beg the Buyer to take notice that the Folia from 52 to 62 are mistaken by the Printer; As for other Errata's in the Musick (whereof all Books have some) they are so very few, small and inconsiderable, that I hope I shall need onely to crave the Judicious to mend with their Pen.

A Catalogue of MUSICK Books sold by John Playford at his Shop in the Temple.

Books for Vocal MUSICK.

1. Mr. Wilby's Madrigals of 3,4,5 and 6 Voyces.
2. Orlando Gibon's 5 Parts for Viols and Voyces.
3. Dr. Champian's Ayres for 1,2, or 3 Voyces.
4. Mr. Walter Porter's first set of Ayres and Madrigals for 2, 3, 4, and 5 Voyces; with a Through Bass; for the Organ or Theorbo Lute, the Italian way: Printed 1639.
5. Mr. Walter Porter's second Set of Psalms or Anthems for two voyces to the Organ or Theorbo-Lute: Printed 1657.
6. Mr. William Child (late Organist of his Majesties Chappel at Windsor) his Psalms for three voyces, after the Italian way, to be sung to the Organ, the which are Engraven on Copper plates: Printed 1656.
7. Select Ayres and Dialogues by Dr. Wilson, Dr. Colman, Mr. Henry Lawes, and others: Reprinted with large Additions 1659.
8. Ayres and Dialogues set forth by Mr. H. Lawes, viz. his { First Book fol. Printed 1653.
Second Book fol. Printed 1655.
Third Book fol. Printed 1658. }
9. Mr. John Gamble his first and second book of Ayres and Dialogues; first printed 1657, second 1659.
10. A Book of Catches and Rounds collected and published by John Hilton 1651, and now with large additions by John Playford, newly Reprinted 1658.
11. An Introduction to the Skill of Musick, Vocall and Instrumentall, with Instructions for the Violin by J. Playford, newly Reprinted 1658.
12. The Art of Descant, or composing Musick in parts, written by Dr. Champian, and enlarged by Mr. Christopher Simpson, printed 1655.

Books for Instrumental MUSICK.

1. Mr. East Set of Fancies for Viols, containing 6 Fantasies for two Bass-Viols, 9 Fantazies for two Trebles and a Bass, and 12 Fantazies of 4 parts.
2. Court Ayres, of two parts, Bass and Treble, Viols or Violins, containing 245 Ayres, Corants and Sarabands, Composed by Dr. Coleman, Mr. William Lawes, Mr. John Jenkins, Mr. Ben. Rogers of Windsor; Mr. Christopher Sympson, and others: Printed 1656.
3. Mr. Matthew Lock his Little Consort of Three parts, Pavans, Almains, Corants and Sarabands, for Two Trebles and a Bass, for Viols or Violins: Printed 1657.
4. Musicks Recreation on the Lyra Viol, Containing 100 Lessons, viz. Preludiums, Almains, Corants, Sarabands, and several new and pleasant Tunes for the Lyra Viol, with Instructions for beginners: printed 1656.
5. A Book of New Lessons for the Cithren and Gittern, containing many new and pleasant Tunes, with plain and easie Instructions for Beginners thereon: Printed 1659.
6. The Dancing Master, containing 132 New and Choice Country Dances, Directing the Learner the manner how to understand the several Figures and Movements thereof; Also the Tunes set over each Dance, very usefull to such as Practise on the Treble Violin; In which Book is added 42 French Corants, and other Tunes to be plaid on the Treble Violin: printed 1657.

All sorts of Rul'd Paper for Musick ready Ruled, also Books of several Sizes ready bound up of very good Ruled Paper; Also very good Inke to prick Musick.

Musick Books shortly to come forth.

A most Excellent Treatise of Musick, Entituled, The Violist, or an Introduction to play Division to a Ground, Teaching all things necessary to the Knowledge of the Viol, as also the Rudiments of Composition by a Method more short and easie then hath been heretofore delivered. Written by the most Knowing Master of that Instrument, Mr. Christopher Simpson.

Also a Book for the Virginals, containing variety of new and choice Lessons, also Toys, and Jigs, Fitted for the practice of young Learners.

[1]

A Lovers Melancholy Repose.

Like Hermit poor in pensive place obscure, I mean to spend my days of endless doubt, to wail such woes as *time* cannot recure, where none but *love* shal ever find me out. And at my gates, and at my gates *despair* shal linger still, to let in *death*, to let in *death* when *love* and *fortune* wil.

Mr. *Nich. Lancare.*

A Gowne of gray my body shall attire,
My staffe of broken hope whereon I'le stay,
Of late repentance linkt with long desire,
The Couch is fram'd whereon my limbs I lay,
And at my gates, &c.

My food shall be of care and sorrow made,
My drink nought else but tears faln from mine eyes,
And for my light in this obscure shade,
The flame may serve, wh ch from my heart arise,
And at my gates,

Loves ingratitude.

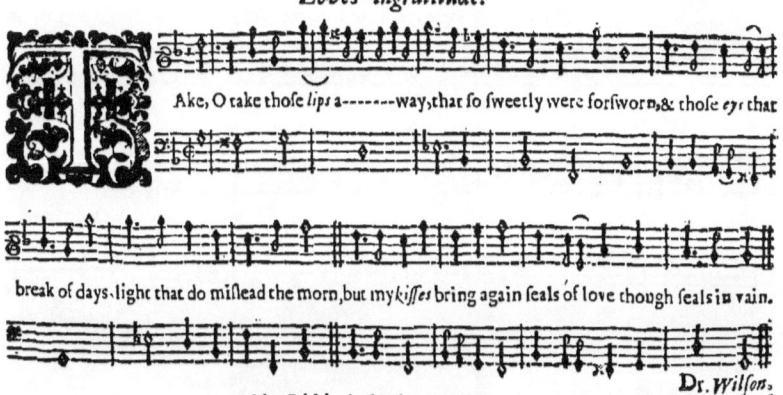

Take, O take those *lips* a-------way, that so sweetly were forsworn, & those *eys* that break of days, light that do mislead the morn, but my *kisses* bring again seals of love though seals in vain.

Dr. *Wilson.*

Hide, O hide those Hils of Snow
That thy frozen Blossome bears;
On whose tops the Pinks that grow,
Are yet of those that April wears:
But first set my poor heart free,
Bound in those Icy Chaines by thee.

B

Cupid's weak Artillery.

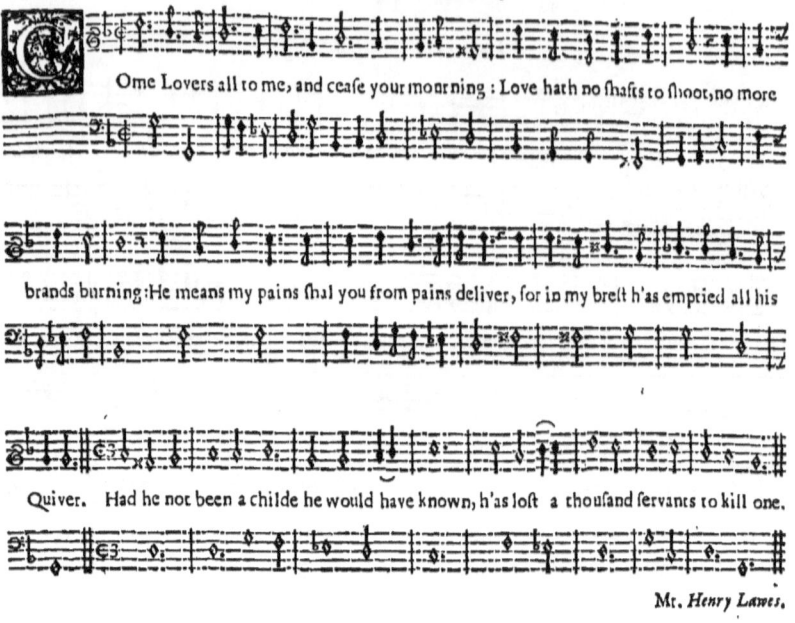

Come Lovers all to me, and cease your mourning: Love hath no shafts to shoot, no more brands burning: He means my pains shal you from pains deliver, for in my brest h'as emptied all his Quiver. Had he not been a childe he would have known, h'as lost a thousand servants to kill one.

Mr. *Henry Lawes.*

Love preferring Virtue above Wealth.

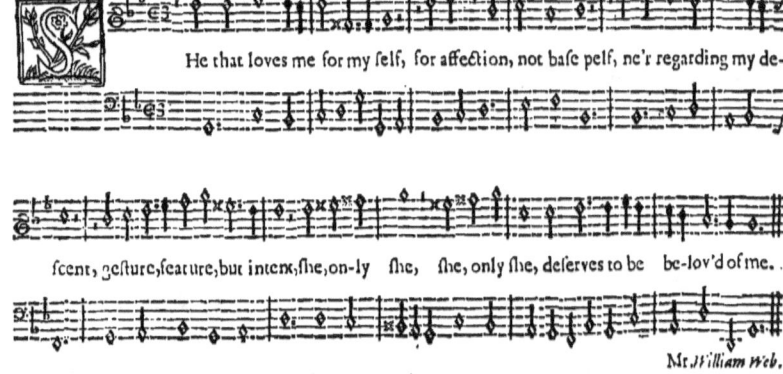

He that loves me for my self, for affection, not base pelf, ne'r regarding my descent, gesture, feature, but intent, she, on-ly she, she, only she, deserves to be be-lov'd of me.

Mr. *William Web.*

She that loves me for no end,
But because I am her friend;
Never doubting my desire,
But believ'd it sacred fire;
She, only she, deserves to be belov'd of me.

She that loves me with resolve
Ne're to alter till dissolve;
Slighting all things, that stern fate
May hereafter seem to threat:
She, only she, deserves to be belov'd of me.

A strife betwixt two Cupids reconciled.

'Bout the sweet Bag of a Bee, two Cupids fell at ods; and whose the pretty prize should be, they vow'd to ask the gods: which *Venus* hearing thither came, and for their boldness stript them, and taking thence from each his flame, with rods of Mirtle whipt them: which done, to still their wanton cryes, and quiet grown sh'ad seen them, she kist and dry'd their dove-like eyes, and gave the Bag between them.

Mr. *Henry Lawes*.

[4]

Venus *lamenting her lost* Adonis.

Wake my *Adonis*, do not die, one life's enough for thee and I; where are thy looks, thy wiles thy fears, thy frowns, thy smiles? a---las, in vain I call, one death hath snatcht them all; yet death's not deadly in that face, death in those looks it self hath grace; 'twas this, 'twas this I fear'd, when thy pale ghost appear'd, this I presag'd, when thun———dering *Jove* tore the best Mirtle in my grove, when my sick rose buds lost their smel, & from my temples untoucht fell, and 'twas for some such thing, my Dove first hung her wing. Whither art thou my Deity gone?

On his Loves Absence.

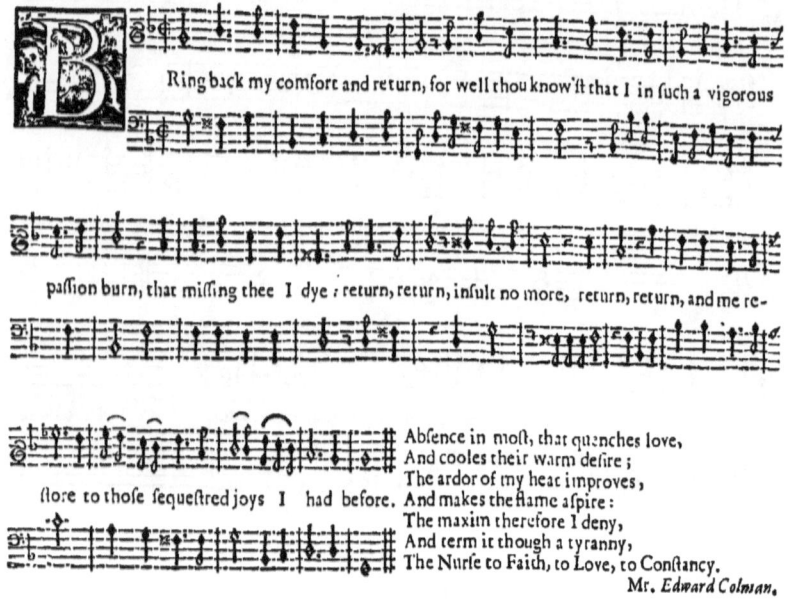

Bring back my comfort and return, for well thou know'ſt that I in ſuch a vigorous paſſion burn, that miſſing thee I dye: return, return, inſult no more, return, return, and me re-ſtore to thoſe ſequeſtred joys I had before.

Abſence in moſt, that quenches love,
And cooles their warm deſire;
The ardor of my heat improves,
And makes the flame aſpire:
The maxim therefore I deny,
And term it though a tyranny,
The Nurſe to Faith, to Love, to Conſtancy.

Mr. Edward Colman.

Beauty clouded with grief.

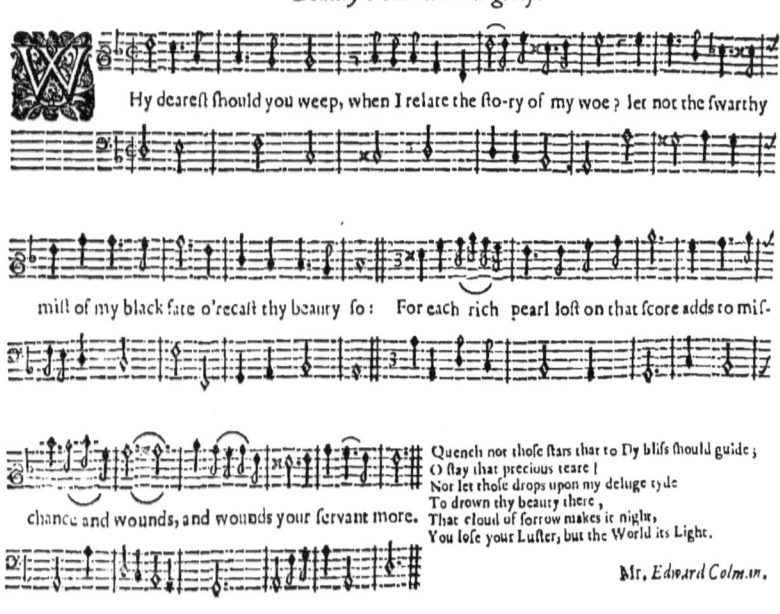

Why deareſt ſhould you weep, when I relate the ſto-ry of my woe? let not the ſwarthy mill of my black fate o'recaſt thy beauty ſo: For each rich pearl loſt on that ſcore adds to miſ-chance and wounds, and wounds your ſervant more.

Quench not thoſe ſtars that to Dy bliſs ſhould guide;
O ſtay that precious teare!
Nor let thoſe drops upon my deluge tyde
To drown thy beauty there,
That cloud of ſorrow makes it night,
You loſe your Luſter, but the World its Light.

Mr. Edward Colman.

On Loves Artillery.

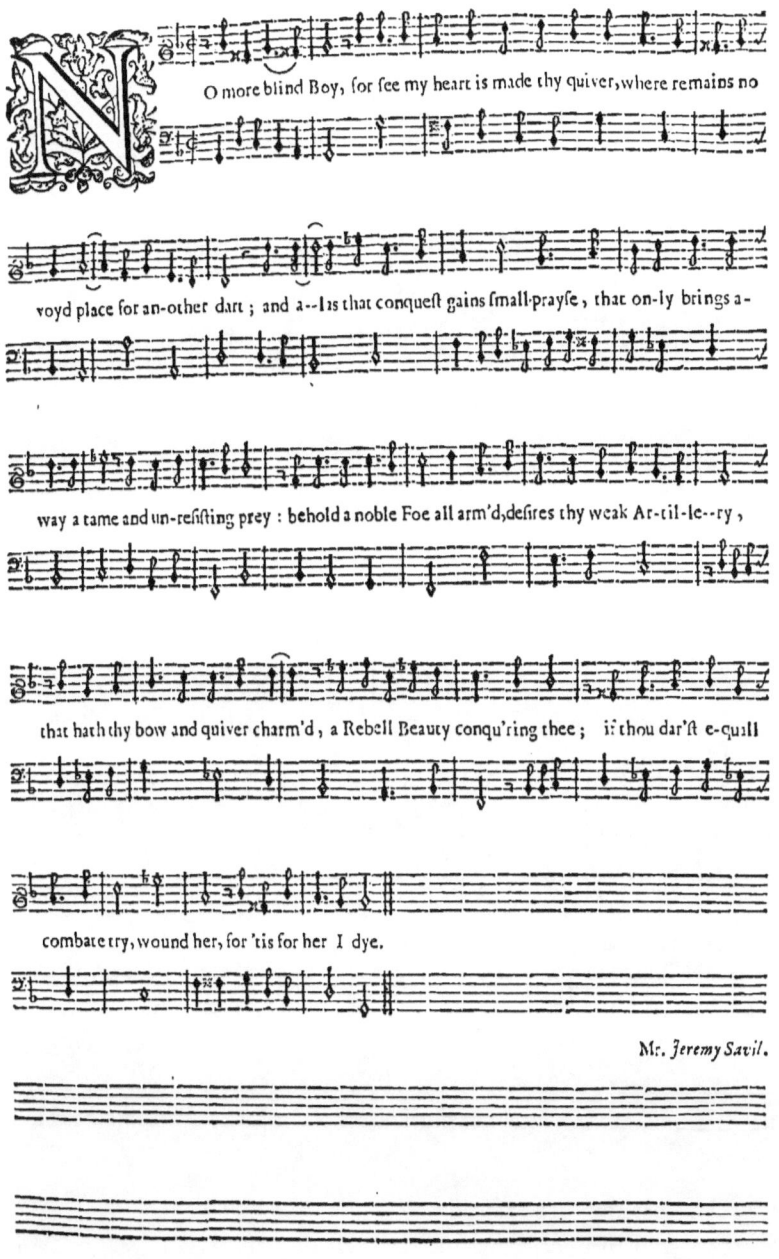

NO more blind Boy, for see my heart is made thy quiver, where remains no voyd place for an-other dart; and a--las that conquest gains small prayse, that on-ly brings a-way a tame and un-resisting prey: behold a noble Foe all arm'd, desires thy weak Ar-til-le--ry, that hath thy bow and quiver charm'd, a Rebell Beauty conqu'ring thee; if thou dar'st e-quall combate try, wound her, for 'tis for her I dye.

Mr. *Jeremy Savil*.

On the Vicissitudes of Love.

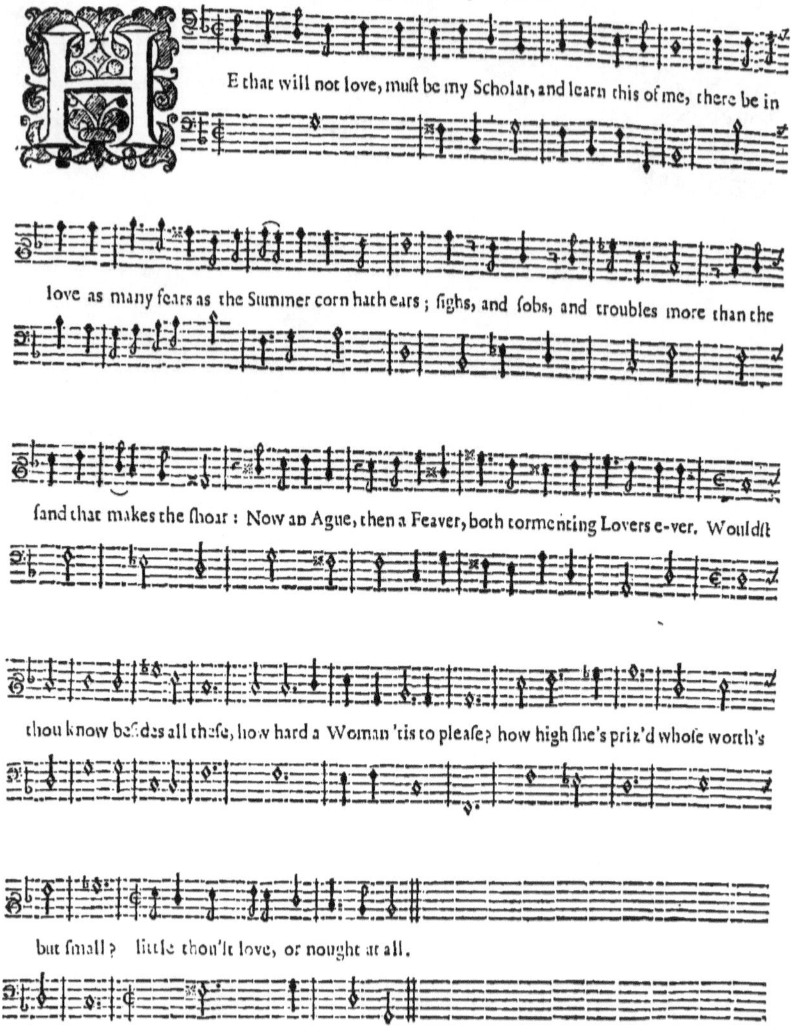

He that will not love, must be my Scholar, and learn this of me, there be in love as many fears as the Summer corn hath ears; sighs, and sobs, and troubles more than the sand that makes the shoar: Now an Ague, then a Feaver, both tormenting Lovers e-ver. Wouldst thou know besides all these, how hard a Woman 'tis to please? how high she's priz'd whose worth's but small? little thou'lt love, or nought at all.

Mr. William Lawes.

[9]

A false designe to be cruel.

IN vain fair *Chloris*, you designe, to be cruel, to be kind ; for we know with all your arts, you never hold but willing hearts; men are too wise grown to expire with broken shafts, and painted fire.

The Lady *Deerings* Composing.

II.

And if among a thousand Swains
Some one of Love, or Fate complains;
And all the stars in heav'n defie,
With *Cloro's* lip, or *Celia's* eye :
'Tis not their love the Youth would chuse,
But the glory to refuse.

III.

Then wisely make your prize of those
Want wit, or courage to oppose ;
But tempt me not that can discover
What will redeem the fondest Lover ;
And flie the list, lest it appear
Your pow'r is measur'd by our fear.

IV.

So the rude wave securely shocks
The yeelding Bark, but the stiff rocks
If it atempt, how soon again
Broke and dissolv'd it fills the Main :
It foams and roars , but we deride
Alike its weaknes, and its pride.

D

[10]

Constancy in Love.

Is not ith' pow'r of all thy scorn or un-relenting hate, to quench my flames, or make them burn with heat more temperate: still do I struggle with despair, and ever court disdain; and though you ne'r prove lesse severe, Ile dote up--on my pain.

(2) Yet meaner beauties cannot claime
In Love this tyranny,
They must pretend an equall flame,
Or else our passions die :
You faire Clarinda you alone
Are priz'd at such a rate,
To have a Votary of one
Whom you do reprobate.

Mr. *Henry Lawes*.

On Inconstancy.

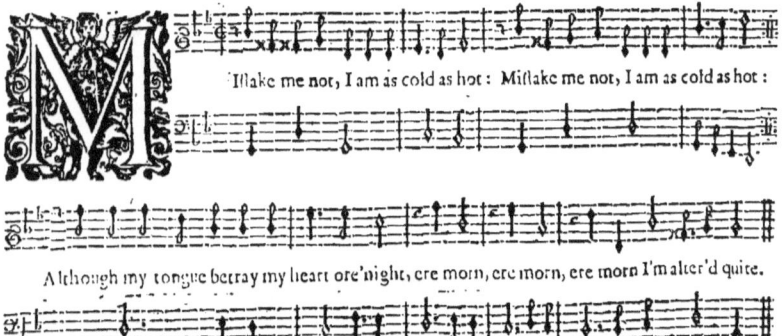

Mistake me not, I am as cold as hot : Mistake me not, I am as cold as hot : Although my tongue betray my heart ore'night, ere morn, ere morn, ere morn I'm alter'd quite.

II. Sometime I burn, and straight to Ice I turn,
Ther's nothing so inconstant as my mind,
I change ♯ ♭ with every wind.

III. Perhaps in jest, I said I lov'd thee best ,
But 'twas no more, then what not long before
I vow'd ♯ ♭ to twenty more.

IV. Then prethee see, thou giv'st no heed to me ;
For when I cannot keep my word a day,
What hope ♯ ♭ hadst thou to stay.

Mr. *Thȯ. Brewer*.

On Womens Inconstancy.

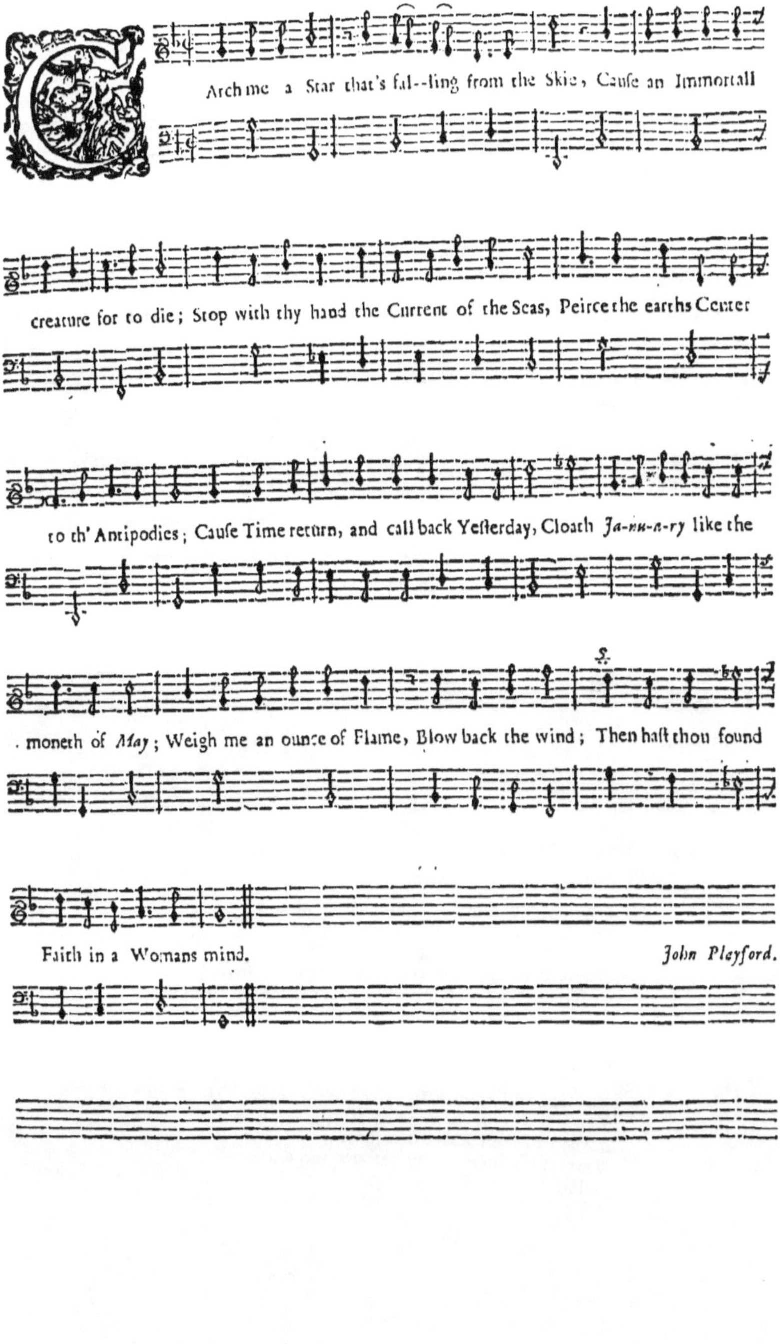

Arch me a Star that's fal--ling from the Skie, Cause an Immortall creature for to die; Stop with thy hand the Current of the Seas, Peirce the earths Center to th' Antipodies; Cause Time return, and call back Yesterday, Cloath *Ja-nu-a-ry* like the moneth of *May*; Weigh me an ounce of Flame, Blow back the wind; Then hast thou found Faith in a Womans mind.

John Playford.

A Resolution not to Love.

Love I must tell thee, Ile no longer be a Victive to thy beardless Deitie; nor shall this heart of mine, now 'tis return'd, be offer'd at thy shrine, or at thy Altar burn'd, Love like Religions made an Ayrie name, to awe those souls whom want of wit makes tame.

John Playford.

II.

Ther's no such thing as Quiver, Shaft, or Bow,
Nor do's Love wound, but we Imagine so:
Or if it do's perplex and grieve the mind,
'Tis the poor masculine sect: women no sorrow find.
   'Tis not our parts or person that can move 'um,
   Nor is't mens worth, but wealth, makes women love 'um.

III.

Reason henceforth, not Love, shall be my guide,
Our fellow Creatures shan't be deifide:
Ile now a Rebell be, and so pull down
That disloffe Hierarchy and females fanci'd crown.
   In these unbridled times who will not strive
   To free his neck from all prerogative.

A Forsaken Lovers Complaint.

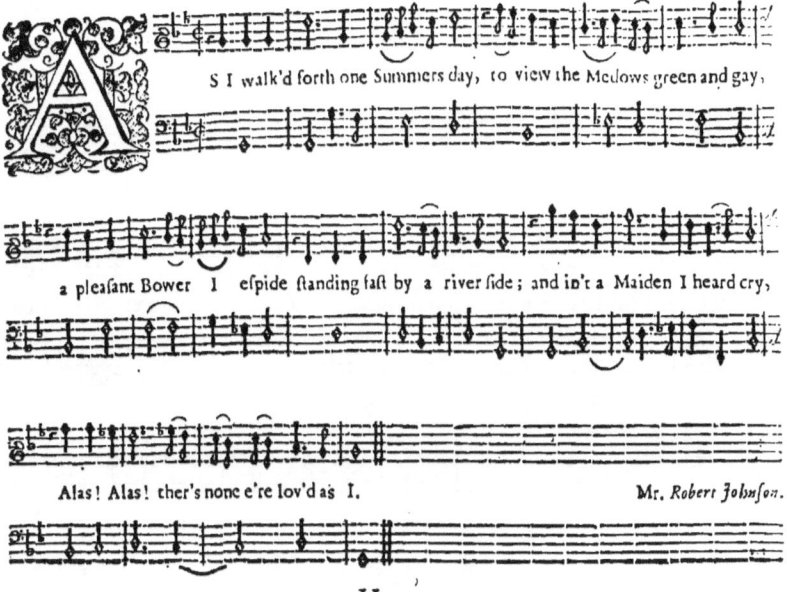

AS I walk'd forth one Summers day, to view the Medows green and gay, a pleasant Bower I espide standing fast by a river side; and in't a Maiden I heard cry, Alas! Alas! ther's none e're lov'd as I.

Mr. *Robert Johnson*.

II.
Then round the medow did she walk,
Catching each flower by the stalk;
Such flowers as in the medow grew,
The *Dead-mans Thumb*, an Hearb all blew.
 And as she pull'd them, still cry'd she,
 Alas! Alas! none e're lov'd like me.

III.
The Flowers of the sweetest sents
She bound about with knotty Betts,
And as she bound them up in Bands
She wept, she sight'd and wrung her hands,
 Alas! Alas! Alas! cry'd she,
 Alas! none was e're lov'd like me.

IV.
When she had fill'd her Apron full
Of such green things as she could cull,
The green leaves serv'd her for a Bed
The Flowers were the Pillow for her head:
 Then down she laid, ne'r more did speak;
 Alas! Alas! with Love her heart did break.

At a Masque, to invite the Ladies to Dance.

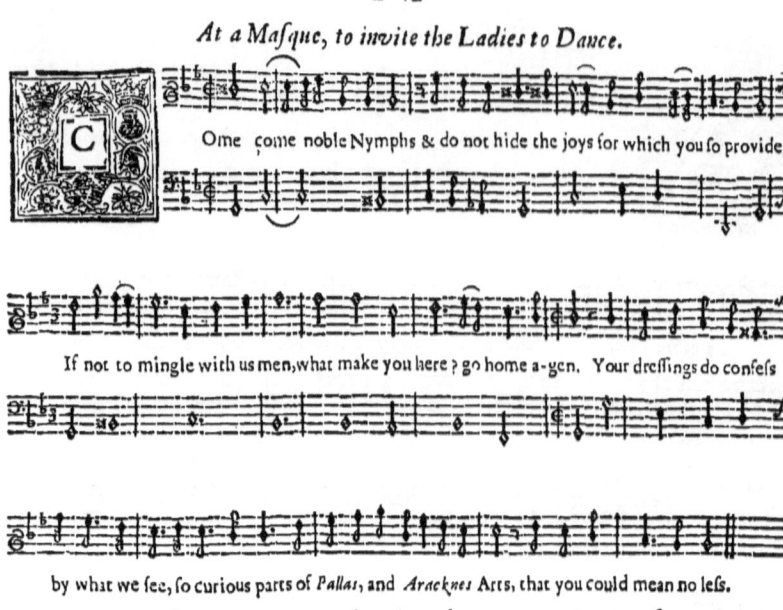

Come come noble Nymphs & do not hide the joys for which you so provide;
If not to mingle with us men, what make you here? go home a-gen. Your dressings do confess
by what we see, so curious parts of *Pallas*, and *Aracknes* Arts, that you could mean no less.

II.   Mr. *William Webb*.

Why do you were the Silk-worms toyls?
Or glory in the Shel-fish spoils?
Or strive to shew the grains of Ore
That you have gathered long before?
   Whereof to make a Stock
To graff the greener Emrauld on,
Or any better water'd Stone,
   Or Ruby of the Rock.

III.

Why do you smell of Amber-greece,
Whereof was formed *Neptunes* Neece,
The Queen of Love? unlesse you can
Like Sea-born-*Venus*, love a man?
   Try, put your selves unto't:
Your Looks, and Smiles, and Thoughts that meet;
Ambrosian-hands, and Silver-feet,
   Do promise you will do't.

An Italian Ayre.

Ug-gi, fuggi, fuggi, da lieti aman i empia dona cagion de-pi-an-ti. Che non gia per essere Crudele ma per essere ingrata & infidele egni core t'ha ni horrore, fuggi, fuggi, fuggi, che chiti mira perche vivi pe-ange e sos pira.

Fuggi, fuggi, fuggi, fallace fera
Frede in fernale empia ma gera
Che se bene hai di donna l' aspetto
Di furia un corte nascendi nel petto
Tutta danno tutt' inganno
Fuggi, fuggi, fuggi, ch'ogn un che t'ama
Il tuo ben piange, e il tuo mal brama.

A French Ayre.

Amor merere, che d' amor merere, amor merere che d' amor merere; amor me fuge, amor me struge, non pos a pue, non pos a pue.

[16]

Loves Scrutiny.

Why shouldst thou swear I am forsworn, since thine I vow'd to be? Lady it is already morn, it was last night I swore to thee, this fond impos-si-bi-li-tie.   Mr. *Henry Lawes*.

II.
Have I not lov'd thee much and long,
A tedious twelve houres space?
I should all other Beauties wrong,
And rob thee of a new imbrace,
Should I still dote upon thy face.

III.
Not that all Joyes in thy brown hair
By others may be found;
But I will search the black, the fair,
Like skilfull Mineralists that found
For treasuers in unplowed ground.

IV.
Then if when I have lov'd thee round,
Thou prove the pleasant she,
In spoyle of meaner Beauties crown'd,
I laden will return to thee,
Ev'n sated with varietie.

No Beauty without Love.

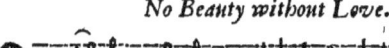

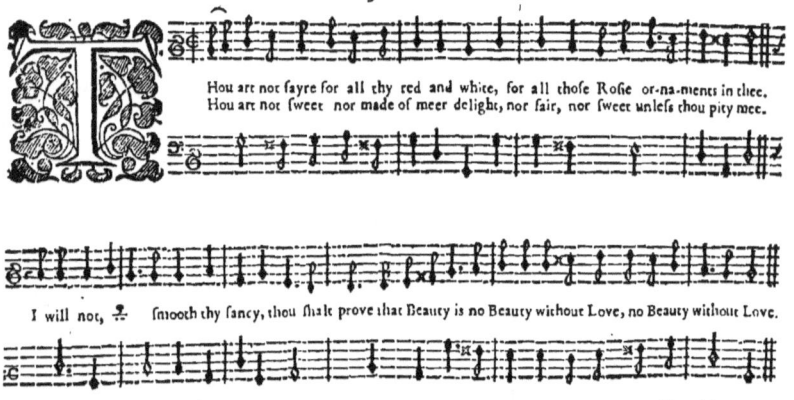

Thou art not fayre for all thy red and white, for all those Rosie or-na-ments in thee. Thou art not sweet nor made of meer delight, nor fair, nor sweet unless thou pity mee. I will not, smooth thy fancy, thou shalt prove that Beauty is no Beauty without Love, no Beauty without Love.

Mr. *Nich. Lanneere*.

II.
Yet love not me, nor seek thou to allure
My thoughts with beauty, were it now divine;
Thy smiles and kisses I cannot indure,
I'le not be wrapt up in those armes of thine.
Now shew if thou be a woman right,
Imbrace, and kisse, and love me in dispite.

[17]

Delayes in Love breeds Danger.

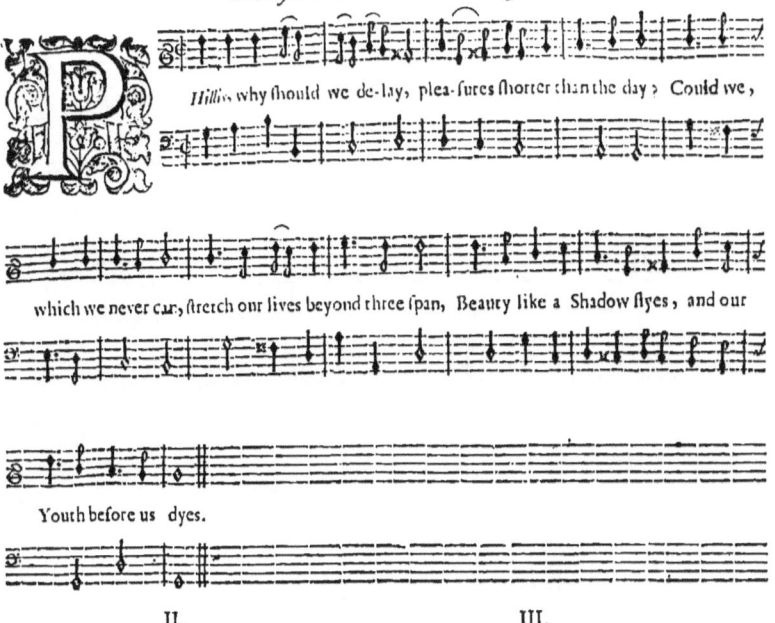

Phillis, why should we de-lay, plea-sures shorter than the day? Could we, which we never can, stretch our lives beyond three span, Beauty like a Shadow flyes, and our Youth before us dyes.

II.

Or would Youth and Beauty stay,
Love ha's wings, and will away;
Love ha's swifter wings than time,
Change in love too oft do's chime;
Gods that never change their state,
Very oft their love and hate.

III.

Phillis, to this truth we owe
All the love betwixt us now;
Let not you and I require
What ha's been our past desire;
On what Shepherds you have smil'd,
Or what Nymphs I have beguil'd.

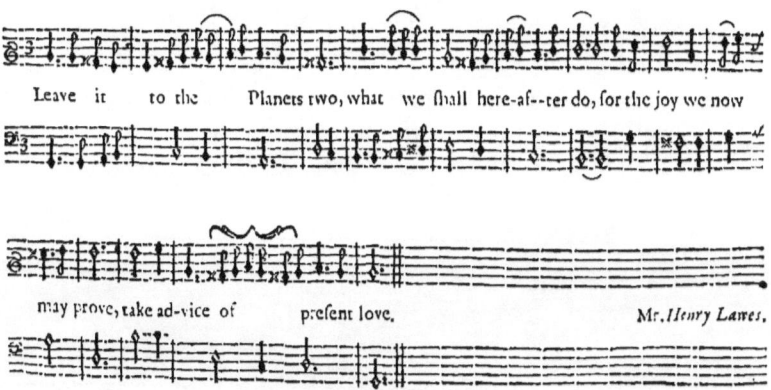

Leave it to the Planets two, what we shall here-af--ter do, for the joy we now may prove, take ad-vice of present love.

Mr. Henry Lawes.

On Cælia's Coynesse.

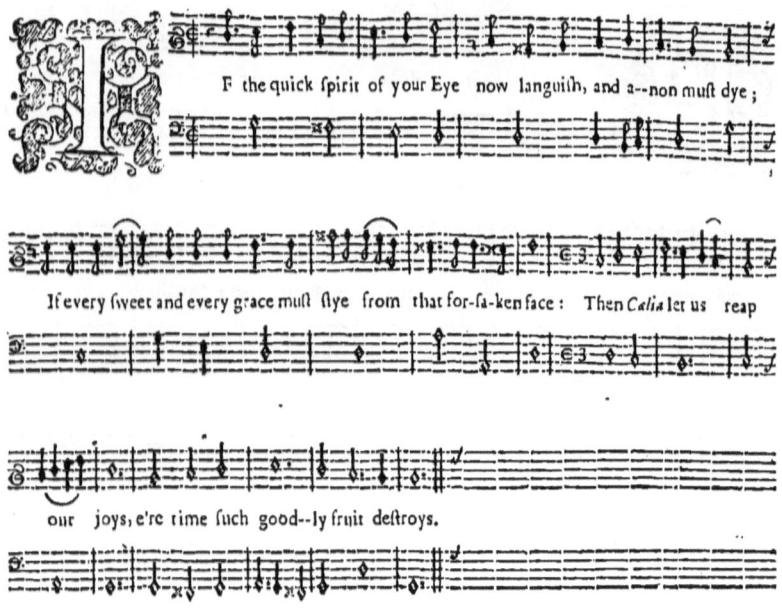

F the quick spirit of your Eye now languish, and a--non must dye;
If every sweet and every grace must flye from that for-sa-ken face: Then *Cælia* let us reap
our joys, e're time such good--ly fruit destroys.

II.

Or if that Golden Fleece must grow, for ever free from aged Snow;
If those bright Suns must know no shade, nor your fresh Beauty ever fade;
Then *Cælia* feare not to bestow,
What still being gather'd, still must grow.

Thus either Time his fickle brings in vain, or else in vain his wings.   Mr. *Henry Lawes.*

Loves sweet Repose.

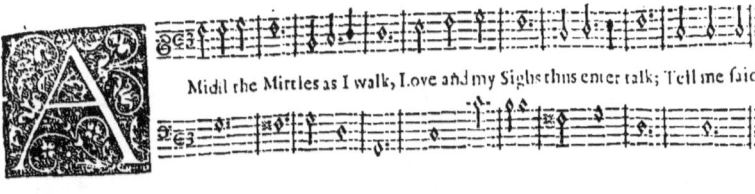

Midſt the Mirtles as I walk, Love and my Sighs thus enter talk; Tell me ſaid I, in deep diſtreſs, where I may find my Shepherdeſs.

Mr. *Henry Lawes*.

Then Fool (ſaid Love) know'ſt thou not this,
In every thing that's good ſhe is,
In yonder Tulip go and ſeek,
There thou ſhalt find her Lip and Cheek.

In that inamell'd Fancy by
There ſhalt thou find her curious Eye;
In bloom of Peach, in Roſes bud
There wave the ſtreams of her bloud.

'Tis true, ſaid I, and thereupon,
And went and pluckt them one by one
To make a parts union,
But on a ſuddain all was gone.

At which I ſtopt; ſaid Love, theſe bee
Fond man, reſemblances of thee;
For as theſe Flowers thy joy muſt dye,
Even in the turn'ng of an eye.

And all thy hopes of her muſt wither,
As do thoſe Flowers when knit together.

A Willow Garland ſent for a Newyeers-gift.

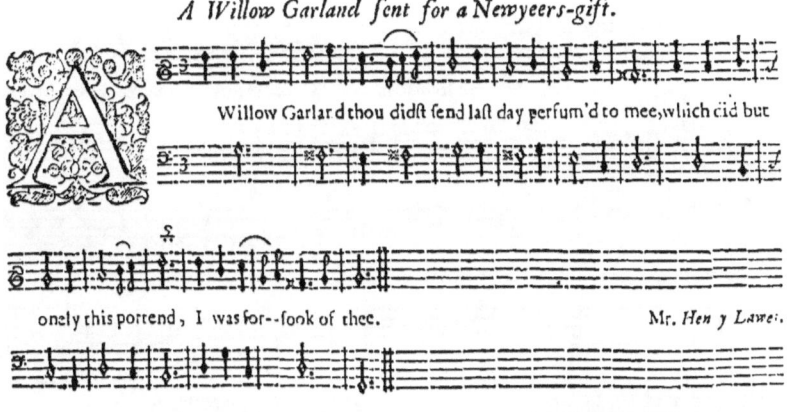

Willow Garland thou didſt ſend laſt day perfum'd to mee, which did but onely this portend, I was for--ſook of thee.

Mr. *Henry Lawes*.

II.
Since that it is, I'le tell thee what,
To morrow thou ſhalt ſee
Me wear the Willow, after that
To dye upon the tree.

III.
As Beaſts unto the Alter go
With Garlands, ſo I
Will with my Willow wreath alſo
Come forth, and ſweetly die.

Loves Victory.

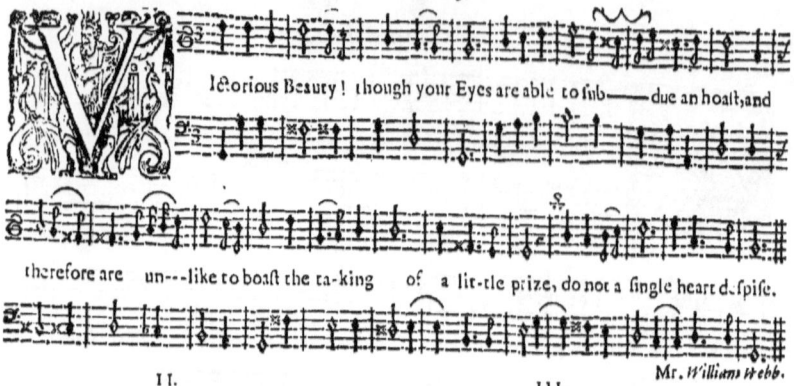

Victorious Beauty! though your Eyes are able to sub——due an hoast, and therefore are un---like to boast the ta-king of a lit-tle prize, do not a single heart despise.

Mr. *Williams Webb.*

II.
I came alone, but yet so arm'd
With former love I durst have sworn
That as that privy coat was worn,
With characters of beauty charm'd,
Thereby I might have scap'd unharm'd.

III.
The Conquest in regard of me,
Alas is small! but in respect
Of her that did my Love protect,
Where it divulg'd, deserv'd to be
Recorded for a Victorie.

IV.
But neither steel nor stony brasse
Are proofs against those looks of thine,
Nor can a beauty lesse divine,
By any heart be long possest,
Where you intend an interest.

V.
And such a one as chance to view
Her lovely face, perhaps may stay,
Though you have stole my heart away;
If all your servants prove not true,
May steal a heart or two from you.

Diswasion from Presumption.

Ladies, you that seem so nice, and as cold in shew as Ice, and perhaps have held out thrice, do not think but in a trice one or other may entice, and at last by some device set your honours at a price.

Mr. *Henry Lawes.*

You whose smooth and dainty skin,
Rosie lips, or cheeks, or chin,
All that gaze upon you win;
Yet insult not, sparks within,
Slowly burn ere flames begin,
And presumption still hath bin
Held a most notorious sin.

The Careless Lovers Resolution.

LET longing Lovers sit and pine, and the forsaken Willow wear Love shal not blast this heart of mine, with ling'ring hope or killing fear: He never love till I enjoy, or lose my time on her that's coy.

Mr. *Henry Lawes.*

If Ladies call us to the field,
And all their Colours there display,
Alasse! they needs must to us yield,
Since we are better arm'd than they;
'Tis folly then to beg or whine
For us that are born Masculine.

Then Lovers learn your strength to know,
And you may overcome with ease,
Your enemy fights with a Bow
That cannot wound, unlesse you please;
And he that pines because shee's coy,
Wants wit, or courage, women say.

Disdain.

TAke heed fair *Chloris*, how you tame (with your disdain) *Amintor's* flame. A noble heart, when once despis'd, swels unto such a height of pride, 'twil rather burst than deign to be a worshipper of crueltie.

II.
You may use common shepherds so,
My flames at last to storms will grow,
And blow such scorn upon thy pride,
Will blast all I have magnifi'd:
You are not fair when Love you lack,
Ingratitude makes all things black.

III.
O do not for a flock of sheep,
A golden showre when as you sleep;
Or for the tales ambition tells,
Forsake the house where honor dwels,
In *Damons* palace you'l ne'r shine
So bright as in these armes of mine.

Mr. *Henry Lawes.*

[22]

Loves Fruition.

Tell me not I my time mispend, 'tis time lost to reprove me: Enjoy thou thine, I have my End, so *Chloris* one-ly love me.

Mr. *Henry Lawes.*

Tell me not others flocks are full,
Mine poor, let them despise me
That more abound with Milk, and Wool,
So *Chloris* only prize me.

For pity thou that wiser art,
Whose thoughts lies wide of mine;
Let me alone with my one heart,
And I'le ne'r envy thine.

Try other easier eares with these
Unappertaining Stories;
He never feels the Worlds disease,
That cares not for her Glories.

Nor blame whoever blames my wit,
That seek's no higher prize
Then in unenvy'd Shades to sit,
And sing of *Chloris* Eyes.

Loves Drollery.

Love thee for thy Fickleness, and great Inconstancy; for had'st thou been a constant Lass, then thou had'st ne'r lov'd mee.

Mr. *Henry Lawes.*

I love thee for thy Wantonesse,
And for thy Drollerie;
For if thou had'st not lov'd to sport,
Then thou had'st ne're lov'd mee.

I love thee for thy poverty,
And for thy want of Coyne;
For if thou hadst been worth a Groat,
Then thou had'st ne'r been mine.

I love thee for thy Uglynesse,
And for thy foolerie;
For if thou had'st been fair or wise,
Then thou had'st ne'r lov'd mee.

Then let me have thy heart a while,
And thou shalt have my mony;
Ile part withall the wealth I have,
T'enjoy a Lass so Bonny.

Disdain returned.

HE that loves a Ro——sie cheek, or a Corall lip admires; or from Star-like eyes doth seek fu-el to maintain his fires, as old Time makes these de-cay, so his flames must waste a-way.

II.
But a smooth and stedfast mind,
Gentle thoughts, and calm desires,
Hearts with equall love combin'd,
Kindle never-dying fires:
Where these are not, I despise
Lovely Cheeks, or Lips or Eyes.

III.
Celia, now no tears can win
My resolv'd heart to return;
I have search'd thy soul within,
And find nought but pride and scorn:
I have learn'd those Arts, and now
Can disdain as much as thou.

Some God in my revenge con---vey that Love to her I cast a-way. Mr. *Henry Lawe*.

Loves Content.

Dear, leave thy home, and come with mee, that scorn the world for love of thee: Here we will live within this Park, a Court of joy and pleasures Ark. Mr. *Henry Lawes*.

To his Forsaken Mistresse.

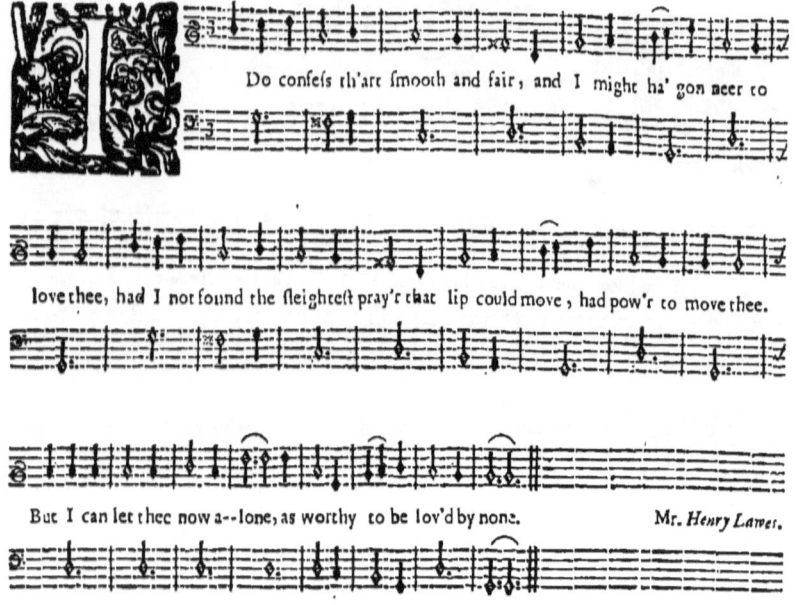

I Do confess th'art smooth and fair, and I might ha' gon neer to love thee, had I not found the sleightest pray'r that lip could move, had pow'r to move thee. But I can let thee now a--lone, as worthy to be lov'd by none.

Mr. *Henry Lawes*.

II.

I do confess th'art sweet, yet find
Thee such an Unthrift of thy Sweets;
Thy favours are but like the wind,
Which kisseth ev'ry thing it meets :
And since thou can'st with more than one,
Th'art worthy to be kiss'd by none.

III.

The morning Rose that untoutch'd stands,
Arm'd with her briars, how sweet shee smels!
But pluck'd, and strain'd through ruder hands,
Her sweets no longer with her dwels ;
But Sent and Beauty both are gone,
And Leaves fall from her one by one.

IV.

Such Fate e're long will thee betide,
When thou hast handled been a while,
With sear Flow'rs to be thrown aside ;
And I shall sigh when some will smile,
To see thy love to ev'ry one
Hath brought thee to be lov'd by none.

Two Songs in the Play of The Royal Slave.

Come from the Dungeon to the Throne, to be a King, and straight be none:

Reign then a while, that thou mayst be fitter to fall by majestie: So Beasts for sacrifice we

feed, first they are crown'd, and then they bleed, they bleed.   Mr. *Henry Lawes.*

Love and Musick.

Come my Sweet, whilest ev'ry Strain cals our Souls in-to the Ear; where the greedy

listning fain would turn in--to the sound they hear; lest in desire to fill the quire, themselves they

tie to harmo---ny, let's kiss and call them back a-gain.   Mr. *Henry Lawes.*

A Resolution in choice of a Mistresse.

Ert thou yet fairer then thou art, which lies not in the pow'r of Art; o: had'st thou in thine Eyes more Darts, then *Cupids* e----ver shot at Hearts; yet if they were not thrown at me, I would not cast a Thought at thee.

Mr. *Henry Lawes.*

II.

I'de rather marry a disease,
Then court the thing I cannot please:
She that would cherish my desires
Must court my flames with equall fires:
What pleasure is there in a Kiss
To him that doubts the Heart's not his?

III.

I love thee not 'cause thou art fair,
Softer than down, smoother than air;
Not for the *Cupids* that do lye
In either corner of thine Eye:
Would you then know what it might be?
'Tis I love you 'cause you love me.

Inconstancy in Love.

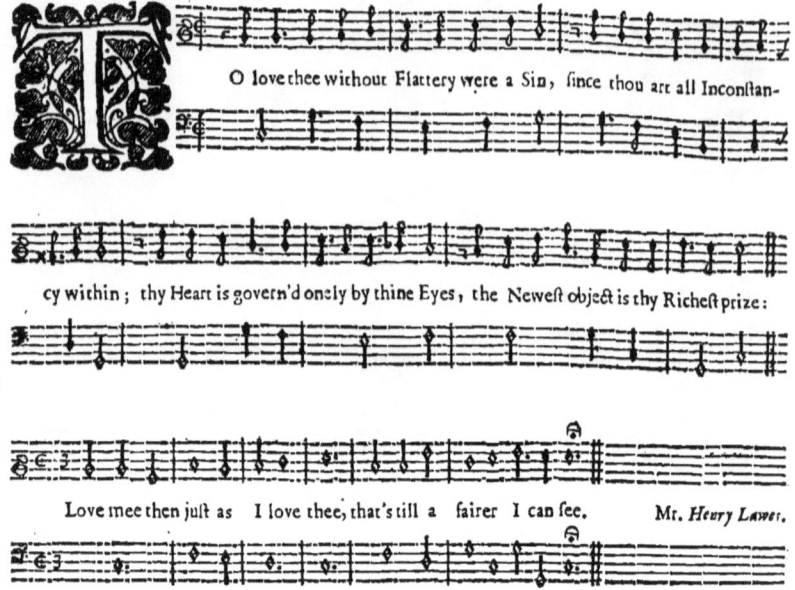

TO love thee without Flattery were a Sin, since thou art all Inconstancy within; thy Heart is govern'd onely by thine Eyes, the Newest object is thy Richest prize: Love mee then just as I love thee, that's till a fairer I can see.   Mr. *Henry Lawes.*

II.

My thoughts are now at liberty, and can
Love all that's fair, as you can all that's man;
I never will hereafter think it strange
To see thee please thy Apperite with change:
   No! love me just as I love thee,
   That's till a fairer I can see.

III.

I hate this constant doting on a Face,
Content ne're dwelt a Week in any place;
Why then should you and I love one another
Longer then we can be content together?
   Love mee then just as I love thee,
   That's till a fairer I can see.

Discontent.

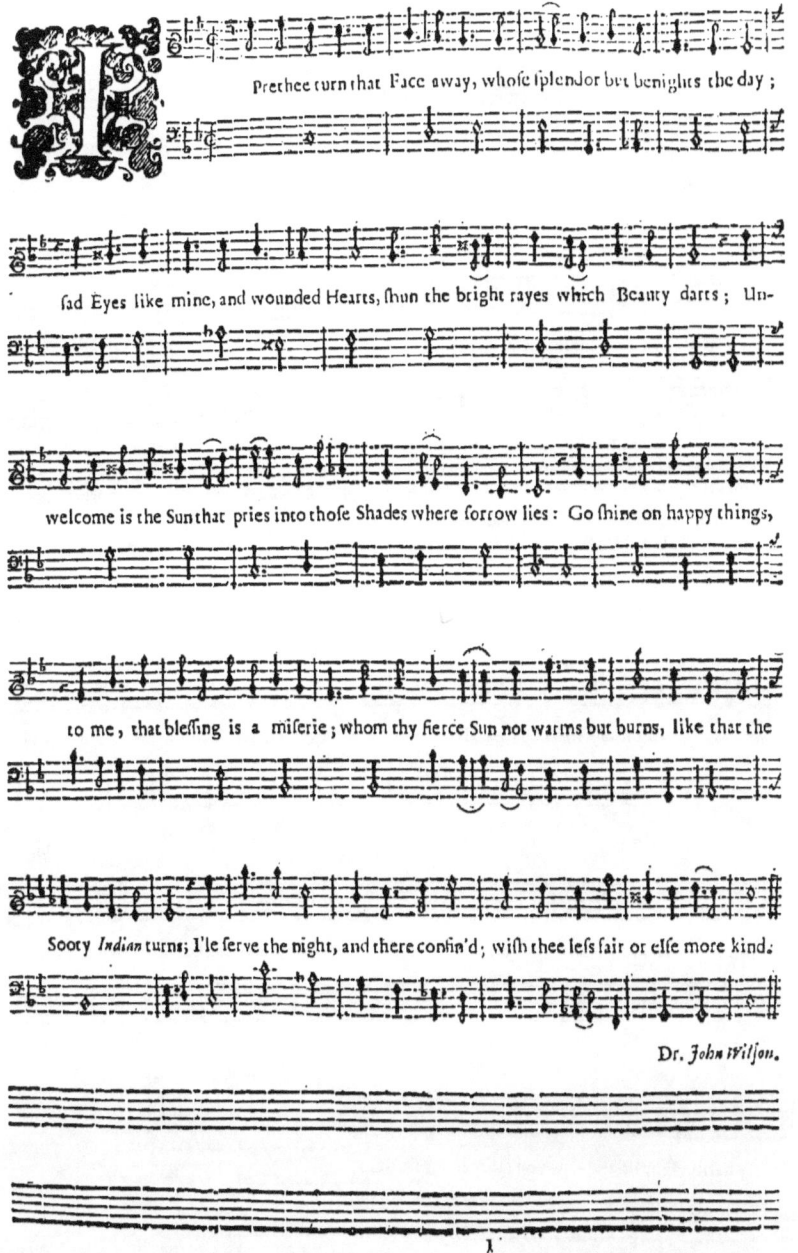

Prethee turn that Face away, whose splendor but benights the day; sad Eyes like mine, and wounded Hearts, shun the bright rayes which Beauty darts; Unwelcome is the Sun that pries into those Shades where sorrow lies: Go shine on happy things, to me, that blessing is a miserie; whom thy fierce Sun not warms but burns, like that the Sooty *Indian* turns; I'le serve the night, and there confin'd, wish thee less fair or else more kind.

Dr. *John Wilson.*

Loves Votary.

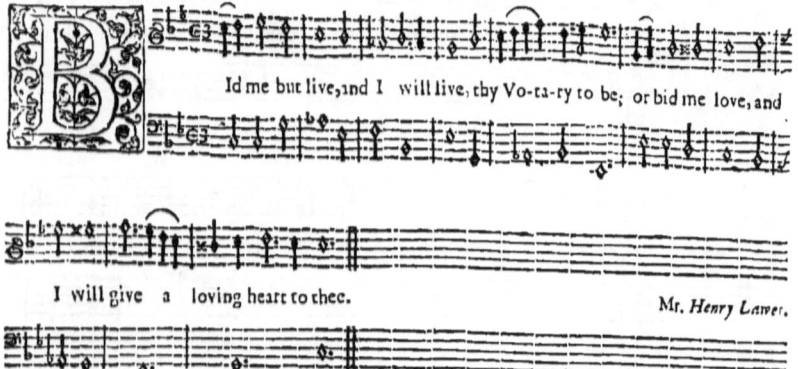

Bid me but live, and I will live, thy Vo-ta-ry to be; or bid me love, and I will give a loving heart to thee.

Mr. *Henry Lawes*.

A heart as soft, a heart as kind, a heart as soundly free
As in the world thou canst not find, that heart I'le give to thee.

Bid that heart stay, and it shall stay, and honour thy decree,
Or bid it languish quite away and it shall do't for thee.

Bid me to weep, and I will weep, while I have eyes to see,
Or having none, yet I will keep a heart to weep for thee.

Thou art my love, my life my heart, the very eye of mee,
And hast command of every part, to live and dye for thee.

To Aurelia.

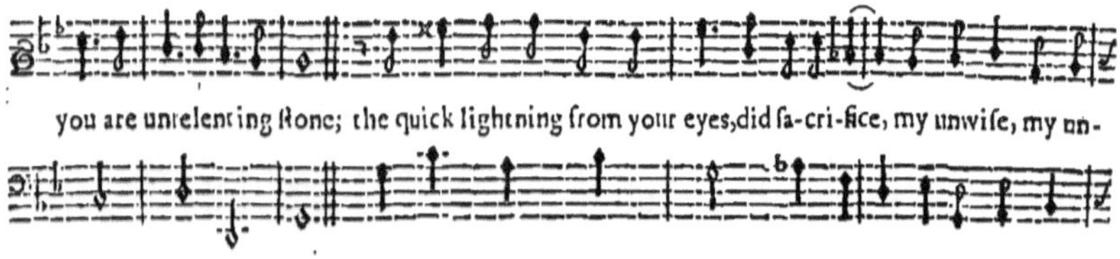

Right *Aurelia*, I do owe all the woe I can know to those glorious looks alone, though you are unrelenting stone; the quick lightning from your eyes, did sa-cri-fice, my unwise, my un-wary harmless heart, and now you glory in my smart.

How unjustly you do blame
That pure flame,
From you came.
Vext with what your selfe may burn,
Your scorns to tinder did it turn.

The least sparke now Love can call
That does fall
On the small
Scorcht remainder of my heart,
Will make it burn in every part. Dr. *Colman*.

[31]

Loves Flattery.

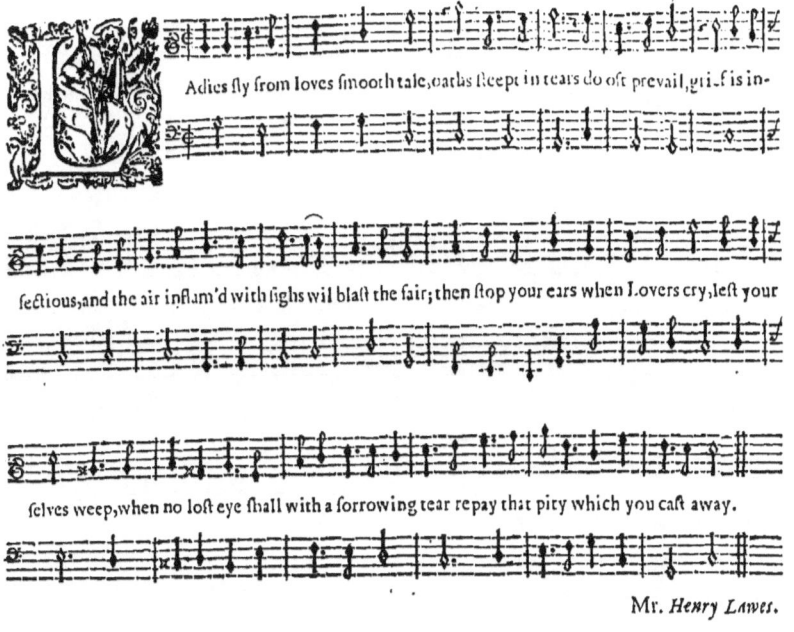

Adieu fly from loves smooth tale, oaths steept in tears do oft prevail, grief is infectious, and the air inflam'd with sighs wil blast the fair; then stop your ears when Lovers cry, lest your selves weep, when no lost eye shall with a sorrowing tear repay that pity which you cast away.

Mr. *Henry Lawes*.

To Chloris.

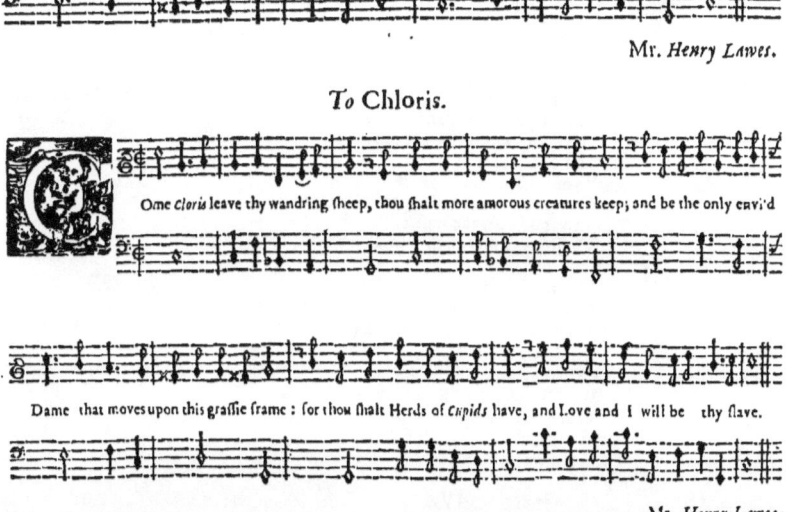

Come *Cloris* leave thy wandring sheep, thou shalt more amorous creatures keep; and be the only envi'd Dame that moves upon this grassie frame : for thou shalt Herds of *Cupids* have, and Love and I will be thy slave.

Mr. *Henry Lawes*.

II.
Nymphs, Satyres, and the Sylvian Fawns,
Shall leave the Woods and narrow Lawns
To wait on *Cloris*, and adore
Their *Cytherea*; now no more
The name of *Cloris* shall create
A servitude in every state.

III.
In yonder Mirtle grove wee'l dwell
With more content then tongue can tell,
Where hungry Moles shall not affright
Thy tender Lambs or thee by night :
There we the wanton sheeves will play,
And steal each others hearts away.

Seeming Coyness.

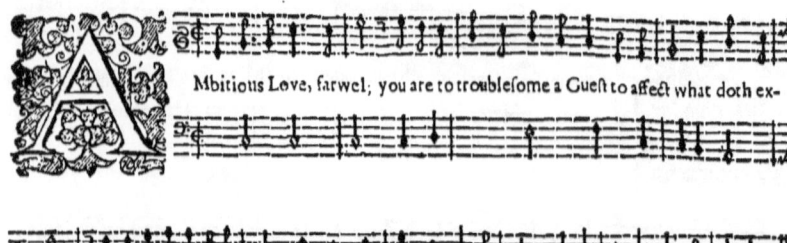

Ambitious Love, farwel; you are to troublesome a Guest to affect what doth ex-

cell; and to be ever at a Feast; is not the cheapest freest diet, less in joy and less in quiet:

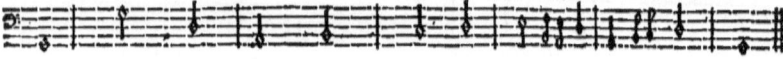

Be proud who list Fetters of Gold to wear, I like no tedious ceremonious cheer.

II.

I'le take such as I find,
So it be good, and handsome drest,
Pretty, looking freely, kinde,
To a good appetite is best.
If your Usage do not please you,
  Change is near you Change will ease you:
Tempest and Feasts the wisest disaffect,
Let it suffice you find no disrespect.

Dr. Charls Colman.

III.

Seek not the highest place,
The lowest commonly is most free
Less subject to disgrace,
Others eyes, or your jealousies.
Bold Freedome will improve your taste,
  When awe imbitters a repast:
A doating fancy is a foolish Guest,
The freest welcome makes the sweetest Feast.

IV.

It is not Natures way,
She made Love no such busie thing,
She meant it a short lay,
A Common-Weal without a King.
Her love on ev'ry edge doth grow,
  Her Fruits are best in Taste and Shew;
Her Sweets extend unto the meanest Clown,
Often most fair, though in a Russet Gown.

Loves Bacchinall.

Ay that sullen Garland by thee, keep it for th' Elizium shades; take my wreath of lusty I-vy, not of that faint Mirtle made; when I see thy soul descending to that cold unfertile Plain of sad fools the Lake attending, thou shalt wear this Crown a-gain. Now drink wine, and know the ods 'twixt that *Lethe,* 'twixt that *Lethe,* 'twixt that *Lethe,* and the Gods.

Rouse thy dull and drowsie spirits,
Here's the soul reviving streams,
The stupid Lovers brain inherits
Nought but vain and empty dreams.

Think not thou these dismall trances,
Which our raptures can content,
The Lad that laughs, sings and dances,
Shall come soonest to his end.

Cho. Sadnesse may some pity move,
  Mirth and courage, mirth and courage,
  Mirth and courage conquers love.

Fy then on that cloudy fore-head,
Ope thou vainly crossed armes;
Thou mayst as well call back the buried
As raise Love by such like charmes.

Sacrifice a glasse of Clarret
To each letter of her name;
Gods have oft descended for it,
Mortals must do more the same.

If she comes not at that flood,
  Sleep will come, sleep will come,
  Sleep will come and that's as good.

Platonick Love.

Hange Platonicks, change for shame, get your selves a-no-ther name. This is but a thin disguise, and betray'd to common eyes: Dim and purblind though they bee, your Philo-so-phy they see is but Lay Hypocrisie, and a kind of He-re-sie.

Dr. *Colman*.

II.

Plato ne'r allow'd a Kiss,
Nor the like fantastick bliss,
All the day fit and Ca Goll
With Sir Amorous La Fool;
Ne'r dream't of that delight
Which a Ball presents at night,
To apt you to what follows next,
Only you corrupt the Text.

III.

Yet must *Plato* justifie
All your wanton vanitie,
When indeed the truth to say,
'Tis Opinion that doth sway.
Is a meer Court-Frippery,
You act but yet most formerly
What your Sex was wont to do
Many hundred years ago.

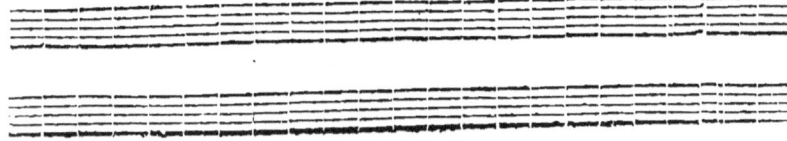

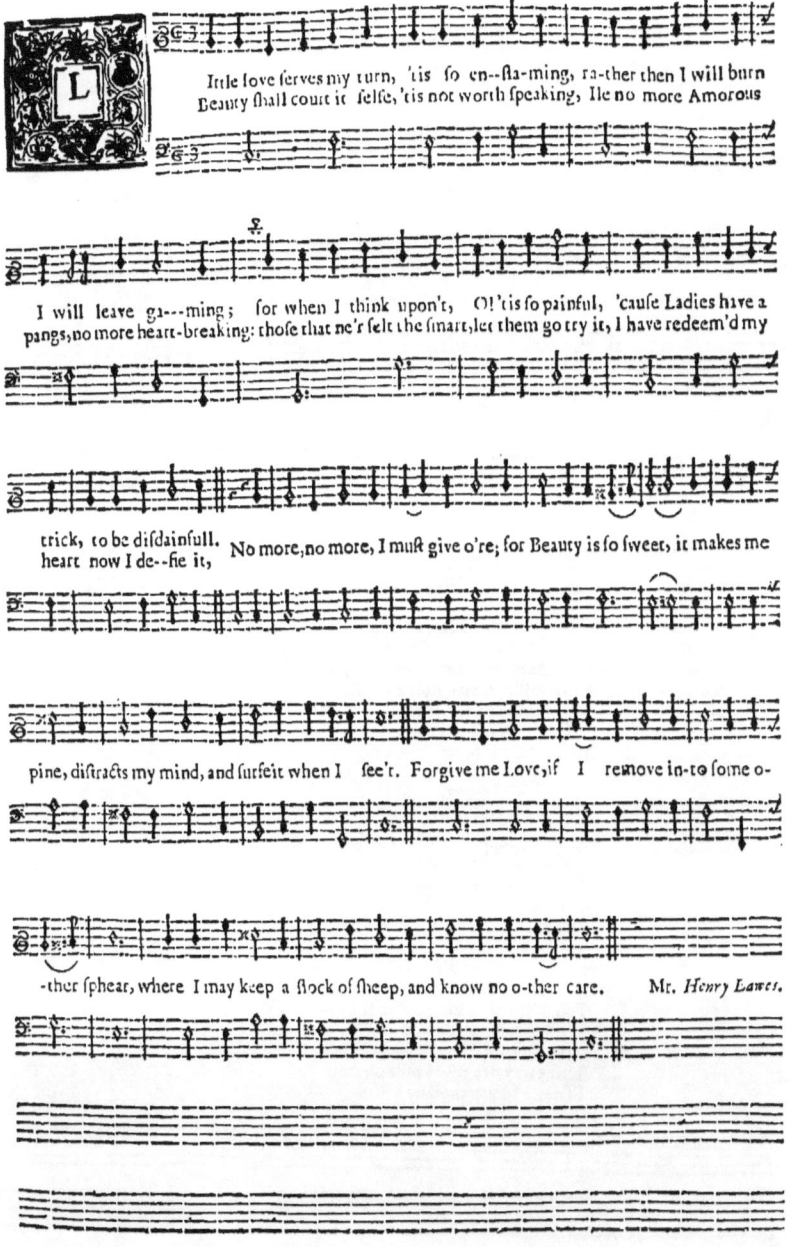

Love Neglected.

Ittle love serves my turn, 'tis so en‑fla‑ming, ra‑ther then I will burn Beauty shall court it selfe, 'tis not worth speaking, Ile no more Amorous I will leave ga‑‑‑ming; for when I think upon't, O! 'tis so painful, 'cause Ladies have a pangs, no more heart‑breaking: those that ne'r felt the smart, let them go try it, I have redeem'd my trick, to be disdainfull. No more, no more, I must give o're; for Beauty is so sweet, it makes me heart now I de‑‑fie it, pine, distracts my mind, and surfeit when I see't. Forgive me Love, if I remove in‑to some o‑ther sphear, where I may keep a flock of sheep, and know no o‑ther care.   Mr. *Henry Lawes*.

Lovers Wantonneſſe.

See, how carleſs men are grown of Love and Loving in our days, Every ones Heart is now his owne; his Eyes upon no object ſtays, but baits a while and goes his ways.

Mr. *Henry Lawes.*

II.

Shall Beauty that was wont to reign
Un-ri vall'd in each noble breaſt,
Command by turns, or elſe in vain;
And by new faſhion'd minds depreſt,
Become an Inn, and love a Gueſt.

III.

Sure they ſuppoſe her of Glaſſe,
And let her firſt on purpoſe fall,
Then peice-meal would pick up this Maſſe,
That for one Beauty bow to all,
And change of Fetters, Freedome call.

IV.

Though lowly minded, I will ſtand
With ſuch for place, and at no rate
Give Rebell Lovers th'upper hand,
That every day new Lords create;
I ſerve a Monarch, they a State.

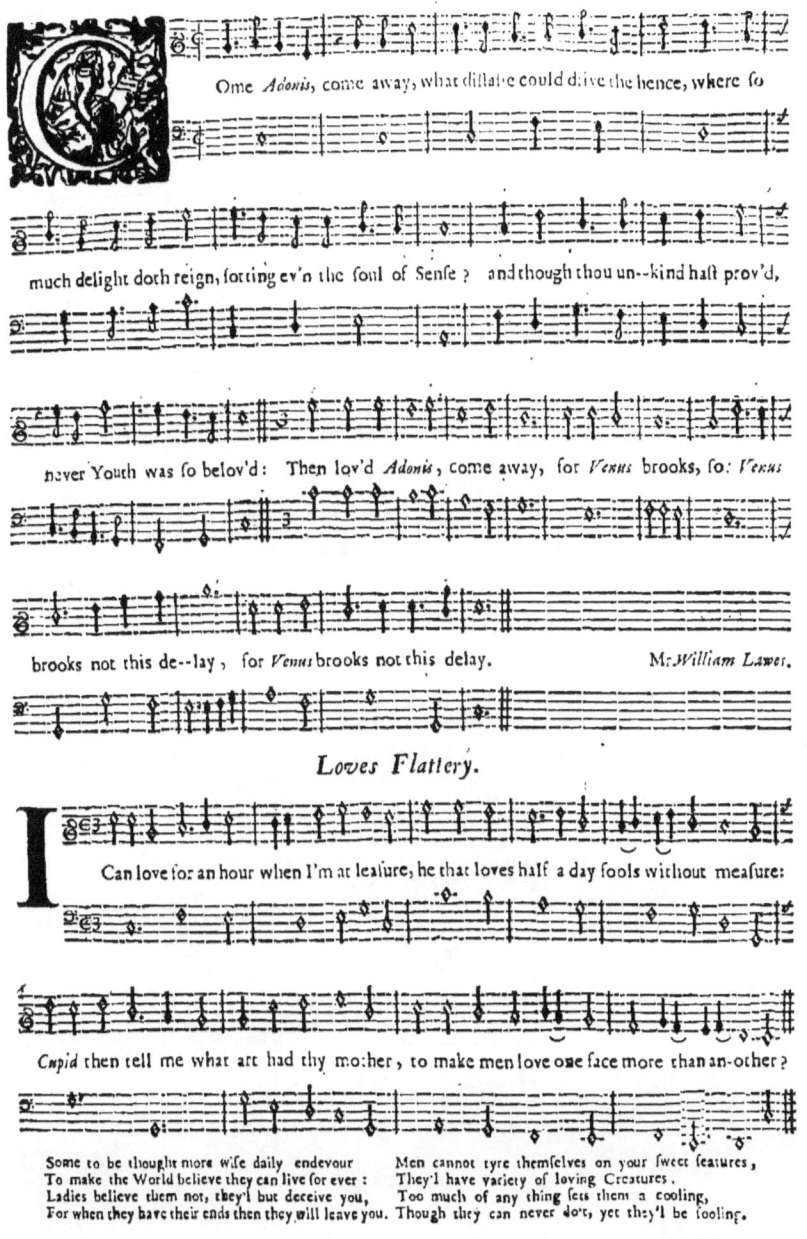

Venus to her Adonis.

Come *Adonis*, come away, what distaste could drive thee hence, where so much delight doth reign, sotting ev'n the soul of Sense? and though thou un--kind hast prov'd, never Youth was so belov'd: Then lov'd *Adonis*, come away, for *Venus* brooks, so: *Venus* brooks not this de--lay, for *Venus* brooks not this delay.

Mr. *William Lawes.*

Loves Flattery.

I Can love for an hour when I'm at leasure, he that loves half a day fools without measure: *Cupid* then tell me what art had thy mother, to make men love one face more than an-other?

Some to be thought more wise daily endevour
To make the World believe they can live for ever :
Ladies believe them not, they'l but deceive you,
For when they have their ends then they will leave you.

Men cannot tyre themselves on your sweet features,
They'l have variety of loving Creatures.
Too much of any thing sets them a cooling,
Though they can never do't, yet they'l be fooling.

Mr. *William Lawes.*

Inconstancie in Women.

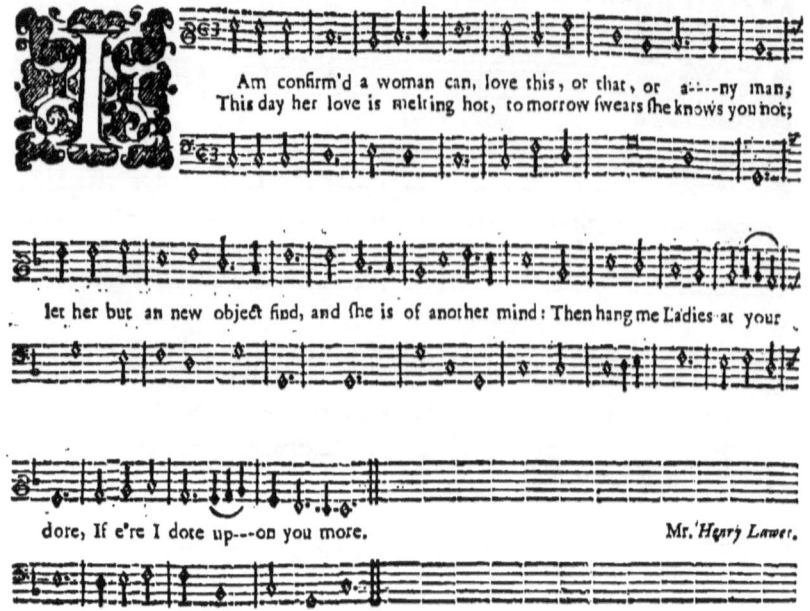

I Am confirm'd a woman can, love this, or that, or a---ny man;
This day her love is melting hot, tomorrow swears she knows you not;
let her but an new object find, and she is of another mind: Then hang me Ladies at your
dore, If e're I dote up---on you more.

Mr. *Henry Lawer.*

II.

Yet still I'le love the fair one, why?
For nothing but to please mine eye;
And so the fat and soft skinn'd Dame
I'le flatter, to appease my flame;
 For her that's Musicall I long,
 When I am sad to sing a Song:
But hang me Ladies, &c.

III.

I'le give my fancy leave to range
Through every face to find out change:
The black, the brown, the fair shall be
But objects of varietie:
 I'le court you all to serve my turn,
 But with such flames as shall not burn:
For hang me Ladies, &c.

A Lovers Legacy.

Ain would I *Chloris* e're I die, bequeath you such a Legacie, as you might say when I am gon, None has the like! My heart alone were the best gift I could bestow, but that's already yours you know: So that till you my Heart resigne, or fill with yours the place of mine; and by that grace my store renew, I shall have nought worth giving you, whose Brest has all the wealth I have, save a faint Carcase, and a Grave: But had I as many Hearts as Hairs, as many Loves as Love has Fears, as many Lives as Years have Hours, they should be all and only yours.

Mr. *Henry Lawes.*

Loves Martyr.

How long shall I a Martyr be to Love and Womans cru--el-ty? Or why doth sullen Fate confine my heart to one that is not mine: had I er'e lov'd as others do, but only for an hour or two, then there had store of reason bin why I should suffer for my sin.

Mr. *Henry Lawes.*

II.

But Love, thou knowest with what a flame
I have ador'd my Mistress name:
How I ne'r offered other fires
But such as rose from chaste desires:
Nor have I ere prophaned thy shrine
With an inconstant fickle minde,;
Yet thou combining with my Fate,
Hath forc'd my love and her to hate.

III.

O Love! if her supremacie
Have not a greater power then thee,
For pity sake then once be kind,
And throw a dart to change her mind:
Thy deity we shall suspect,
If our reward must be neglect.
Then make her love, or let me be
Inspir'd with scorn as well as she.

Amintor *for his* Chloris *absence.*

Tell me you wan-dering spirits of the Air, did you not see a Nymph more bright, more fair than Beauties darling, or of parts more sweet than stolne conrent? If such a one you meet, wait on her hourly where so e're she flies, and cry, and cry, A-mintor for her absence dies.

Mr. *Henry Lawes.*

II.

Go search the Vallies, pluck up every Rose,
You'l find a sent, a blush of her in those:
Fish, fish for Pearle, or Corall, there you'l see
How orientall all her colours bee.
   Go call the Ecchoes to your aide, and cry,
Chloris, Chloris, for that's her name for whom I dy.

III.

But stay a while, I have inform'd you ill,
Were shee on earth she had been with me still:
Go fly to Heaven, examine every Sphere,
And try what Star hath lately lighted there;
   If any brighter than the Sun you see,
Fall down, fall down, and worship it, for that is shee.

Chloris,   *Chloris,*
Fall down, fall down, &c.

Love in a Calme.

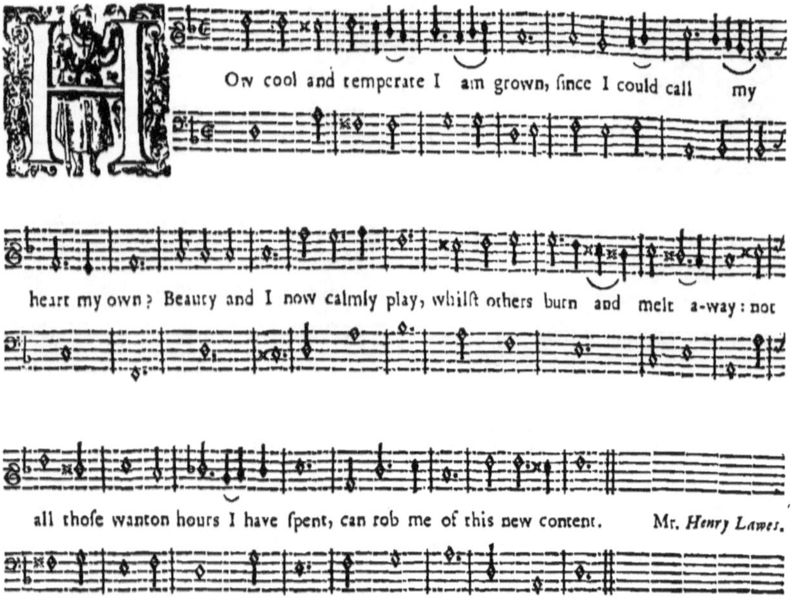

How cool and temperate I am grown, since I could call my heart my own? Beauty and I now calmly play, whilst others burn and melt a-way: not all those wanton hours I have spent, can rob me of this new content.

Mr. *Henry Lawes.*

II.
Loves mists are scattered from my sight,
Which flattered me with new delight,
And now I see 'tis but a face
That stole my heart out of its place:
 Then Love forgive me, I'le no more
 Thine Altars or thy Shrine adore.

III.
Farewell to all heart-breaking eyes,
Farewell each look that can surprize,
Farewell those curls and amorous spels,
Farewell each place where *Cupid* dwels;
 And farewell each bewitching smile,
 I must enjoy my selfe a while.

Loves Shepherdesse.

In faith I cannot keep my Sheep, since first I grew to be in love: whilst my poor Flock a wandring creep, and I to Face a Shepherd am, Love, first in love, in love, I first began.

Love without Additionals.

Mr. *William Webb.*

II.

There's no such thing as that, we Beauty call,
It is meer couzenage all;
For though some long ago
Lik't certain colours mingled so and so,
That doth not tie me now from chusing new,
    If I a fancy take
    Too black and blew,
That fancy doth it Beauty make.

II.

'Tis not the meat, but 'tis the appetite
Makes eating a delight;
And if I like one dish
More than another, that a Phesant is:
What in our Matches, may in us be found,
    So to the height, and nick
    We up be bound,
No matter by what hand or trick,

A Frozen Heart made warm by Love.

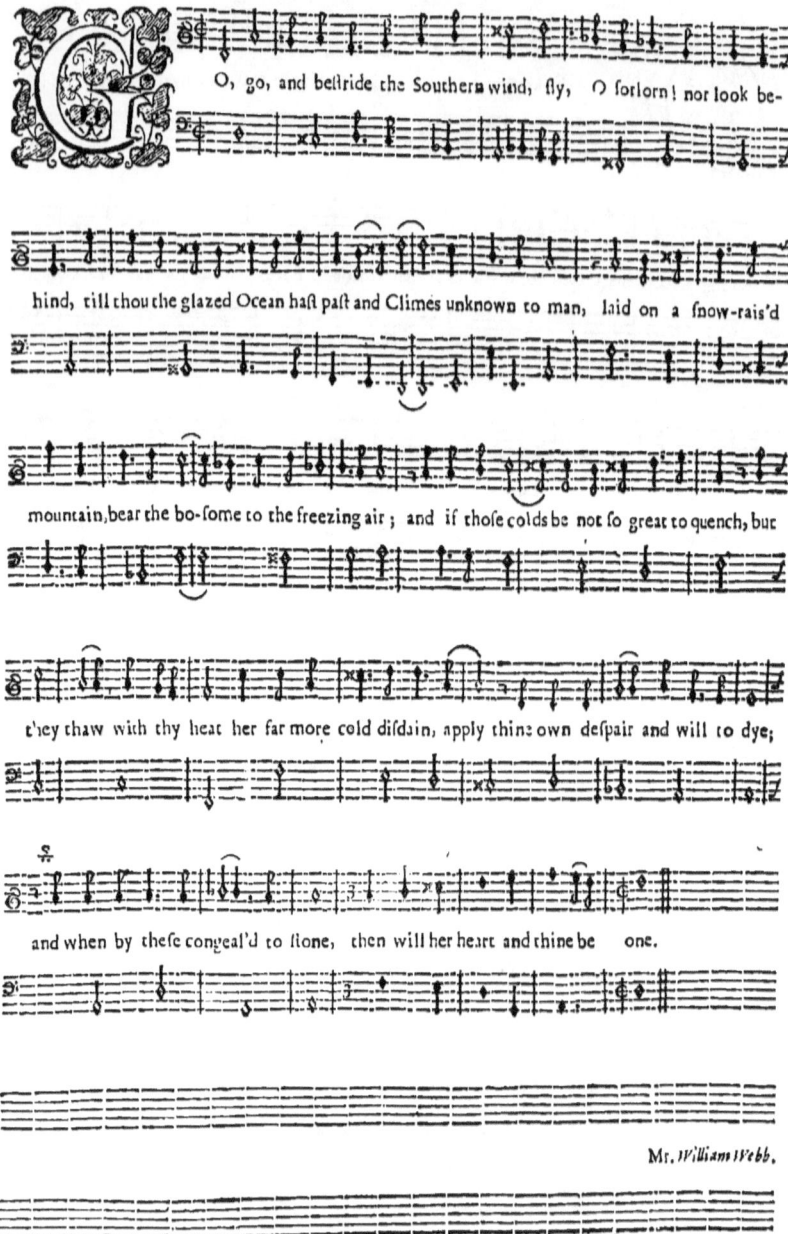

Go, go, and beſtride the Southern wind, fly, O forlorn! nor look behind, till thou the glazed Ocean haſt paſt and Climes unknown to man, laid on a ſnow-rais'd mountain, bear the boſome to the freezing air; and if thoſe colds be not ſo great to quench, but they thaw with thy heat her far more cold diſdain, apply thine own deſpair and will to dye; and when by theſe congeal'd to ſtone, then will her heart and thine be one.

Mr. William Webb.

False Love reproved.

BY all thy Glories willingly I go, yet could have wish'd thee constant in thy love; but since thou needs must prove uncertain as is thy Beauty, or as the Glass that shews it thee, my hopes thus soon to o-verthrow, shows thee more fickle; but my flames by this are easier quencht than his, whom flattering smiles betray; 'tis tyrannous delay breeds all the harm, and makes that fire consume, which should but warm.

Mr. *Henry Lawes*.

II.

Till time destroy those blossomes of thy youth,
Thou art our Idol-worship, at that rate,
    But who can tell thy fate?
And say that when this Beauties done,
This Lovers Torch shall still burn on;
I could have serv'd thee with such truth
Devourest Pilgrims to their Saints do show,
   'Departed long ago;
   And at this ebbing tyde,
   Have us'd thee as a Bride
   Who's only true
Whilst you are fair, he loves himself, not you.

Loves torrid Zone.

O, no, fair Heretick, it cannot be, but an ill love in mee, and worse for thee; for were it in my pow'r to love thee now this hour, more than I did the last, 'twould then so fall, I might not love at all: Love that can flow, and can admit encrease, admits as well an ebb, and may grow lesse.
Mr. *Henry Lawes*.

II.

True love is still the same
The Torrid Zones,
And those more frigid ones
It must not know:
For love grown cold, or hot
Is lust and friendship, not
The think we have, for that's a flame would dye,
Held down, or up too high;
Then think I love, more than I can expresse,
And would know more, could I but love thee lesse.

To his Chloris at Parting.

Fain would I *Chloris* whom my heart adores, longer a while between thine arms remain; but loe, the jealous morn her Ro-fie does to fpight me ope's, and brings the day a-gain. Farewell, farewell, *Chloris*, 'tis time I dy'd, the night de-parts, yet ſtill my woes abide.

Dr. *John Wilſon*.

II.

Hence ſaucy flearing Candle of the Skies,
Let us alone we, have no need of thee:
Our eyes are ever day, where *Chloris* eyes
Shine, that a pair of brighter Tapers bee.
Farewell, farewell, &c.

III.

O night! whoſe fable vaile was wont to be
More friend to Lovers, than the noiſefull day:
Wherefore, O wherefore do'ſt thou fly from me,
And carry with thee all my joys away?
Farewell, farewell, &c.

Coyness in Love.

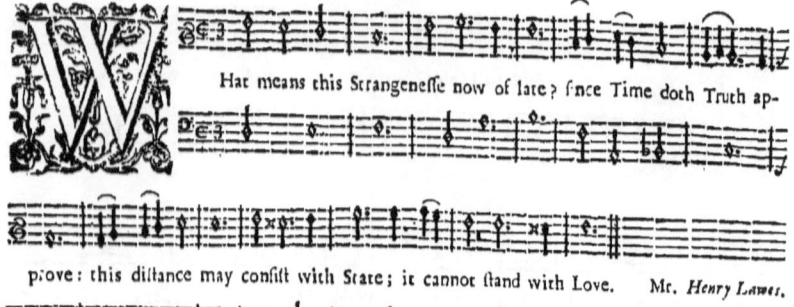

What means this Strangenesse now of late? since Time doth Truth approve: this distance may consist with State; it cannot stand with Love. Mr. *Henry Lawes.*

'Tis either cunning or distrust,
That do such ways allow:
The first is base, the last injust;
Let neither blemish you.

Speak but a word, or do but cast
One Look that seems to frown,
I'le give you all the love that's past,
The rest shall be mine own.

If you intend to draw me on,
You over act your part:
And if it be to have me gon,
You need not halfe this Art.

And such a faire and equall way
On both sides none can blame,
Since every man is bound to play
The fairest of his Game.

Love possest.

Wish no more thou shouldst love mee, my joys are full in loving thee; my heart's too narrow to contain my blisse, if thou shouldst love me a-gain. Mr. *Warner.*

Thy scorn may wound me, but my fate
Leads me to love, and thee to hate;
Yet I must love while I have breath,
For not to love were worse than death.

Then shall I sue for scorn or grace,
A lingring life, or death embrace;
Since one of these I needs must try,
Love me but once and let me dy.

Such mercy more thy fame shall raise,
Than cruell life can yield thee praise;
It shall be counted who so dies,
No murder, but a sacrifice.

A Lovers Resolution.

Tell not I dye, or that I live by thee, and as thou points my doom, so it must be: Or that my life (didst thou but leave to love,) would like a long disease, as weary prove: Since he whose mind is proof a---gainst his fate, makes himself happy at the worst estate.

Mr. *Tho. Brewer.*

II.

'Tis vanity for a man to build his blisse
On the frail favour of a womans kisse;
And most unmanly to enthrall his eye,
When Heaven and Nature gives it liberty:
Since Womens fancies with their fashions change,
To love for fashion to each face that's strange.

III.

I know the humour of your Sex is such
You ne'r could value any one thing much;
For should thy brest with constant flames be fir'd,
'Twere more then I expected, although desir'd:
Then think me not so fond, although I love,
But as thou stear'lt thy course, so mine shal move.

IV.

He that hath wealth, and can that wealth for-goe,
Is his own man, not slave to any he,
Thus arm'd with resolution, I am
Still o'recommer of my destinie:
Yet know I love, thou I can leave the state,
He best knows how to love, knows how to hate.

O

The Primrose.

Ask me why I send you here, this first-ling of the Infant year? Ask me why I send to you, this Primrose all be-pearl'd with dew? I must whisper to your Eares, the sweets of Love are wash'd with tears.

Ask me why this Rose doth show
All yellow, green, and sickly too?
Ask me why the stalk is weak,
And yeelding each way, yet not break?
I must tell you, These discover
What doubts and fears are in a Lover.

Cupid's Embassage.

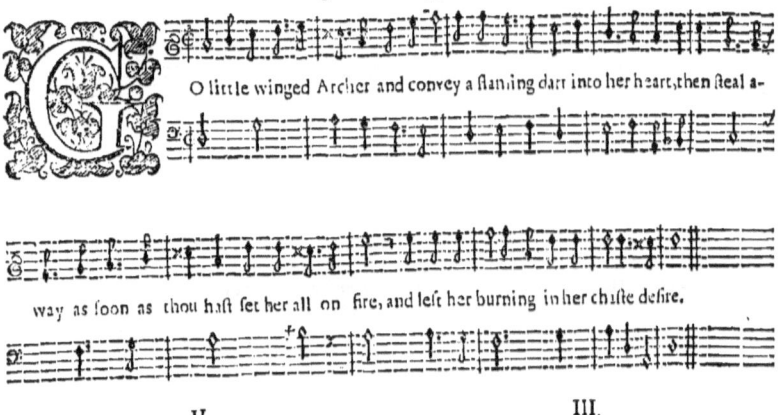

GO little winged Archer and convey a flaming dart into her heart, then steal away as soon as thou hast set her all on fire, and left her burning in her chaste desire.

II.   III.

Coridon *to his* Phillis.

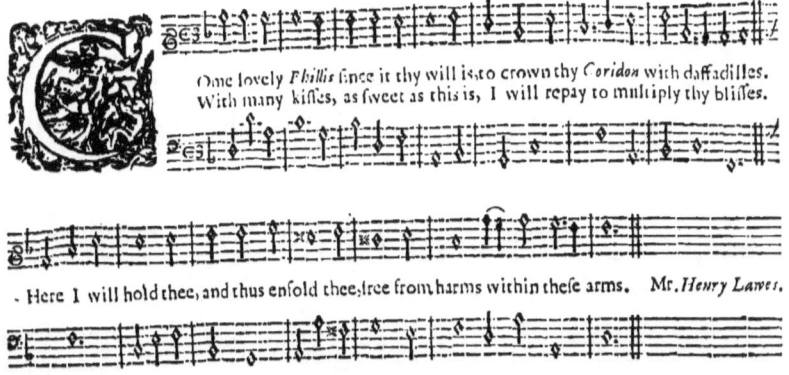

Come lovely *Phillis* since it is thy will is, to crown thy *Coridon* with daffadilles.
With many kisses, as sweet as this is, I will repay to multiply thy blisses.
Here I will hold thee, and thus enfold thee, free from harms within these arms.   Mr. *Henry Lawes*.

Sweet, still be smiling, 'tis sweet beguiling
Of tedious hours and sorrows best exiling;
For if you lowre, the bankes no power
Will have to bring forth any pleasant flower;
   Your eyes not granting
   Their raies enchanting,
Mine may raine, but 'twere in vain.

Thine eyes may wonder that mine asunder
Do from the Sun-shine draw thine to sit under;
Hold me unblam'd, to be enflam'd,
Where not to be so, youth were rather sham'd:
   Since that the oldest
   That thou beholdest
May feele fire of loves desire.

On Chloris *attractive Beauty.*

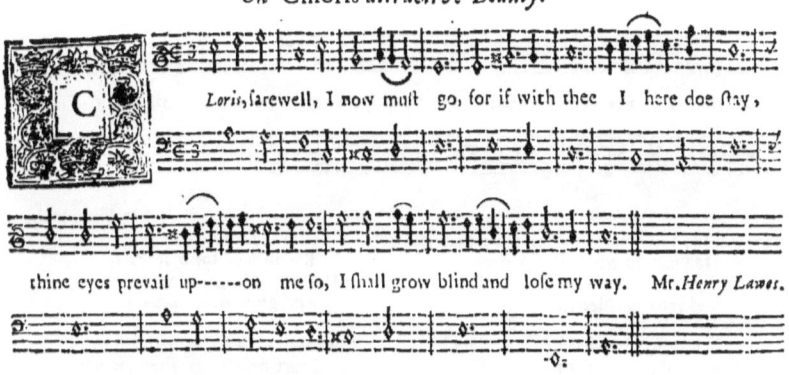

*C*loris, farewell, I now must go, for if with thee I here doe stay,
thine eyes prevail up------on me so, I shall grow blind and lose my way.   Mr. *Henry Lawes*.

Fame of thy Beauty, and thy Youth
  Amongst the rest me hither brought;
Finding this fame fall short of truth,
  Made me stay longer than I thought.

For I'm engag'd by word and oath
  A servant to anothers will;
Yet for thy love would forseit both,
  Could I be sure to keep it still.

But what assurance can I take,
  When thou fore-knowing this abuse,
For some more worthy Lovers sake,
  May'st leave me with so just excuse.

For thou may'st say 'twas not thy fault
  That thou did'st thus unconstant prove;
Thou wert by my example taught
  To break thy oath, to mend thy love.

No *Chloris*, no, I will return,
  And raise thy story to that height,
That Strangers shall at distance burn,
  And she distrust me Reprobate.

Then shall my love this doubt displace,
  And gain such trust, that I may come
And banquet sometimes on thy face,
  But make my constant meals at home.

[52]

Clora *forsaken, thus complains.*

Cloris false love made Clora weep, and by a river side her flock which she was wont to keep, neglecting thus she cry'd: Is't not In--ju--stice, O ye Gods! to kin--dle my desire, and to leave his at so much ods, as there's no mutual fire. Poor victo-ry, to peirce a heart that was a ten-der one, but cowardise to spare your dart from his that was a stone.

Dr. *John Wilson.*

As she thus mourn'd, the tears that fell
  Down from her love-sick eyes,
Did in the water drop and swell,
  And into bubbles rise.

Wherein her bloubard face appears,
  Now out alas, said she,
How do I melt away in tears
  For him that loves not me.

Yet as I lessen multiply,
  But in lesse form appears,
Thus do I languish from mine eye,
  And grow new in my tears.

Break not that Christall, circles me
  Sweet streams by your fair side,
My love perhaps may walking be,
  And I may be espi'd.

And thus in little drawn and drest
  In sad tears attire,
May force such passions from his brest,
  Shall equall my desire.

Reciprocal Love.

I Love a Lasse, but cannot show it, I keep a fire that burns with-in, rak'd up in em-bers: Ah could she know it, I might per-haps be lov'd a-gain: For a true love may justly call for friendship love reciprocall.   Dr. *John Wilson*.

II.

Some gentle courteous winde betray me,
   A sigh by wispering in her ear,
Or let some pitious shower convey me,
   By dropping on her breast a tear,
     Or two, or more; the hardest flint,
     By often drops receives a dint.

III.

Shall I then vex my heart and rend it,
   That is already too too weak ;
No, no, they say, Lovers may send it,
   By writing what they cannot speak:
     Go then my Muse, and let this verse
     Bring back my Life, or else my Hearse.

On Loves deceitful Charmes.

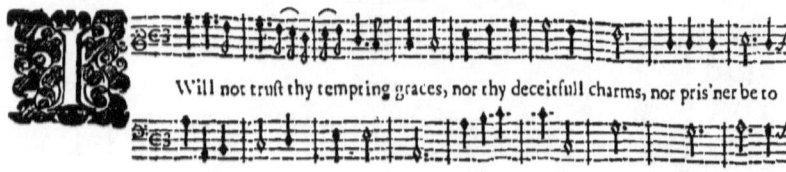

I Will not trust thy tempting graces, nor thy deceitfull charms, nor pris'ner be to

thy imbraces, or fet-ter'd in thine arms: No *Celia*, no, not all thy art can wound or captivate my heart.

Mr. *Jeremy Savill*.

II.
I will not gaze upon thine eyes,
Nor wanton with thy haire,
Lest those should burn me by surprize,
Or these my soul insnare:
Nor with those smiling dangers play,
Or fool my liberty away.

III.
Since then my weary heart is free,
And unconfin'd as thine;
If thou would'st mine should captive be,
Thou must thine own resigne:
And Gratitude shall thus move more
Than Love or Beauty could before.

Beauty a fading Ornament.

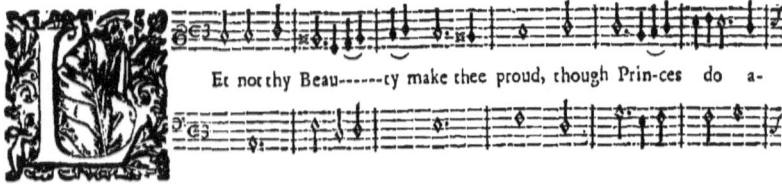

Et not thy Beau------ty make thee proud, though Prin-ces do a-

dore thee, since time and sickness were alow'd to mow such flowers before thee. Mr. *Henry Lawes*.

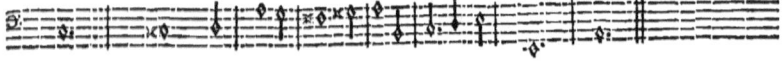

II.
Nor be not shy to that degree
Thy friends may hardly know thee,
Nor yet so coming, or so free,
That every fly may blow thee;
A state in every Princely brow,
As decent is requir'd,
Much more in thine, to whom they bow
By Beauties lightnings fir'd.

III.
And yet a state so sweetly mixt
With an attractive mildness;
It may like Vertue sit betwixt
The extreams of pride and vileness.
Then every eye that sees thy face
Will in thy Beauty glory,
And every tongue that wags will grace
Thy vertue with a story.

Beauty in Eclipse.

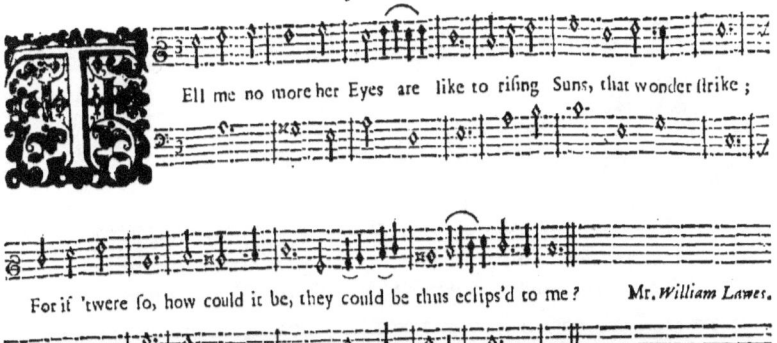

Tell me no more her Eyes are like to rising Suns, that wonder strike; For if 'twere so, how could it be, they could be thus eclips'd to me?

Mr. *William Lawes*.

Tell me no more her Breasts do grow
Like rising Hills of melting Snow;
For if 'twere so, how could they lye
So near the Sun-shine of her eye?

No, say her Eyes Portenders are
Of ruine, or some blazing starre,
Else would I feel from that fair fire
Some heat to cherish my desire.

Say that although like to the Moon,
She heavenly fair, yet chang'd as soon;
Else she would constant once remain
Either to pity or disdain.

Tell me no more the restless Spheares
Compar'd to her voyce, fright our ears;
For if 'twere so, how then could death
Dwell with such discord in her breath?

Say that her Breasts, though cold as Snow,
Are hard as Marble, when I wooe;
Else they would soften and relent
With sighs inflamed, from me sent.

That so by one of them I might
Be kept alive, or murther'd quite;
For 'tis no less cruell there to kill,
Where life doth but increase the ill.

Cupid detected.

Silly Heart forbear, those are murd'ring Eyes, in the which I swear *Cupid* lur-king lies: See his Quiver, see his Bow; to see his Dart, fly, O fly! thou foolish Heart.

Greedy Eyes, take heed, they are scorching Beams
Causing Hearts to bleed,& your Eyes spring streams:
Love lies watching with his Bow bent,and his Dart
For to wound both Eyes and Heart.

Think and gaze your fill, foolish Heart and Eyes,
Since you love your ill, and your good despise:
Cupid Shooting, *Cupid* Darting, and his Band
Mortal powers cannot withstand.

Loves Flattery.

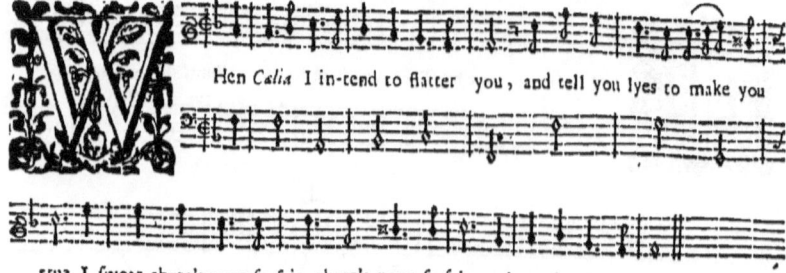

When *Celia* I in-tend to flatter you, and tell you lyes to make you true, I swear there's none so fair, there's none so fair, and you beleive it too.   Dr. *Colman.*

Oft have I matcht you with the Rose, and said
No twins so like hath nature made,
            But 'tis
Only in this,
You prick my hand and fade.

Oft have I said there is no pretious stone
But may be found in yon alone;
          Though I
No stone espy,
Unlesse your heart be one.

When I praise your skin I quote the wooll
That Silk-worms from their Entrailes pull,
          And show
That new fallen snow,
Is not more beautifull.

Yet grow not proud by such Hyperboles
Were you as excellent as these
          Whilst I
Before you ly,
They might be had with ease.

Loves Theft.

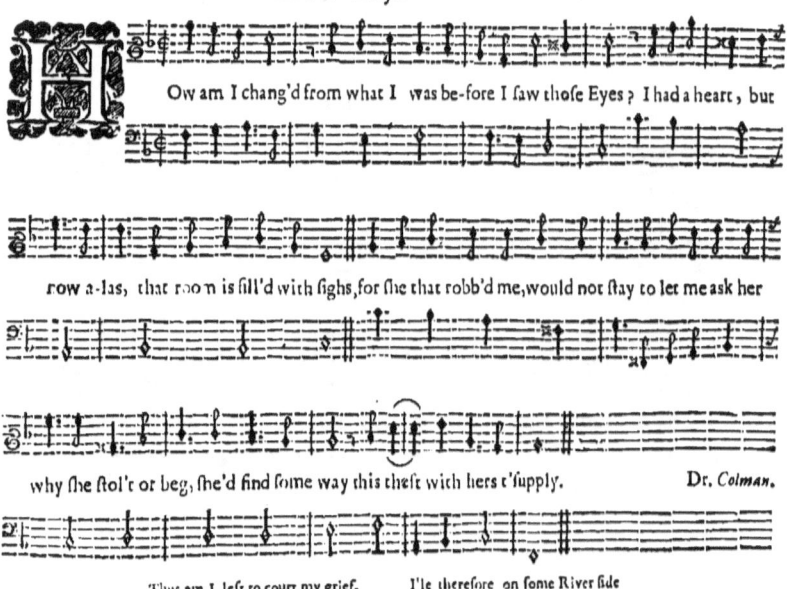

How am I chang'd from what I was be-fore I saw those Eyes? I had a heart, but row a-las, that room is fill'd with sighs, for she that robb'd me, would not stay to let me ask her why she stol't or beg, she'd find some way this theft with hers t'supply.   Dr. *Colman.*

Thus am I left to court my grief,
For when she's out of sight,
There can on earth be no relief,
Or ought that's true delight.

I'le therefore on some River side
Wander to breath my woe,
And ask those Nymphs how *Hylas* dy'd
That I might do so too,

Dr. *John Wilson.*

II.

So when the jealous Eye and Ear
   Are shut or turn'd aside,
Our Tongues, our Eyes, may talk sans fear
   Of being heard or spi'd.
What though our Bodies cannot meet
   Loves fuels more divine;
The fixt stars by their twinkling greet,
   And yet they never joyn.

III.

False Meteors that do change their place,
   Though they shine fair and bright;
Yet when they covet to embrace,
   Fall down and lose their light.
Thus while we shall preserve from waste
   The flame of our desire,
No vestall shall maintain more chaste,
   Or more immortal fire.

IV.

If thou perceive thy flame decay,
   Come light thine Eyes at mine;
And when I feel mine waste away
   I'le take new fire from thine.

A Motive to Love.

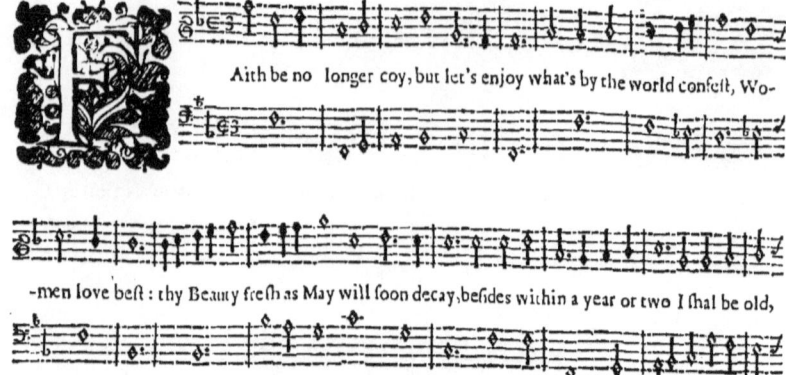

Faith be no longer coy, but let's enjoy what's by the world confest, Women love best: thy Beauty fresh as May will soon decay, besides within a year or two I shal be old,

 and cannot doe.

Do'st think that nature can
For every man,
Had she more skill, provide
So fair a Bride?
Who ever had a Feast
For a single Guest?
No, without she did intend
To serve the Husband and his friend.

To be a little nice
Sets better price
On Virgins, and improves
Their Servants loves;
But on the riper years
It ill appears:
After a while you'l find this true,
I need provoking more then you.

On Liberty.

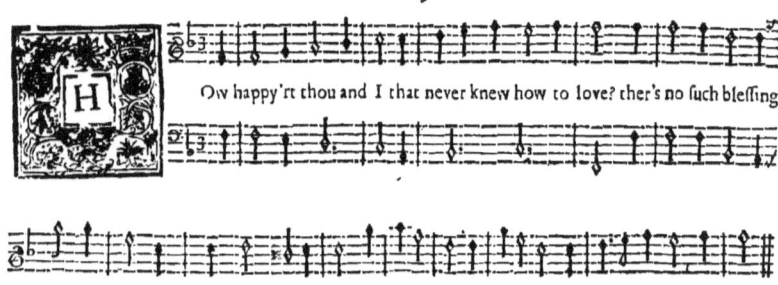

How happy'rt thou and I that never knew how to love? ther's no such blessing here beneath, what e're there is above; 'tis li-berty, 'tis liberty, that e-very wise man loves.

Out, out upon those Eyes, that think to murder mee,
And he's an Asse beleives her fair, that is not kind and free:
Ther's nothing sweet, ther's nothing sweet to man, but Liberty.

I'le tye my Heart to none, nor yet confine mine Eyes,
But I will play my Game so well, I'le never want a prize:
'Tis liberty, 'tis liberty, has made me now thus wise.

[55]

Beauty and Love at ods.

Beauty and Love once fell at ods, and thus revil'd each other: Quoth Love, I am one of the gods, and you wait on my mother; thou hast no pow'r ore man at all, but what I gave to thee; nor art thou longer fair or sweet, then men acknowledge me. Mr. *Henry Lawes.*

Away fond Boy, then Beauty said,
We see that thou art blind,
But men have knowing eyes, and can
My graces better find:
'Twas I begot thee, Mortals know,
And call'd thee Blind desire;
I made thy Arrows, and thy Bow,
And Wings to kindle fire.

Love here in anger flew away,
And straight to *Vulcan* pray'd
That he would tip his shafts with scorn,
To punish this proud Maid:
So Beauty ever since hath bin
But courted for an hour,
To love a day is now a fin
'Gainst Cupid and his power.

Love admits no Delay.

Come, O come, I brook no stay, she doth not love that can delay; see how the stealing Night hath blotted out the light, and Tapers do supply the day. Mr. *Henry Lawes.*

To be Chaste is to be Old,
And that foolish Girle that's cold
Is fourscore at fifteen,
Desires do write us green;
And loofer Flames our Youth unfold.

See the first Taper's almost gon,
Thy flame like that will straight be none,
And I as it expire,
Not able to hold fire;
She loseth Time that lyes alone.

Let us cherish then these powers
Whiles we yet may call them curs;
Then we best spend our Time,
When no Dull Zealous Chime,
But sprightfull kisses strike the hour.

The Anglers Song.

Mans Life is but vain, for 'tis subject to pain and sorrow, and short as a Bubble; Tis a Hodg Pody of businesse, and Money and Care, and Care and Mony, and trouble. But we'l take no Care when the Weather proves Fair, nor will we Vex now though it Rain; wee'l banish all Sorrow, and Sing till to morrow, and Angle and Angle again.

Mr. *Henry Lawes.*

On Attractive Beauty.

Oh see how unregarded now that piece of Beauty passes? There was a time when I did vow to that alone, but mark the fate of Faces; That Red and White works now no more on me, than if it could not charm, or I not see.   Mr. *John Goodgroome*.

II.

And yet the Face continues good,
   And I have still desires;
Am still the self-same Flesh and Blood,
   As apt to melt, and suffer for those fires:
Oh some kind power unriddle where it lyes,
Whether my Heart be faultie or her Eyes.

III.

She every day her man doth kill,
   And I as often dye;
Neither her Power then, nor my Will
   Can question'd be, what is the Mysterie?
Sure Beauties Empires, like to greater States,
Have certain Periods set, and Hidden Fates.

[64]

Power of Love.

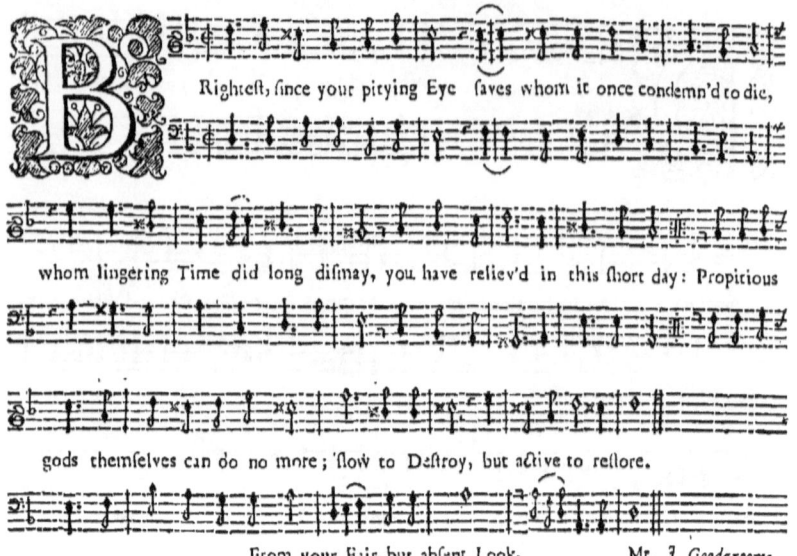

Brighteft, fince your pitying Eye faves whom it once condemn'd to die, whom lingering Time did long difmay, you have reliev'd in this fhort day: Propitious gods themfelves can do no more; flow to Deftroy, but active to reftore.

From your Fair, but abfent Look,
Cold Death her Pale Artilory took;
Till Gentle Love that Dart impreft,
And Lodg'd a Milder in your breft;
Like Fam'd *Acchillis* myftick fpear, thus you
Both fcatter Wounds, and fcatter Balfame too.

Mr. *J. Goodgroome*.

The Jovial Begger.

From Hunger and Cold who liveth more free, and who fo richly choathed as we? Our Bellies are full, and our Flefh it is Warm, and againft Pride our Rags is a Charm: Enough is a Feaft to Morrow, Let rich men take care, we feel no Sorrow.

A Protest against Love.

O, no, I never was in Love, nor ever hope to be; I have an Art protects my Heart from that fond Lu-na-cie. And yet I know that I have seen a world of Taking Faces; and spent much time in finding out their several hidden Graces.   Mr. H. Lawes.

This Lady for her pretty Shape
I often have admir'd:
That for her Fancy and her Wit;
I sometimes have desir'd.
But yet I never was in Love,
Nor ever hope to be:
Unless some Stronger Influence
Do draw my heart to thee.

The Excellency of Wine.

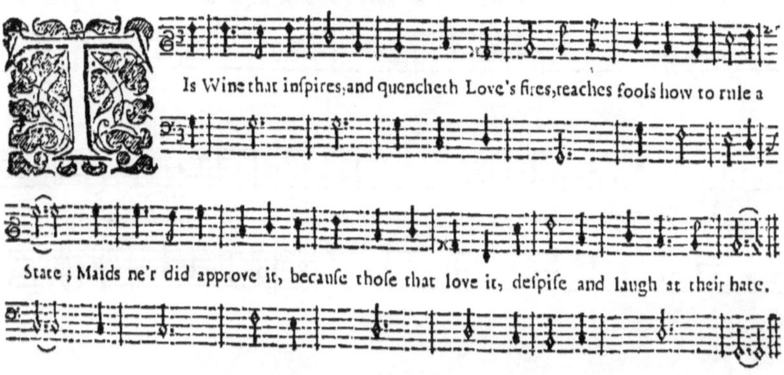

'Is Wine that inspires, and quencheth Love's fires, teaches fools how to rule a State; Maids ne'r did approve it, because those that love it, despise and laugh at their hate.

An Italian Ayre.

[67]

An Italian *Ayre for two Voyces.*

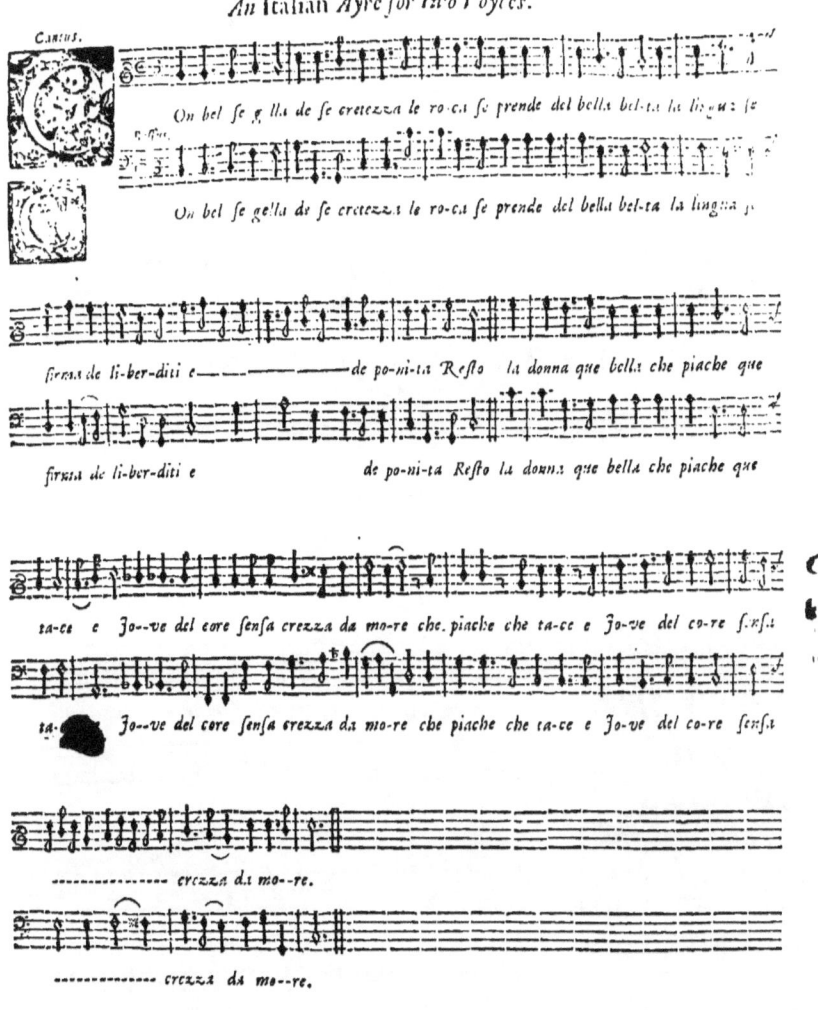

Here endeth the AYRES for One or two Voyces to the *Theorbo-Lute*, or *Basse-Viol*.

S

[68]

SECOND BOOK:
CONTAINING
DIALOGUES
For TWO VOYCES:
To be Sung to the *Theorboe-Lute* or *Basse-Viol*.

A Dialogue betwixt Phillis *and* Clorillo.

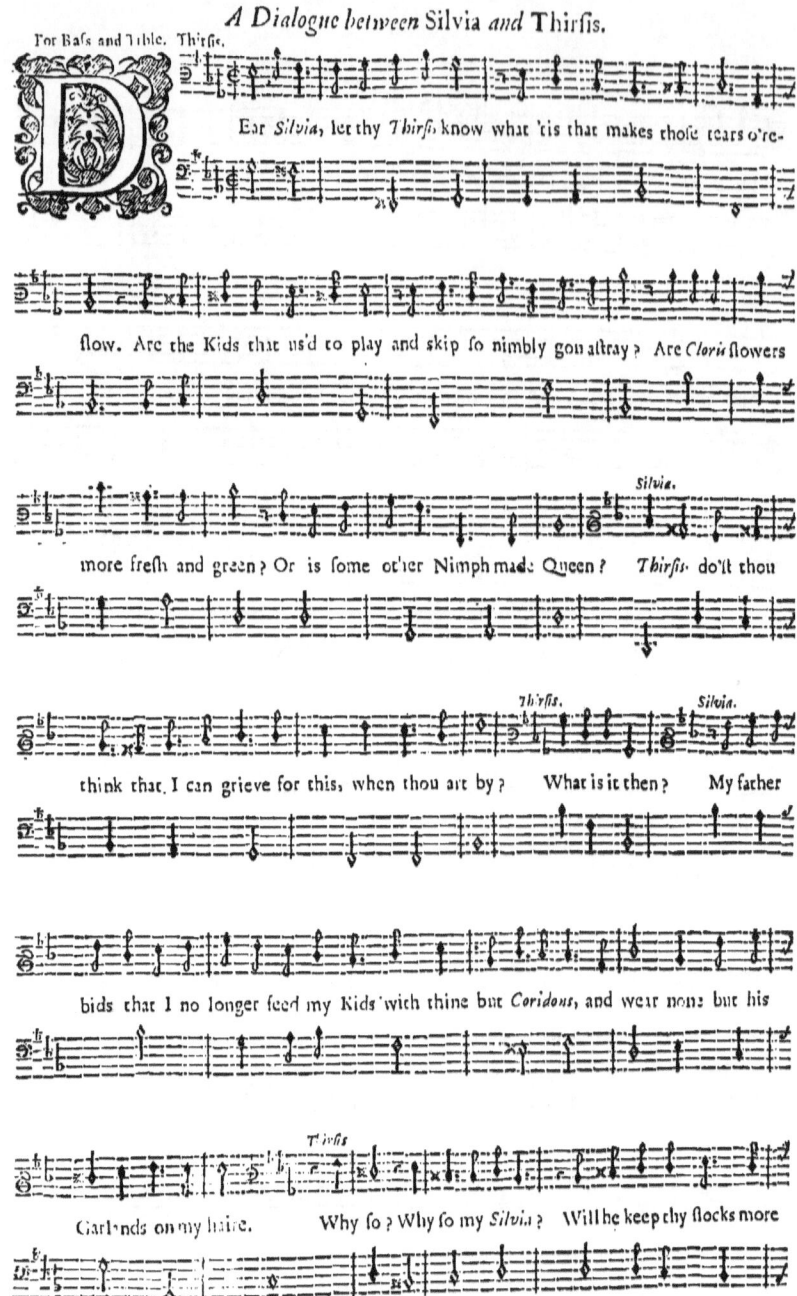

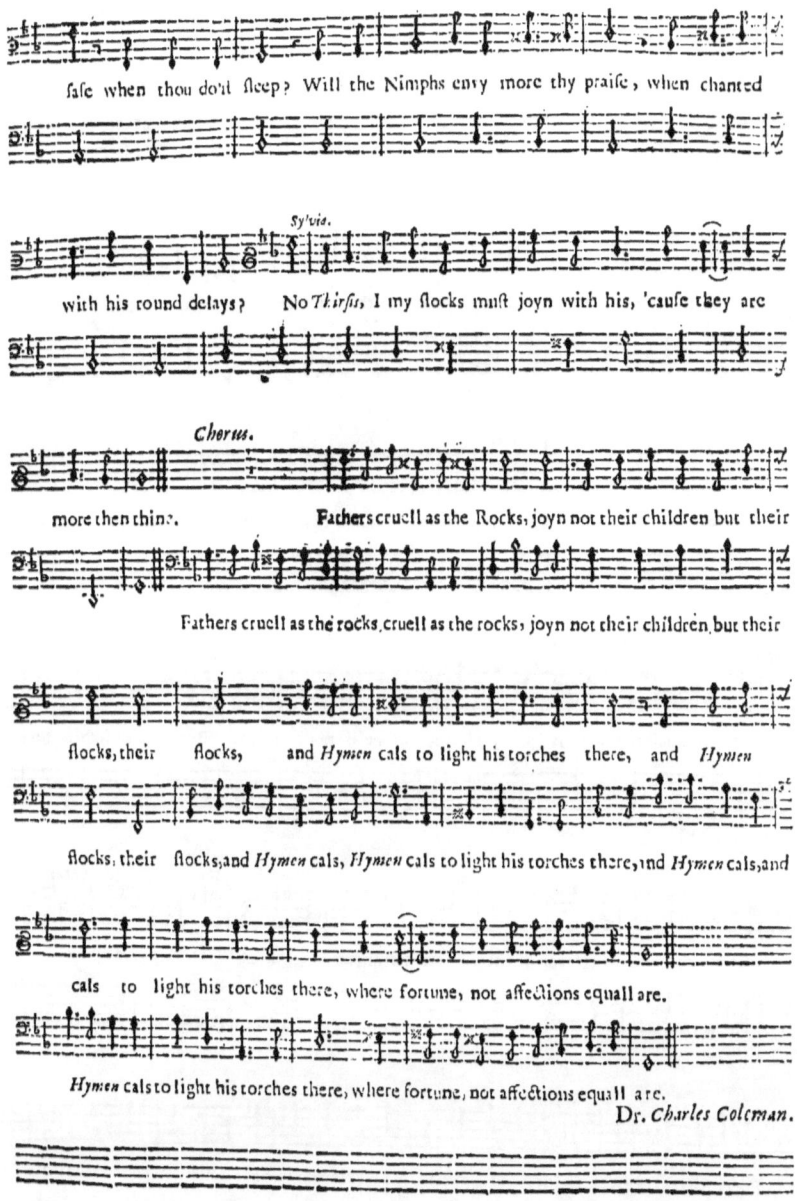

[74]

A Dialogue between Daphne and Strephon.

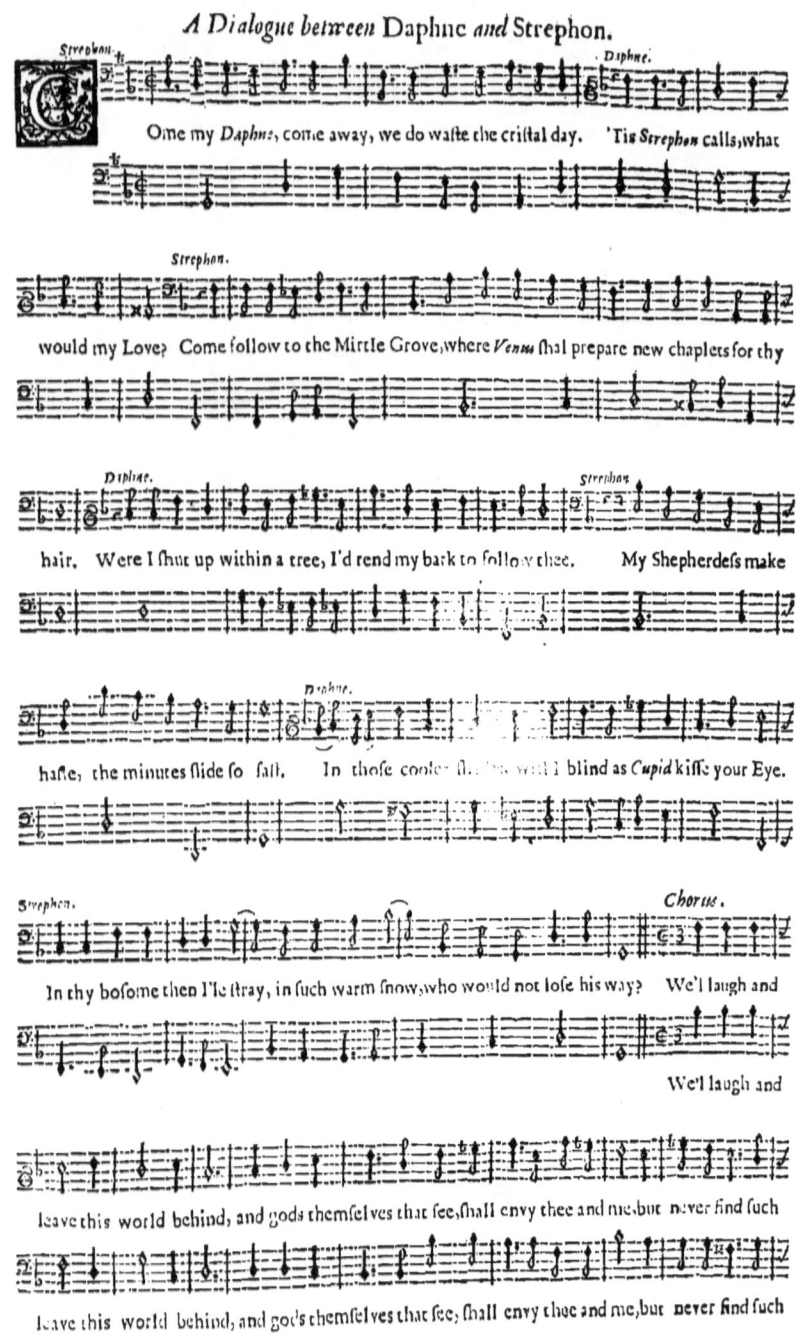

Come my *Daphne*, come away, we do waste the cristal day. 'Tis *Strephon* calls, what would my Love? Come follow to the Mirtle Grove, where *Venus* shal prepare new chaplets for thy hair. Were I shut up within a tree, I'd rend my bark to follow thee. My Shepherdess make haste, the minutes slide so fast. In those cooler shades will I blind as *Cupid* kisse your Eye. In thy bosome then I'le stray, in such warm snow, who would not lose his way? We'l laugh and leave this world behind, and gods themselves that see, shall envy thee and me, but never find such

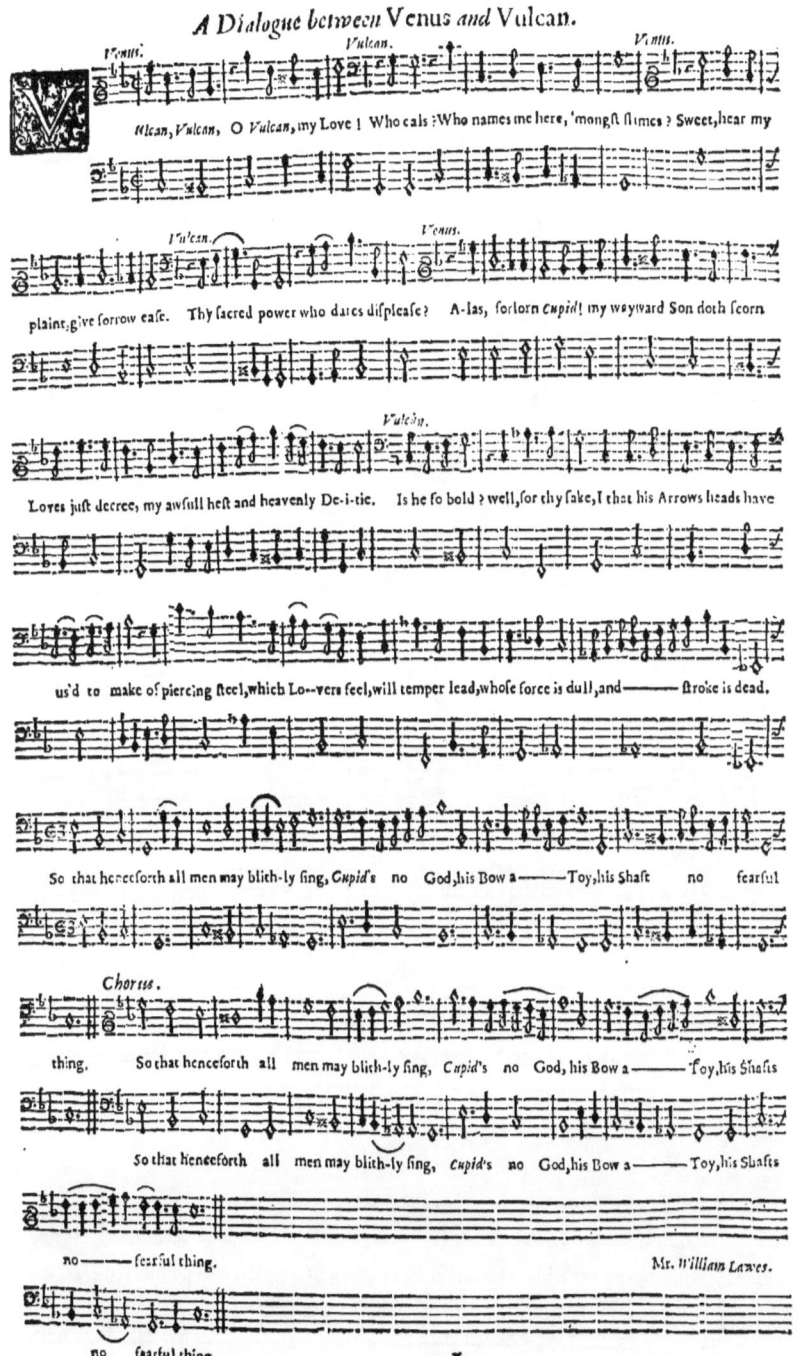

A Dialogue between Charon and Philomel.

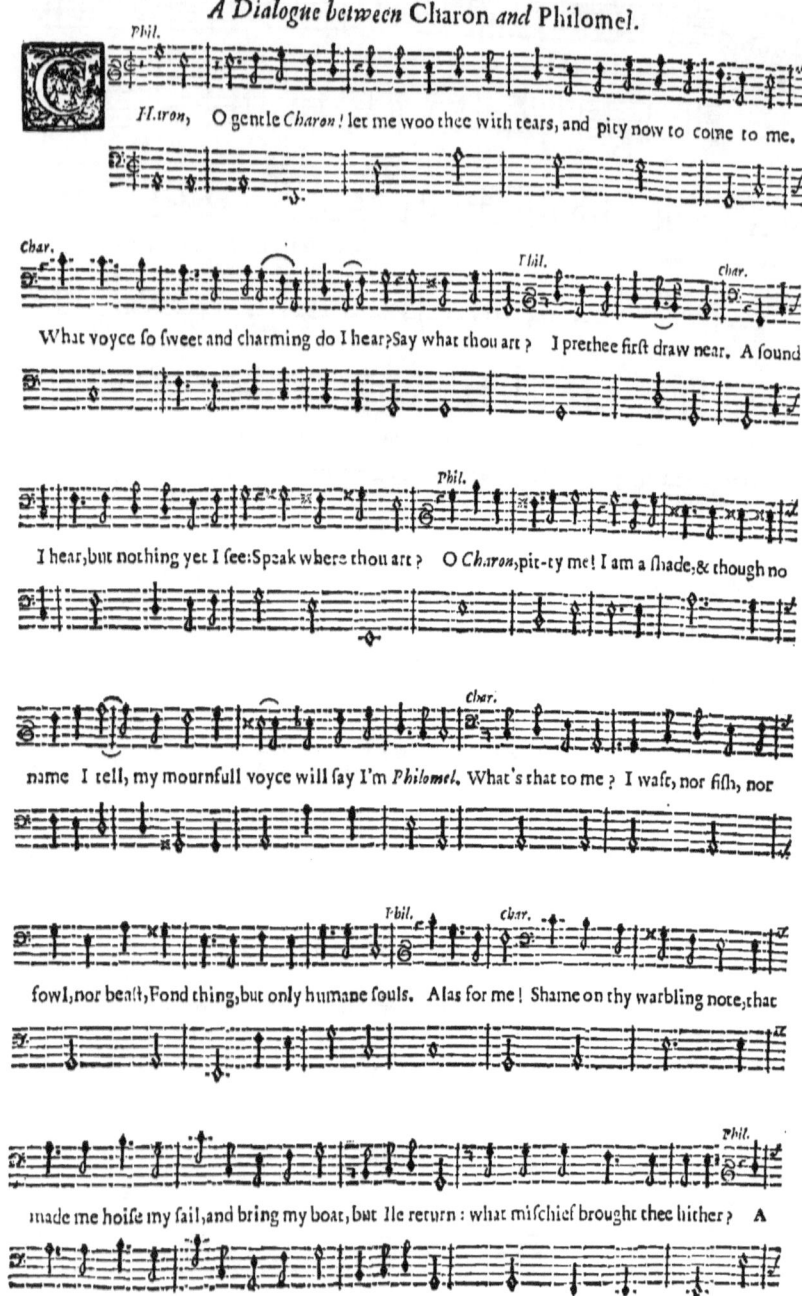

O gentle *Charon!* let me woo thee with tears, and pity now to come to me. What voyce so sweet and charming do I hear? Say what thou art? I prethee first draw near. A sound I hear, but nothing yet I see: Speak where thou art? O *Charon*, pit-ty me! I am a shade,& though no name I tell, my mournfull voyce will say I'm *Philomel.* What's that to me? I waft, nor fish, nor fowl, nor beast, Fond thing, but only humane souls. Alas for me! Shame on thy warbling note, that made me hoise my sail, and bring my boat, but Ile return: what mischief brought thee hither? A

A Dialogue between Thyrſis and Damon.

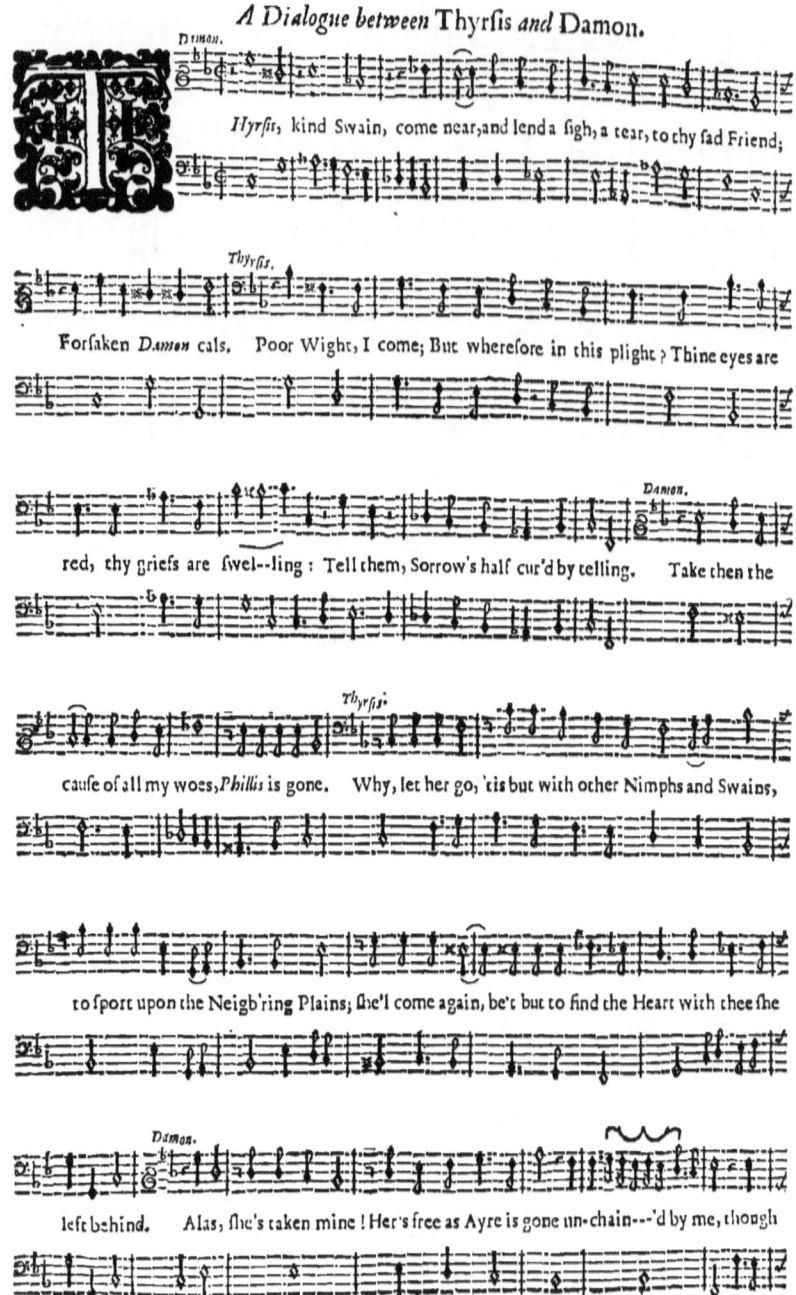

Thyrſis, kind Swain, come near, and lend a ſigh, a tear, to thy ſad Friend; Forſaken *Damon* cals. Poor Wight, I come; But wherefore in this plight? Thine eyes are red, thy griefs are ſwel--ling: Tell them, Sorrow's half cur'd by telling. Take then the cauſe of all my woes, *Phillis* is gone. Why, let her go, 'tis but with other Nimphs and Swains, to ſport upon the Neigb'ring Plains; ſhe'l come again, be't but to find the Heart with thee ſhe left behind. Alas, ſhe's taken mine! Her's free as Ayre is gone un-chain---'d by me, though

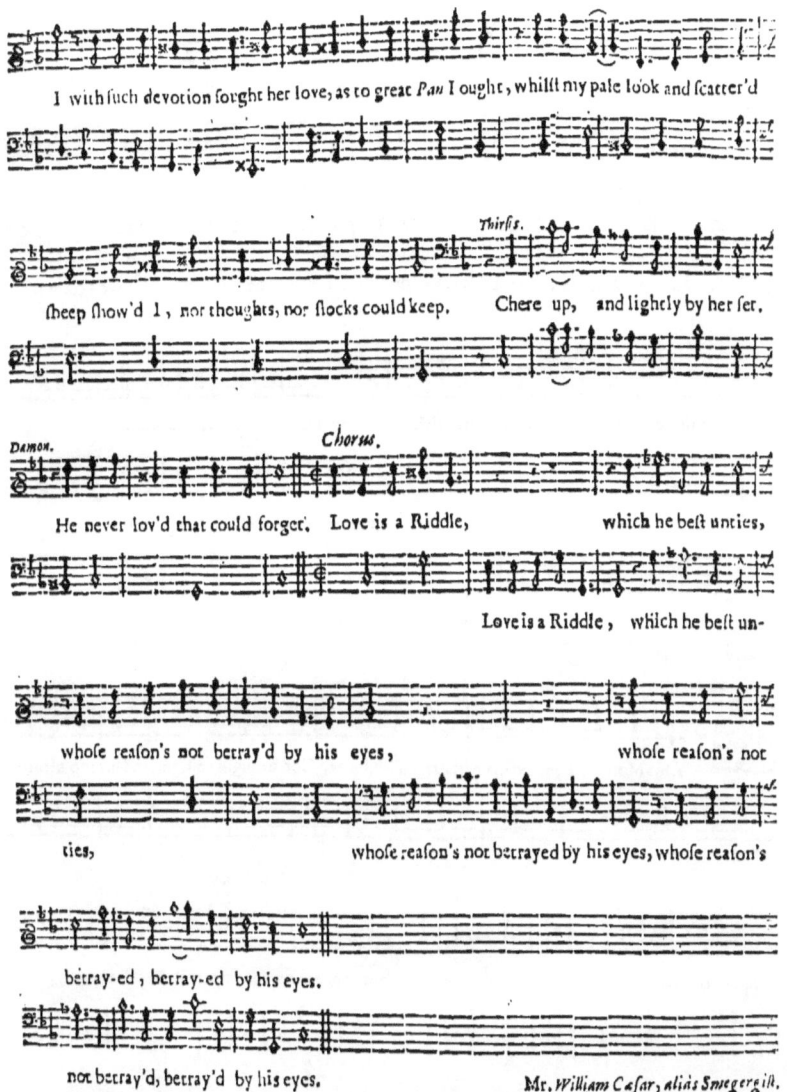

[84]

A Glee to Bachus *with* Chorus *for Three voyces to be sung between every verse.*

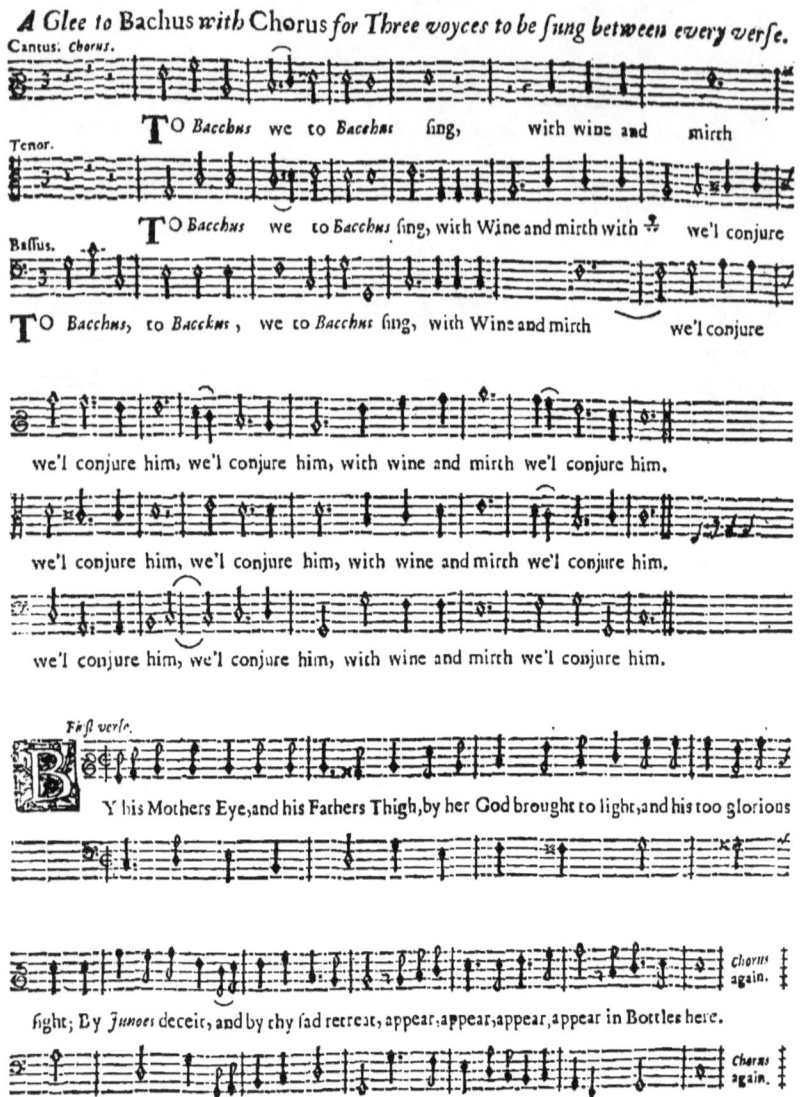

Cantus: *Chorus.*

Tenor.

TO Bacchus we to Bacchus sing, with wine and mirth

Bassus.

TO *Bacchus* we to *Bacchus* sing, with Wine and mirth with ♯ we'l conjure

TO Bacchus, to Bacchus, we to Bacchus sing, with Wine and mirth we'l conjure

we'l conjure him, we'l conjure him, with wine and mirth we'l conjure him.

we'l conjure him, we'l conjure him, with wine and mirth we'l conjure him.

we'l conjure him, we'l conjure him, with wine and mirth we'l conjure him.

First verse.

BY his Mothers Eye, and his Fathers Thigh, by her God brought to light, and his too glorious

fight; By *Junoes* deceit, and by thy sad retreat, appear, appear, appear, appear in Bottles here. *Chorus again.*

Chorus again.

[85]

A Glee with Chorus *for three voyces to be sung to every verse.*

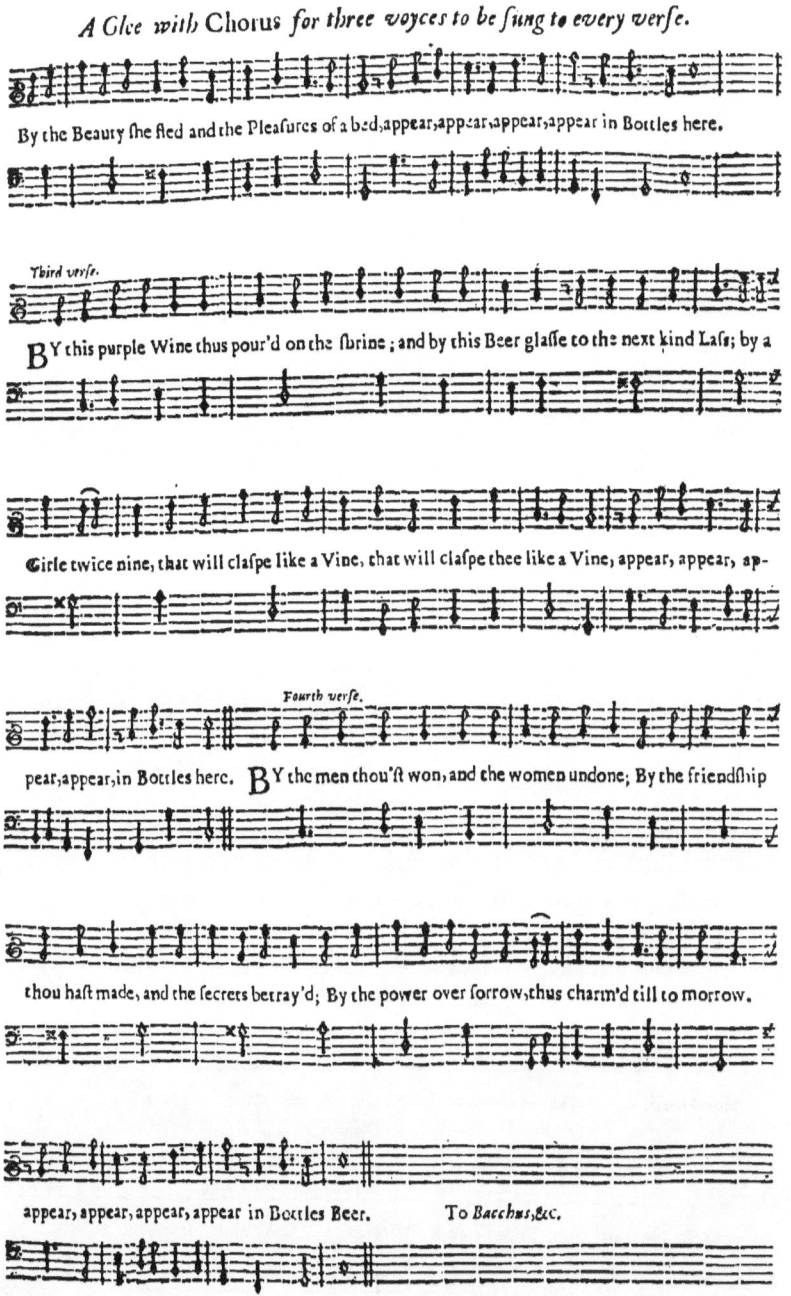

By the Beauty she fled and the Pleasures of a bed, appear, appear, appear, appear in Bottles here.

Third verse.

BY this purple Wine thus pour'd on the shrine; and by this Beer glasse to the next kind Lass; by a

Girle twice nine, that will claspe like a Vine, that will claspe thee like a Vine, appear, appear, ap-

Fourth verse.

pear, appear, in Bottles here. BY the men thou'st won, and the women undone; By the friendship

thou hast made, and the secrets betray'd; By the power over sorrow, thus charm'd till to morrow.

appear, appear, appear, appear in Bottles Beer.   To *Bacchus*, &c.

Dr. *Charles Colman.*

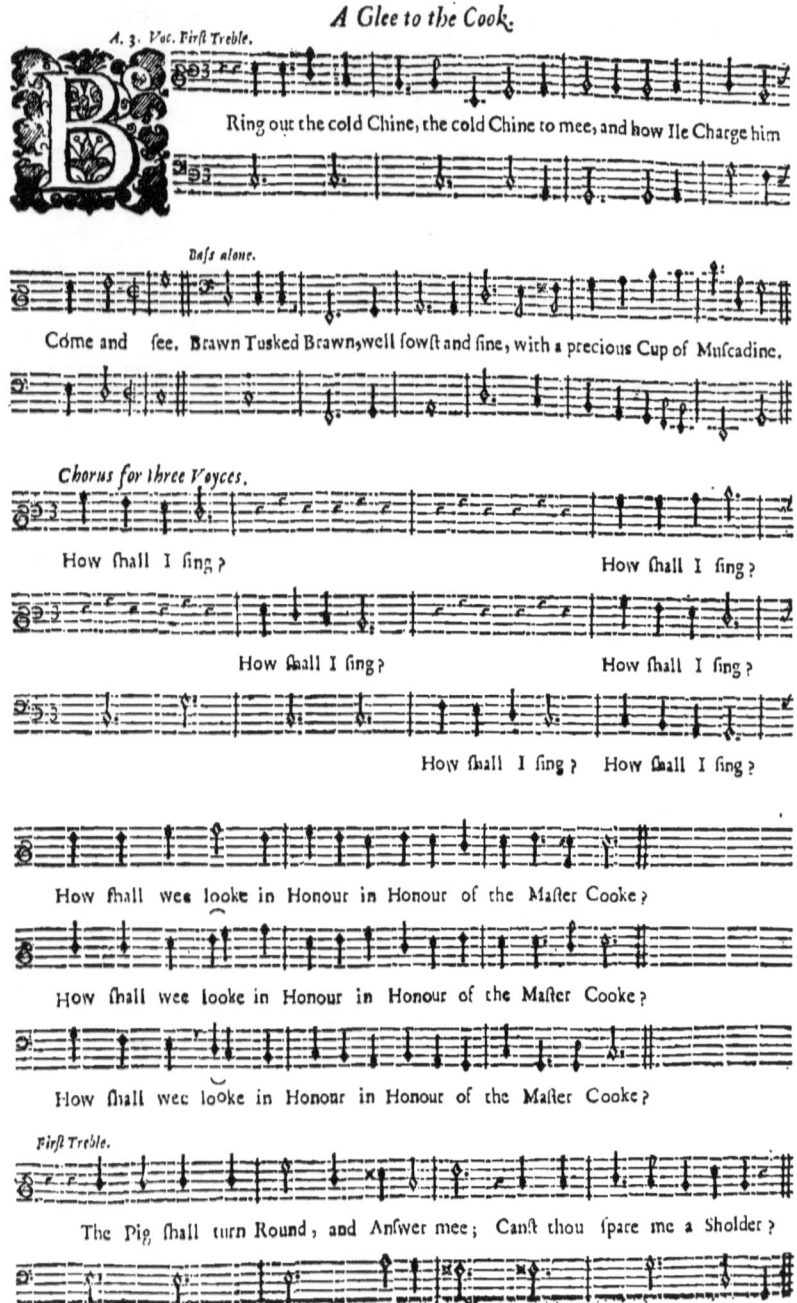

A Glee to the Cook.

A. 3. Voc. First Treble.

Ring out the cold Chine, the cold Chine to mee, and how Ile Charge him

Bass alone.

Come and see, Brawn Tusked Brawn, well sowst and fine, with a precious Cup of Muscadine.

Chorus for three Voyces.

How shall I sing?   How shall I sing?

How shall I sing?   How shall I sing?

How shall I sing?   How shall I sing?

How shall wee looke in Honour in Honour of the Master Cooke?

How shall wee looke in Honour in Honour of the Master Cooke?

How shall wee looke in Honour in Honour of the Master Cooke?

First Treble.

The Pig shall turn Round, and Answer mee; Canst thou spare me a Sholder?

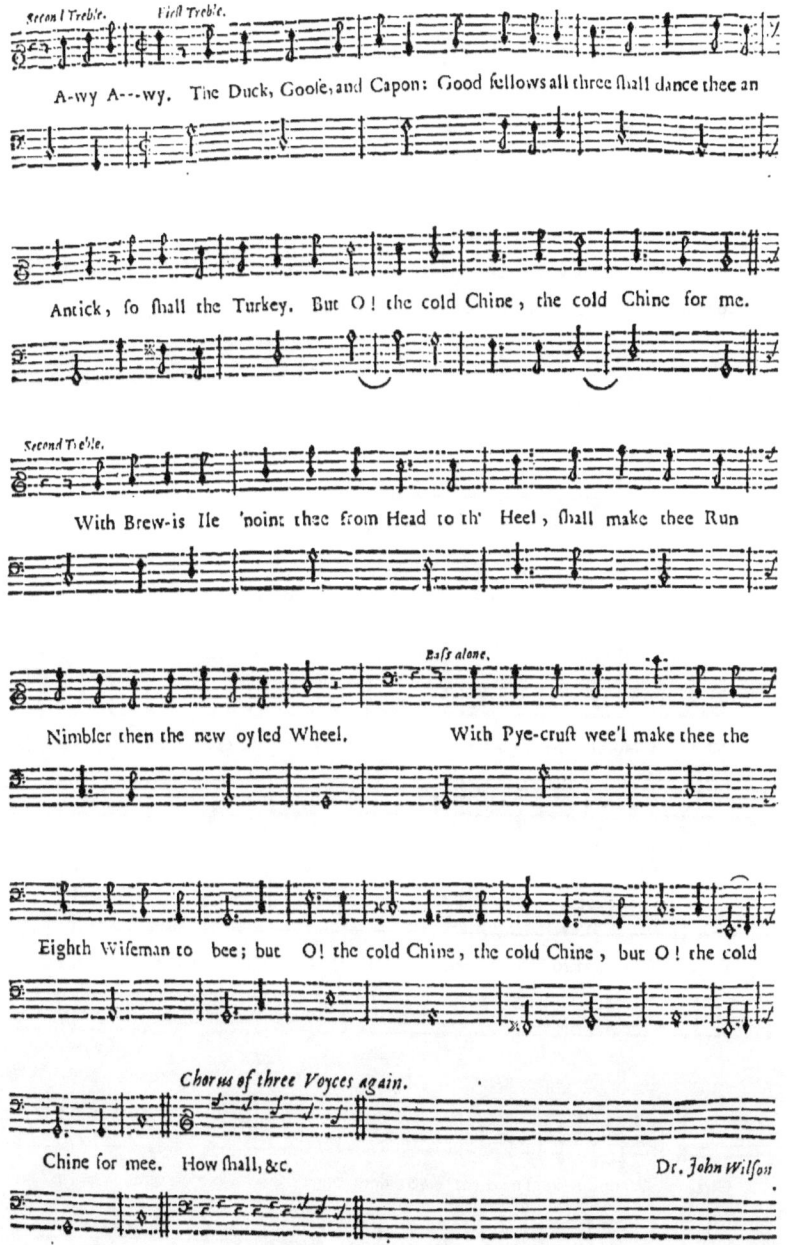

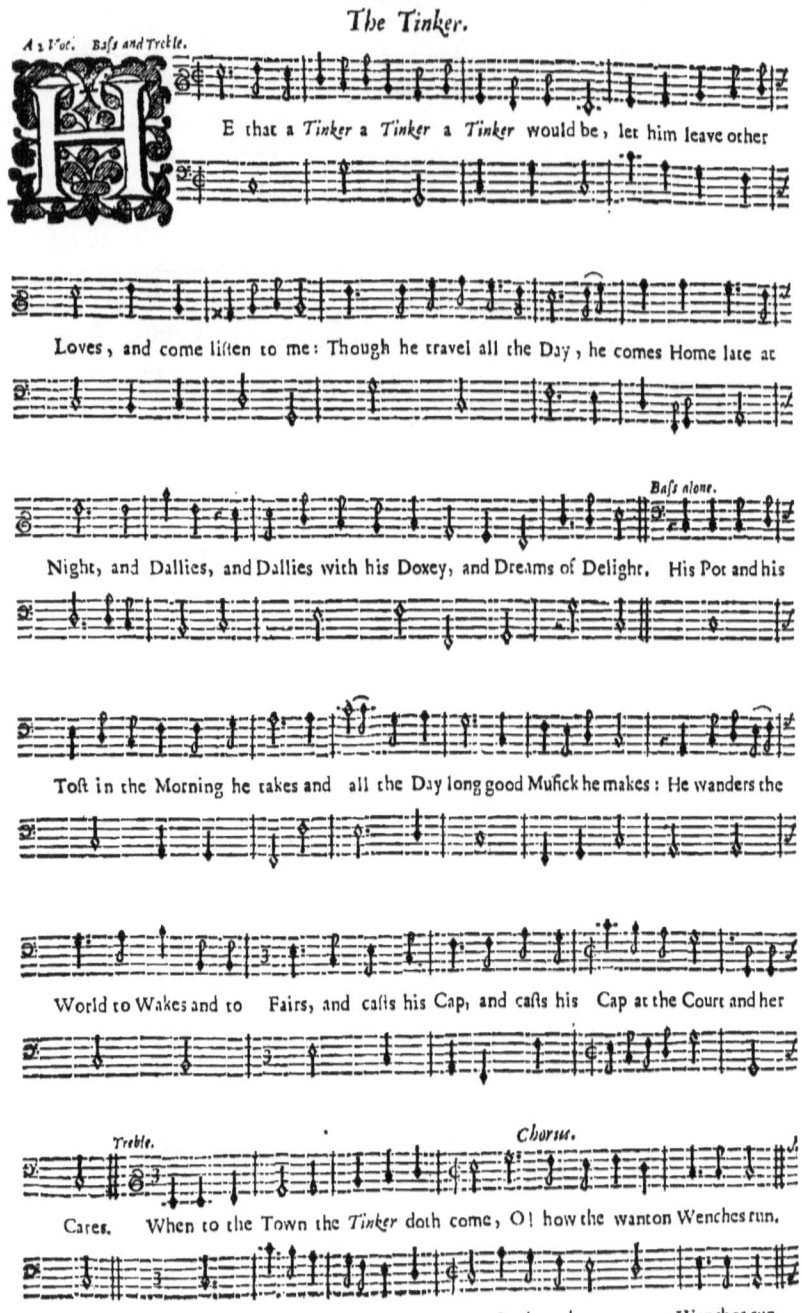

[89]

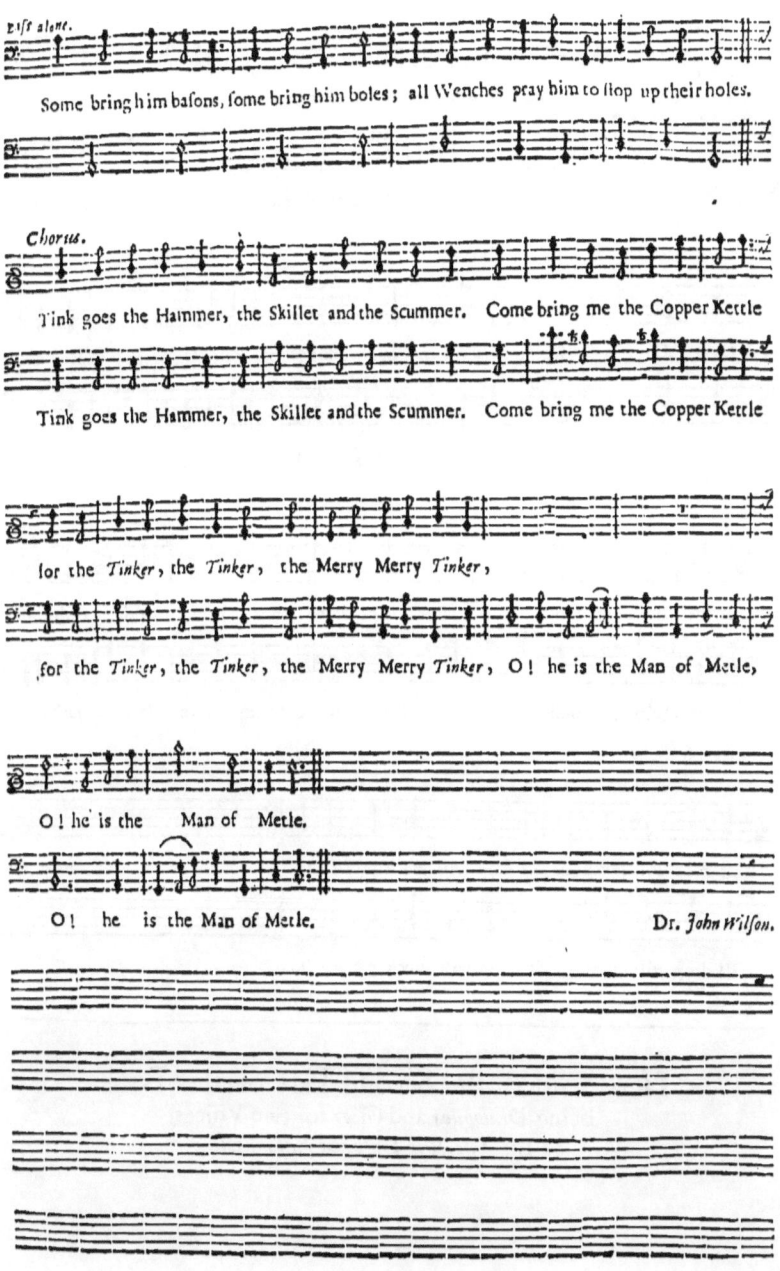

Dr. *John Wilson.*

[90]

A Glee.

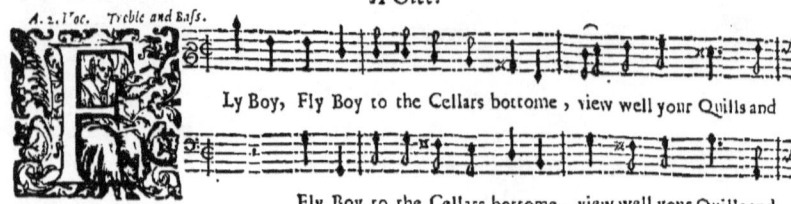

Ly Boy, Fly Boy to the Cellars bottome, view well your Quills and

Fly Boy to the Cellars bottome, view well your Quills and

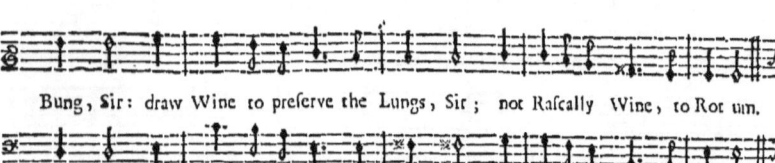

Bung, Sir: draw Wine to preserve the Lungs, Sir; not Rascally Wine, to Rot um.

Bung, Sir: draw Wine to preserve the Lungs, Sir; not Rascally Wine, to Rot um.

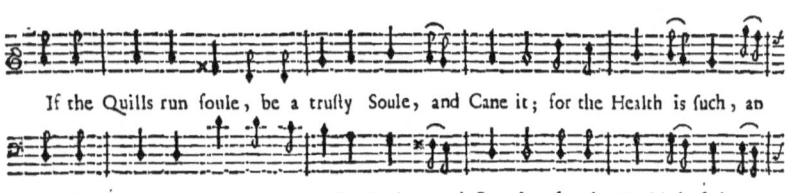

If the Quills run foule, be a trusty Soule, and Cane it; for the Health is such, an

If the Quills run foule, be a trusty Soule, and Cane it; for the Health is such, an

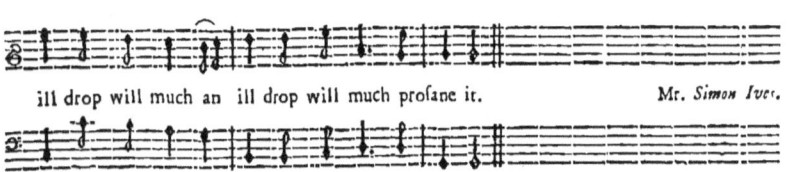

ill drop will much an ill drop will much profane it.   Mr. *Simon Ives.*

ill drop will much an ill drop will much profane it.

Here Endeth the Second Part of this Book;
being *Dialogues* and *Glees* for two Voices,
to the *Theorboe-Lute,* or *Bass-Viol.*

[91]

THIRD BOOK.
CONTAINING
Short *AYRES* or *BALADS* for Three Voyces:
Which may be sung either by a Voyce alone, or by Two or Three Voyces.

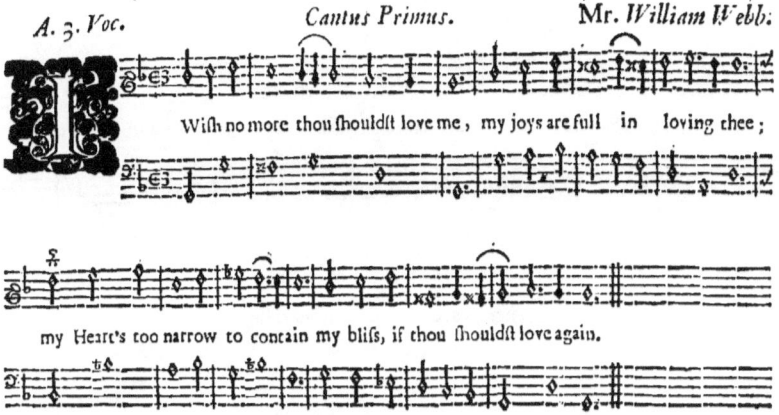

A 2

[92]

A. 3. Voc. *Cantus Primus.* Mr. *Nicholas Lanneare.*

Hough I am young and cannot tell, either what love or death is well; and then again I have been told, love wounds with heat, love wounds with heat, and death with cold

Yet I have heard they both bear darts,
And both do aime at humane hearts;
So that I fear they do but bring
Extreams to touch, and mean one thing.

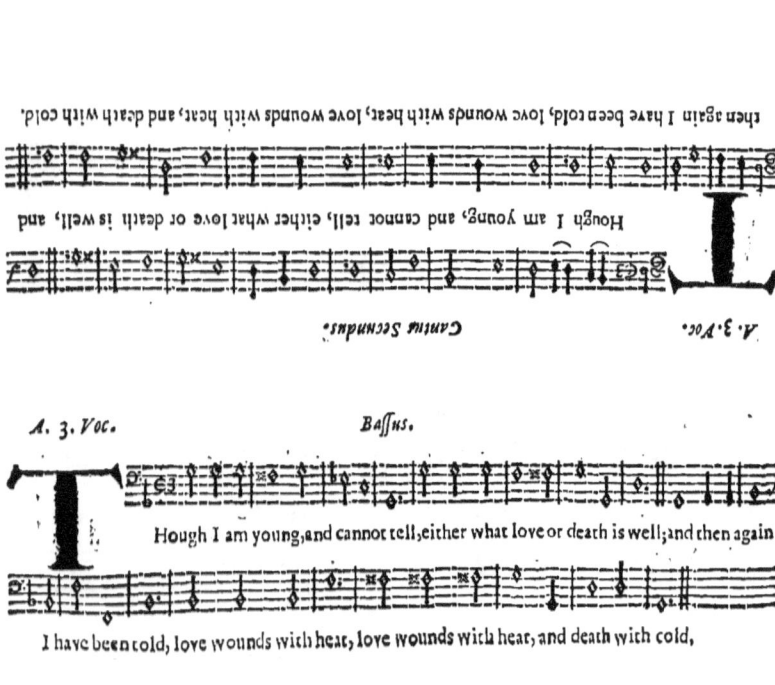

Cantus Secundus. *A. 3. Voc.*

then again I have been told, love wounds with heat, love wounds with heat, and death with cold.
Hough I am young, and cannot tell, either what love or death is well, and

A. 3. Voc. *Bassus.*

Hough I am young, and cannot tell, either what love or death is well; and then again I have been told, love wounds with heat, love wounds with heat, and death with cold,

[93]

A.3.Voc. Chloris *taking the Ayre.* Mr. Henry Lawes.

Ome *Chloris*, hie we to the Bow'r to sport us ere the day be done; such is thy Pow'r, that ev'ry Flow'r will ope to thee as to the Sun.

II.

And if a Flow'r but chance to dye
 With my sighs blasts, or mine Eyes rain,
Thou can'st revive it with thine Eye,
 And with thy breath mak't sweet again.

III.

The wanton Suckling and the Vine
 Will strive for th' honour, who first may
With their green Arms incircle thine,
 To keep the burning Sun away.

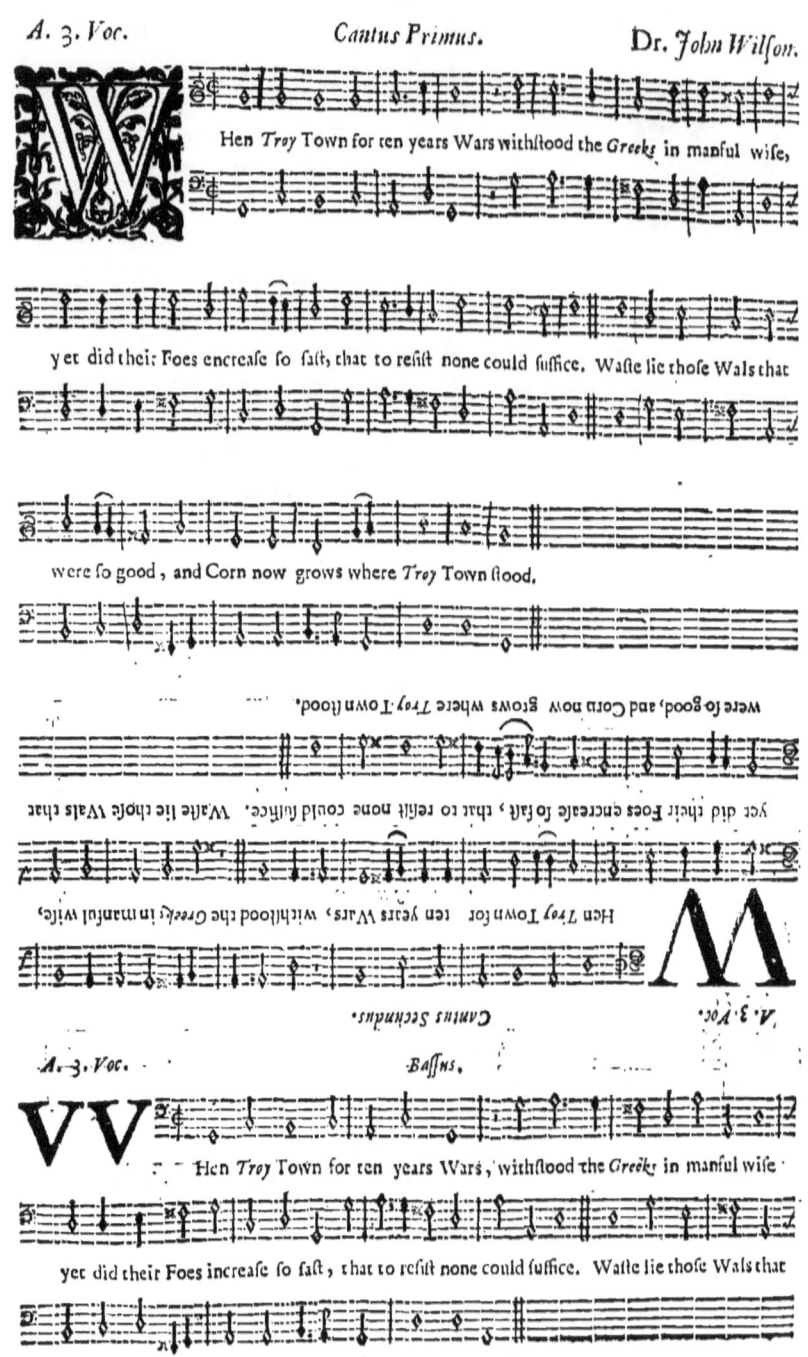

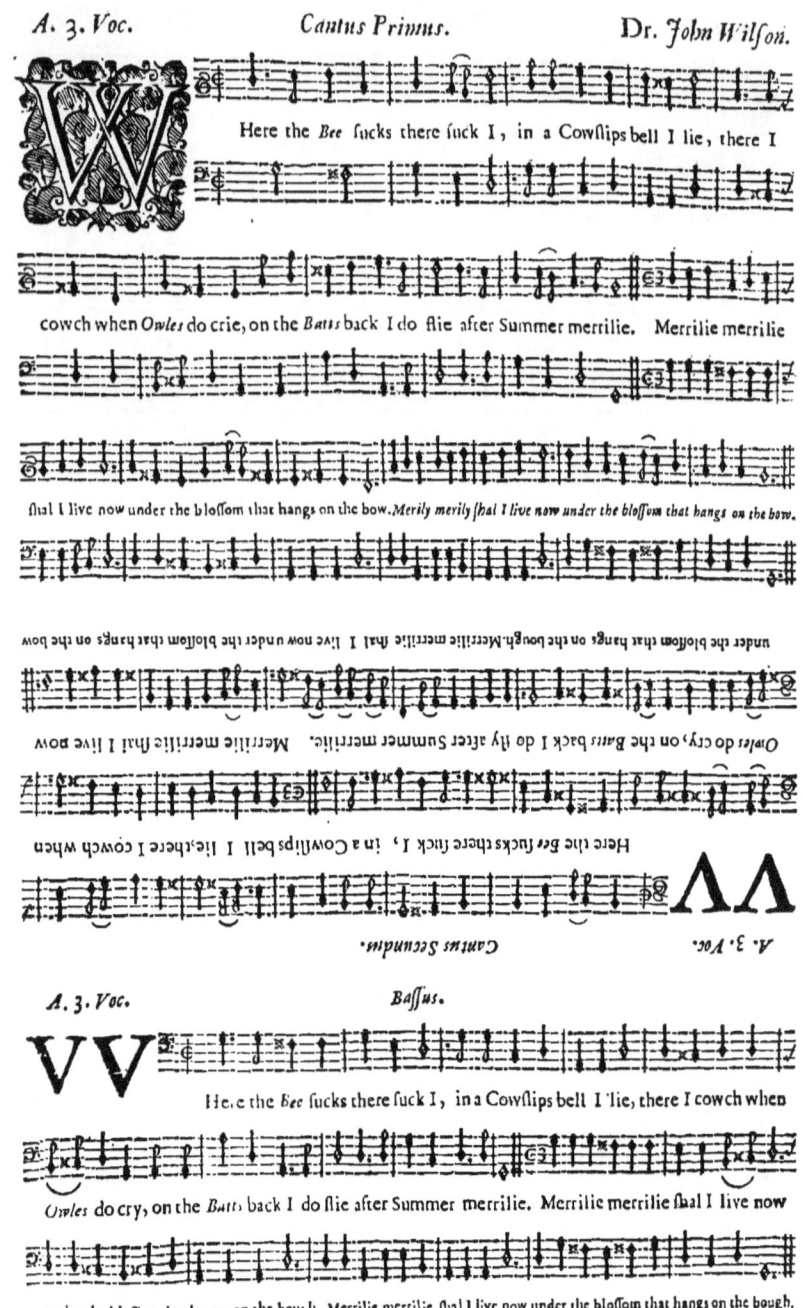

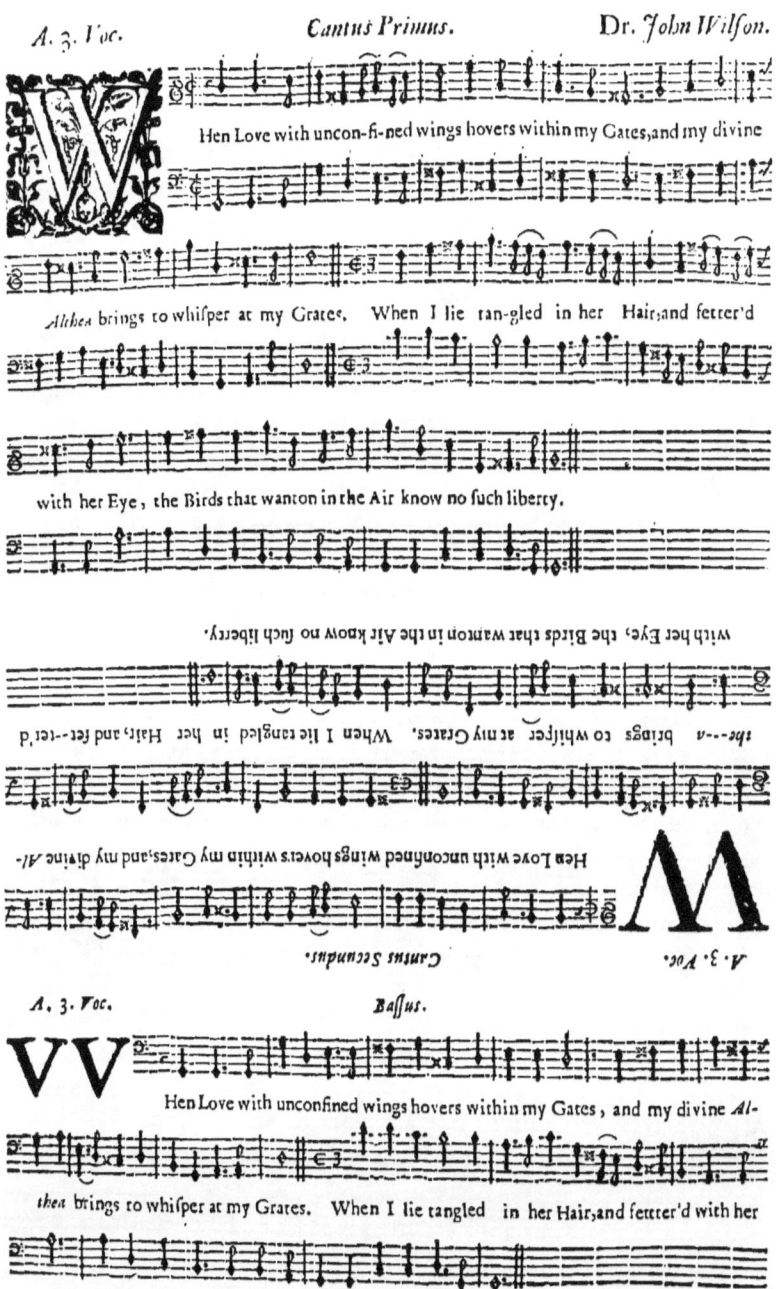

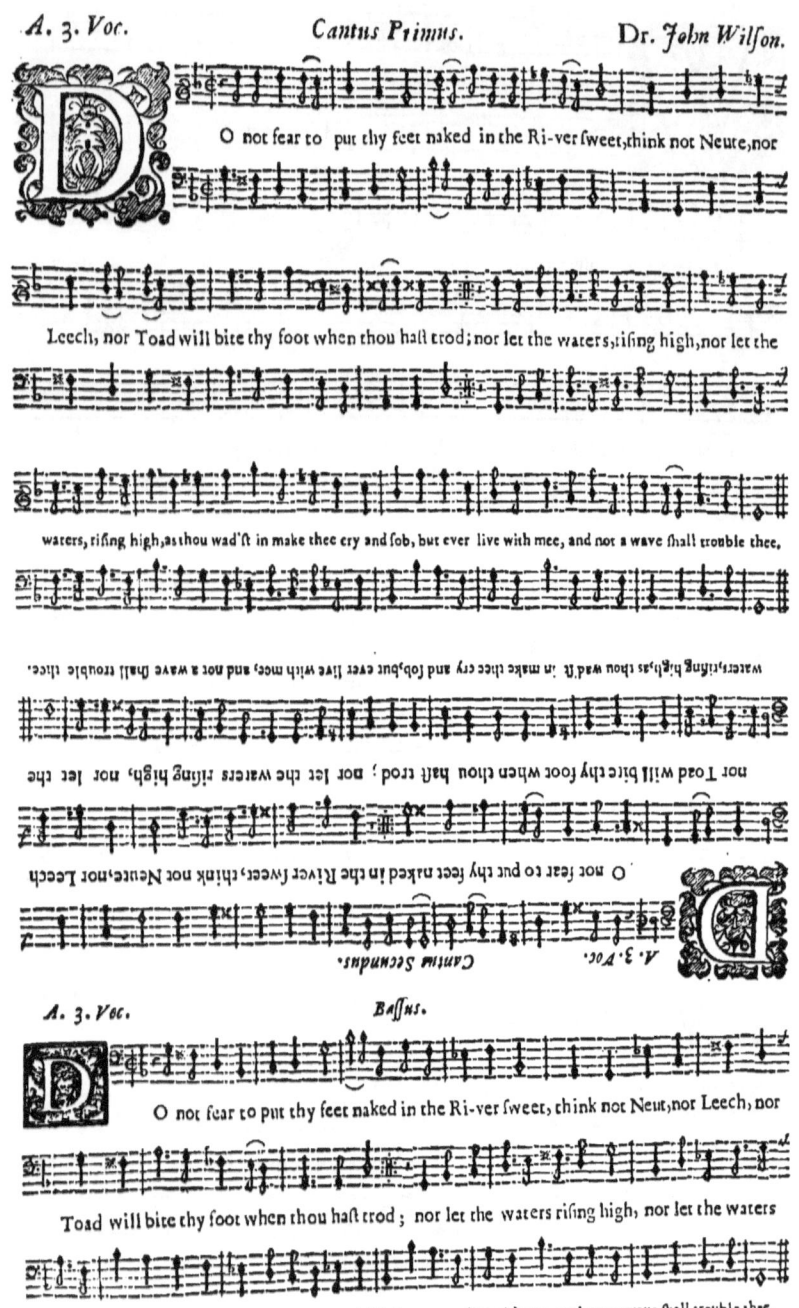

[99]

A. 3. Voc.　　　　　　Cantus Primus.　　　　　Dr. John Wilson.

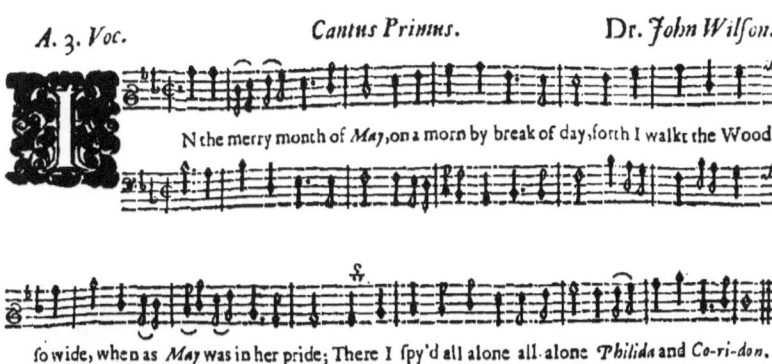

IN the merry month of May, on a morn by break of day, forth I walkt the Wood so wide, when as May was in her pride; There I spy'd all alone all alone Philida and Co-ri-don.

Much adoe there was, God wot,
He did love, but she could not;
He said his love was to woo,
She said none was false to you;
He said, he had lov'd her long,
She said, love should take no wrong.

Coridon would have kist her then,
She said, Maids must kisse no Men,
Till they kisse for good and all;
Then she bad the Shepherd call
All the Gods to witnesse truth,
Ne'r was loved so fair a youth.

    Then with many a pretty Oath,
    As Yea and Nay, and Faith and Troth;
    Such as silly Shepherds use
    When they would not love abuse;
    Love which had been long deluded,
    Was with kisses sweet concluded.

      And Phillida with Garlands gay
      Was Crowned the Lady May.

Cantus Secundus.　　　　　　A. 3. Voc.

A. 3. Voc.　　　　　　Bassus.

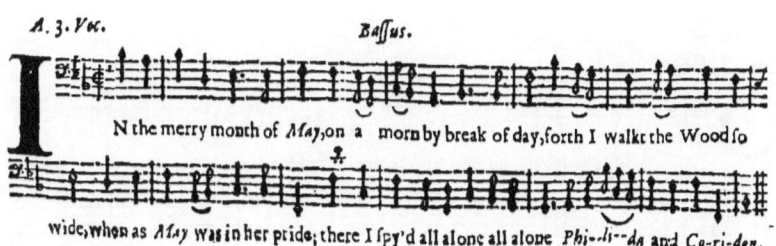

IN the merry month of May, on a morn by break of day, forth I walkt the Wood so wide, when as May was in her pride; there I spy'd all alone all alone Phi-li-da and Co-ri-don.

C c

A. 3. Voc.   Cantus Primus.   Mr. William Lawes.

My *Clarissa!* thou cruel Fair, bright as the Morning, and soft as the Air;

Fresher than Flow'rs in *May*, yet far more sweet than they ; Love is the subject of my prayer.

When first I saw thee, I felt a flame,
Which from thine Eyes like lightning came ;
Sure it was Cupid's Dart,
It peirc'd quite through my heart;
Oh, could thy breast once feele the same !

A wound so powerfull would urge thy soule,
Spight of a froward heart, coyness controule,
And make thy love as fixt
As is the heart thou prik'st,
Forcing thee with me to condole.

Let not such Fortune my Love betide ;
Oh, let your rocky breast be mollifi'd !
Send me not to my Grave
Unpittyed like a slave ;
How can love such usage abide ?

Sympathize with me a while in grief,
This passion quickly will find out relief;
Cupid wil from his Bowers
Warm these chill hearts of ours,
And make his power rule there in chief.

Then would the God of Love equall bee,
Giving me ease, as by wounding thee ;
Then would you never scorn,
When like to me you burn ;
At least not prove unkind to mee.

[101]

A. 3. Voc.   *Cantus Primus.*   Mr. *William Lawes.*

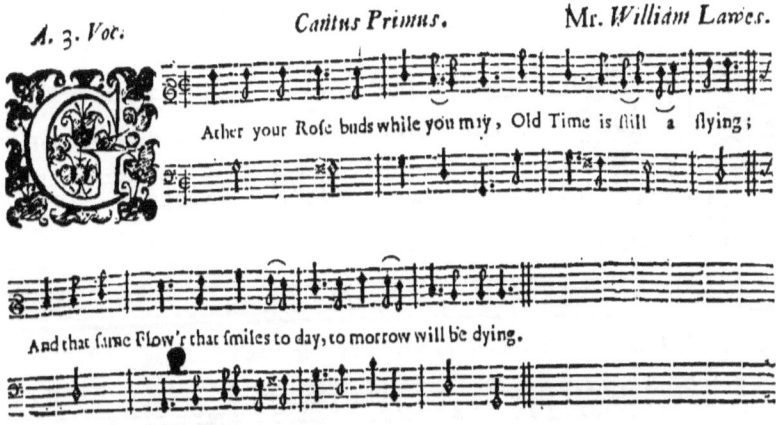

Gather your Rose buds while you may, Old Time is still a flying;
And that same Flow'r that smiles to day, to morrow will be dying.

The glorious Lamp of Heaven, the Sun,
  The higher he is getting,
The sooner will his race be run,
  And nearer he's to setting.

That Age is best that is the first,
  While your' and blood are warmer;
Expect not the last and worst,
  Time still succeeds the former.

Then be not coy, but use your time,
  While you may go marry,
For having once but lost your prime,
  You may for ever tarry.

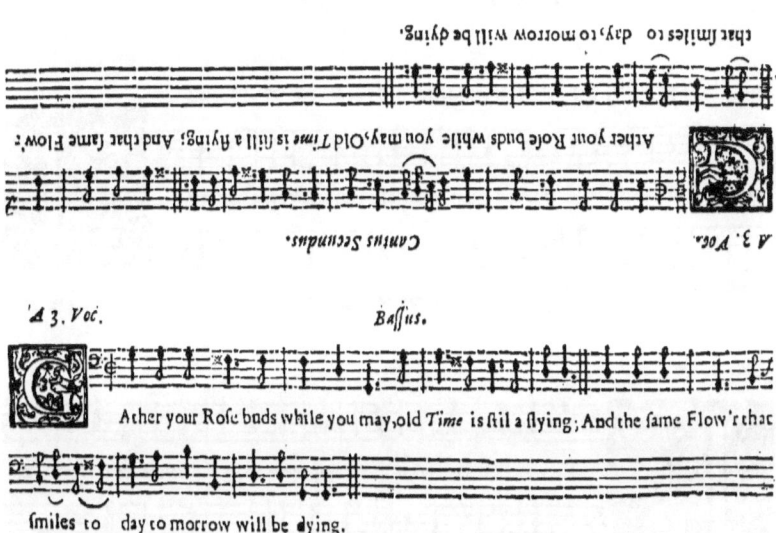

A 3. Voc.   *Bassus.*

Gather your Rose buds while you may, old *Time* is still a flying; And the same Flow'r that smiles to day to morrow will be dying.

A. 3. Voc.   Cantus Primus.   Mr. Henry Lawes.

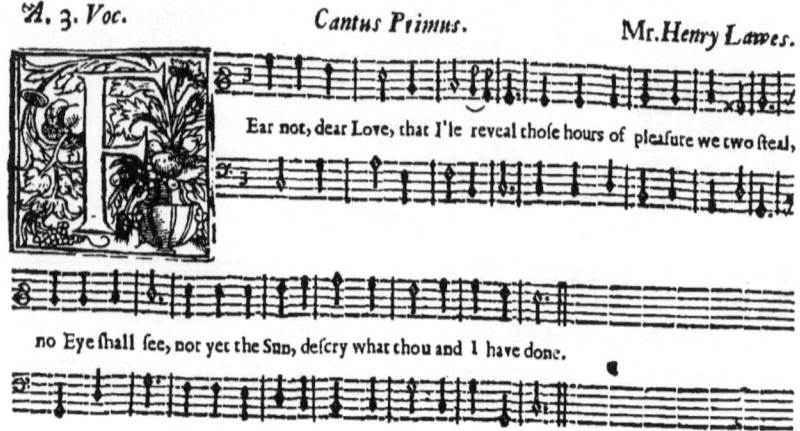

Ear not, dear Love, that I'le reveal those hours of pleasure we two steal, no Eye shall see, nor yet the Sun, descry what thou and I have done.

No ear shall hear our Love, but we
As silent as the night will be,
The God of Love himself, (whose dart
Did first wound mine, and then thy heart.)

Shall never know that we can tell,
What sweets in stoln embraces dwell;
This onely means may find it out,
If when I die, Physicians doubt.

What caus'd my death, and then to view
Of all their judgments which was true;
Rip up my heart, O then I fear
The world will see thy picture there.

Cantus Secundus.   A. 3. Voc.

Ear not, dear Love, that I'le reveal those hours of pleasure we two steal, no Eye shall see, nor yet the Sun, descry what thou and I have done.

A. 3. Voc.   Bassus.

Ear not, dear Love, that I'le reveal those hours of pleasure we two steal, no Eye shall see, nor yet the Sun, descry what thou and I have done.

A. 3. Voc. *Cantus Primus.* Mr. *William Tompkins.*

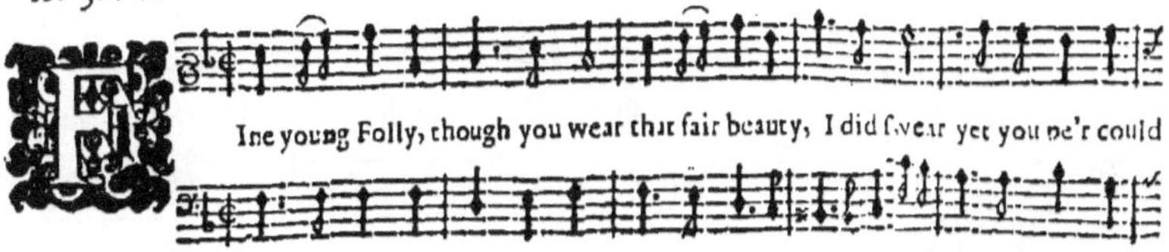

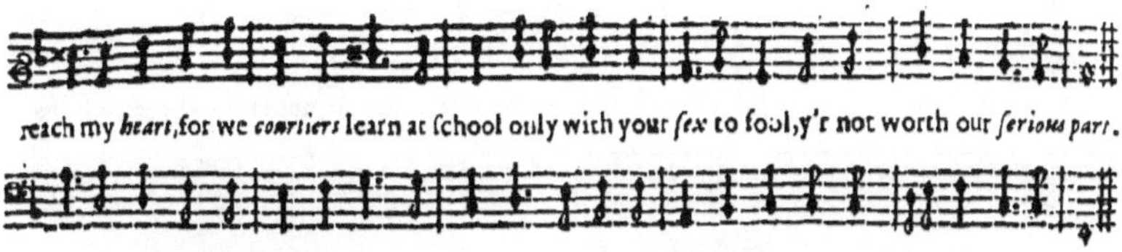

F
Ine young Folly, though you wear that fair beauty, I did swear yet you ne'r could

reach my *heart*, for we *courtiers* learn at school only with your *sex* to fool, y'r not worth our *serious part.*

When I sigh and kiss your hand,
Crosse mine Armes, and wondring stand,
Holding fairly with your eye:
Then dilate on my desires,
Swear the Sun ne'r shot such fires,
All is but a handsome lye.

When I eye your Curles or Lace,
Gentle soul, you think your face
Straight some murder doth commit;
And your conscience doth begin
To be scrup'lous of my sin,
When I court to shew my wit.

Wherefore, Madam, wear no cloud,
Nor to check my flames grow proud;
For insooth I much do doubt,
'Tis the powder in your hair,
Not your breath perfumes the Air,
And your cloaths that set you out.

Yet though truth hath this confest,
And I swear I love in jest,
Courteous soul, when next I court,
And protest an amorous flame
You I vow, I in earnest am,
Bedlam, this is pretty sport.

A. 3. Voc. *Cantus Secundus.*

F
Ine young Folly, though you wear that fair beauty, I did swear yet you ne'r, you ne'r could
reach my *heart*, for we *courtiers* learn at school only with your *sex* to fool, y'r not worth our *serious part.*

A 3. Voc. *Bassus.*

F
Ine young Folly, though you wear that fair beauty, I did swear yet you ne'r you ne'r could
reach my *heart*, for we *courtiers* learn at school only with your *sex* to fool, y'r not worth our *serious part.*

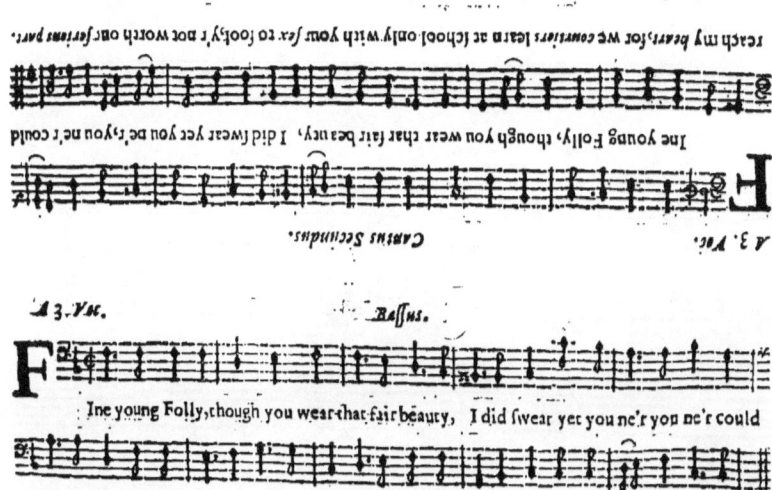

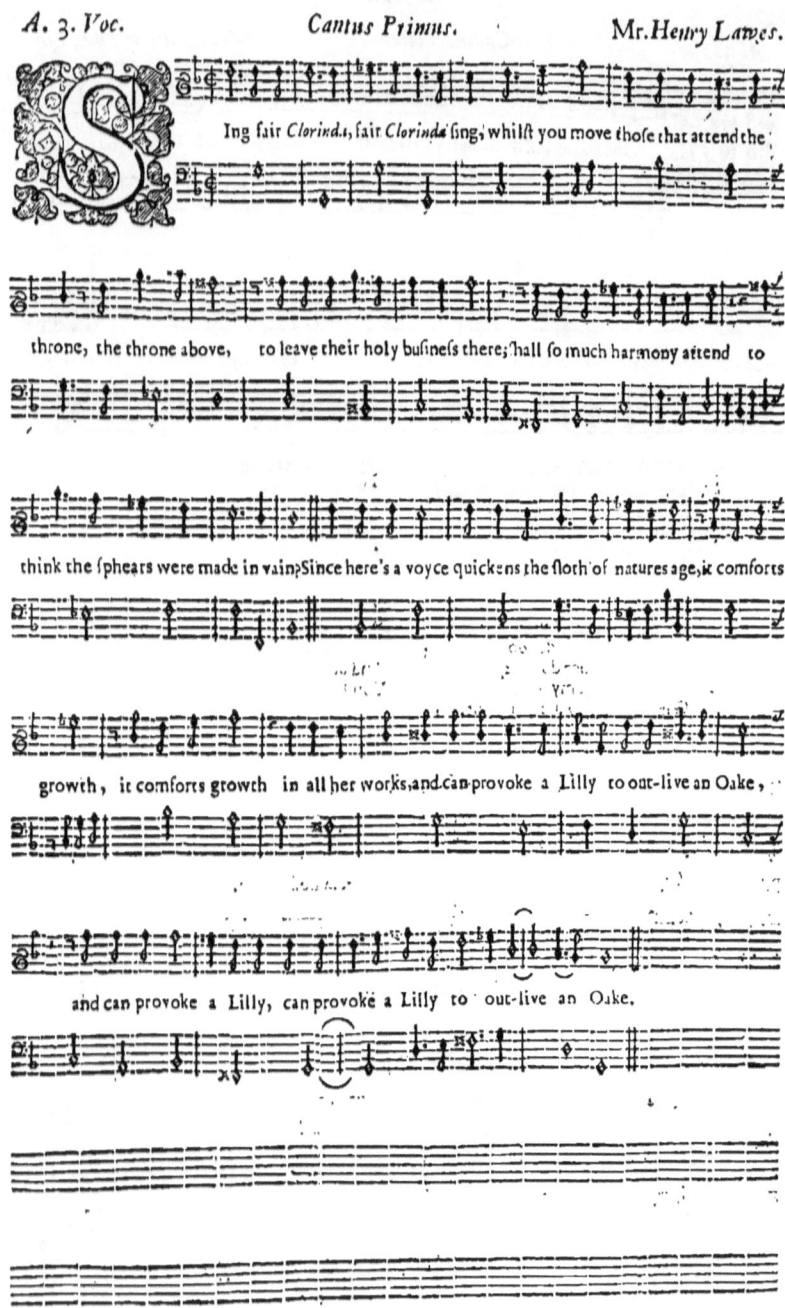

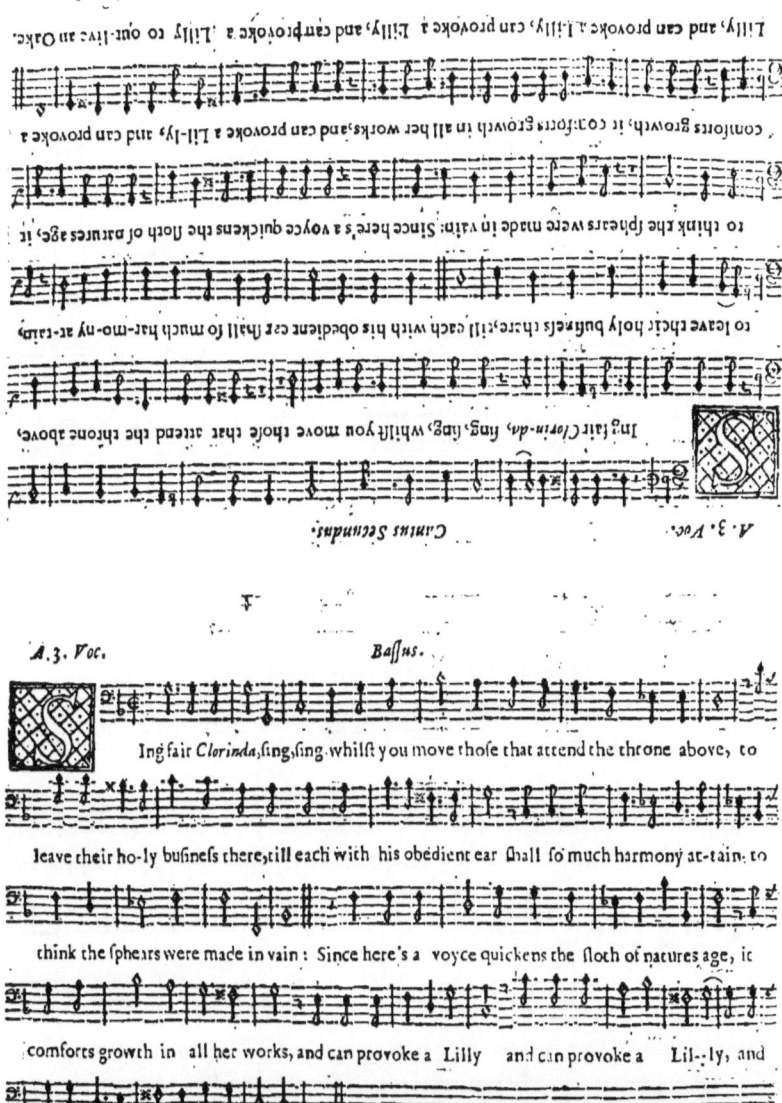

A. 3. Voc.   *Baſſus.*

Ing fair *Clorinda*, ſing, ſing, whilſt you move thoſe that attend the throne above, to leave their ho-ly buſineſs there, till each with his obedient ear ſhall ſo much harmony at-tain, to think the ſphears were made in vain: Since here's a voyce quickens the ſloth of natures age, it comforts growth in all her works, and can provoke a Lilly and can provoke a Lil-ly, and can provoke a Lil-ly to out-live an Oake.

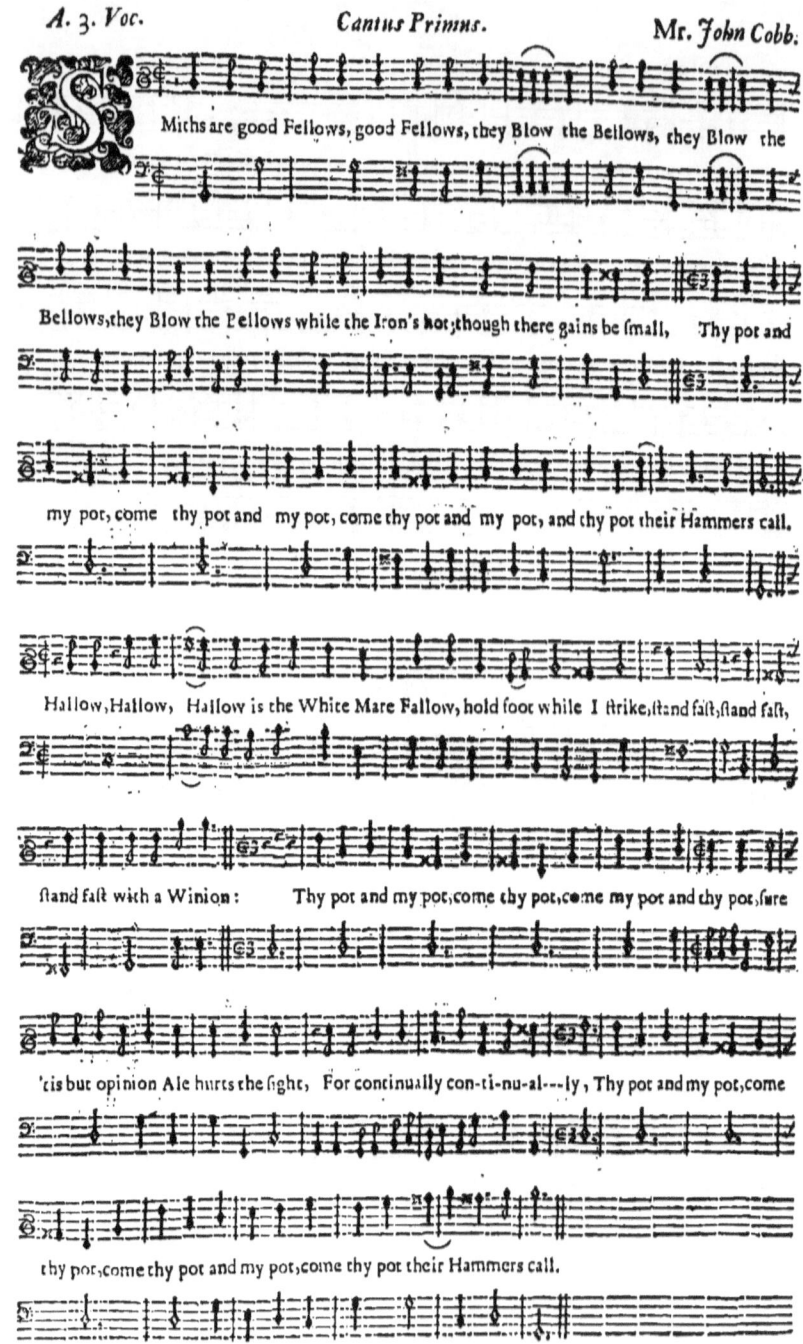

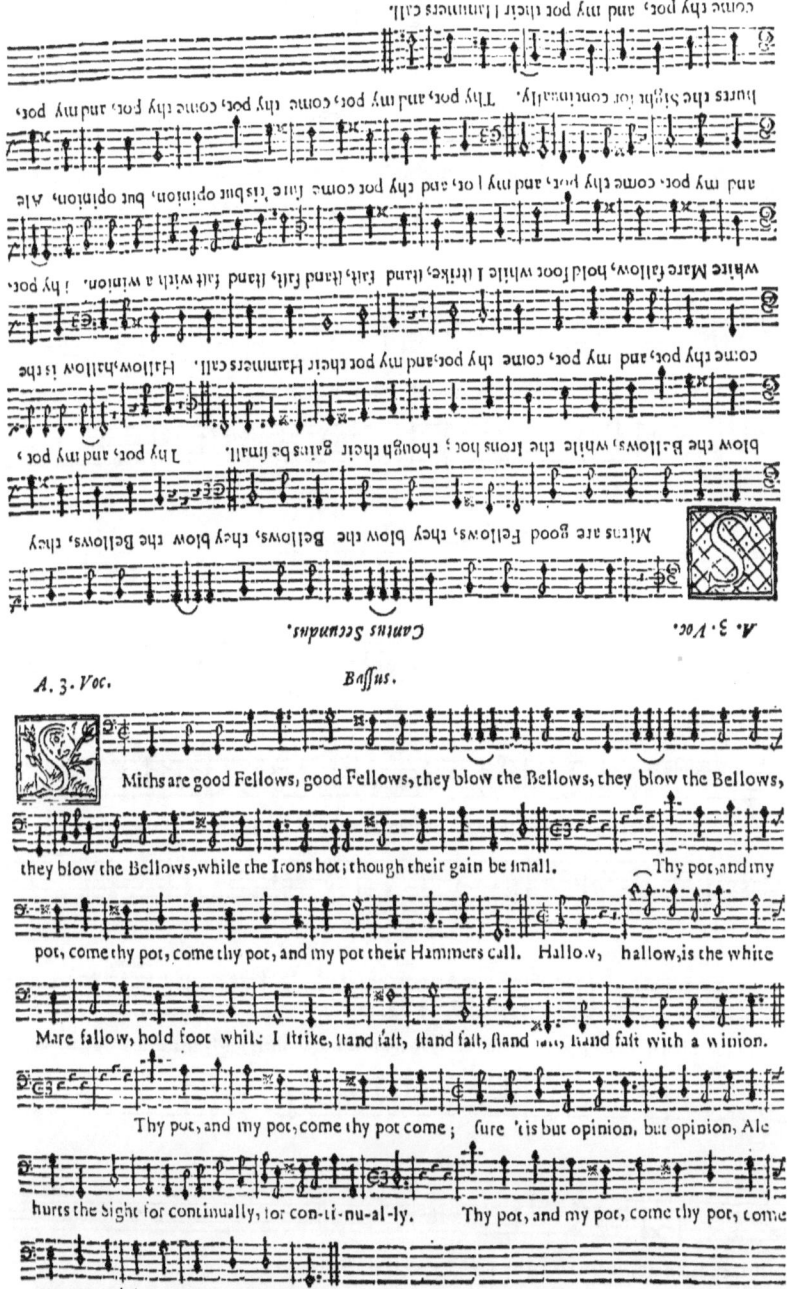

A. 3. Voc. *Bassus.*

Miths are good Fellows, good Fellows, they blow the Bellows, they blow the Bellows, they blow the Bellows, while the Irons hot; though their gain be small. Thy pot, and my pot, come thy pot, come thy pot, and my pot their Hammers call. Hallo.v, hallow, is the white Mare fallow, hold foot while I strike, stand fast, stand fast, stand fast, stand fast with a winion. Thy pot, and my pot, come thy pot come; sure 'tis but opinion, but opinion, Ale hurts the sight for continually, for con-ti-nu-al-ly. Thy pot, and my pot, come thy pot, come my pot; and thy pot their Hammers call.

E e

[105]

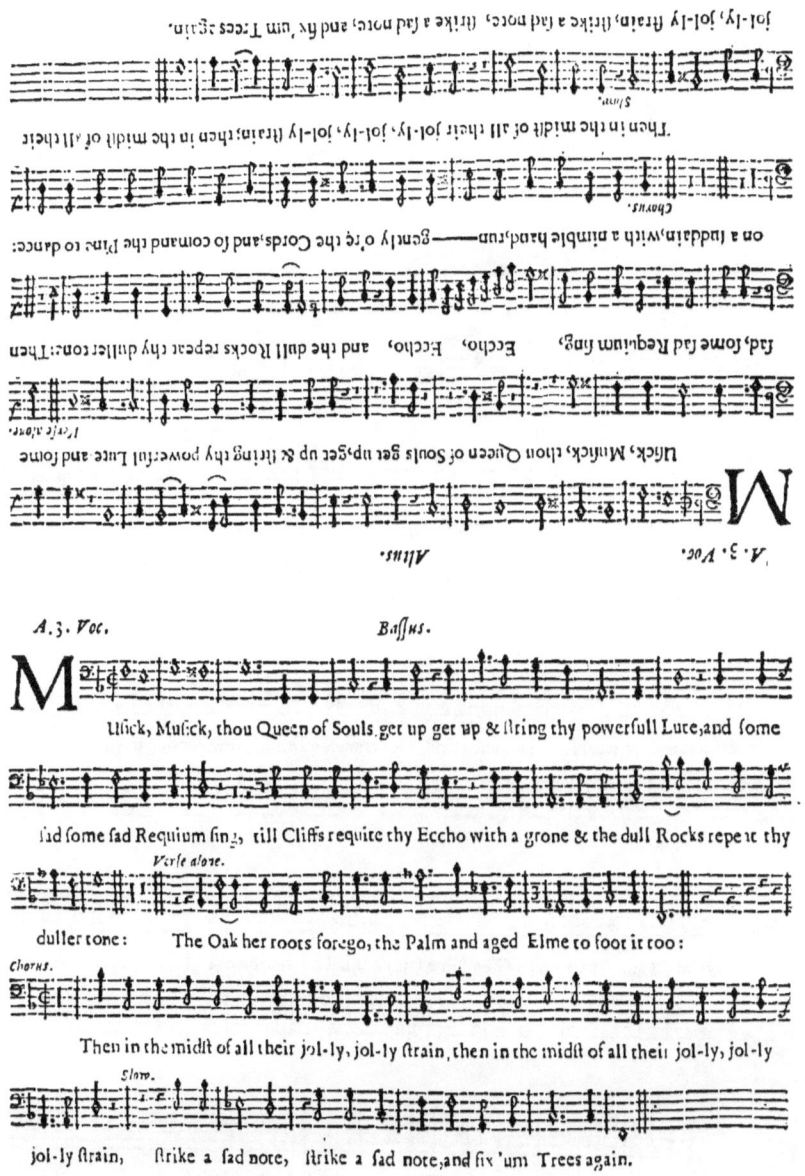

A. 3. Voc.   Bassus.

MUsick, Musick, thou Queen of Souls, get up get up & string thy powerfull Lute, and some sad some sad Requiem sing, till Cliffs requite thy Eccho with a grone & the dull Rocks repeat thy

Verse alone.

duller tone: The Oak her roots forego, the Palm and aged Elme to foot it too:

Chorus.

Then in the midst of all their jol-ly, jol-ly strain, then in the midst of all their jol-ly, jol-ly

Slow.

jol-ly strain,   strike a sad note,   strike a sad note, and fix 'um Trees again.

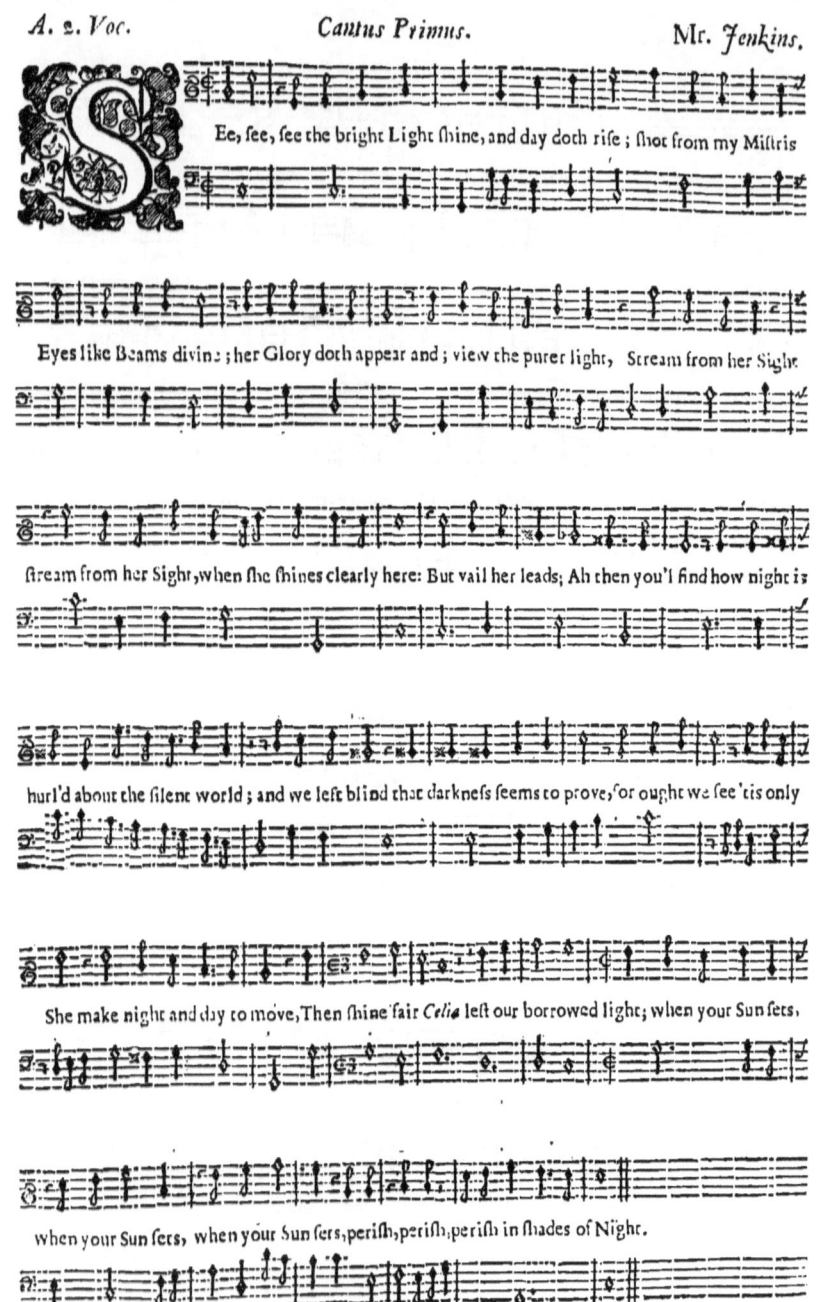

[111]

A. 2. Voc.   *Bassus.*   Mr. *Jenkins.*

See, see the bright, bright Light shine, and day doth rise; shot from my Mistris Eyes, like Beams divine her Glories doe appear; and view the purer light Stream from her Sight, whilest she shines clearly here: But veil her lids: Ah then you'l find how Night is hurl'd about the silent World, and we left blind; that Darkness seems to prove, for ought we see, 'tis only She makes Night and Day to move. Then shine fair *Celia*, lest our borrow'd Light, when your Sun sets, when your Sun sets, when your Sun sets; Perish, perish, perish in Shades of Night.

F f

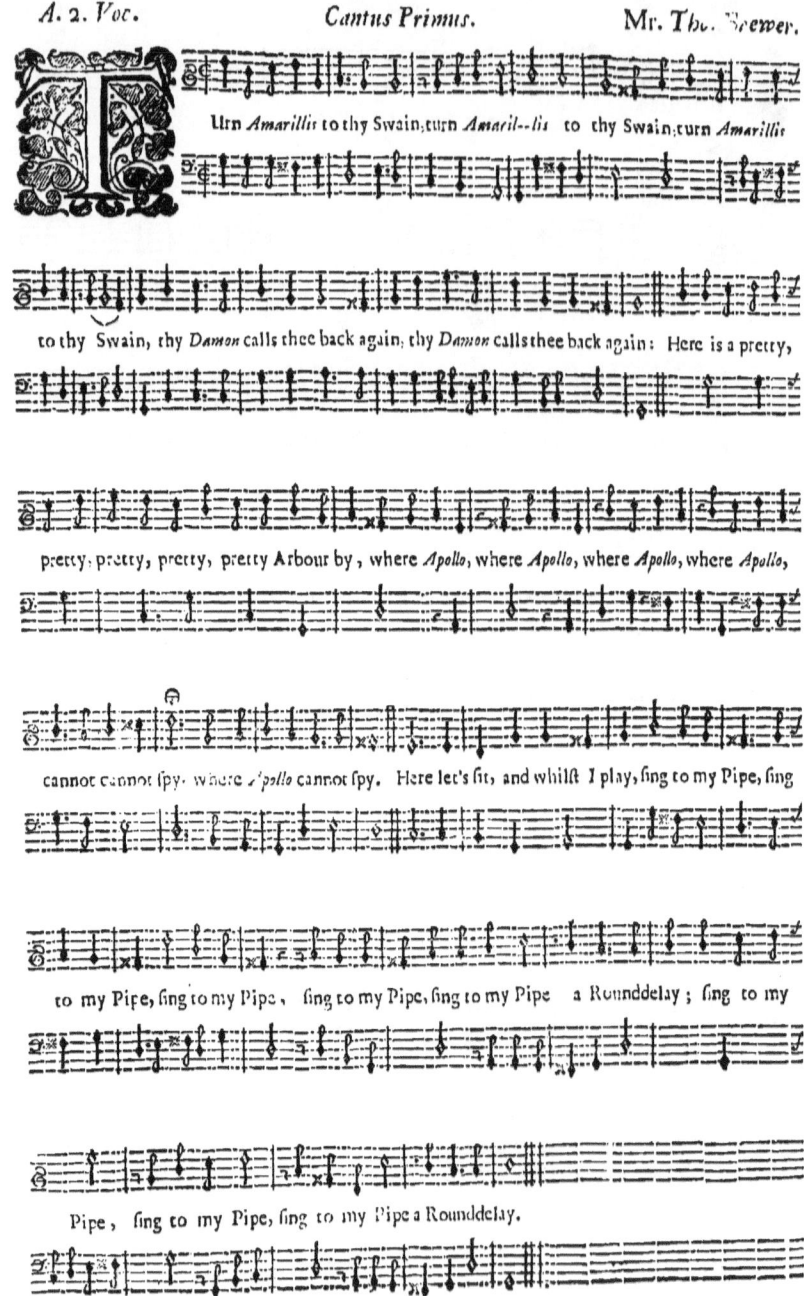

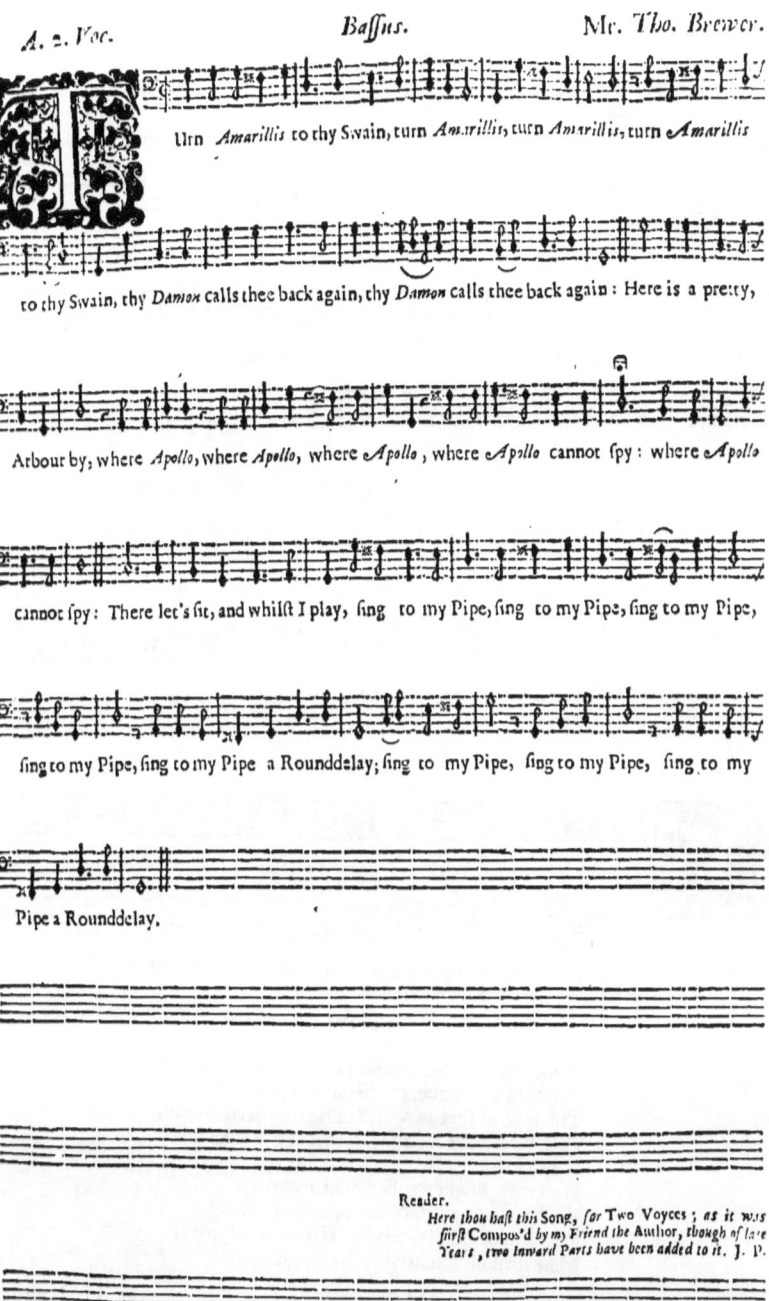

In praise of Musick.

Musick miraculous *Rhethorick*! that speak'ſt Sence
Without a Tongue, excellent Eloquence:
The love of thee in wild Beaſts have been known,
And Birds have lik'd thy Notes above their own.

How eaſie might thy Errors be excus'd,
Wert thou as much beloved, as th'art abus'd;
Yet although dull Souls thy Harmony diſprove,
Mine ſhall be fixt in what the Angels love.

FINIS.   *W. D.* Knight.

SELECT
AYRES
AND
DIALOGUES
To Sing to the
THEORBO-LUTE
OR
BASSE-VIOL.

COMPOSED
By Mr *HENRY LAWES*, late Servant to His Majesty in His Publick and Private MUSICK:
And other Excellent *MASTERS*.

The Second BOOK.

LONDON,
Printed by *William Godbid* for *John Playford*, and are to be Sold at his Shop in the *Temple*, near the Church Dore. 1669.

OF
Vocal MUSICK.

GENTLEMEN,

THis second Book of SELECT AYRES doth chiefly consist of Mr. Henry Lawes Composition, being Transcribed from his Originals, a short time before his Death, and with his free consent for me to Publish them, if occasion offer'd : I need not make any Apology for their Excellency, the Authors Name is enough, having (while he liv'd) Published three several Books of this Nature with great Esteem and Approbation; and the Impressions of the two first, being long since Sold off, many have since sought to have them, for some particular Songs in them; but considering, that to Reprint them both again would not answer the expectation either of Buyer or Seller, I have therefore selected out of them both the best and most desired Songs, and added them to those many other in this Book of Mr. Lawes and other Authors, which were never Printed till now, together with some few Italian Ayres which have formerly passed with good Fame among our English Masters. And since it is so stored with variety, I hope it will and may please most Ears, though, I fear, not all; for our new A la mode Gallants will Object, They are old, and after the English Mode; had I fill'd it with the light Ayres of the French, or the wanton Songs of the Stage, it would have liked their Humour much better : But I study not to please such. But with sober and judicious Understanders of Musick, it will (I doubt not) gain Credit and Repute. Those are the true Lovers of Musick, who do embrace it for the Excellency therein, moving the Passions to Noble and Virtuous Ends; but others there are, who affect it for no other ends but to stir their Minds to Wantonness and Lasciviousness. Mr. Owen Feltham's Expression in his Resolves, is worth our observation, Musick (says he) is an helper both to good and ill; and therefore I honour it when it moves to Virtue, and will beware of it when it would flatter into Vice. To conclude, My intent is to bind many of these with my first Book of Select Ayres and Mr. Lawes his third Book together; which will be an intire Volume of the most choice Songs that have been Composed for Forty Years past, and I doubt not but will retain their Fame for many more to come. I must confess when I began this Book, my design was to have it comprized in fewer Sheets; but finding my Stock was large, and my resolution to make this Book the last that ever I intend to Publish of this Nature, hath swell'd it into so large a Volume. And if my pains herein, may be advantageous and acceptable to any, it will further encourage me to proceed in things of this Nature, for the publick benefit of all sober and judicious Lovers of Musick; To whose Service I devote my self, and remain their Well-wisher and Servant,

J. P.

A TABLE of the SONGS and DIALOGUES in this BOOK.

A.

	fol.
AT Dead low Ebb of Night.	5
Am I despis'd because you say	13
A Lover once I did espie	21
Amarillis tear thy Hair	25
Art thou in Love it cannot be	45
Ah Cloris would the gods allow	63
Admit thou Darling of mine Eyes	66
Awake my Lute, arise my String	69
Ah Mighty Love what power unknown	82
And must our Tempers ever be at War	86

B.

Behold and listen whilst the fair	36
Black Maid complain not	49
Boast not Blind Boy	50
Be not Proud pretty One for I must Love	59
Beauty have you seen a Toy	75
But that I knew before	42

C

Careless of Love and free from Fear	9
Cloris since first our Calm	14
Canst thou love me and yet doubt	20
Come, Come thou glorious Object	22
Come, Come sad Turtle	35
Come my Lucatia	42
Can so much Beauty own a Mind	44
Cloris 'twil be for eithers rest	66
Cruel Cloris did you know	70
Clear stream who do with equal pace	81
Cupid's no god a wanton Child	91

D

Dearest do not now delay me	10
Death cannot extinguish	31
Delicate Beauty why should you disdain	41
Disdain not fair one since we know	88

F

Farewel fair Saint may not the Sea	7
Fire, loe here I burn	56
For that one glance I wounded lye	58
Fall Dew of Slumbers in a gentle Stream	64
Farewel despairing hope I'le Love no more	78

G

Gaze not on Swans on whose	10
Give me more Love or more Disdain	11
Go lovely Rose tell her that wasts	43

H

Help, Help O Divinity of Love	1
Hark how the Nightingale	38

I

	fol.
It is not that I Love the less	12
If when the Sun at Noon	17
I prethe Sweet to me be kind	19
I laid me down upon a Pillow	28
I Lov'd thee once I'le Love no more	30
I was foretold your Rebel Sex	33
If you will Love know this to be	62
Indeed I never was but once so Mad	65
I never knew what Cupid meant	76
If still Theora you wear this Disguise	79
I had a Cloris my delight	85
If thou wilt know the reason why	92

L

Ladies fly not from Loves smooth Tales	27
Love me no more or else with scorn	90

M

Mark how the blushful Morn	53
Madam your Beauty I confess may	88

N

Now, now Lucatia now	3
No more of Tears	37
No more shall Meads be deckt	54
No more will I contemplate Love	67
Not that I wish my Mistress	72
No more fond Love give o're	73
No, no, I tell thee no though from thee	57

O

Oh how I hate thee now	16
On this swelling bank	41
O King of Heaven and Hell	46
O fairest lights whose clear aspect	87
Oft have I searcht both Court and Town	63

P

Pleasure, Beauty, Youth attend ye	23
Poor Celia once was very fair	96

S

Seek not to know my Love	18
Swift through the yielding Ayr	24
Still to be neat still to be drest	51
Stay silly Heart and do not break	57
Sure 'twas a Dream how long fond Man	61
She which would not I would chuse	68
Strike Sweet Licoris strike	83

T

That flame is born of earthly fire	38
Transcendent Beauty thou that art	40
Tell me no more 'tis Love	43

	fol.		fol.
'Tis Christmass now	45	Why lovely boy why flyest thou me	42
What Herald was but a dull Ass	62	When I am dead and then wouldest	5
When sents to me a Heart was Crown'd	71	Wilt thou begon thou hartless Man	52
The Glories of our Birth and State	74	White though you be yet Lillies know	58
Though you are Young and I am Old	76	Will Cloris cast her Sun-bright Eye	7
Though Silvias Eyes a flame coud raise	89	Wake all ye Dead what hoa	60
The Thirsty Earth sucks up the Rain	94	Well well 'tis true I now am fallen in Love	73
V		What Conscience say is it in the	77
Venus redress a wrong	8	When I taste my Coblet deep	93
Up Ladies prepare your taking Faces	64	Weep not my Dear for I shall go	40
W		Y	
What shall I do I've lost my Heart	26	Yes yes 'tis Cloris Sings	15
When this Flie lived	32	You that think Love can convey	29
When thou fair Cælia	34	Yes I could Love, could I but find a Mistress	72
Whether so gladly and so fast	39	You ask my Dear if I be well	90
Where shall a Man an Object find	46		

A Table of the Italian AYRS in this Book.

1 Dove Dove Corri mio Corri
2 Intencrite voi
3 Occhi Belleo've Imperai
4 Acche Lallo Credero
5 Sio moro, Chi dira
6 Amantea Consiglio
7 Si tocchi Tambuco
8 Si guarde che puo
9 Fugite, Fugite
10 De quei Belleocchi

A Table of the DIALOGUES in this Book.

Sweet Lovely Nimph	Treble and Bass	105
Why sighs thou Shepherd	Treble and Bass	106
Hast you Nimphs	Treble and Bass	108
Charon O Charon draw	Treble and Bass	109
Charon O Charon hear	Treble and Bass	112
This Mossy Bank they prest	Two Trebles	114
Shepherd well met	Two Trebles	118

COURTEOUS FRIENDS,

I Was not negligent in overseeing the Press, yet notwithstanding all my Care some Faults are committed, but they are small, and by the skilful may be easily mended, as happening most in the Through-Bass; two whereof, being too great to pass, I beg you with your Pen to mend,

Page 48 the two last Bars of the fourth line in the Bass, must be thus, And *Page* 89 in the Through-Bass the third Bar must be thus,

---

ADVERTISEMENT.

AT Mr. *Playford*'s Shop is Sold all sorts of Rul'd Paper for Musick, and Books of all sizes ready Bound for Musick.

Also the Excellent Cordial called ELIXIR PROPRIETATIS, a few drops of which drank in a glass of Sack or other Liquors, is admirable for all Coughs and Consumptions of the Lungs and inward Distempers of the Body, a Book of the manner of the taking of it is given also to those who buy the same.

Also, If a Person desire to be furnished with good new Virginals and Harpsicons, if they send to Mr. *Playford*'s Shop, they may be furnished at reasonable Rates, to their Content.

To my much Ingenuous Friend Mr. JOHN PLAYFORD,
upon his late Publication of two Excellent Books for VOCAL MUSICK,
VIZ.
SELECT AYRES *and* DIALOGUES,
AND,
The MUSICAL COMPANION.

TReasurer of *Musick*, how much we
  Do Owe unto thy industrie !
Th' unhappy Science ne'r did found
In a full Chord, 'till thou hadst bound
Up in one Book, the whole Consent
Of scatter'd *Musick's* Ornament.
The Choice Composers of our Age
Did each one in a private Page
Whisper unto his Muse, till now
They're made a Publick Quire by you ;
Where, like to joyful Birds by th' Spring
Call'd to a pleasant Grove, they sing
Not more their own felicitie,
And Notes, than just Applause to thee.
For why ? *Musick* ('tis true) has been
Dispos'd to Harmony, but when
Were the Musicians so much like
To be a Body Politique ?
Their Corporation incompleat
Appear'd, before thou did'st the feat :
The Order of thy Book shall be
The List of their Societie,
And none shall dare t' intrude himself,
But such into their Common-wealth.
Dispers'd *Absyrtus's* useless Parts
Might be reduc'd with half the Arts
That thou hast exercis'd upon
Thy *Musical Companion* ;
A Piece so choice, so trim, so drest,
Who would not covet such a Guest ?
Nor let vain *Momus* Carp and Cry
This Work speaks thee a *Plagiary*,
For don't we know thy depth, and skill
In *Musick*? Thou dost change, or fill
What pleaseth not, or where it wants,
And regulate the false Descants.
Thou art as ready to translate,
As to transcribe, thy Book can say't.
Thy Composition too doth raise
Equal Advantage to thy praise,

And though thy bashful Muse holds forth
Too small a taste of her own worth,
It shews enough what thou canst do,
And to thy Commendation too,
That in a thing so rare thou art
Content thy Friends should share a part ;
When some like *Cæsar* so high flown,
Resolve t' have all or none their own.
  If pity'd *Ign'rance* yet should cast
Spite at thy Name, Oh ! let him hast
For better Knowledge and Instruction
To *Playford's* famed *Introduction*.
If nimble Wits begin to play,
Thou'rt full of *Catches* too, as they,
And more than they can prove, or sing,
Thy Notes give Life to what they bring.
Th' Ingenuous Lover, when he looks
For Am'rous pastime in thy Books,
He'l Court thy *Ayres* with all Respect,
Thou countenanc'st none, but are *Select*.
And when the *Virtuosi* come ,
For that sage Train thou fittest some
Good Entertainment, then set on
Thy *Musical Companion*.
A Man against the World, what shall
I say ? How shall I *Playford* call ?
The Field's too large, *Helicon's* too scant
To pay a drop to every plant
That sprouteth forth : And then I hear
(Methinks) thy *Genius* drawing near,
To check my vain attempt, and tell
Thy self does only speak thee well.
I will not therefore Gaul with Baies
Thy tender Brows, nor clog with Praise
Thy fertile Merit , only here
Take leave to pay my thanks, for fear
I tempt thy Native Modesty
To flush into too deep a Dye.

Cha. Pigeon. Soc. Gra. In.

To my Beloved Friend and Fellow
Mr. HENRY LAWES,
On his Books of AYRES,
lately Published.

NOw I have view'd this Book of thine,
And find sweet Language, Notes more
And see thy *Fuges* wrought in the chime,(fine
Thy Weaving far excells the Rhime ;
And still thy choice of Lines are good,
Not like to those who get their Food
As Beggars Rags from Dunghills take ,
(Such as comes next) ill Songs to make ;
Who by a witty blind pretenfe
Take words that creep half way to sense ;
Hippocrates or *Galen's* Feet ,
And sing them too with Notes as meet ;
Songs as all th' way to *Gammut* tend ,
But in F Fa *ut* make an end ;
With killing notes which ever must [**Coriat.*]
Squeez the Spheres, and intimate the Dust :
These with their brave *Chromaticks* bring
Noise to the Ear, but mean No-thing :
Yet these will censure, when indeed
Shew them good Lines, They cannot read ;
Or read them so, that in the close
You'll hardly judge them Rhime from Prose.
  But why do I write this to Thee ?
This is for shop-sale Frippery ;
Thy richer store hath truly hit
The whole Age for their want of wit :
Live freely , and thy Phansie please ,
We shall be censur'd by such Things as these.

John Wilson, *Doct. in Musick.*

To my much Honoured Friend,
Mr. HENRY LAWES,
On his Books of AYRES,
lately Published.

THings that are thus, thus excellently good ,
Are hardly prais'd, 'cause hardly understood :
For though at the first hearing all admire ,
Yet when into the severals men inquire ,
(which make up the *Composure*) they are lost ,
Such Ayr, Wit, Spirit, *Harmony engross'd*
In every piece, as makes each piece the best ;
And yet (as good as 'tis) a Foyl to th' rest.
How greedily do the best judgements throng
To hear the Repetition of thy Song ?
Which they still beg in vain ; for when Re-sung
So much new Art and Excellence is flung
Round thy Admirers (unobserv'd before)
As makes the newly-ravish'd ravish'd more :
For comprehend thee fully none can do
Till like thy Musick th' are Eternal too.
  'Tis Thou hast honour'd Musick, done her right,
Fitted her for a strong and useful Flight ;
Shee droop'd and flaggd before, as Hawks complain
Of the sick Feathers in their Wing and Train :
But thou hast imp'd the Wings She had before.
Musick does owe Thee much, the Poet more ;
Thou lift'st him up, and dost new Nature bring,
Thou giv'st his noblest Verse both *Feet* and *Wing*.
  Live then above our Praise, immortal here ,
The *Atlas,* the Support of Musicks Sphere :
To what a darkness would our Art decline,
Robb'd of thy glorious and diurnal Shine ?
These fixed Tapers cannot do Thee right ,
Nor fully speak thy Rays which gave them Light ,
But as small Stars by Night in Consort met ,
Would only tell the World, *Our Sun is Set.*

Charles Colman, *Doct. in Musick.*

A Catalogue of late Printed MUSICK BOOKS, Sold by *John Playford* at his Shop in the *Temple*.

Books for Vocal MUSICK.

Dr. *William Child* his Pſalms for Three Voyces to the Theorbo or *Organ*, Engraved on Copper Plates.

Mr. *Walter Porter* his Pſalms for Two Voyces to the *Organ*.

Mr. *Henry* and Mr. *William Laws* Pſalms for Three Voyces to the *Theorbo* or *Organ*.

Mr. *Richard Deering* his *Latin* Hymns for Two and Three Voyces to the *Organ* with *Halleluiahs*.

Dr. *John Wilſons* Ayrs or Ballads for Three Voyces to the *Theorbo*, lately Printed at *Oxford*.

Select *Ayres* and *Dialogues* to Sing to the *Theorbo*, firſt Volume.

Select *Ayres* and *Dialogues* to Sing to the *Theorbo*, ſecond Volume.

The *Muſical-Companion* in two Books, the Firſt contains *Catches* and *Rounds* for Three Voyces, the Second, *Dialogues* and *Ayres* for Two Three and Four Voyces.

A *Brief Introduction* to the skill of Muſick, by *John Playford*, being a moſt plain and eaſie Method for the underſtanding the Principles and Grounds of Muſick both *Vocal* or *Inſtrumental*.

Books for Inſtrumental MUSICK.

Mr. *Michael Eaſt's Fantaſies* for Viols of Two, Three and Four parts.

Mr. *Wil. Young* his *Fantaſies* for Viols of Three parts.

Mr. *Matthew Leck's Little Conſort* of Three parts for Viols or Violins.

Court Ayres of Two parts, Treble and Baſs, for Viols or Violins, Compoſed by ſeveral excellent *Engliſh* Maſters.

Muſicks Recreation on the *Lyra Viol*, containing eaſie and pleaſant Leſſons for Beginners, with Inſtructions for Learners, newly Reprinted.

Mr. *Chriſtopher Simpſon's Diviſion Violiſt*, or a Guide to play Diviſion upon any Ground.

The *Dancing-Maſter*, containing Rules for the Dancing *Country-Dances*, with the Tunes to each Dance; to which is added the Tunes of the new *French-Dances*, and other new and delightful Tunes for the *Treble-Violin*.

Muſiks Solace, containing Leſſons and Inſtructions for the *Ciſhren*, newly Printed in a more eaſie Method than it was formerly.

Muſicks Handmaid, preſenting new and pleaſant Leſſons for the *Virginals* fitted for the Practice of young Beginners, Engraven on Copper Plates.

Books which are now fitted for the Preſs.

1. *A Book for the* Flagelet, *containing many new and pleaſant Tunes and Inſtructions for Learners.*

2. *A Book for the* Treble Violin, *containing all the late Tunes of the* French Dances, *and other new* Theatre Tunes.

3. *A Book of* Divine Hymns *and* Dialogues, *for One and Two Voyces to Sing to the* Theorbo-Lute *or* Organ, *Compoſed by Mr.* Henry Lawes *and others*.

A STORM:

CLORIS *at Sea, near the Land, is surprized by a Storm:* AMINTOR *on the Shore, expecting her Arrival,*
THUS COMPLAINS:

Elp, help, O help, Di-vi-ni—-ty of Love! or Neptune will commit a Rape upon my *Cloris*; She's on his bosome, and without a wonder cannot scape. See, see, the Winds grow drunk with Joy, and throng so fast to see Loves *Argo*, and the wealth it bears, that now the tackling and the sails they tear: They fight, they fight! who shall convey *Amintor*'s Love into her Bay; and hurl whole Seas at one another, as if they would the Welkin smother. Hold *Boreas*, hold; He will not hear;

The Rudder cracks, the Main-mast falls; the Pilot swears, the Skipper bawls; a showre of Clouds in

dark—ness fall, to put out *Cloris* light withall. Ye gods, where are ye? where are ye? Are ye all a-

sleep, or drunk with *Nectar*: Why do you not keep a watch upon your Ministers of Fate? Tie up the

Winds, or they will blow the Seas to heav'n, and drown your Deities. A calm, a calm! Miracle of

Love; the Sea-born Queen, that sits a—bove, hath heard *Amintor*'s cryes, and *Neptune* now must

lose his prize. Welcome, welcome *Cloris* to the Shore; Thou shalt go to Sea no more: We to *Tempe*'s

Groves

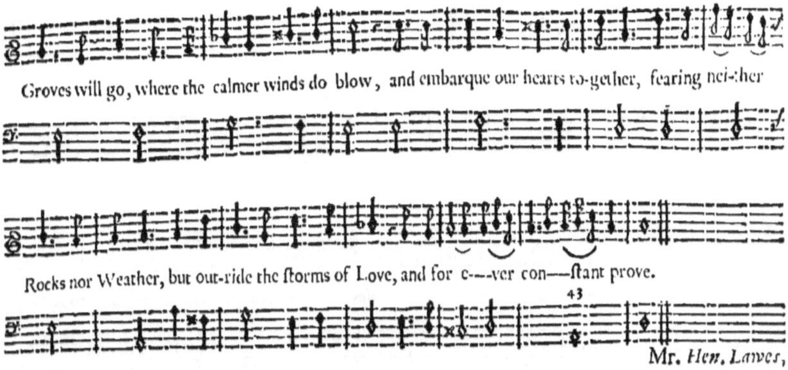

[3]

Groves will go, where the calmer winds do blow, and embarque our hearts to-gether, fearing nei-ther Rocks nor Weather, but out-ride the storms of Love, and for e---ver con----ftant prove.

Mr. *Hen. Lawes*,

No *REPRIEVE.*

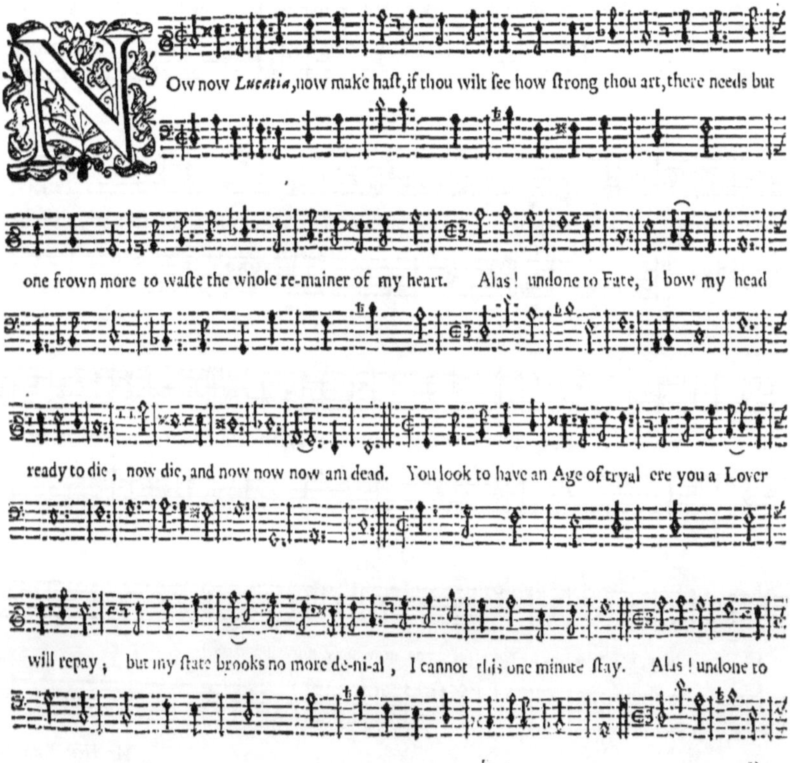

Now now *Lucretia*, now make haft, if thou wilt fee how ftrong thou art, there needs but one frown more to wafte the whole re-mainer of my heart. Alas! undone to Fate, I bow my head ready to die, now die, and now now now am dead. You look to have an Age of tryal ere you a Lover will repay; but my ftate brooks no more de-ni-al, I cannot this one minute ftay. Alas! undone to Fate

[4]

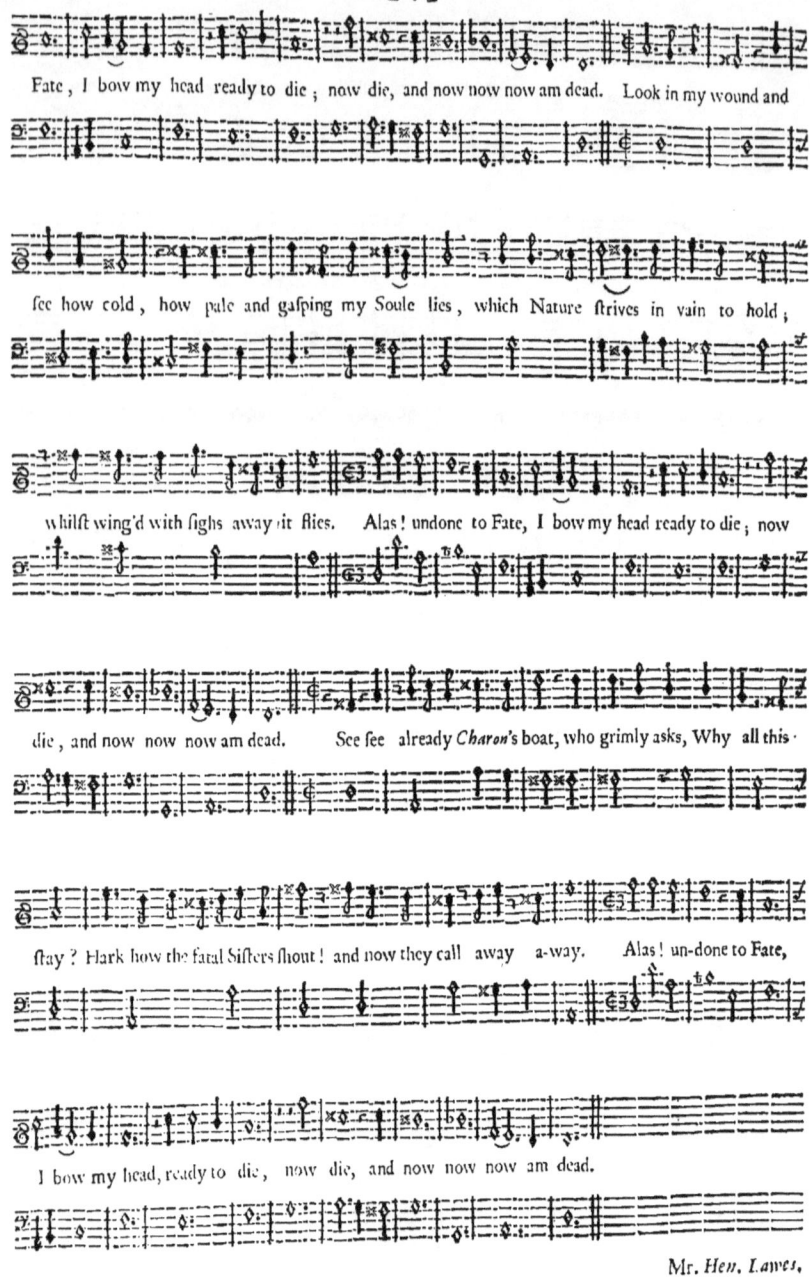

Mr. *Hen. Lawes.*

A TALE out of ANACREON.

AT dead low ebb of night, when none but Great *Charles* Wayn was driven on; When Mortals strict cessation keep, to re-recruit themselves with sleep; 'Twas then a Boy knockt at my gate. Who's there, said I, that calls so late? O let me in, he soon reply'd, I am a Childe; and then he cry'd, I wander without guide or light, lost in this wet, blind, Moonless night.

In pity then I rose, and straight unbarr'd my dore, and sprang a light: Behold, It was a Lovely Boy, a sweeter sight ne're bless'd mine Eye: I view'd him round, and saw strange things; a

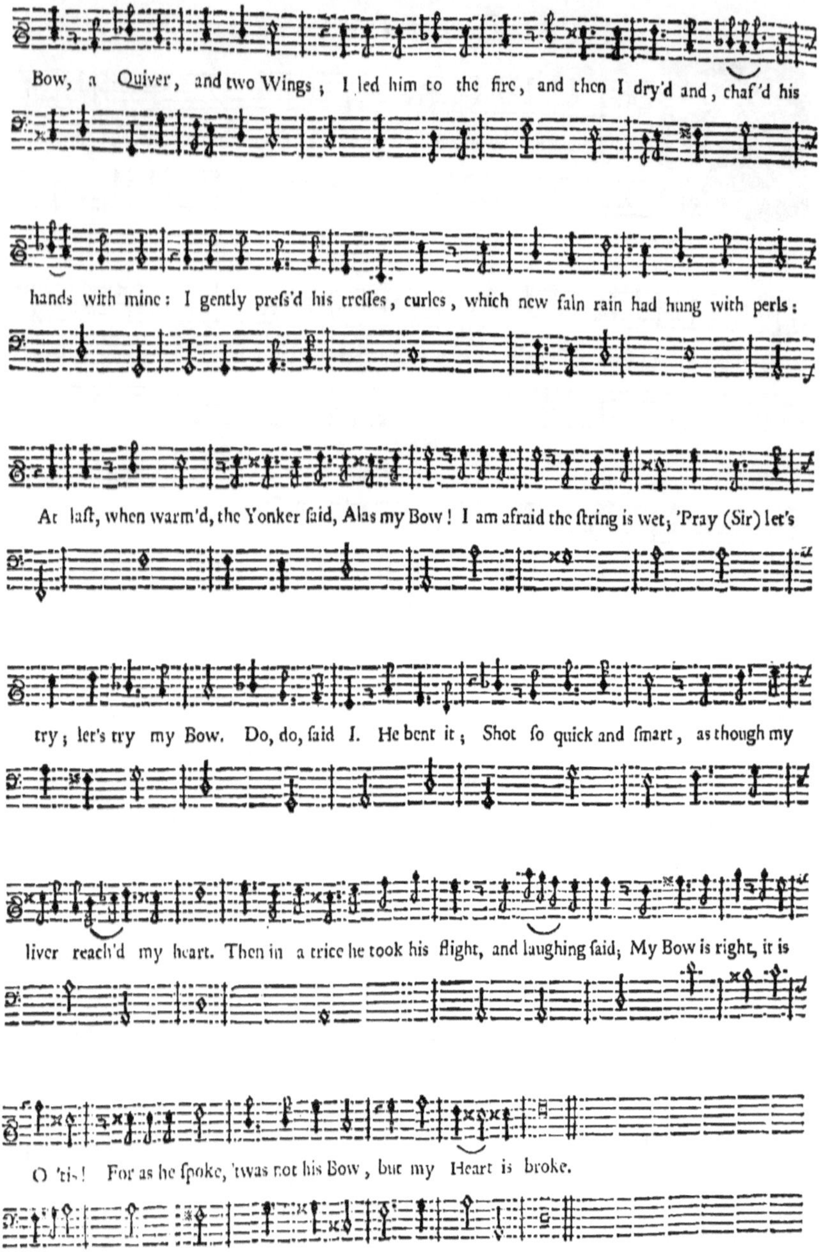

[6]

Bow, a Quiver, and two Wings; I led him to the fire, and then I dry'd and, chaf'd his

hands with mine: I gently press'd his tresses, curles, which new faln rain had hung with perls:

At last, when warm'd, the Yonker said, Alas my Bow! I am afraid the string is wet, 'Pray (Sir) let's

try; let's try my Bow. Do, do, said I. He bent it; Shot so quick and smart, as though my

liver reach'd my heart. Then in a trice he took his flight, and laughing said, My Bow is right, it is

O 'tis! For as he spoke, 'twas not his Bow, but my Heart is broke.

Mr. Hen. Lawes.

To his MISTRESS going to SEA.

Farewell, fair Saint! May not the Sea and Wind swell like the Hearts and Eyes you leave behind; but calm and gentle as the Looks you bear, smile in your face, and whisper in your ear. Let no bold Billow offer to arise, that it may never look upon your Eyes; lest wind and wave, enamour'd of your form, should throng and crowd themselves into a Storm. But if it be your Fate, vast Seas! to Love; of my becalmed breast learn how to move: Move then but in a gentler Lovers pace; no furrows nor no wrinkles in your face: And ye fierce winds, see that you tell your

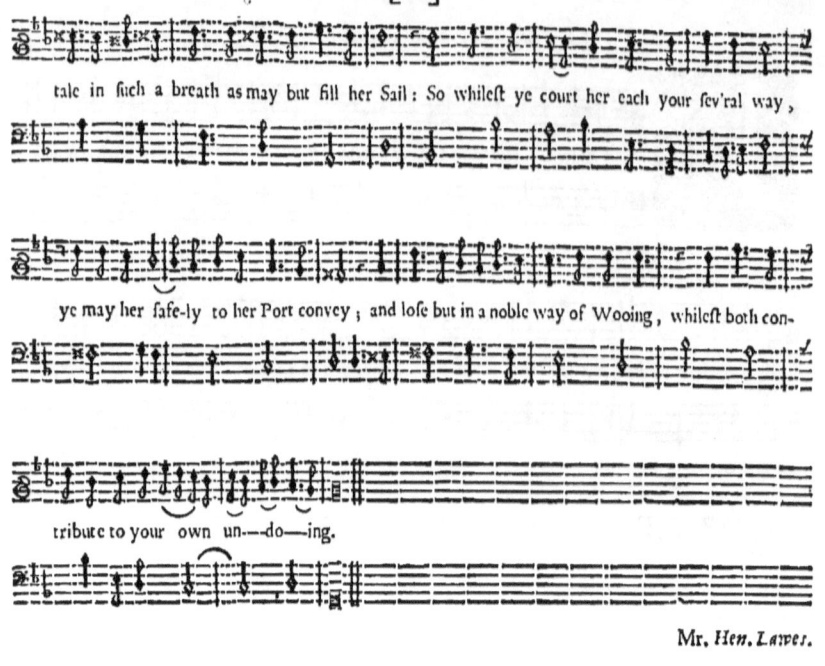

tale in such a breath as may but fill her Sail: So whilest ye court her each your sev'ral way, ye may her safe-ly to her Port convey; and lose but in a noble way of Wooing, whilest both con-tribute to your own un---do---ing.

Mr. *Hen. Lawes.*

A Complaint against CUPID.

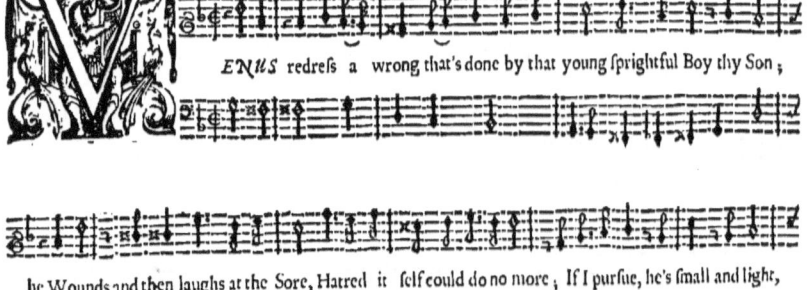

VENUS redress a wrong that's done by that young sprightful Boy thy Son; he Wounds and then laughs at the Sore, Hatred it self could do no more; If I pursue, he's small and light,

both

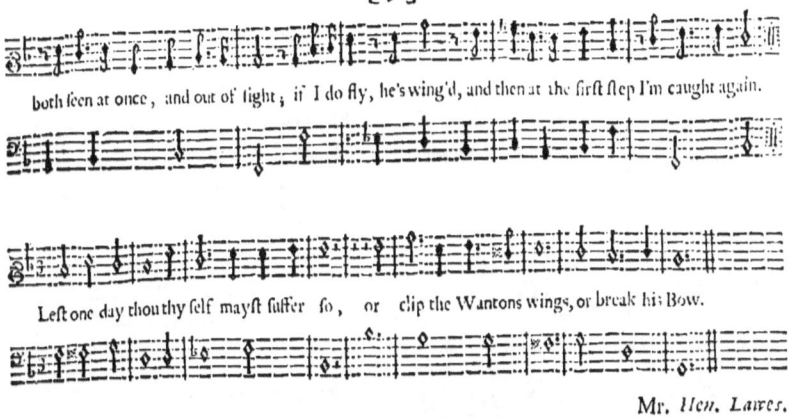

both seen at once, and out of sight; if I do fly, he's wing'd, and then at the first step I'm caught again.

Left one day thou thy self mayst suffer so, or clip the Wantons wings, or break his Bow.

Mr. Hen. Lawes.

The SURPRISE.

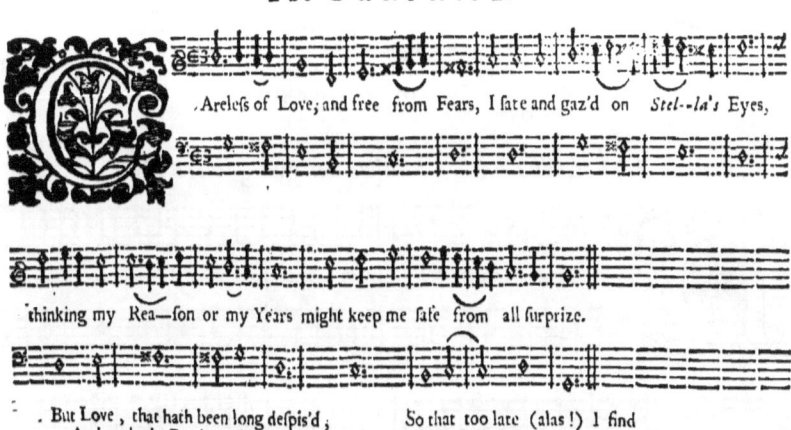

Careless of Love; and free from Fears, I sate and gaz'd on Stel--la's Eyes,

thinking my Rea—son or my Years might keep me safe from all surprize.

But Love, that hath been long despis'd;
And made the Baud to others trust,
Finding his Deity surpriz'd,
And chang'd into degenerate Lust;

Summon'd up all his strength and power;
Making her Face his Magazine,
Where Virtue's grace, and Beauty's flower
He plac'd his Godhead to redeem.

So that too late (alas!) I find
No steeled Armour is of proof,
Nor can the best resolved mind
Resist her Beauty and her Youth.

But yet the folly to untwist,
That loving I deserve no blame;
Were it not Atheisme to resist
Where Gods themselves conspire her flame.

Mr. Hen. Lawes.

BEAUTIES *Excellency.*

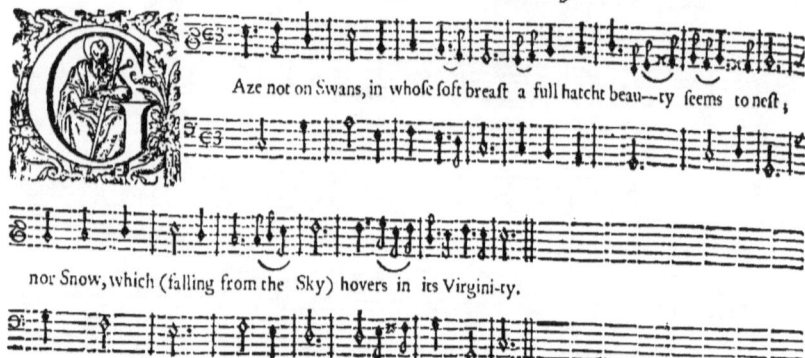

Aze not on Swans, in whose soft breast a full hatcht beau—ty seems to nest,
nor Snow, which (falling from the Sky) hovers in its Virgini-ty.

Gaze not on Roses, though new blown,
Grac'd with a fresh complexion;
Nor Lillies, which no subtle Bee
Hath rob'd by kissing Chymistrie.
Gaze not on that pure Milky way
Where night uses splendour with the day;
Nor Pearl, whose silver walls confine
The Riches of an Indian Mine.

For if my Emp'ress appears,
Swans moultring dye, Snow melts to tears;
Roses do blush and hang their heads,
Pale Lillies shrink into their beds.
The Milky way rides post, to shroud
Its baff'ed glory in a Cloud;
And Pearls do climb into her ear,
To hang themselves for Envy there.

So have I seen Stars big with light
Prove Lanthorns to the Moon-ey'd night;
Which when *Sol*'s Rays were once display'd,
Sink in their Sockets, and decay'd.

To his MISTRES *upon his going to travel.*

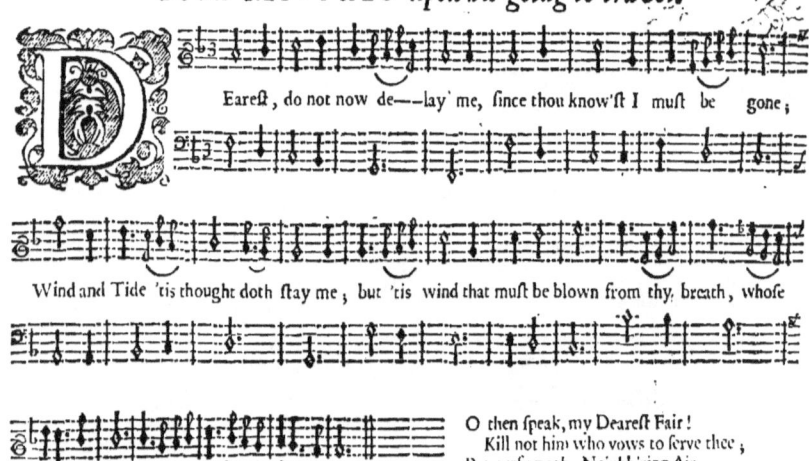

Earest, do not now de—lay' me, since thou know'st I must be gone;
Wind and Tide 'tis thought doth stay me; but 'tis wind that must be blown from thy breath, whose
na-tive smell In—dian Odours doth ex-cel.

O then speak, my Dearest Fair!
Kill not him who vows to serve thee;
But perfume the Neighb'ring Air,
For dumb silence else will starve me:
'Tis a word is quickly spoken,
Which restrain'd, a heart is broken.

Mediocrity

Mediocrity in Love rejected.

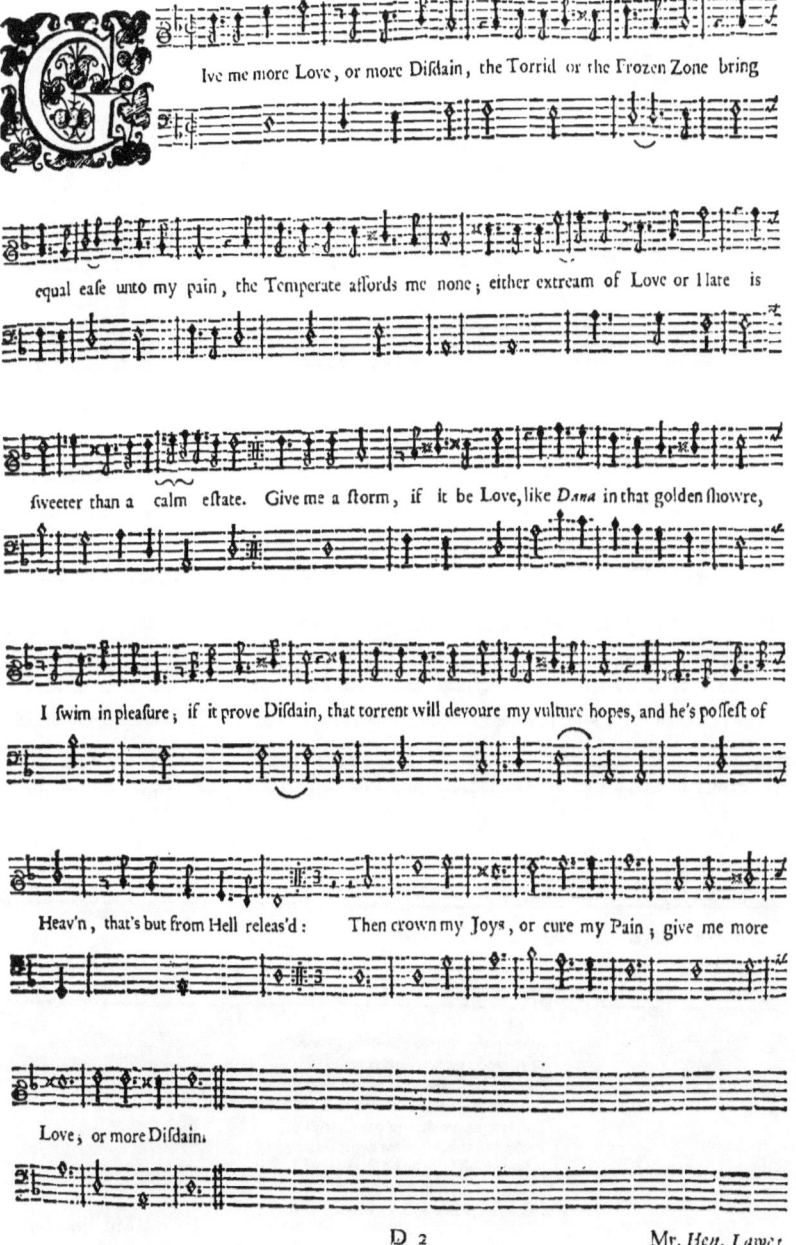

Mr. *Hen. Lawes.*

[12]
The Self-Banished.

'T is not that I love you less then when before your feet I lay, but to pre-vent the sad encrease of hopeless Love I keep away: In vain a-las! for ev'ry thing that I have known be-long to you, your form dares to my fan-cy bring, and make my old wounds bleed a-new.

But I have vow'd, and never must your banish'd Ser--vant trouble you; for if he break, you may distrust the vow he made to love you too.

Who in the Spring from the new Sun
  Already hath a Feaver got;
Too late begins those shafts to shun
  Which *Phœbus* through his veins hath shot;
Too late he would the pains asswage,
  And to thick shadows does retire,
About with him he bears the rage,
  And in his tainted bloud the fire.
     But I have vow'd, &c.

Mr. *Hen. Lawes*.

[13]

To his MISTRES objecting his Age.

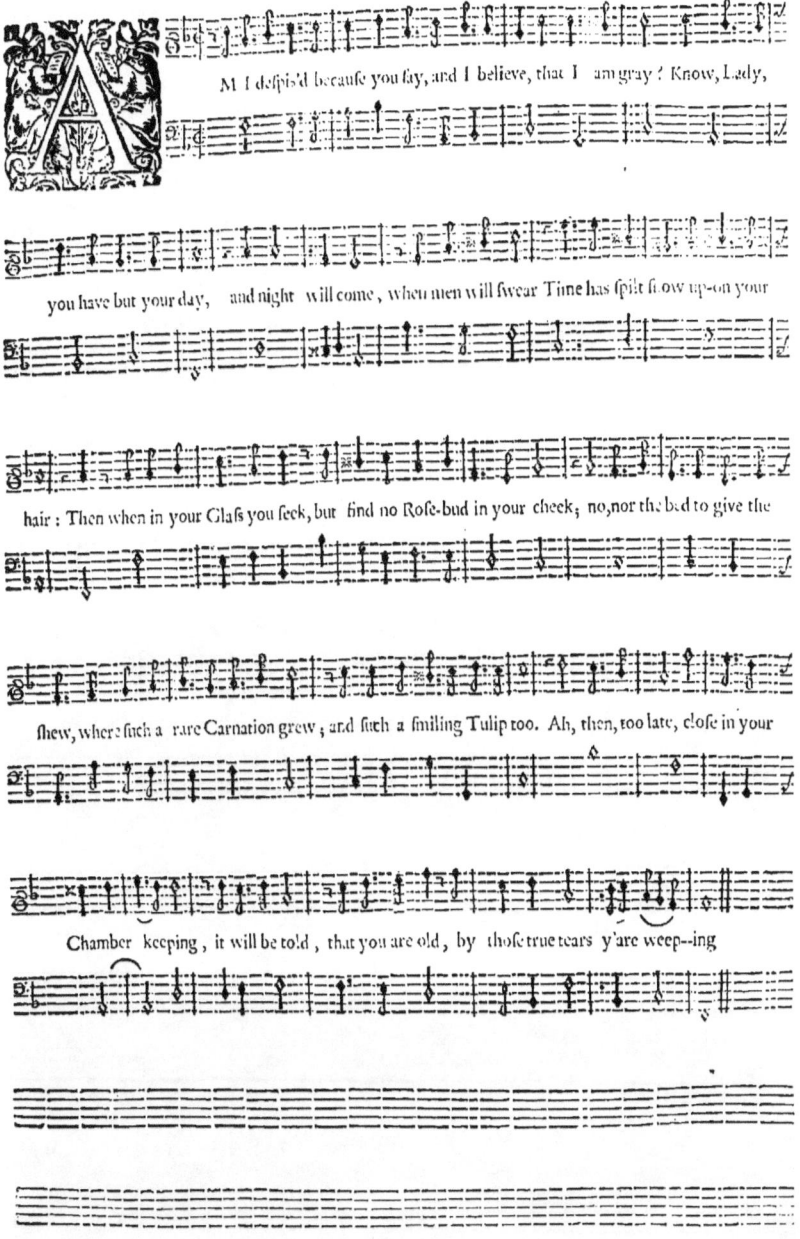

AM I despis'd because you say, and I believe, that I am gray? Know, Lady, you have but your day, and night will come, when men will swear Time has spilt snow up-on your hair: Then when in your Glass you seek, but find no Rose-bud in your cheek; no, nor the bud to give the shew, where such a rare Carnation grew; and such a smiling Tulip too. Ah, then, too late, close in your Chamber keeping, it will be told, that you are old, by those true tears y'are weep--ing

To a Lady, more affable since the War began.

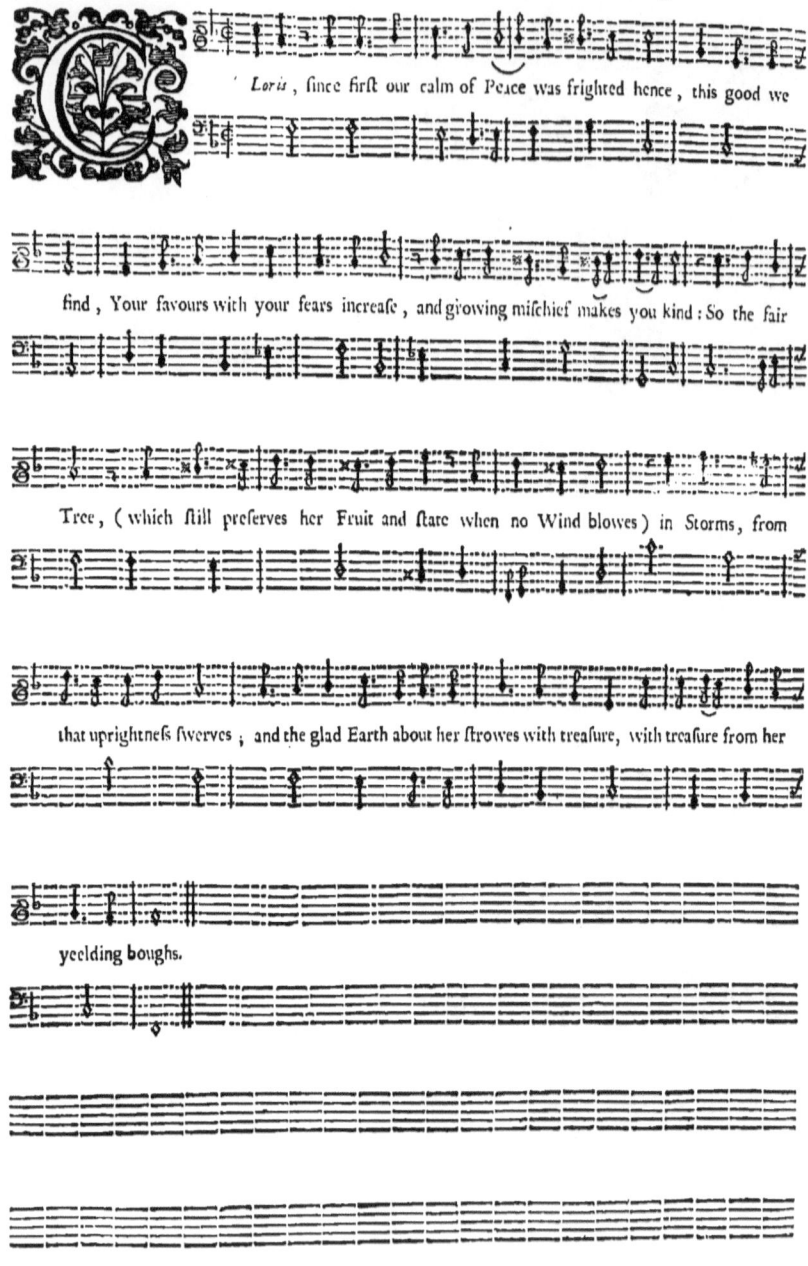

Cloris, since first our calm of Peace was frighted hence, this good we find, Your favours with your fears increase, and growing mischief makes you kind: So the fair Tree, (which still preserves her Fruit and state when no Wind blowes) in Storms, from that uprightness swerves; and the glad Earth about her strowes with treasure, with treasure from her yeelding boughs.

Cloris Singing.

Es, yes, 'tis *Cloris* sings, 'tis she ; Mark how the Nymphs and Shepherds all flock to her : so the Master Bee the swarm leads with his awful call; so to the *Thracian* Lyre the floods resor.ed, and the listning woods: so shoals of Dolphins on the green waves spring, when *Doris* or her Sea-born Daughters sing, and so her Notes their hearts benum : one looks pale, others eyes ore-flow with tears of

The Unconstant Lover.

How I hate thee now, and my self too, for loving such a false, false thing as thee! who hour-ly canst depart from heart to heart, to take new har-bour as thou didst in me; but when the world shall spie, and know thy shifts as well as I, they'l shut their hearts and take thee in no more; he that can dwell with none, must out of dore.

II.

Thy pride hath overgrown
All this great Town
Which stoops, and bowes as low as I to you;
Thy falshood might support
All the new Court
Which shifts, and turn, almost as oft as thou.
But to express thee by,
There's not an object low, or high,
For 'twill be found, when ere the measures tride,
Nothing can read thy falshood, but thy pride.

Night and day to his MISTRES.

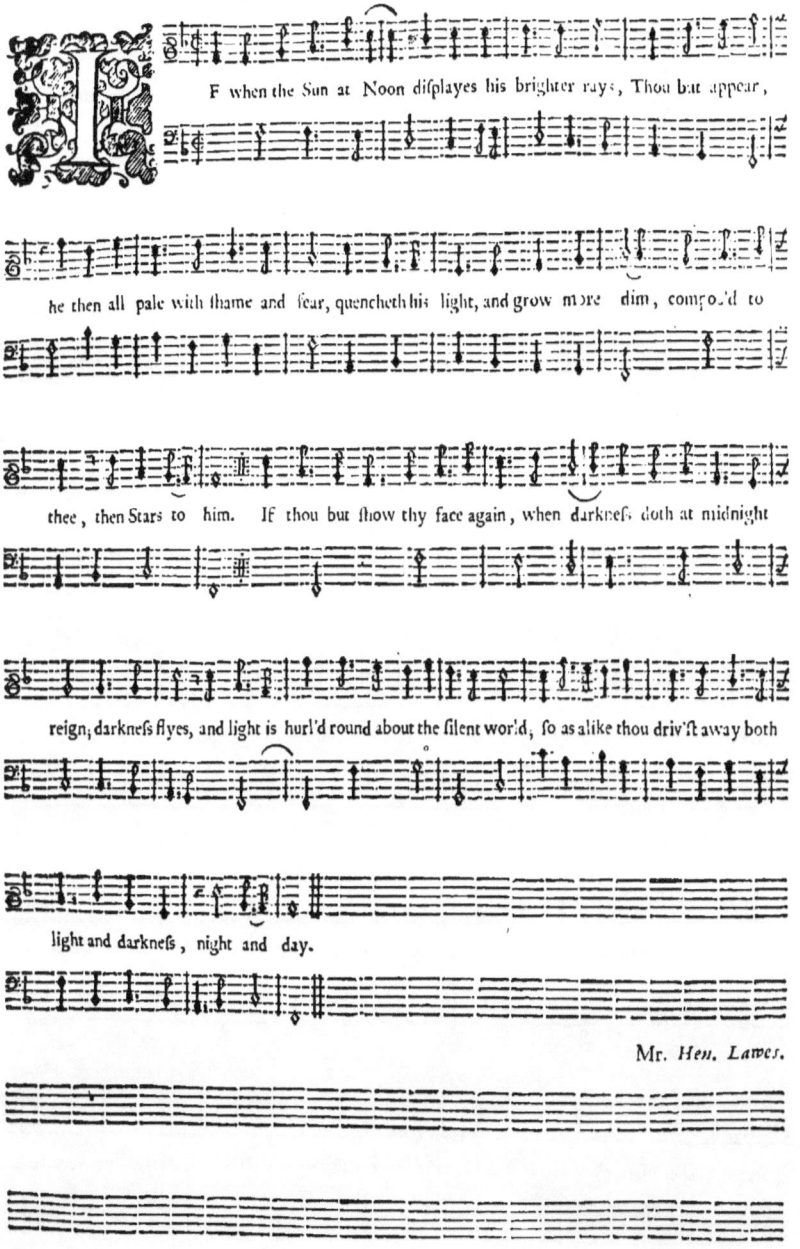

F when the Sun at Noon displayes his brighter rays, Thou but appear, he then all pale with shame and fear, quencheth his light, and grow more dim, compo..'d to thee, then Stars to him. If thou but show thy face again, when darkness doth at midnight reign; darkness flyes, and light is hurl'd round about the silent world, so as alike thou driv'st away both light and darkness, night and day.

Mr. *Hen. Lawes.*

To his RIVALL.

Seek not to know my Love, for she hath vow'd her Constant faith to me: her milde Aspects are mine, and thou shalt onely find a Stormy brow; for if her Beauty stir desire in mee, her Kisses quench the fire: Or I can to Loves Fountain goe, or dwell upon her Hills of Snow; But when thou burn'st, shee shall not spare one gentle Breath to cool the Air; thou shalt not climbe those Alps, nor spie where the sweet Springs of *Venus* lie: Search hidden Nature, and there find a treasure to enrich thy mind: Discover Arts not yet reveal'd,

But

The Heart Intire.

Anſt thou love me, and yet doubt ſo much Falſhood in my heart, that a way I ſhould find out to impart fragments of a broken Love to you, more then all b'ing leſs then due: O, no! Love muſt clear Diſtruſt, or be eaten with that Ruſt; ſhort Love liking may find Jars, the Love that laſteth knows no Wars.

There Belief begets Delight,
And ſo ſatisfies Deſire,
That in them it ſhines as Light
   No more Fire;
All the burning Qualities appeas'd,
Each in others joying pleas'd;
Not a whiſper, not a thought
But 'twixt Both in common's brought;
Even to ſeem Two they are loath,
Love being only Soul to both.

Mr. *Hen. Lawes.*

[21]
Love in Despair.

A Lover once I did espie with bleeding Heart and weeping Eye; he sigh'd and groan'd, and curst the Boy that planted woe, supplanted joy; he wept and cry'd, How great's his pain that lives in Love, and loves in vain! Can there (says he) no Cure be found, but by the hand that gave the wound. Then let me die, which Ile endure, since she wants Charity to Cure: Yet let her one day feel the pain to wish sh' had cur'd, but wish in vain; for wither'd cheeks may chance recover some sparks of Love, but not a Lover.

Mr. Hen. Lawes.

[22]

Loves Fruition.

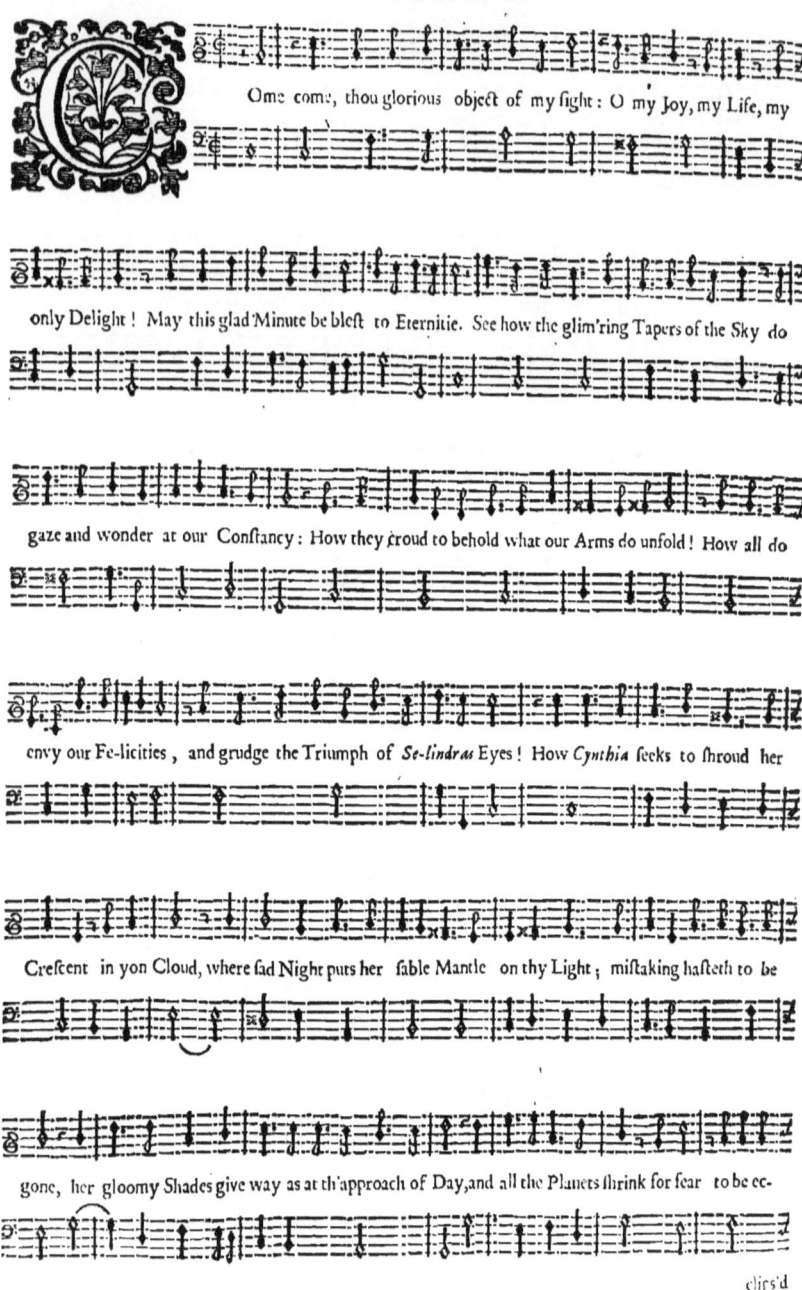

Come come, thou glorious object of my sight: O my Joy, my Life, my only Delight! May this glad Minute be bleft to Eternitie. See how the glim'ring Tapers of the Sky do gaze and wonder at our Conftancy: How they proud to behold what our Arms do unfold! How all do envy our Fe-licities, and grudge the Triumph of *Se-lindra's* Eyes! How *Cynthia* feeks to fhroud her Crefcent in yon Cloud, where fad Night puts her fable Mantle on thy Light; miftaking hafteth to be gone, her gloomy Shades give way as at th'approach of Day, and all the Planets fhrink for fear to be ec-

clips'd

[23]

clips'd by a brighter De-i-tie. Look, O look, how the small Lights do fall and adore what before the

Heavens have not shown, nor their godhead known. Such a Faith, such a Love as may move Mighty

Jove from a-bove to descend and re-main amongst Mortals again.

Mr. *Hen. Lawes.*

Love in the Spring.

Pleasure, Beauty, Youth attend ye; Love and Melting thoughts befriend ye:

[24]
The LARK.

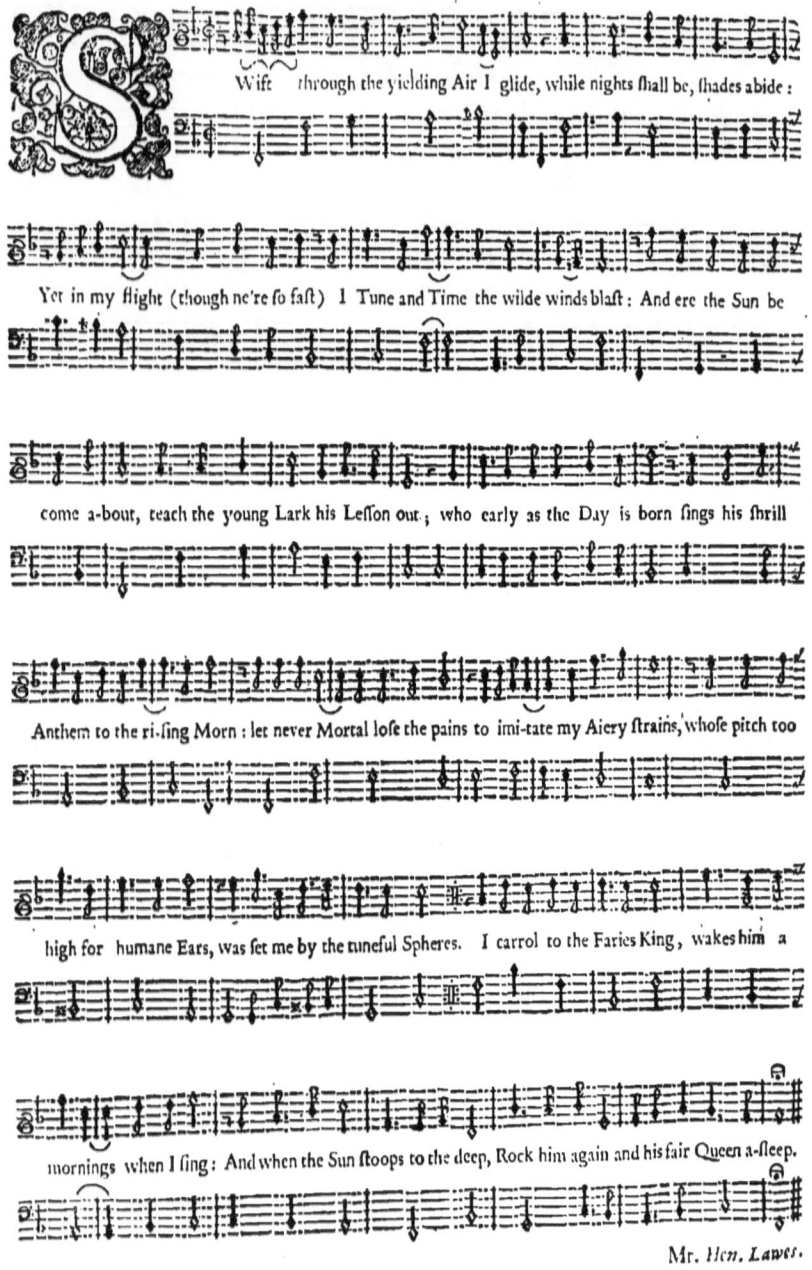

Swift through the yielding Air I glide, while nights shall be, shades abide: Yet in my flight (though ne're so fast) I Tune and Time the wilde winds blast: And ere the Sun be come a-bout, teach the young Lark his Lesson out ; who early as the Day is born sings his shrill Anthem to the ri-sing Morn : let never Mortal lose the pains to imi-tate my Aiery strains, whose pitch too high for humane Ears, was set me by the tuneful Spheres. I carrol to the Faries King, wakes him a mornings when I sing: And when the Sun stoops to the deep, Rock him again and his fair Queen a-sleep.

Mr. Hen. Lawes.

Loves Dying Passion.

Amarillis tear thy hair, beat thy breast, sigh, weep, despair; cry cry Ay me! Is *Daphne* dead? I see a paleness on his brow, and his cheeks are drown'd in snow; Whether, whether, whether are those Roses fled? O my heart! how cold, how cold he's growne? Sure his Lips are turn'd to stone. Thus, Thus then I offer up my blood, and bathe my body in his shrowd. Since living accents cannot move, Know *Amarillis*, know *Amarillis* dy'd for Love.

Mr. Hen. Lawes.

On a lost Heart.

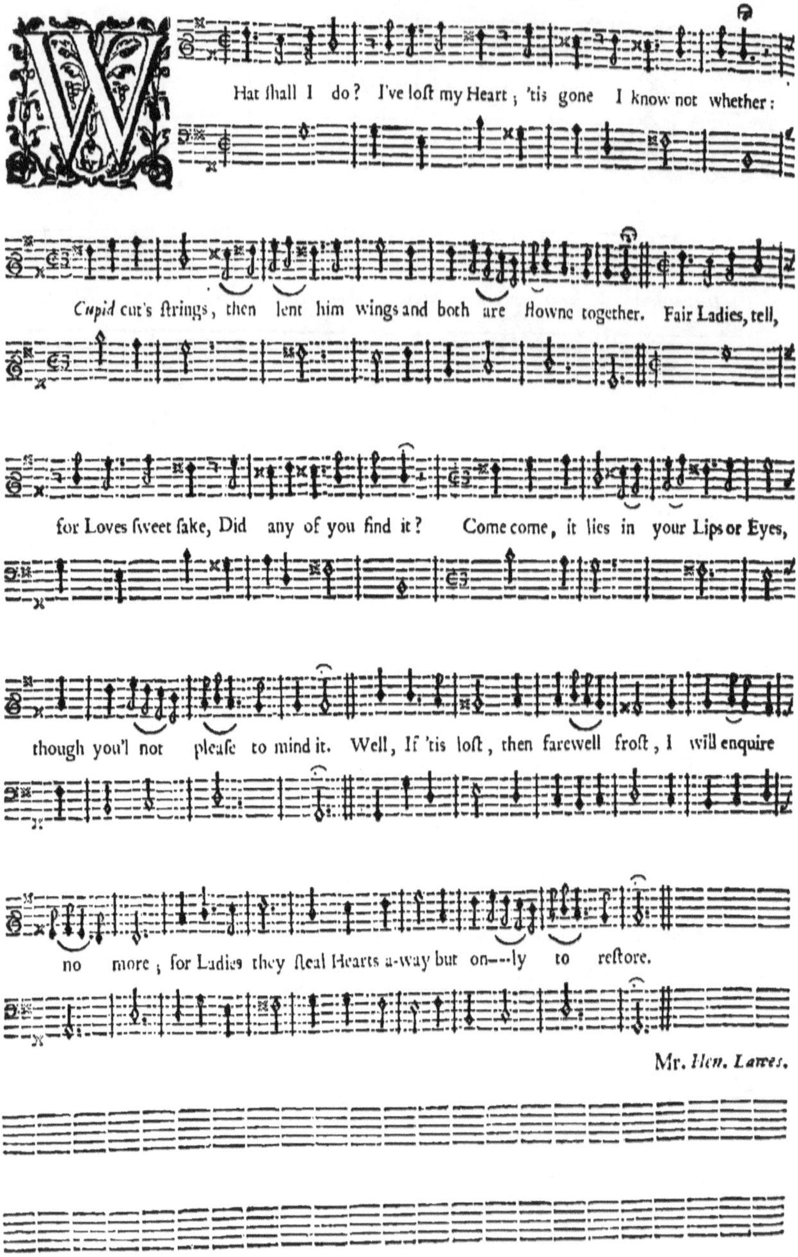

What shall I do? I've lost my Heart; 'tis gone I know not whether: Cupid cut's strings, then lent him wings and both are flowne together. Fair Ladies, tell, for Loves sweet sake, Did any of you find it? Come come, it lies in your Lips or Eyes, though you'l not please to mind it. Well, If 'tis lost, then farewell froft, I will enquire no more; for Ladies they steal Hearts a-way but on---ly to restore.

Mr. *Hen. Lawes*.

Loves Flattery.

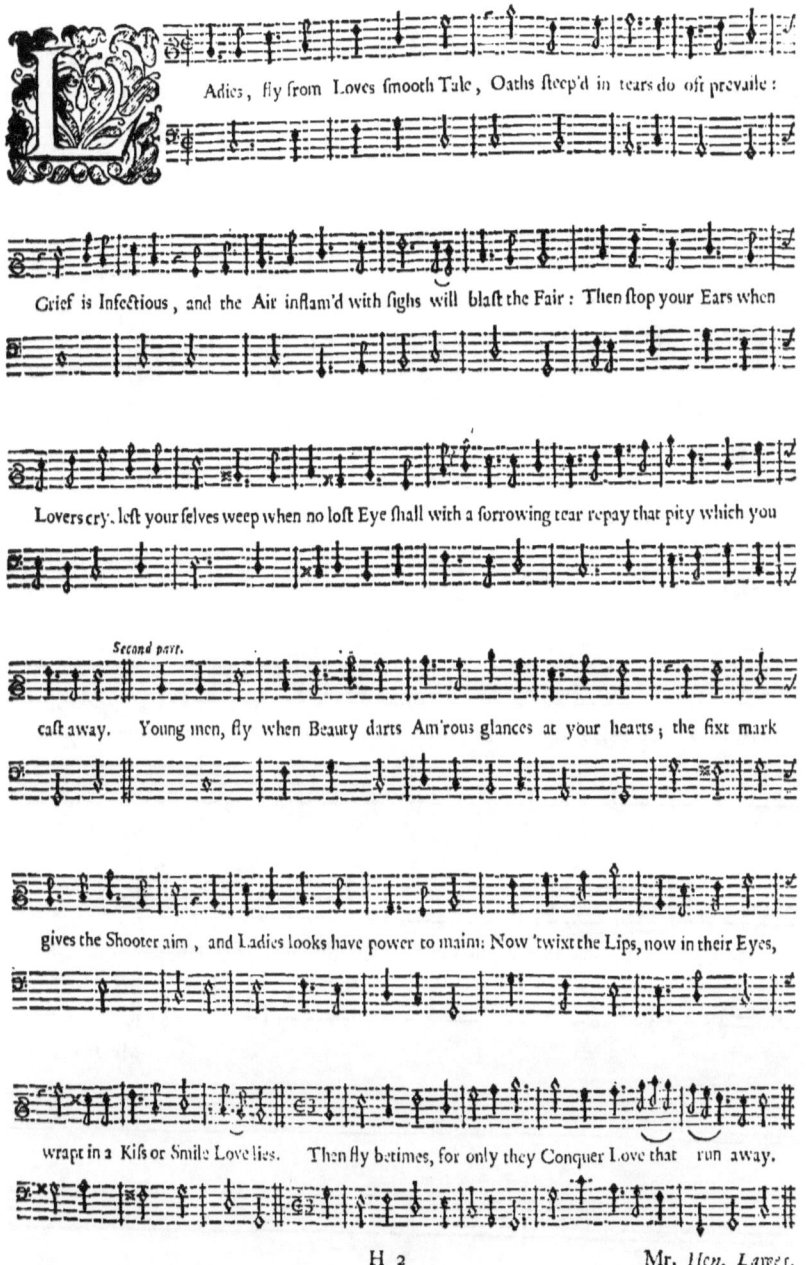

Mr. *Hen. Lawes.*

A Dream.

I Laid me down up—on a pillow soft, and dream'd I clypt and kist my Mistress oft: She cry'd, Fie fie, away, you are too bold. I pray'd her be content, though she were cold, my veins did burn with flames of hot desire, and must not leave till she had quench'd my fire. Well, since (said she) I may not from you fly, do what you please, I give you liberty. With that I wak'd, but found I was deceiv'd; for which I storm'd like one of sense bereav'd.

Mr. Hen. Lawes.

Upon the Hearing Mrs. MARY KNIGHT Sing.

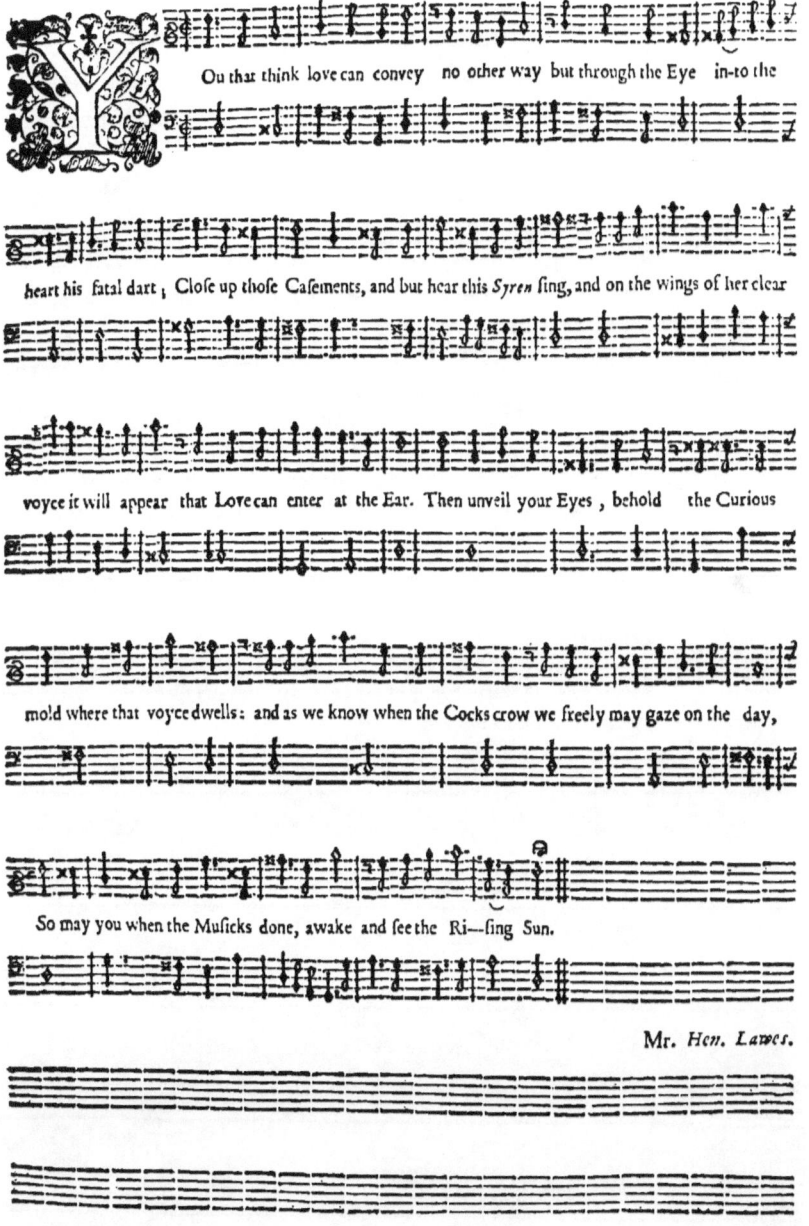

You that think love can convey no other way but through the Eye in-to the heart his fatal dart; Close up those Casements, and but hear this *Syren* sing, and on the wings of her clear voyce it will appear that Love can enter at the Ear. Then unveil your Eyes, behold the Curious mold where that voyce dwells: and as we know when the Cocks crow we freely may gaze on the day, So may you when the Musicks done, awake and see the Ri---sing Sun.

Mr. *Hen. Lawes.*

The Thrifty LOVER.

I Lov'd thee once, Ile love no more; thine be the grief as is the blame: Thou art not what thou wert before; What rea--son I should be the same? He that can love un-lov'd again, hath better store of Love than Brain. God send me Love my Debts to pay, whilest Unthrifts fool their Love away.

Mr. *Hen. Lawes.*

A LOVER on his Dying MISTRESS.

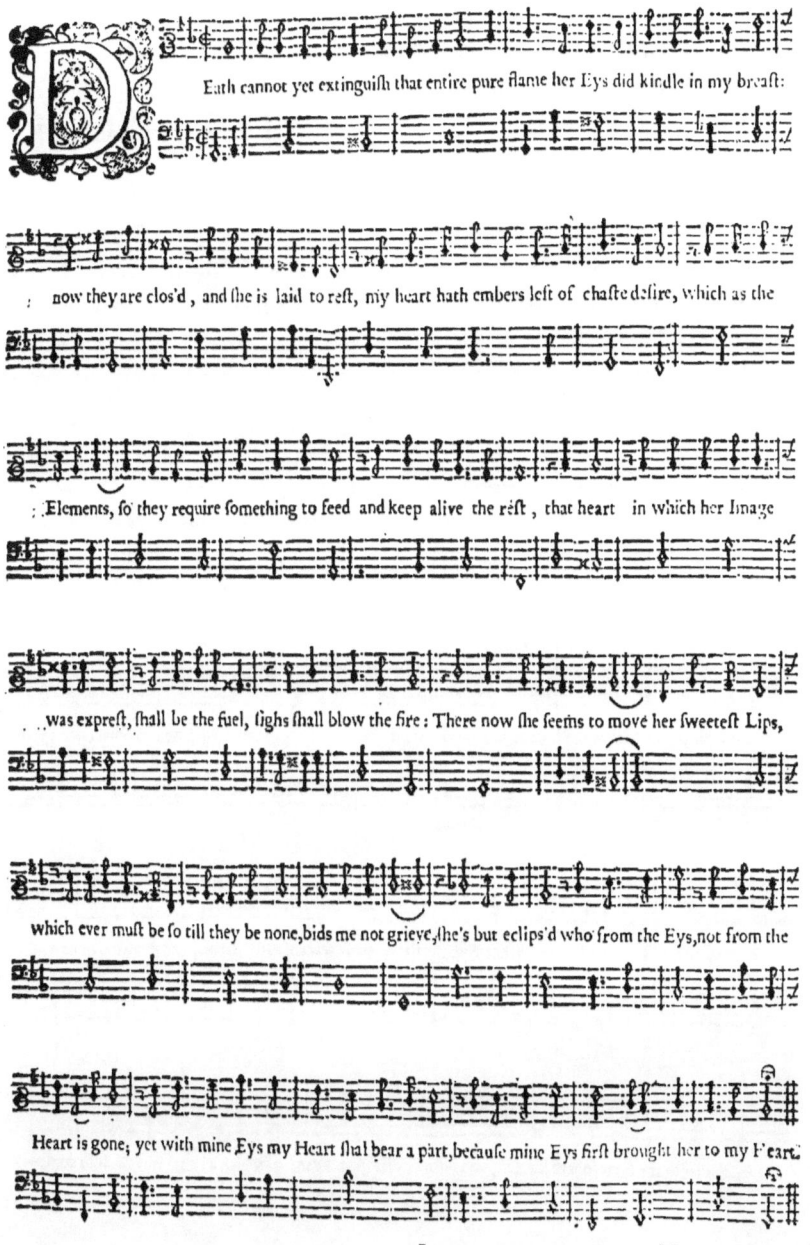

Mr. Hen. Lawes.

The FLY.

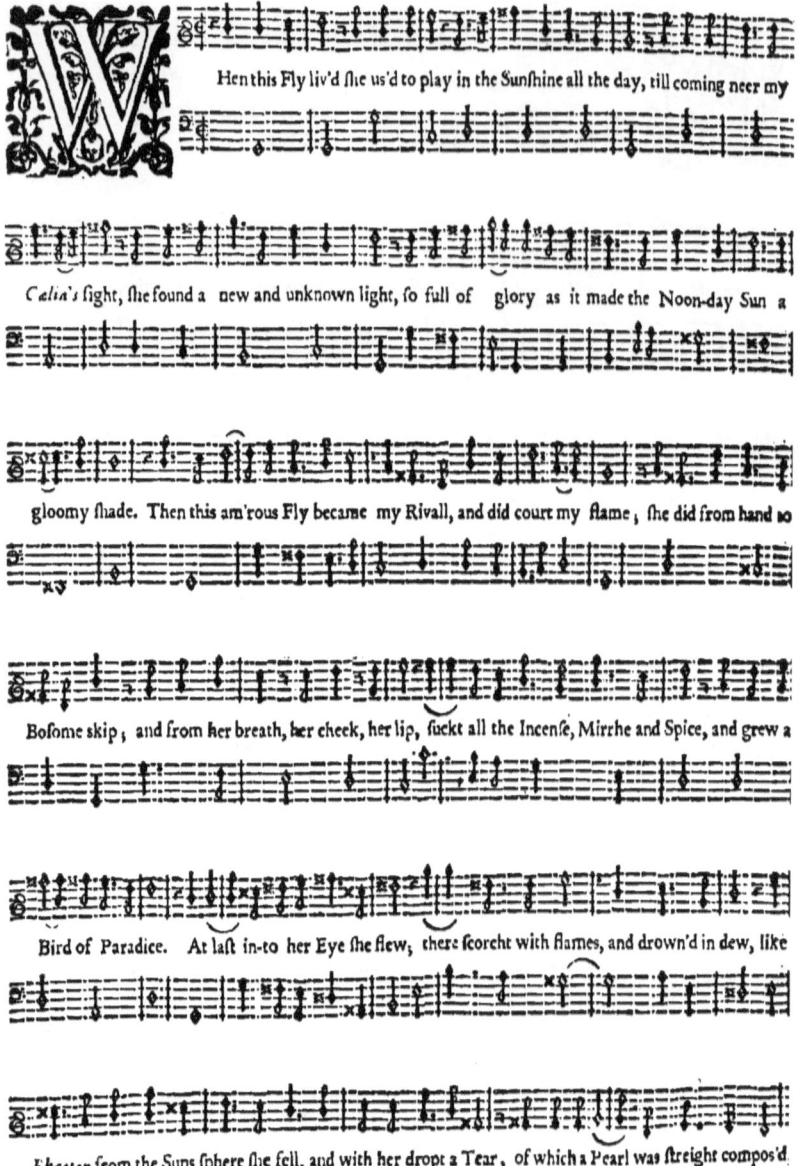

When this Fly liv'd she us'd to play in the Sunshine all the day, till coming neer my Celia's sight, she found a new and unknown light, so full of glory as it made the Noon-day Sun a gloomy shade. Then this am'rous Fly became my Rival, and did court my flame, she did from hand to Bosome skip, and from her breath, her cheek, her lip, suckt all the Incense, Mirrhe and Spice, and grew a Bird of Paradice. At last in-to her Eye she flew, there scorcht with flames, and drown'd in dew, like Phaeton from the Suns sphere she fell, and with her dropt a Tear, of which a Pearl was streight compos'd wherein her Ashes lie inclos'd: Thus she receiv'd from *Celia's* Eye, Funeral flame, Tombe Obsequie.

Loves Torment.

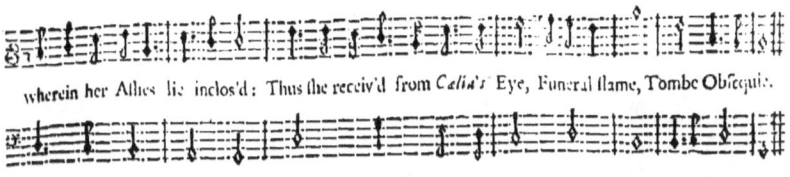

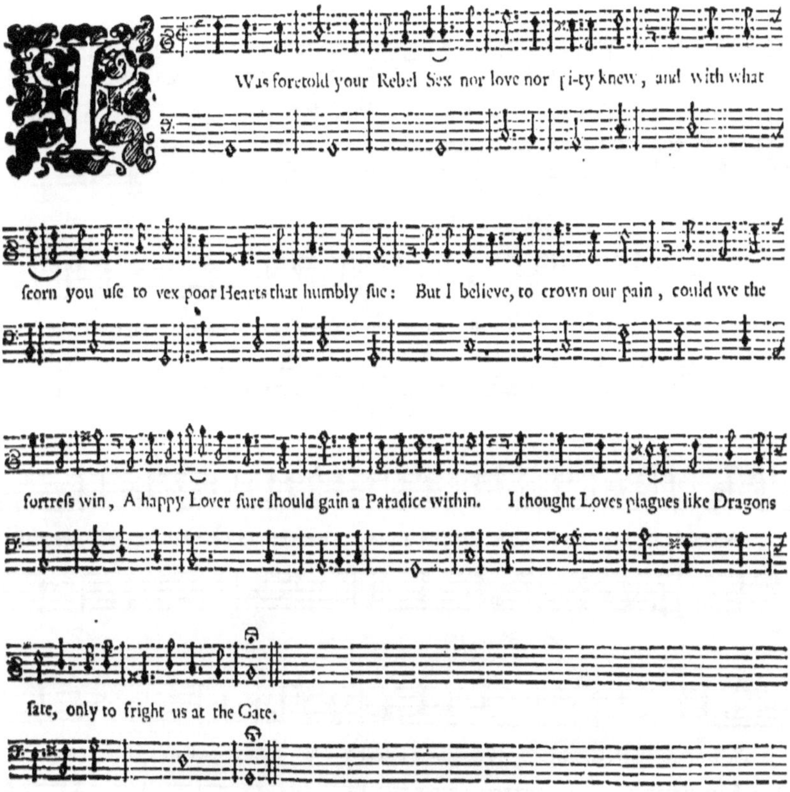

I Was foretold your Rebel Sex nor love nor pi-ty knew, and with what scorn you use to vex poor Hearts that humbly sue: But I believe, to crown our pain, could we the fortress win, A happy Lover sure should gain a Paradice within. I thought Loves plagues like Dragons fate, only to fright us at the Gate.

If I did enter and enjoy what happy Lovers prove,
I would Kiss, and Sport, and Toy, and taste those Sweets of Love:
Or had they but a lasting fate, or if in *Celia's* breast,
Or of Love might not abate, *Jove* was too mean a Guest:
   But now her breach of faith far more
   Afflicts than did her Scorn before.

Hard Fate! to have been once possest as Victor of a Heart,
Atchiev'd with labour and unrest, and then forc'd to Depart.
If the stout foe will not resigne when I besiege a Town,
I lose but what was never mine; but he that is cast down
   From Injoy'd Beauty, feels a woe
   Only depoied Kings can know.

K

Love Unveil'd

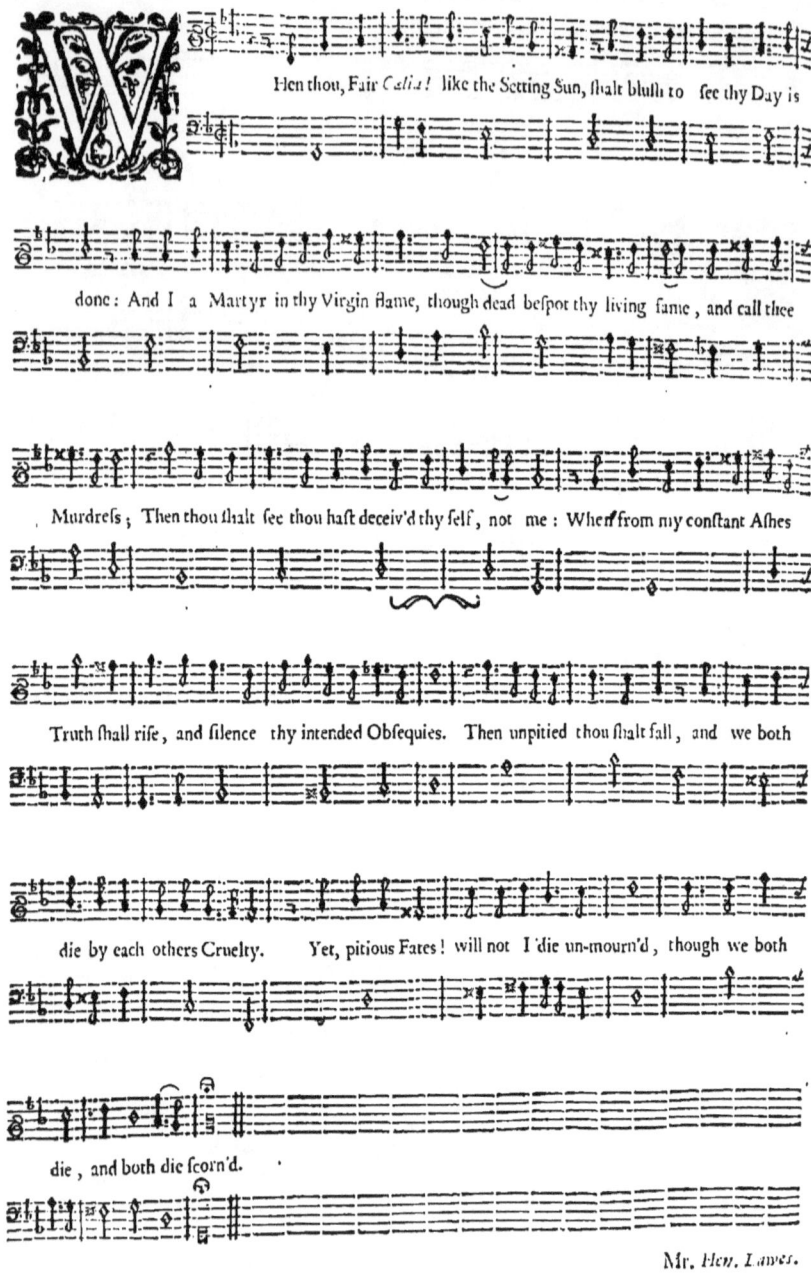

When thou, Fair Cælia! like the Setting Sun, shalt blush to see thy Day is done: And I a Martyr in thy Virgin flame, though dead bespot thy living fame, and call thee Murdress; Then thou shalt see thou hast deceiv'd thy self, not me: When from my constant Ashes Truth shall rise, and silence thy intended Obsequies. Then unpitied thou shalt fall, and we both die by each others Cruelty. Yet, pitious Fates! will not I die un-mourn'd, though we both die, and both die scorn'd.

Mr. Hen. Lawes.

The Mournful Lovers.

Come, come, sad Turtle, matcheless moaning; droop no more for want of Owning: Here's a Breast for your Nest, like an Altar Cypress drest, sa-cri-fi-cing griefful groaning.

Come, sad Turtle, O come hither, our fate's a-like, let's die to-gether. Come come, and use sigh-soothing skill, and with Loving gently kill, soon as Asps fatal clasps, whilest your sad glad feeder gasps, feed on woe, and feast your fill. Come, sad Turtle, O come hither; our Fate's alike,

Let's die to-ge-ther.

Mr. Hen. Lawes.

Loves Power.

Mr. *Hen. Lawes.*

Loves Ardency.

No more of Tears, I've now no more to quench my flame, but make it scorch the more: My sighs that should have cool'd my hot desire, blow my flame high, and set me all on fire. No remedy to Cure me? Yes, there's one: If thou wilt girt me in thy Frozen Zone, then may I be as thou art, or make thee melt thy white snow, and turn to fire like me.

Mr. *Hen. Lawes.*

The NIGHTINGALE.

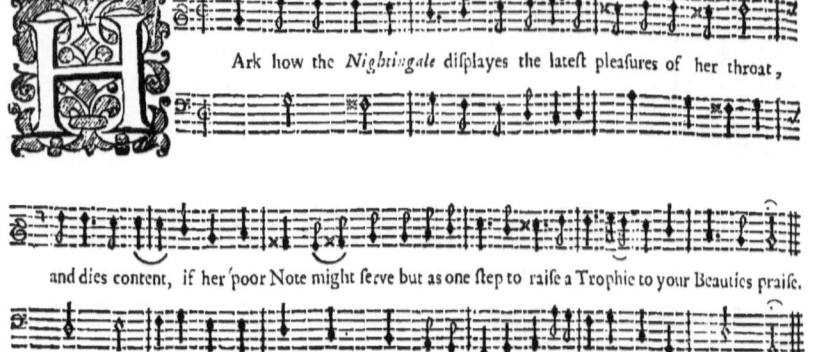

Ark how the *Nightingale* displayes the latest pleasures of her throat, and dies content, if her poor Note might serve but as one step to raise a Trophie to your Beauties praise.

Mr. Hen. Lawes.

The Rose, in whose rich Odours lie
The perfum'd Treasures of the Year,
Doth blush to death when you appear,
And Martyr-like towards you doth fly,
To wear your Cheeks fresh Livery.

Aurora weeps to see a light
Outvie her splendour in your Eyes,
The Sun's asham'd to walk the skies,
And th' Envious Moon, grown pale for spight,
Vows ne're to Revel but with Night.

The saucy Wind with senseless care
(Seeming to feel soft sense of bliss)
Steals through your hair, your lips to kiss,
So Rivals me, who now despair
To touch your Lip, Cheek, Eye or Hair.

Loves Constancy.

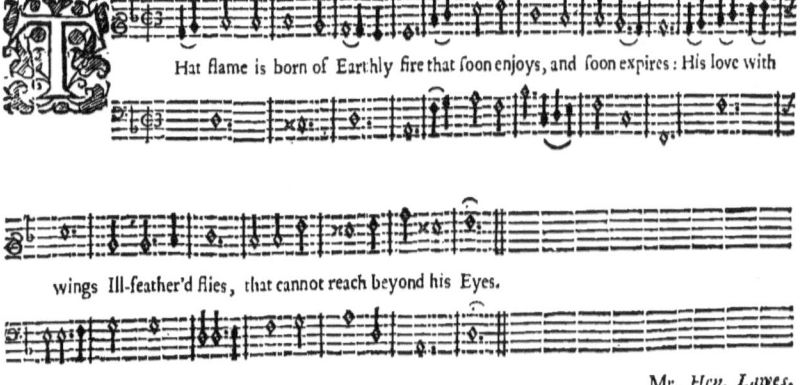

Hat flame is born of Earthly fire that soon enjoys, and soon expires: His love with wings Ill-feather'd flies, that cannot reach beyond his Eyes.

Mr. Hen. Lawes.

Where Hope doth fan the Idle fire
'Tis easie to Maintain desire;
But that's the Noble Love that dare
Continue Constant in Despare.

Cupid's Alarm

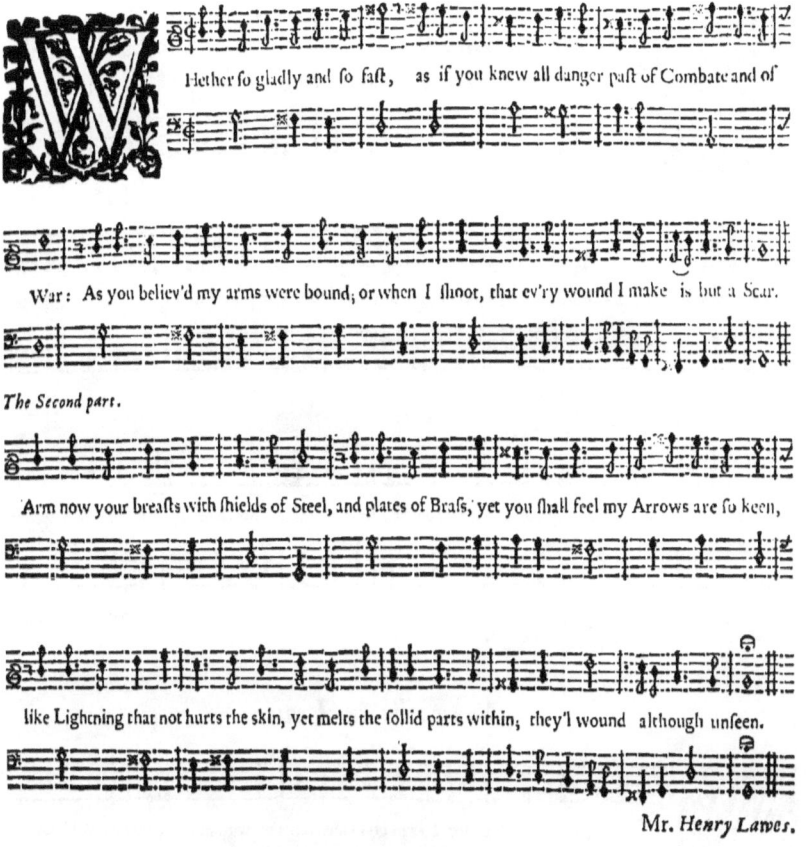

Hether so gladly and so fast, as if you knew all danger past of Combate and of War: As you believ'd my arms were bound, or when I shoot, that ev'ry wound I make is but a Scar.

The Second part.

Arm now your breasts with shields of Steel, and plates of Brass, yet you shall feel my Arrows are so keen, like Lightning that not hurts the skin, yet melts the sollid parts within; they'l wound although unseen.

Mr. *Henry Lawes.*

My Mother taught me long ago
To aim my Shafts, and draw my Bow,
When She did *Mars* subdue:
And now you must resigne to Love
Your warlike Shafts, that She may prove
Those Antique stories true.

Beauties Excellency.

Ranscendent Beauty! thou that art light to mine Eyes, life to my Heart: And in whose Virtue rests alone the only true Phi-lo--so-phers Stone: For as th' Elixir can restore Nature de-cay'd as 'twas before, thy power hath wrought a stranger thing, by changing Autumn to a Spring.

Mr. Hen. Lawes.

Sympathy in Love.

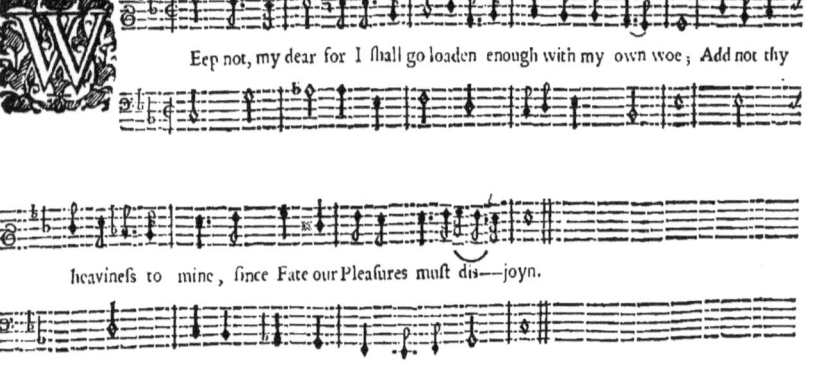

Eep not, my dear for I shall go loaden enough with my own woe; Add not thy heaviness to mine, since Fate our Pleasures must dis-—joyn.

Why should our Sorrows meet, if I
Must go and leave thy Company?
I wish not there's it shall relieve
My Heart, to think thou dost not grieve.

Yet grieve and weep, that I may bear
Every Sigh and every Tear;
And it shall glad my Heart to see
Thou wert thus loth to part from mee.

A Remembrance.

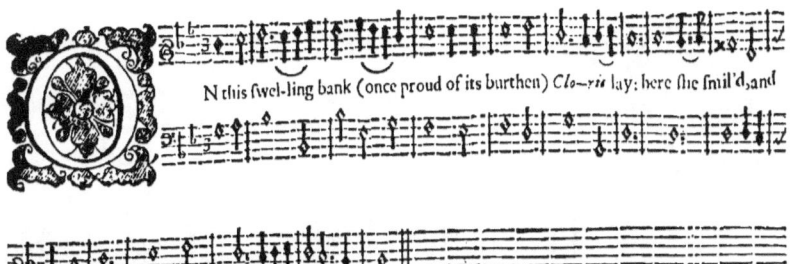

ON this swel-ling bank (once proud of its burthen) Clo—ris lay: here she smil'd, and did uncloud those bright Suns ec—clipse the day.

(2)
Here we sate, and with kind art
She about me twin'd her arms,
Clasp'd in hers my hand and heart
Fetter'd by those pleasing charms.

(3)
Here my love and joys she crown'd
Whil'st the hours stood before me,
With a killing glance did wound
And a melting kiss restore me.

(4)
On the doun of either breast
Whil'st with joy my soul retir'd,
My resigning heart did rest
Till her lips new life inspir'd.

(5)
The renewing of these sights,
Doth with grief and pleasure fill me,
And the thought of those delights
Both at once revive and kill me.

Sufferance.

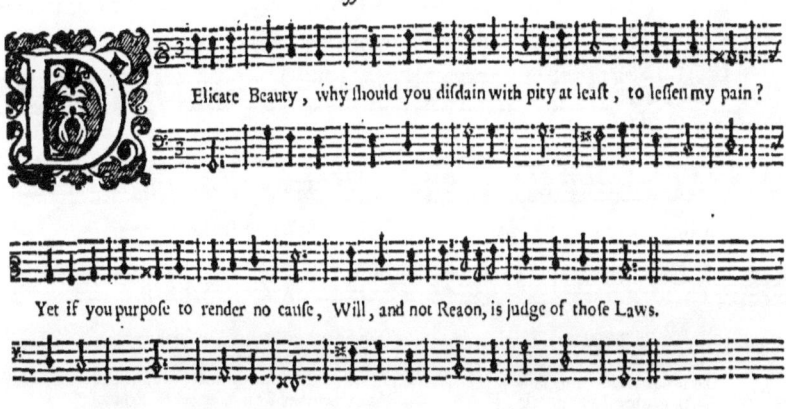

DElicate Beauty, why should you disdain with pity at least, to lessen my pain? Yet if you purpose to render no cause, Will, and not Reason, is judge of those Laws.

(2)
Suffer in silence I can with delight
Courting your anger to live in your sight;
Inwardly languish, and like my disease,
Always provided my sufferance please.

(3)
Take all my comforts in present away,
Let all but the hope of your favour decay;
Rich in reversion I'le live as content,
As he to whom Fortune her fore-lock hath lent.

Mutual affection between ORINDA and LUCATIA.

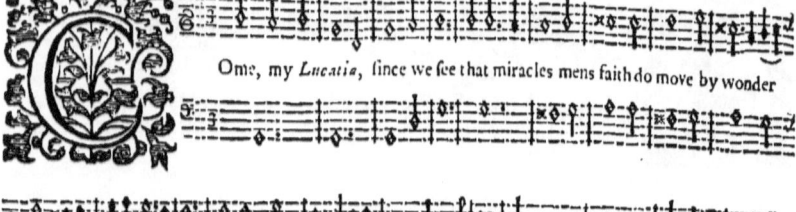

Ome, my *Lucatia*, since we see that miracles mens faith do move by wonder

and by prodi- gie: to the fierce an—gry world let's prove there's a Re-li-gi-on in our Love.

Mr. *Hen. Lawes.*

For though we were defign'd t'agree,
That Fate no liberty deftroys,
But our Election is as free
As Angels, who with greedy choice
Are yet determin'd to their joys.

We court our own captivity,
Then Thrones more great and innocent;
'Twere banifhment to be fet free,
When we wear fetters, whofe intent
Not bondage is, but ornament.

Our hearts are doubled by their lofs,
Here mixture is addition grown,
We both difufe, and both ingrofs,
And we whofe minds are fo much one,
Never, yet ever are alone.

Divided joys are tedious found,
And griefs united eafier grow,
We are our felves but by rebound;
And all our titles fhuffl'd fo,
Both Princes, and both Subjects too.

Loves Parting.

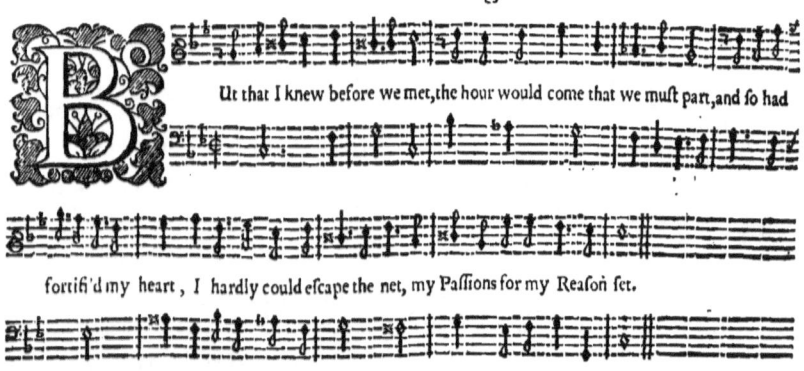

Ut that I knew before we met, the hour would come that we muft part, and fo had

fortifi'd my heart, I hardly could efcape the net, my Paffions for my Reafon fet.

But why fhould Reafon hope to win
A Victory that's fo unkind,
And fo unwelcom to my mind;
To yield is neither fhame nor fin,
Befieg'd without, betray'd within.

And though that night be ne're fo long,
In it they either fleep or wake:
And either way enjoyments take,
In Dreams or Vifions which belong
Thofe to the old: thefe to the young.

But Friends ne're part (to fpeak aright)
For who's but going is not gone;
Friends like the Sun muft ftill move on,
And when they feem moft out of fight,
There abfence makes at moft but night.

I'm old when going; gone 'tis night,
My Parting then fhall be a Dream,
And laft till the aufpicious Beam
Of our next meeting gives new light,
And the beft Vifion that's your fight.

The ROSE.

O lovely Rose, tell her that wasts her time and me, that now she knows when I resemble her to thee, how sweet and fair she seems to be. Tell her that's young, and shuns to have her graces spi'd, that hadst thou sprung in Desarts where no men abide, thou must have uncommended dy'd.

Mr. *Hen. Lawes*

Small is the worth
Of beauty from the light retir'd,
Bid her come forth,
Suffer her self to be desir'd,
And not blush to be admir'd.

Then die, that she
The common fate of all things rare
May read in thee,
How small a part of time they share,
That are so wondrous sweet and fair.

Active Love.

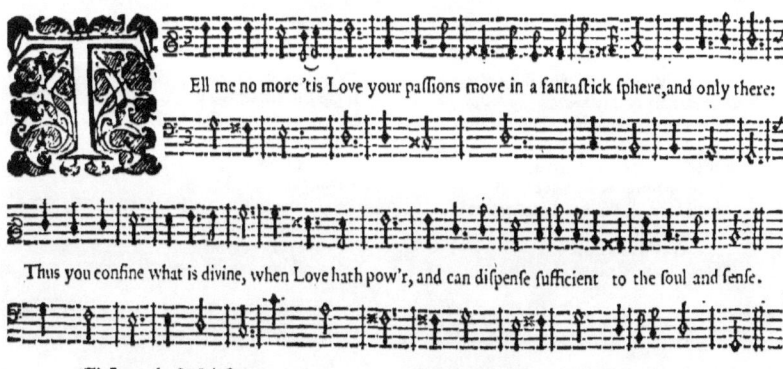

Ell me no more 'tis Love your passions move in a fantastick sphere, and only there: Thus you confine what is divine, when Love hath pow'r, and can dispense sufficient to the soul and sense.

'Tis Love the sense informs,
And cold bloud warms;
Nor gives the soul a Throne
To us alone,

But bids them bend
Both to one end;
And then 'tis Love when thus design'd
They make another of their kind.

M 2

Not to be altred from Affection.

An so much Beauty own a mind? oreswayd by tyranny, as new aflicting ways to find a doubtless faith to try, and all example to out-do, to scorn and make me jealous too: Alass! she knows my fires are too too great; and though she be stone ice to me, her thaw to others cannot quench my heat.

Mr. *Henry Lawes*.

That Law which with such force o're-ran
The Armies of my heart,
When no one thought I could out-man,
That durst once take my part.
For by assault she did invade,
No composition to be made:
Then, since all must yield as well as I
  to stand in aw
    of Victors Law'
There's no prescribing in captivity.

That Love which loves for common ends,
Is but self-loving love;
But nobler conversation tends
Soul mysteries to prove.
And since Love is a passive thing,
It multiplies by suffering.
Then, though she throw life to the waning Moon,
  on him her shine,
    the dark part mine,
Yet I must love her still when all is done.

Policy in Love.

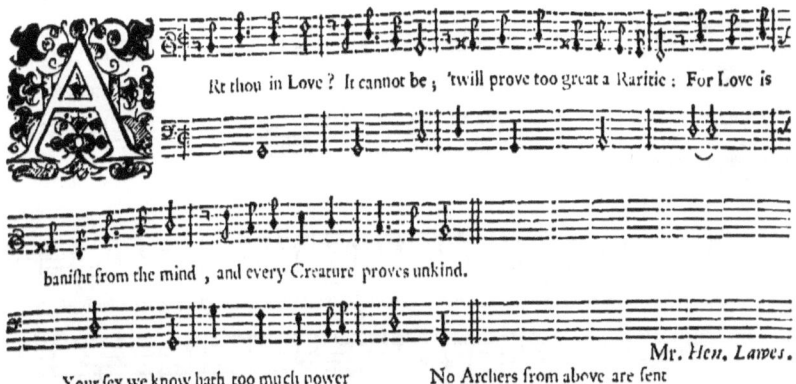

Art thou in Love? It cannot be; 'twill prove too great a Raritie: For Love is banisht from the mind, and every Creature proves unkind.

Mr. Hen. Lawes.

Your sex we know hath too much power
To be confin'd above an hour,
And Ladies are become so wife
They'l please their own, not others Eyes.

No Archers from above are sent
Poor Cupid's Bow lies now unbent,
And Women boast that they can find
A nearer way to please the mind.

    Yet still you sigh and keep adoe
    Only to tempt poor men to wooe:
    But sure if thou a Lover be
    'Tis of thy Self, but not of Me.

A Glee at CHRISTMAS.

Tis Christmas now, 'tis Christmas now, when Cato's self would laugh, and smoothing forth his wrinkled brow, gives li---ber-ty to Quaff, to Dance, to Sing, to Sport and Play; for ev'ry hour's a Holy-day.

Mr. Hen. Lawes.

And for the Twelve days, let them pass
In mirth and jollity:
The Time doth call each Lad and Lass
That will be blithe and merry
    Then Dance, and Sing, &c.

And from the Rising of the Sun
To th' Setting cast off Cares;
'Tis time enough when Twelve is done
To think of our Affairs.
    Then Dance, and Sing, &c.

[46]

The Power of Love.

Here shall a man an object find that may preserve a qui-et mind? Sad sorrow dwells in Loves fair Eyes, and Beauty stirs up Jealousies: A Lovers Hopes are mixt with Fears, and all his Joys, and all his Joys do end in Tears: Yet I must love, though't be my fate to be rewarded still with hate; for by experience now I feel Loves Darts are all Magnetick steel: For when I fly to ease my pain, an Arrow draws me back again.

Mr. *Henry Lawes.*

ORPHEUS *Hymn.*

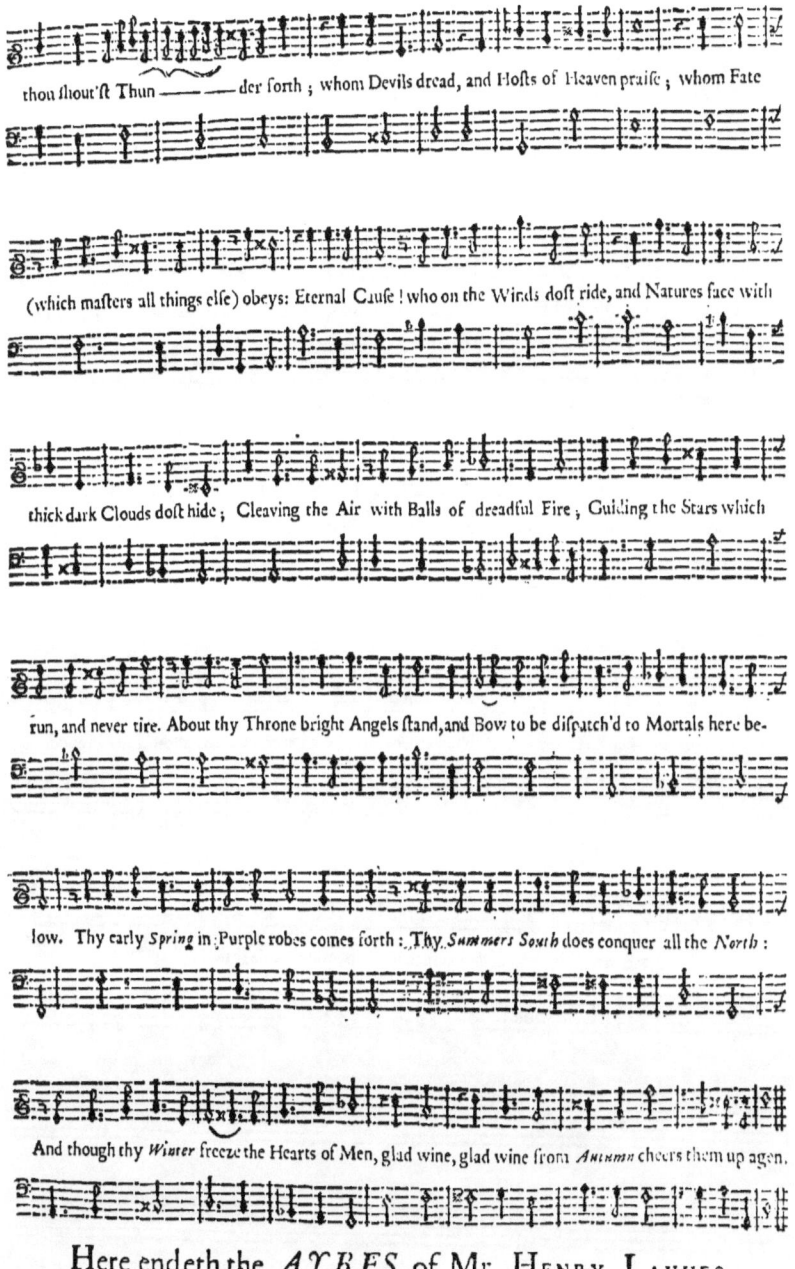

Here endeth the *AYRES* of Mr. HENRY LAWES.

[48]
A Blackmore Maid wooing a Fair Boy.

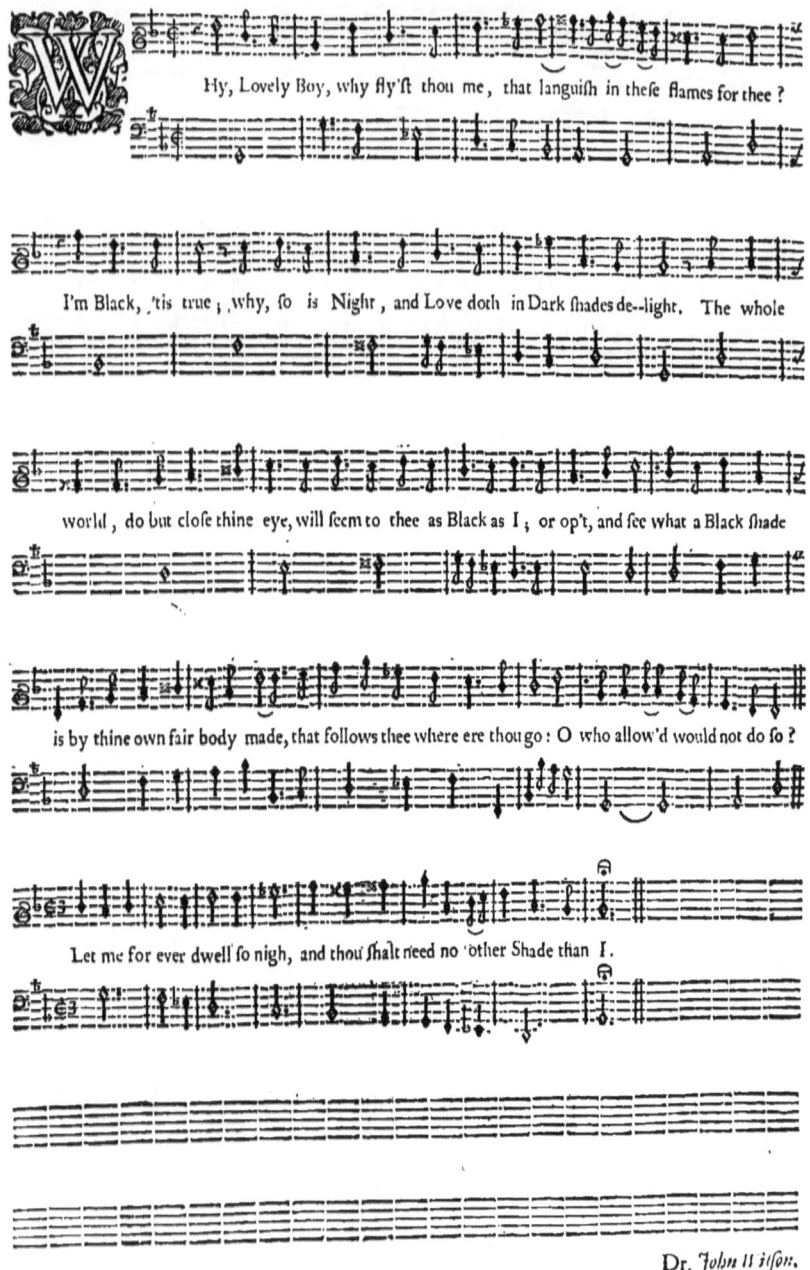

Hy, Lovely Boy, why fly'ſt thou me, that languiſh in theſe flames for thee?
I'm Black, 'tis true; why, ſo is Night, and Love doth in Dark ſhades de--light. The whole
world, do but cloſe thine eye, will ſeem to thee as Black as I; or op't, and ſee what a Black ſhade
is by thine own fair body made, that follows thee where ere thou go: O who allow'd would not do ſo?
Let me for ever dwell ſo nigh, and thou ſhalt need no other Shade than I.

Dr. John Wilſon.

The Boys Answer to the Blackmore Maid.

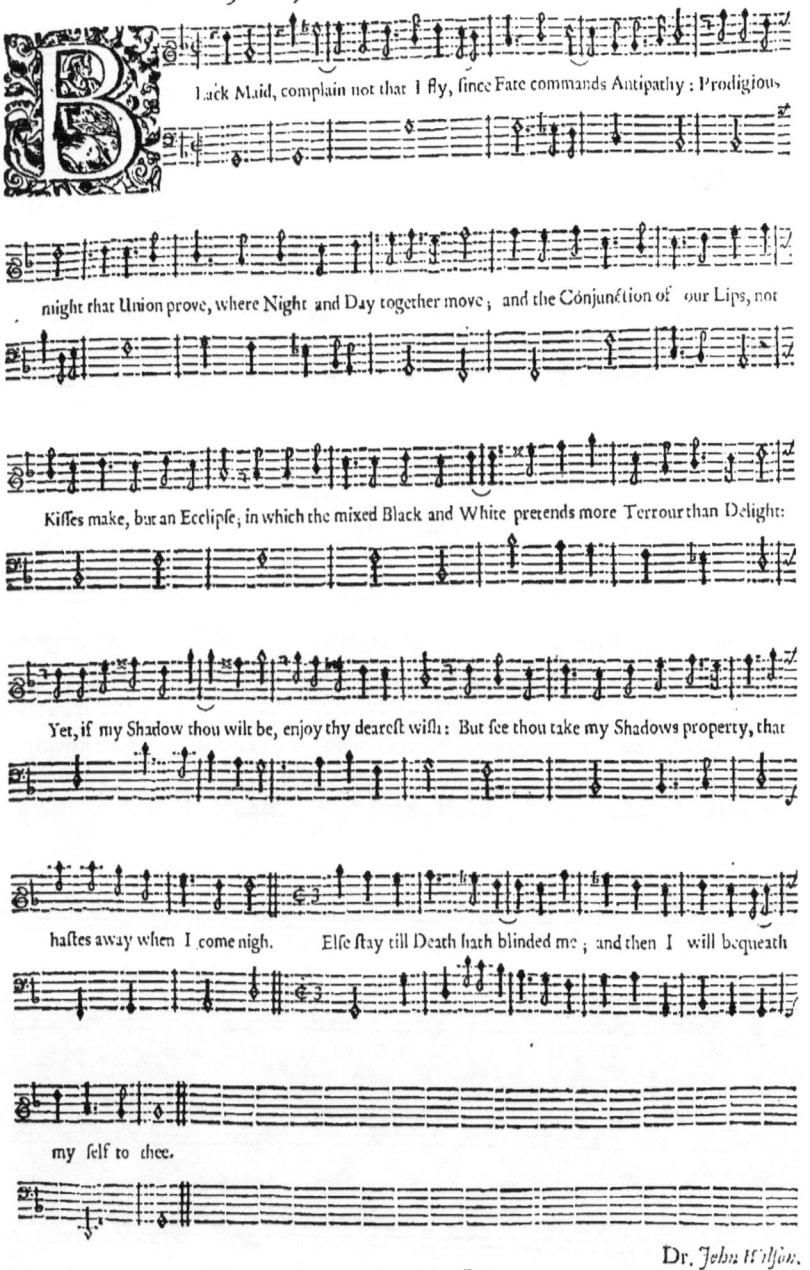

Black Maid, complain not that I fly, since Fate commands Antipathy: Prodigious night that Union prove, where Night and Day together move; and the Conjunction of our Lips, not Kisses make, but an Ecclipse; in which the mixed Black and White pretends more Terrour than Delight: Yet, if my Shadow thou wilt be, enjoy thy dearest wish: But see thou take my Shadows property, that hastes away when I come nigh.   Else stay till Death hath blinded me; and then I will bequeath my self to thee.

Dr. *John Wilson*.

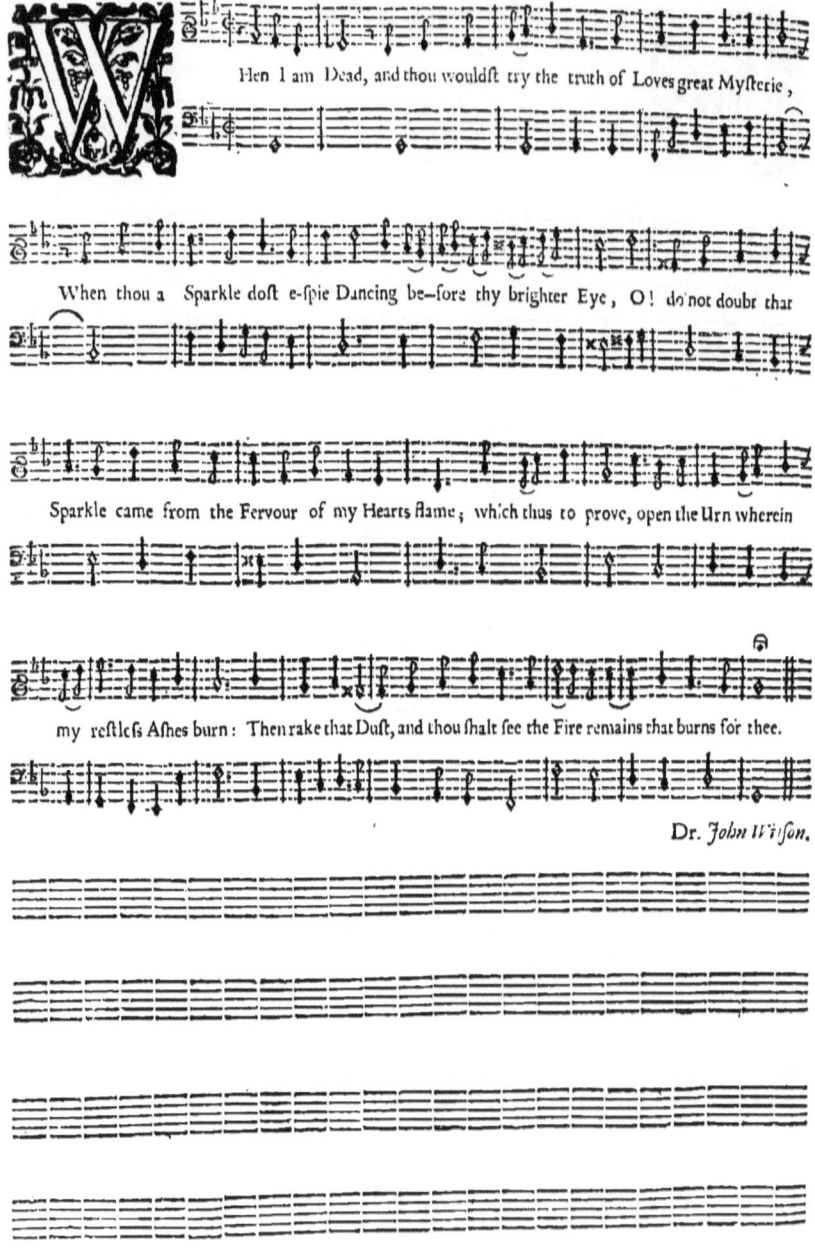

Cupid Scorned.

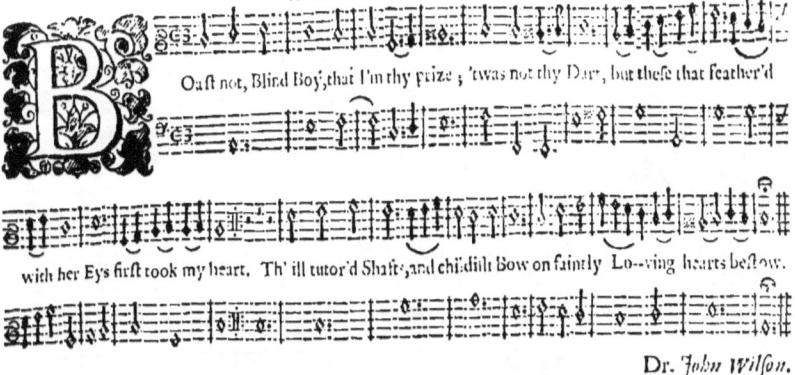

Boast not, Blind Boy, that I'm thy prize; 'twas not thy Dart, but these that feather'd with her Ey's first took my heart. Th' ill tutor'd Shafts, and childish Bow on faintly Lo--ving hearts bestow.

Dr. *John Wilson.*

I vaunt my Flames, and dare defie
Those Bug-bear Fires
Which only serve to satisfie
Fools fond Desires;
Hord up for such thy Painted flame
As tremble when they hear thy Name.

My Heart thy Fires nor Shafts could peirce,
But holy Flashes
Swifter than Lightnings, or more fierce,
Burnt mine to Ashes;
Where let them sleep in unknown rest,
Since Fate concludes thy Urn her Breast.

On a Proud Lady.

Still to be Neat, still to be Drest as you were going to a Feast: Still to be powder'd still perfum'd! Lady, it is to be presum'd, Though Arts hid Causes are not found, All is not sweet, All is not sweet, All is not found.

Give me a Look, give me a Face
That makes Simplicity a Grace;
Robes Loosly flowing, Hair as Free;
Such sweet neglects more taketh me
Then all th' Adult'ries of Art;
They strike my Eyes, but not my Heart.

To an Inconstant Lover.

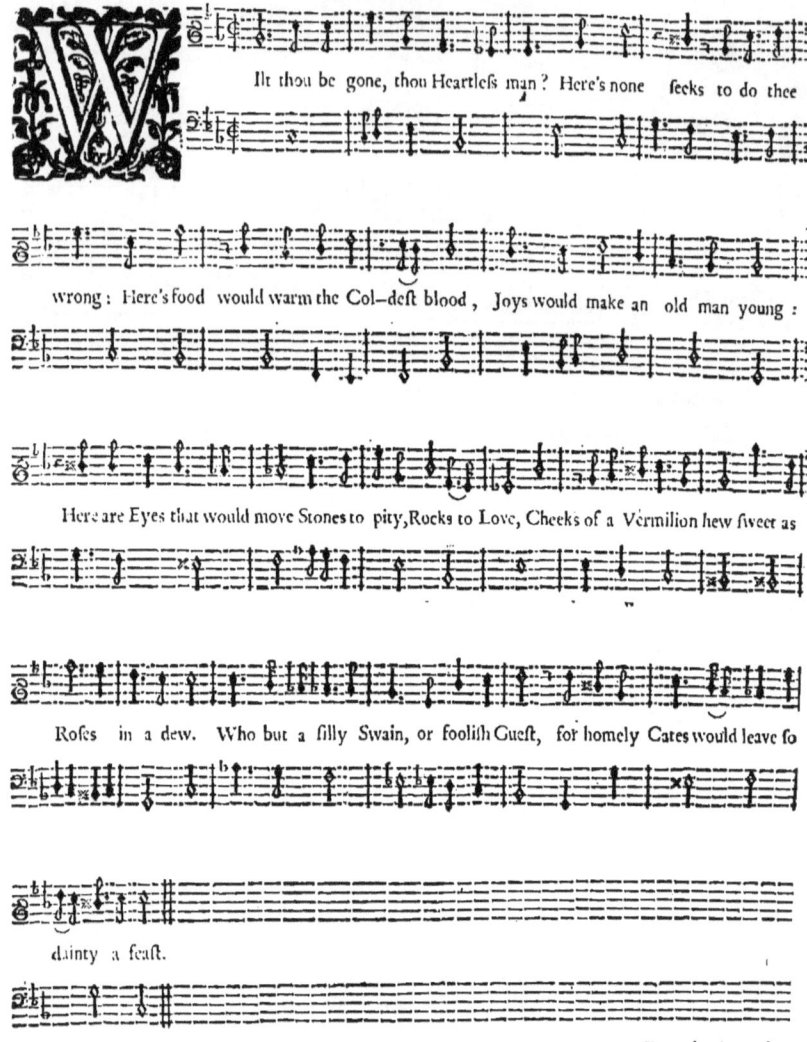

Wilt thou be gone, thou Heartless man? Here's none seeks to do thee wrong: Here's food would warm the Coldest blood, Joys would make an old man young: Here are Eyes that would move Stones to pity, Rocks to Love, Cheeks of a Vermilion hew sweet as Roses in a dew. Who but a silly Swain, or foolish Guest, for homely Cates would leave so dainty a feast.

Dr. *Charles Colm.*

Wilt thou begon, thou Frosty man,
Is not Beauty a fair prize;
Dost rate thy pelf with true Loves wealth:
Foolish man, where are thine Eyes?
Here are Lips both fresh and fair,
Red as Cherries in their prime,
Globe-like Breasts both smooth and white,
Full of pleasure and delight:
Who but Ass would leave such dainty store
To feed on Thistles, when better meat's before.

Go get thee gone, thou Senseless man,
And make Marts with such as thee
Who, both in Kind and Currish mind
Ev'ry way's as base as thee;
That hath Eyelids like some Witch,
Wrinkled Cheeks as black as pitch,
Lips as pale, and for her Breast,
Lank and loathsome as the rest:
May the disgrace her Sex, and thee so far
That thou mayst languish t' death with Loathing!

The MARIGOLD.

Ark how the Blushful morn in vain courts the Amorous *Marigold* with sighing Blush, and weeping Rain, yet she re-fu-ses to unfold. But when the Planet of the Day approacheth with his powerful Ray, then She spreads, then She receives his warmer beams in-to her Virgin Arms.

Mr. *Nich. Lanneare.*

2.
So may'st thou thrive in Love, fond Boy,
If silent tears and sighs discover
Thy grief, thou never shalt enjoy
The just reward of a bold Lover.

3.
But when with moving accent thou
Shalt constant Faith and Service vow,
Thy *Celia* shall receive those charms
With open Ear, and with unfolded Arms.

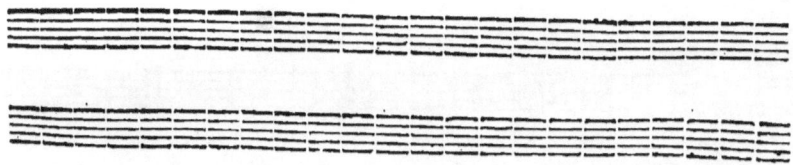

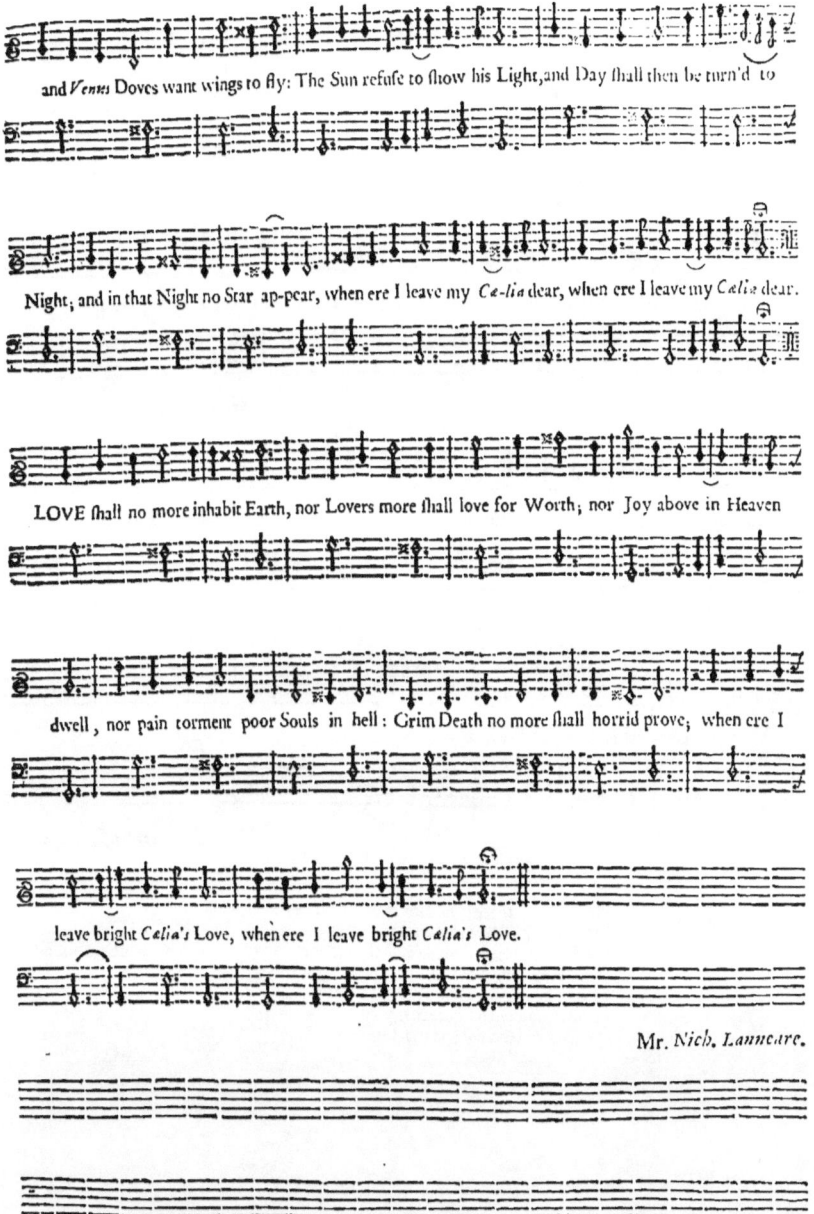

Love Enflamed.

Fire, Fire; Lo here I burn in such desire, that all the tears that I can strain out of my Love-sick empty brain, cannot allay my scorching pain. Come *Humber*, *Trent*, and silver *Thames*: Dread Ocean haste with all thy Streams, and if thou canst not quench my Fire, O drown both me and my Desire.

Mr. *Nich. Lanneare.*

2.
Fire, Fire, there is no Hell to my desire;
See all the Rivers backward fly,
For fear my Heart should drink them dry;
Come Heavenly showers, come pouring down;
Come you that once the World did Drown;
 And if you cannot quench my Fire,
 O Drown both me and my Desire.

Unwilling Parting.

O no, I tell thee no; though from thee I must go, yet my Heart says not so:

It swears by *Stella's* eys, in whose daz'ling surprize it in Loves fetters lies: It swears by those Roses and

Lillies so white, and those Rubies so bright, ne'r to part, ne'r to part from my dear dear Delight.

Mr. *Nich. Lanneare.*

The Dying Lover.

Stay, Silly Heart, and do not break, but give a Lover leave to speak, to tell a

Tale that Stones may move to pity me that dies for Love.

Mr. *Nich. Lanneare.*

2. Thy Heart is harder far than flint,
And will not suffer *Cupid's* print;
But beats his Arrows back to *Jove*,
By which, alas! I die for Love.

4. Then bear me softly by her dore,
And there with Mourning Heads deplore,
Cry loud, look down you Pow'rs above,
On her that slew me for her Love.

3. When I am gone, true Lovers mourn,
Deck all your heads with Wither'd Corn;
Wear on your Hand a Sable Glove,
To testifie I dy'd for Love.

5. Then in an unfrequented Cave
Where Fairies haunt, prepare my Grave
Among wilde Satyrs in a Grove,
That they may sing, I dy'd for Love.

6. Last, build my Tombe of Lovers bones,
Set round about with Marble-stones;
My Scutch'on bearing *Venus Dove*;
My Epitaph, *I dy'd for Love.*

Q

[58]
The LILLY.

Hite though you be, yet Lil-lies know from the firſt ye were not ſo: But Ile tell ye what be-fell ye; *Cupid* and his Mother lay in a Cloud while both did play: He with his prety finger preſt the Ruby Nipple of her Breaſt; out of the which the Cream of Light like to a dew fell down on you, and made you White.

Mr. *Nich. Lanneare.*

Wounded in Love.

Or that one glance I wounded lie, O look again, and let me die: Kill me out-right; I cannot brook to live like one that's Planet ſtrook. Bleſs me again with thoſe bright rays that ſhorten, yet make ſweet my days.

Mr. *John Goodgroome.*

O ſhoot more Glances with thine Eyes
To ſhew th' accept'ſt the Sacrifice
Of my poor Heart, which now doth burn
Whileſt I both Prieſt and Offering turn.
Ile blame no more thoſe Eyes that prove
My ruin, ſince they caus'd my Love.

Loves Affection.

BE not proud, Pretty one, for I muſt love thee; Thou art Fair, but Unkind, yet doſt thou move me. Red is thy Lips, and Cheeks like to thy Bluſhes: The Flame that's in thine Eye burns mine to Aſhes. And on thy Breaſt, the place of Loves abiding, ſits *Cupid* high enthron'd my pain de—ri-ding. O! if a god thou art, wound Her that ſcorns me, or fall from that bright Sphere which ſo adorns thee.

Mr. *Simon Ives.*

Then might my Sighs and Tears move her Compaſſion;
And on her Heart of Flint make ſome Impreſſion;
Knowing her Beauty hath ſo far inſnar'd me,
And all the Joys of Peace hath quite debarr'd me.

O Gentle Nymph! thy Frown now would deſtroy me,
Having liv'd but in hope Once to injoy Thee:
And ſure my Death would add nought to thy Glory;
But rather all your Fame die in the Story.

Cupid's Doomsday.

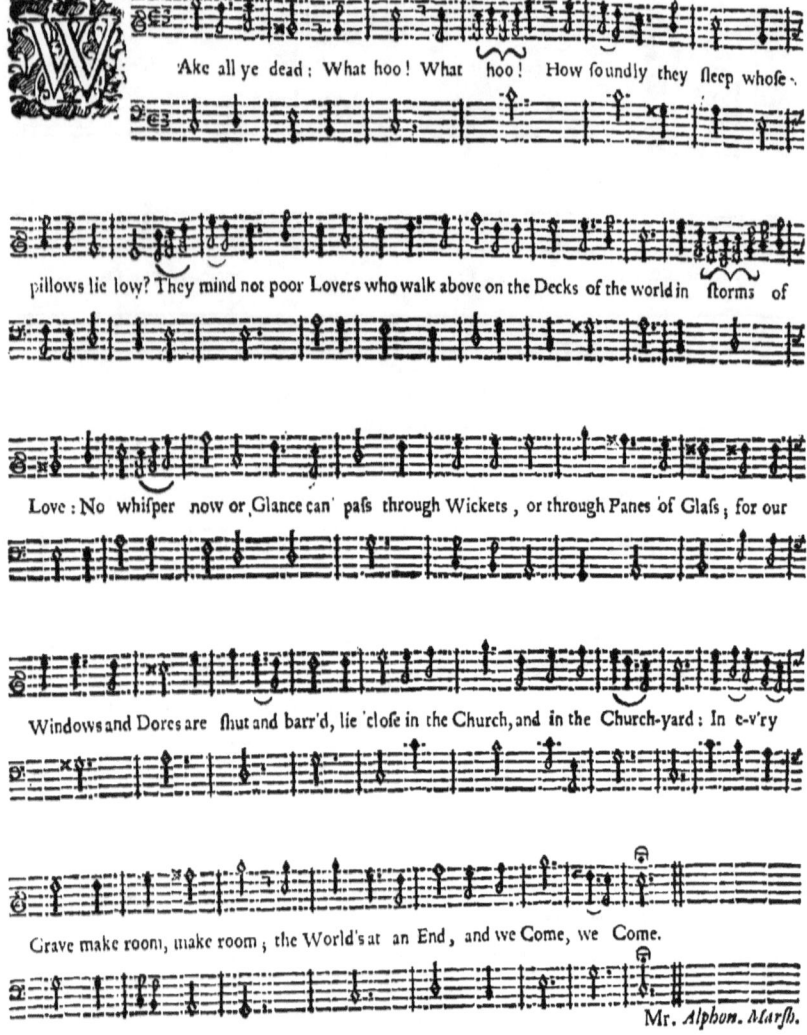

Wake all ye dead: What hoo! What hoo! How soundly they sleep whose pillows lie low? They mind not poor Lovers who walk above on the Decks of the world in storms of Love: No whisper now or Glance can pass through Wickets, or through Panes of Glass; for our Windows and Dores are shut and barr'd, lie close in the Church, and in the Church-yard: In ev'ry Grave make room, make room; the World's at an End, and we Come, we Come.

Mr. *Alphon. Marsh.*

The State is now Loves Foe, Loves Foe;
T'has seiz'd on his Arms, his Quiver and Bow;
T'has pinion'd his Wings, and fetter'd his Feet,
Because he made way for poor Lovers to meet:
  But oh sad chance! his Judge was old;
  Hearts cruel grow, when blood grows cold:
No Man being young, his Process would draw;
Oh Heav'ns! that Love should be subject to Law;
  Lovers go Wooe the Dead, the Dead!
  Lye two in a Grave, and to Bed, to Bed.

Madness in Love.

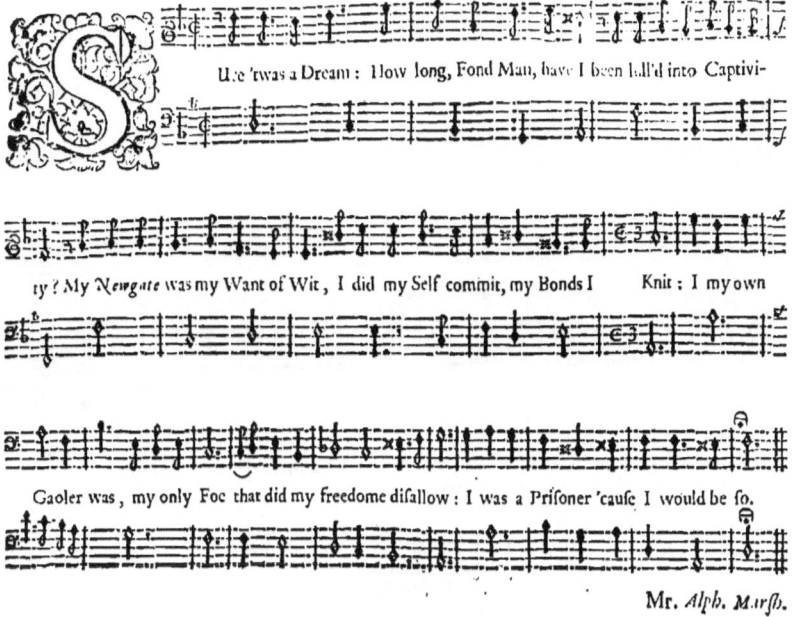

Sure 'twas a Dream: How long, Fond Man, have I been lull'd into Captivity? My Newgate was my Want of Wit, I did my Self commit, my Bonds I Knit: I my own Gaoler was, my only Foe that did my freedome disallow: I was a Prisoner 'cause I would be so.

Mr. *Alph. Marsh.*

II.

'Twas a fine life I liv'd when I did dress
My self to Court your peevishness;
When I did at your foot-stool lye,
Expecting from your eye to live or dye.

Now frowns or smiles, I care not which I have;
Nay, rather than I'le be your slave,
I'le Court the Plague to send me to my grave.

III.

And now I will shake off my chains, and prove
Opinion built the Gaol of Love;
Made all his Bonds, gave him his Bow,
His bloody Arrows too which murder so.

May all the Oaths which idle Lovers dream,
Be all contriv'd to make a Theam
For some carousing Poets drunken Flame.

LOVE and HONOUR.

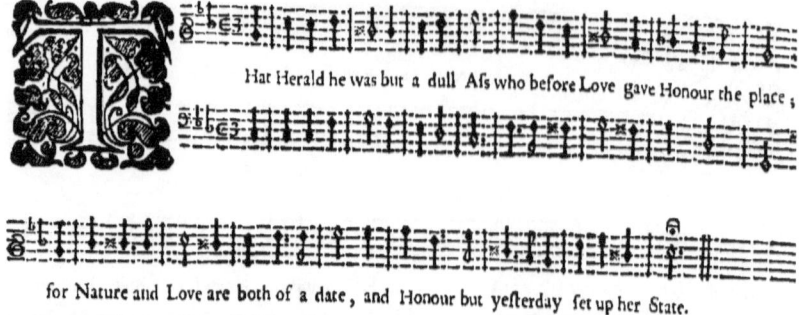

That Herald he was but a dull Aſs who before Love gave Honour the place;
for Nature and Love are both of a date, and Honour but yeſterday ſet up her State.

Mr. *Alph. Marſh.*

Honour we grant's the Daughter of Love,
And this doth them their Precedeſs prove;
For Honour's but Heat, 'tis Love is the Fire;
This may Preſerve, but that Kindles Deſire.

If you take away Love, then Dame Honour muſt
Come down a degree, and lie in the Duſt:
'Tis a Green-ſickneſs fancy to famiſh Love,
And feed upon Honour, which fatal may prove.

    Then you may leave off, for 'tis Labour in vain
    By Reaſon to Cure a True Lovers pain:
    Then farewell dull Mortall, ſince it is moſt true
    That with Honour and Love thou haſt nothing to doe.

CUPID's *Monarchy.*

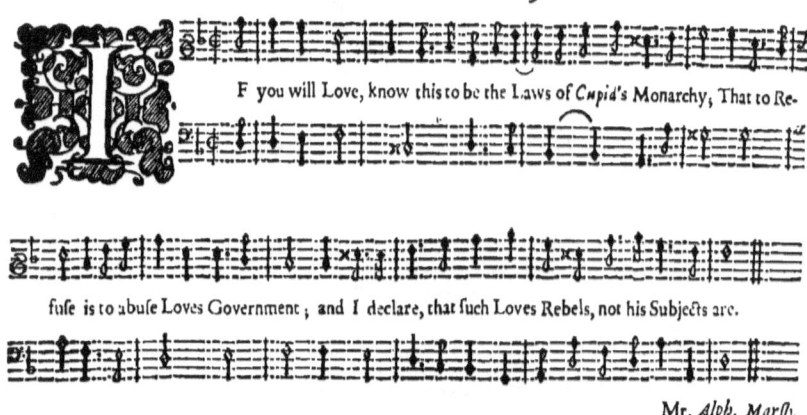

IF you will Love, know this to be the Laws of *Cupid's* Monarchy, That to Refuſe is to abuſe Loves Government; and I declare, that ſuch Loves Rebels, not his Subjects are.

Mr. *Alph. Marſh.*

  To Love is not to be your Owne,
  Love ſtudies to pleaſe them alone
    Whom it affects
    With moſt reſpects
  Of ought beſide; for Love confin'd
  Is but by Uſurpation Love defin'd.

  If you did Love as true as I,
  You nothing would or cold deny,
    But would conceive
    That you receive
  What you beſtow: If this were true,
  Your Heart would dwell in me as I in you.

The Vicissitude of Love.

AH! *Cloris*, would the Gods allow we still might Love as we Love now, what Joys had all the world in store, or Heav'n it self to give us more; for nothing sure so sweet can prove as pleasures of beginning Love.

Mr. *Alphon. Marsh.*

II.
But Love when to its height arriv'd
Of all our Joys is shortest liv'd;
His Morning past, he Sets so soon
That none can find an Afternoon:
And of that little time is lent
Half in Unkindness is misspent.

III.
Since Fate to Love such short Life gives
And Love so tender whilest he lives,
Let us remove Mean fears away,
So to prevent his first decay:
For Love, like blood, let out before,
Will lose his pow'r, and Cure no more.

Loves Hue and Cry.

OFt have I searcht both Court and Town, and Country Village too, the Black, the Fair, the lovely Brown, Bold, Coy and Simple too; yet amongst all I ne'r could find one that's more Constant than the Wind.

Mr. *Alph. Marsh.*

If nobly born, She scorns to be Confined in her Love;
If Riches make her melt, we see varietie she'l prove:
And She whom Want betrays, no less
Counts Change her only happiness.
Since all will try, Ile now no more court dangerous Constancy;
But Ile change Objects, and adore this sweet Variety:
For, taught by their Example, I
Love nothing now but Liberty.

Cupid's Progress.

UP Ladies, Up; prepare your Taking faces; for *Cupid* rides a Hunting to day in Secret places, his Bow is ready bent, to shew you his Intent; his Quiver full of Darts, to wound the chiefest Hearts: Then follow follow me all you that Gamesome be.

Mr. *Alphon. Marsh.*

See where he comes with all his Am'rous Train!
Mark how the Ladies do trip it or'e the Plain!
His Gallants and his 'Squires, all clad in warm desires;
And those that did retire, Come on with fresh desire:
Then follow follow me, all you that Gamesome be.

Endymion's Dream.

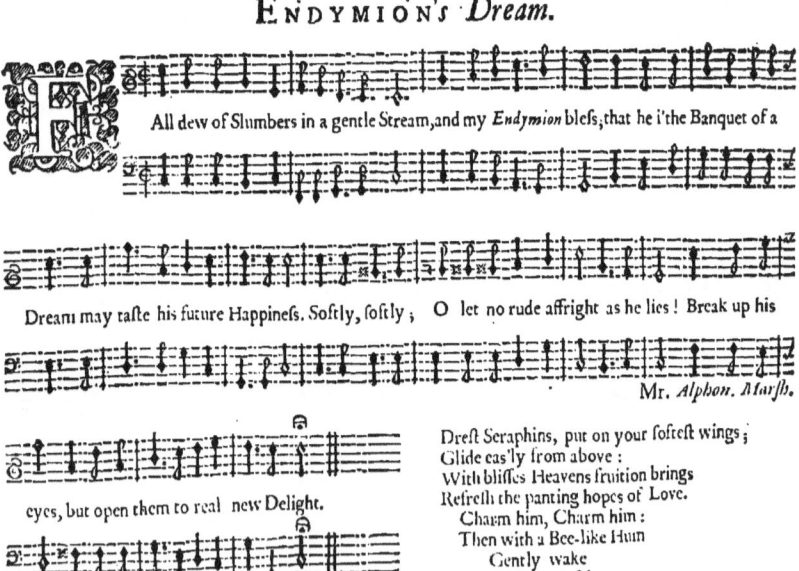

All dew of Slumbers in a gentle Stream, and my *Endymion* bless, that he i'the Banquet of a Dream may taste his future Happiness. Softly, softly; O let no rude affright as he lies! Break up his eyes, but open them to real new Delight.

Mr. *Alphon. Marsh.*

Drest Seraphins, put on your softest wings;
Glide eas'ly from above:
With blisses Heavens fruition brings
Refresh the panting hopes of Love.
 Charm him, Charm him:
 Then with a Bee-like Hum
 Gently wake
 For *Hero*'s sake
Leander from *Elizium.*

LOVE admits no Rivall.

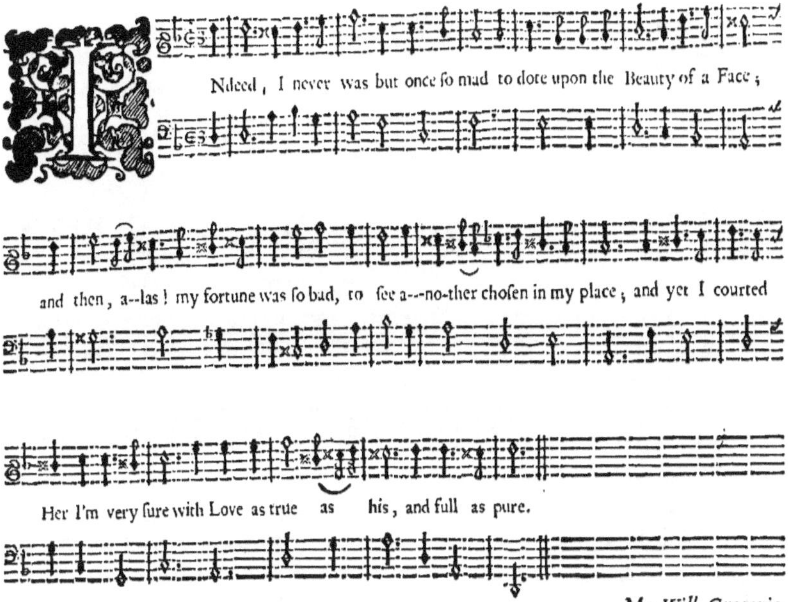

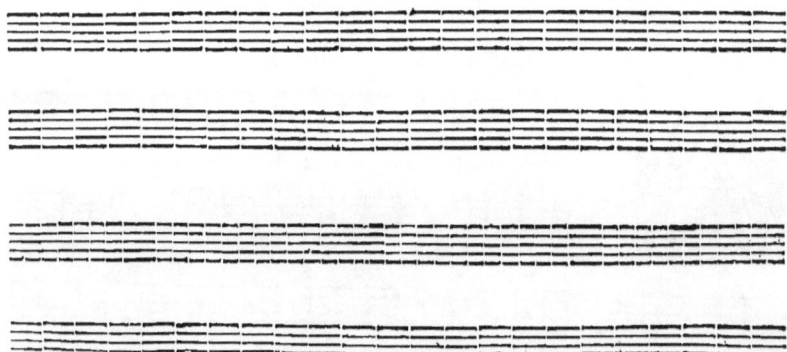

INdeed, I never was but once so mad to dote upon the Beauty of a Face; and then, a--las! my fortune was so bad, to see a---no-ther chosen in my place; and yet I courted Her I'm very sure with Love as true as his, and full as pure.

Mr. Will. Gregorie.

II.

But if I ever be so fond again
To undertake the second part of Love;
Or reassume that most unhappy pain,
Or after Shipwrack do the Ocean prove:
She shall be tender-hearted, kind and free;
Or I'le be as Indifferent as She.

Transparent Love.

Mr. *Roger Hill*.

1. Know then, though you were twice as fair,
   If it could be, as now you are;
   Or if the Graces of the Mind
   With a supportant Beauty shin'd;
   Yet if you love me not, you'l see
   I value those as you do me.

2. Though I a thousand times have sworn,
   My Passion should transcend your Scorn;
   Or that your bright triumphant Eyes
   Creates a flame that never dyes;
   Yet if to me you prove untrue,
   Those Oaths should prove as false to you.

3. Though I should Love, and you should Hate,
   'Twas (I confess) a meer Deceit;
   And that my Flames should Deathless prove,
   'Twas but to render so your Love.
   I brag as, Cowards use to do,
   Of Danger, they ne'r run into.

4. But now my Tenets I have told,
   If you should them too rigid hold;
   T' attempt the Change would be but vain,
   The Conquest not being worth the pain:
   With those I'le other Nymphs persue,
   Cloris too much to lose Time and You.

Love without Flattery.

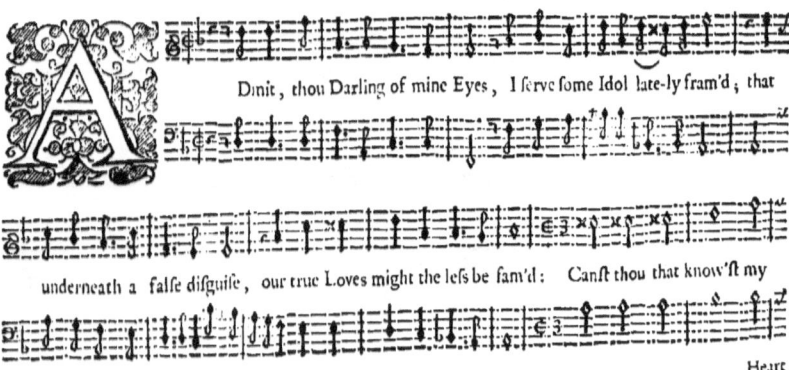

Heart

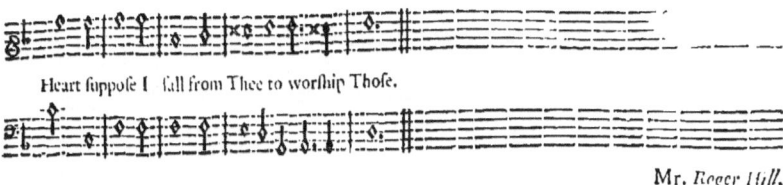

Heart suppose I fall from Thee to worship Those.

Mr. *Roger Hill.*

Remember Dear how loth and slow
I was to cast a Look or Smile;
Or on Love, Lines to misbestow,
Till thou hadst chang'd both Face and Stile:
And art thou now affraid to see
That Mask put on thou mad'st for mee.

I cannot call these Childish fears
That come from Love, much less from Thee;
But wash away with frequent Tears
That Counterfeit Apostacie:
And henceforth kneel to ne'r a Shrine,
To blind the World, but only Thine.

The Crafty Lover.

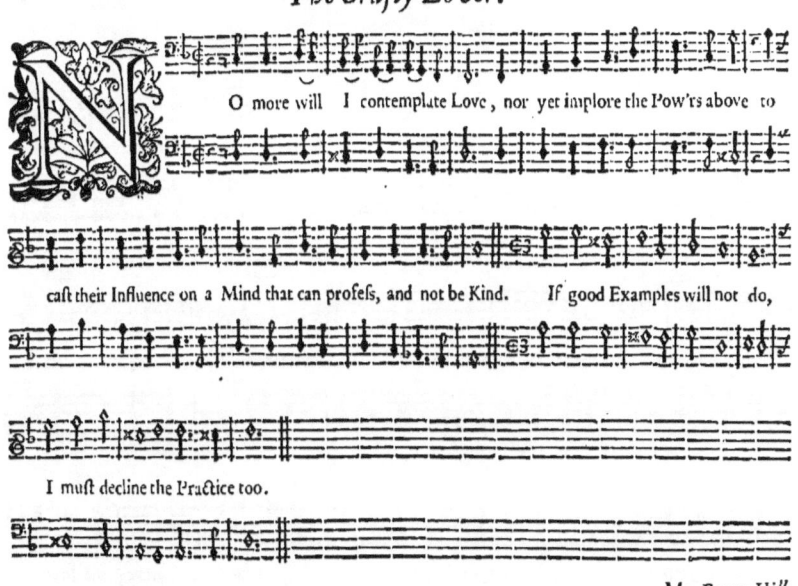

NO more will I contemplate Love, nor yet implore the Pow'rs above to cast their Influence on a Mind that can profess, and not be Kind. If good Examples will not do, I must decline the Practice too.

Mr. *Roger Hill.*

My Mistress I'le no more admire,
Her Beauty or her Love desire;
Though in proportion both agree,
When neither doth reflect on me:
I may without a guilty thought
Esteem those faculties from nought.

Let those who love to spend their days
In speaking Women, or their praise;
Apply their Virtue to their use,
As if 'twere real such abuse:
I can but scorn, 'twill never take;
I honour Virtue for its sake.

I will no longer sacrifice
To such unsacred Miseries,
Nor yet contribute to a pow'r
Exacts Obedience ev'ry hour:
No no, my thoughts are too too free
To fancy Her that Loves not me.

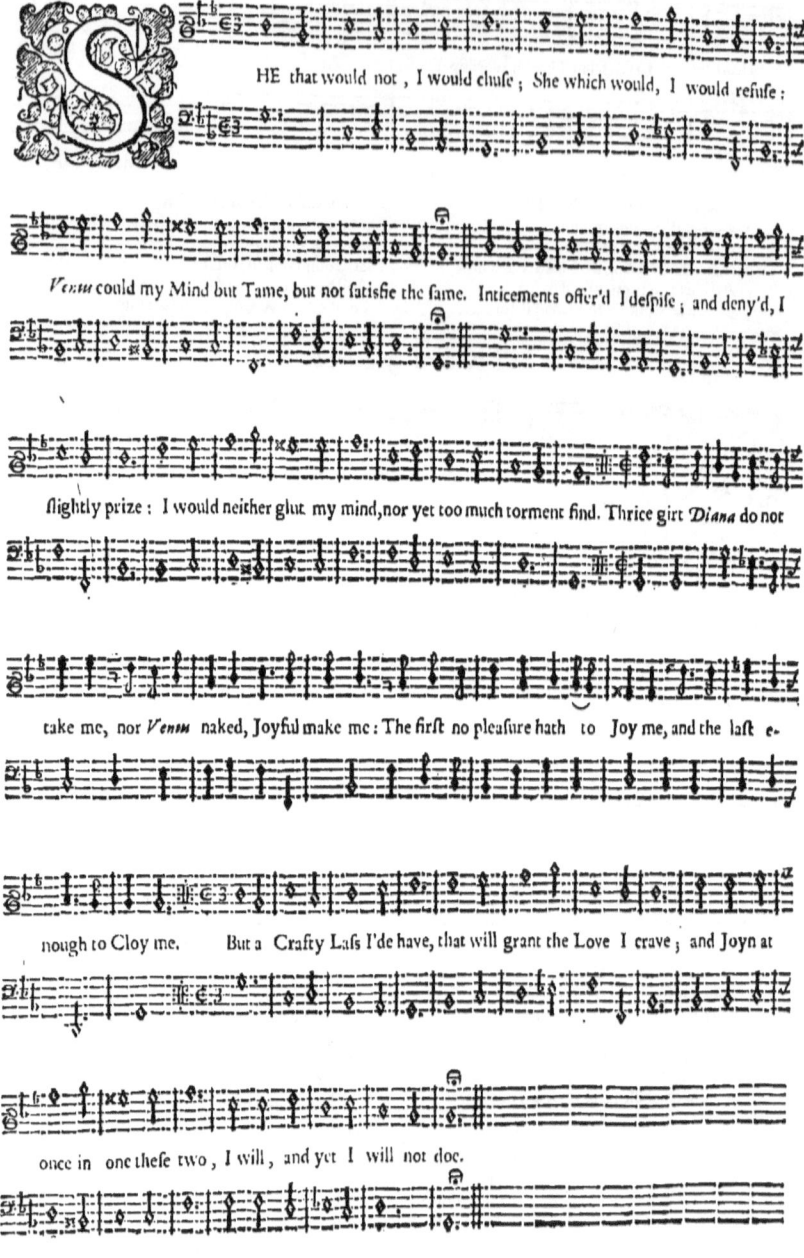

CASSANDRA in Mourning.

Wake my Lute; arise my String, and to my sad *Cassandra* sing; like the old Poets, when the Moon had put her Sa--ble Mourning on, aloud they sounded with a merry strain, until her brightness was re--stor'd again.

Mr. *John* Moss.

II.
Too well I know from whence proceeds
Thy wearing of these Mourning weeds;
In cruel flames for thee I burn,
And thou for me do'st therefore mourn.
So fits a glorious Godess in the Skies;
Clouded i'th' Smoak of her own Sacrifice.

III.
Wear other Virgins what they will!
Cassandra loves her Mourning still:
Thus the milky way so white
Is never seen but in the Night;
The Sun himself, although so bright he seem,
Is black as are the *Moors* that worship him.

IV.
But tell me, thou deformed Cloud,
How dar'st thou such a Body shroud?
So Satyres with black hideous Face
Of old did lovely Nimphs embrace:
That Mourning e're should hide such glorious Maids
Thus Deities of old did live in shades.

V.
Her Words are Oracles, and come
(Like those) from out some dark'ned room:
And her Breath proves that Spices do
Only in Scorched Countries grow:
If she but speak, an *Indian* she appears;
Though all o're black, at Lips She Jewels wears.

VI.
Methinks I now do *Venus* spy
As she in *Vulcan*'s arms did lye;
Such is *Cassandra* and her Shroud:
She looks like Snow within a Cloud:
Melt then, and yield! throw off thy mourning Pall!
Thou never can'st look white, until thou Fall.

The Desparing Lover.

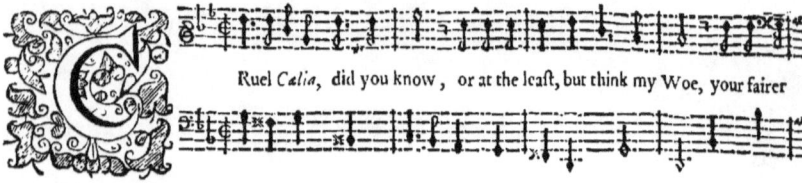

Cruel *Cælia*, did you know, or at the least, but think my Woe, your fairer

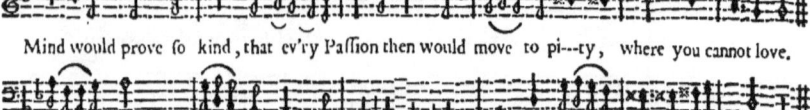

Mind would prove so kind, that ev'ry Passion then would move to pi---ty, where you cannot love.

Mr. *John Mosse.*

II.
Could a Sigh, a Tear, a Grone,
Things pale Passion feeds upon;
 A Midnight Grove,
 Place fit for Love:
Could these but enter in your thought,
You'd then confess Love dearly sought.

III.
Cruel Fairest, there you sit
As unconcern'd, as if my Wit
 To Mirth did move,
 Not to plead Love:
You'r like the Deer, which list'ning stand
To hear me Play, but slight the Hand.

IV.
Fairest, like them, you admire
The Musick, but neglect the Fire,
 The Air that beats
 And gives me heat:
To tell you, Cruel Beauty, you
Have out-done Him that worships You.

CLORIS Yielding.

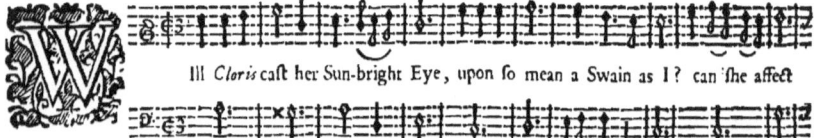

Ill *Cloris* cast her Sun-bright Eye, upon so mean a Swain as I? can she affect

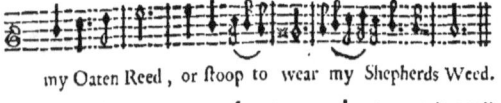

my Oaten Reed, or stoop to wear my Shepherds Weed.

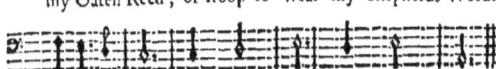

What Rural Sport can I devise
To please her Ears, to please her Eyes;
Fair *Cloris* sees, fair *Cloris* hears,
With Angels Eyes, and Angels Ears.

Mr *John Goodgroome.*

On a Crowned Heart.

Thou sent'st to me a Heart was Crown'd, I thought it had been Thine; but when I saw it had a Wound, I knew that Heart was mine. A Bounty of a strange conceit, to send mine Own to me; and send it in a worse estate than it was sent to Thee. The Heart I sent, it had no stain, but was entirely sound; yet thou hast sent it back again sick of a deadly wound. O Heav'ns! How wouldst thou use a Heart that should Rebellious be, as thus to slay Him with a Dart that ever honour'd Thee.

John Playford.

[72]

Loves Enquiry.

Yes, I could Love, could I but find a Mistress fitting to my mind; who neither Pride nor Gold could move to buy her Beauty, sell her Love: Were Neat, yet car'd not to be Fine; and love me for my self, not mine: Not Lady proud, nor City coy; but full of freedom, full of joy.

J. Playford.

2. Not wise enough to rule a State,
Nor so much Fool to be laugh'd at;
Nor Childish young, nor Beldam old,
Not Fiery hot, nor Icy cold;

Not richly Proud, nor basely Poor;
Not Chast, yet no reputed Whore.
If such a one I chance to find
I have a Mistress to my mind.

The Prudent Lover.

Not that I wish my Mistress or more, or less than what She is, write I these Lines, for 'tis too late, Rules to prescribe unto my Fate.

2. But as the tender Stomachs call
For choice of Meats, yet brook not all;
So queasie Love may here impart
What Mistress 'tis best takes the Heart.

4. Yet this alone will never win,
Unless some Treasure be within;
For where the Spoil's not worth the Prey,
Men raise the Siege and March away.

6. Then would I have her full of wit,
So she knows how to huswife it;
For she whose insolence will dare
To cry her Wit, will shew her ware.

3. First, I would have her richly spread
With Natures Blossom, White and Red;
For flaming heat will quickly dye,
Where is no Jewel for the Eye.

5. I care not much if she be proud,
A little pride may be allow'd;
The amorous Youth will pray and prate
Too freely, where he finds no state.

7. Last, I would have her Loving be,
(Mistake me not) to none but me;
She that loves one, and loves one more,
She'le love a Kingdom o're and o're.

The Humorous Lover.

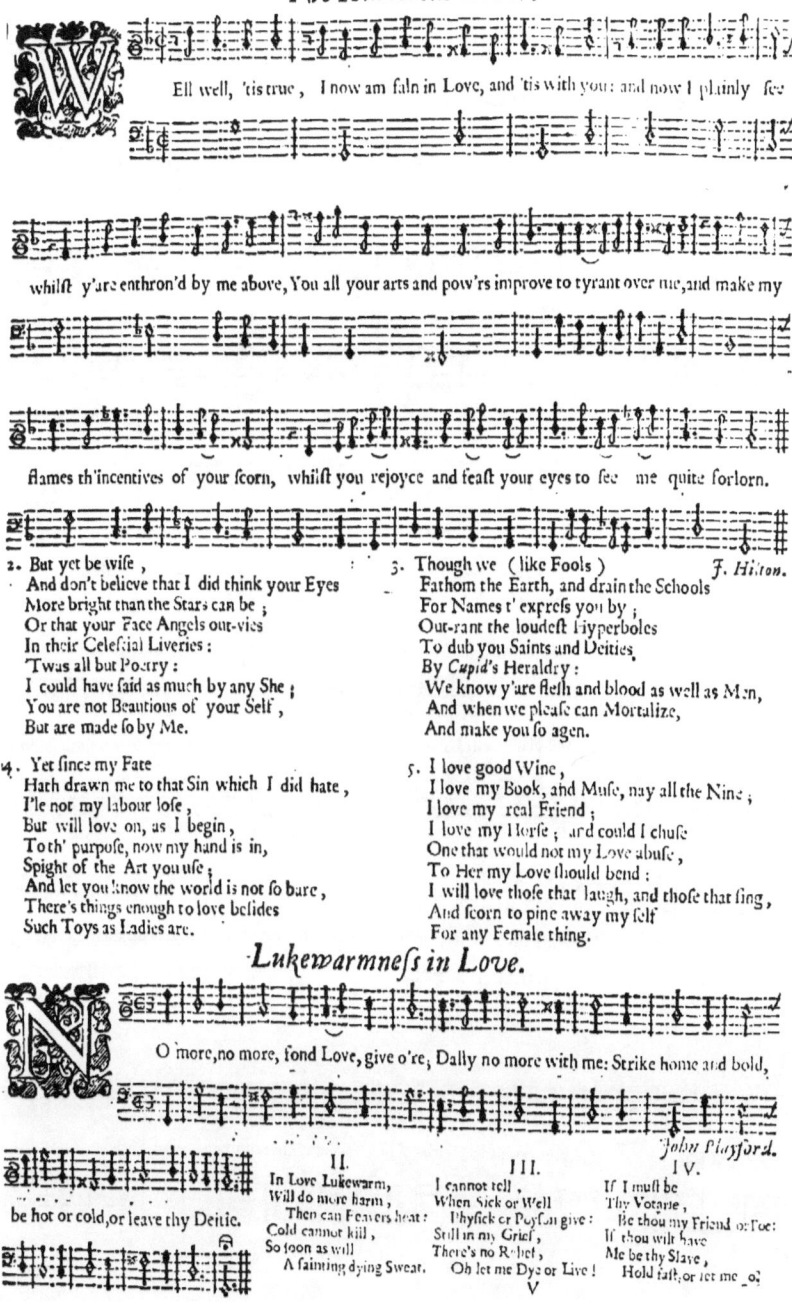

Well well, 'tis true, I now am faln in Love, and 'tis with you: and now I plainly see whilst y'are enthron'd by me above, You all your arts and pow'rs improve to tyrant over me, and make my flames th'incentives of your scorn, whilst you rejoyce and feast your eyes to see me quite forlorn.

J. Hilton.

2. But yet be wife,
And don't believe that I did think your Eyes
More bright than the Stars can be;
Or that your Face Angels out-vies
In their Celestial Liveries:
'Twas all but Poetry:
I could have said as much by any She;
You are not Beautious of your Self,
But are made so by Me.

3. Though we (like Fools)
Fathom the Earth, and drain the Schools
For Names t' express you by;
Out-rant the loudest Hyperboles
To dub you Saints and Deities
By Cupid's Heraldry:
We know y'are flesh and blood as well as Men,
And when we please can Mortalize,
And make you so agen.

4. Yet since my Fate
Hath drawn me to that Sin which I did hate,
I'le not my labour lose,
But will love on, as I begin,
To th' purpose, now my hand is in,
Spight of the Art you use;
And let you know the world is not so bare,
There's things enough to love besides
Such Toys as Ladies are.

5. I love good Wine,
I love my Book, and Muse, nay all the Nine;
I love my real Friend;
I love my Horse; and could I chuse
One that would not my Love abuse,
To Her my Love should bend:
I will love those that laugh, and those that sing,
And scorn to pine away my self
For any Female thing.

Lukewarmness in Love.

No more, no more, fond Love, give o're, Dally no more with me: Strike home and bold, be hot or cold, or leave thy Deitie.

John Playford.

II.
In Love Lukewarm,
Will do more harm,
Then can Feavers heat:
Cold cannot kill,
So soon as will
A fainting dying Sweat.

III.
I cannot tell,
When Sick or Well
Physick or Poyson give:
Still in my Grief,
There's no Relief,
Oh let me Dye or Live!

IV.
If I must be
Thy Votarie,
Be thou my Friend or Foe:
If thou wilt have
Me be thy Slave,
Hold fast, or let me go.

The Triumphs of Death.

THE Glories of our Birth and State Are shadows, not substantial things; There is no Armor 'gainst our fate, DEATH layes his Icy-hand on Kings: Scepters and Crowns must tumble down, And in the Dust be equall layd With the poor crooked Syth & Spade. Some men with Swords may reap the Field, And plant fresh Lawrels where they kill'd; But their strong Nerves at last must yield, They tame but one another still. Early or late they bend to fate, And must give up their murm'ring breath While the pale Captive creeps to Death. The Garland withers on your brow, Then boast no more

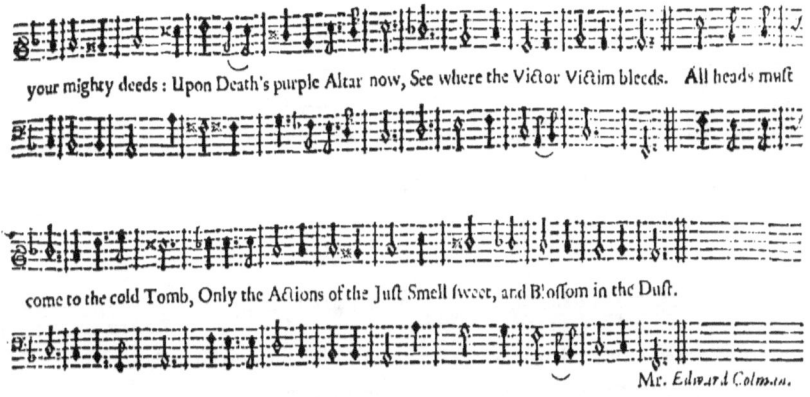

your mighty deeds: Upon Death's purple Altar now, See where the Victor Victim bleeds. All heads must come to the cold Tomb, Only the Actions of the Just Smell sweet, and Blossom in the Dust.

Mr. *Edward Colman.*

Venus *Hue and Cry after* Cupid.

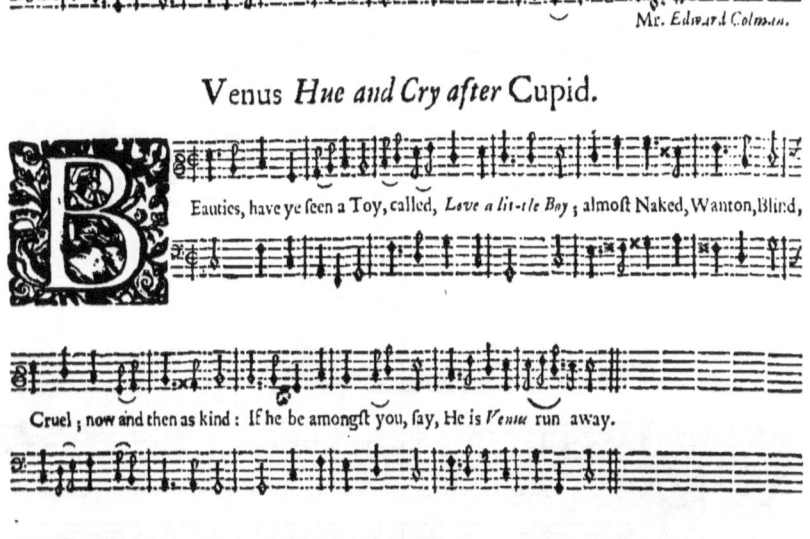

Beauties, have ye seen a Toy, called, *Love a lit-tle Boy*; almost Naked, Wanton, Blind, Cruel; now and then as kind: If he be amongst you, say, He is *Venus* run away.

(2) She that will now but now discover
Where this Winged-wag doth hover,
Shall to night receive a kiss,
How, or where her self would wish;
But who brings him to his Mother,
Shall have that kiss and another.

(3) Marks he hath about him plenty,
You shall know him among twenty;
All his body is a fire,
And his breath a flame entire,
That brings shot (like light'ning) in
Wounds the Heart but not the skin.

(4) Wings he hath which though you clip,
He will leap from Lip to Lip;
Over Liver, Lips, and Heart,
I et ne're stay in any part:
And if by chance his Arrow misses,
He will shoot himself in kisses.

(5) He doth bear a golden Bow,
And a Quiver hanging low,
Full of Arrows that out-brave
Dians Shafts; what if he have
Any head more sharp than other?
With that kiss he strikes his mother.

(6) Still the fairest are his fuel,
When his daies are to be cruel,
Lovers hearts are all his food,
And his Bath's their warmest Blood:
Nought but wounds his hands doth season,
And he hates none like to reason.

(7) Trust him not, his words, though sweet,
Seldom with his heart do meet;
All his practice is deceit,
Ev'ry gift is a bait,
Not a kiss but poyson bears,
And most treason in his tears.

(8) Idle minutes are his reign,
Them the stragler makes his gain,
By presenting Maids with toys,
And would have ye think 'em toys;
'Tis the ambition of the Elfe,
To have all children as himself.

(9) If by these you please to know him,
Beauties be not nice, but show him,
Though you had a will to hide him,
Now I hope ye'le not abide him:
Since ye hear his falser lay,
And that he's *Venus* Run-away.

[76]
Youths Vanity.

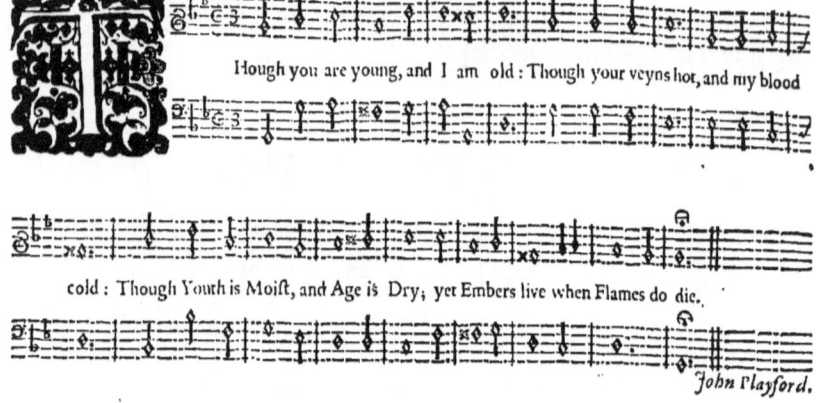

Hough you are young, and I am old: Though your veyns hot, and my blood cold: Though Youth is Moist, and Age is Dry; yet Embers live when Flames do die.

John Playford.

The tender Graft is Easily broke,
But who shall shake the sturdy Oke?
You are more Fresh and Fair than I;
Yet Stubs do live when Flowers do die.

Thou that thy Youth dost vainly boast,
Know Buds are sooner nipt with Frost;
Think that thy Fortune still doth cry,
Fond Youth, To morrow thou must die.

And if to morrow thou Dy'st not,
To Die ere long will be thou lot:
Though thou of late didst Age deny,
Must welcome Death, and learn to Die.

Cupid *Embraced*.

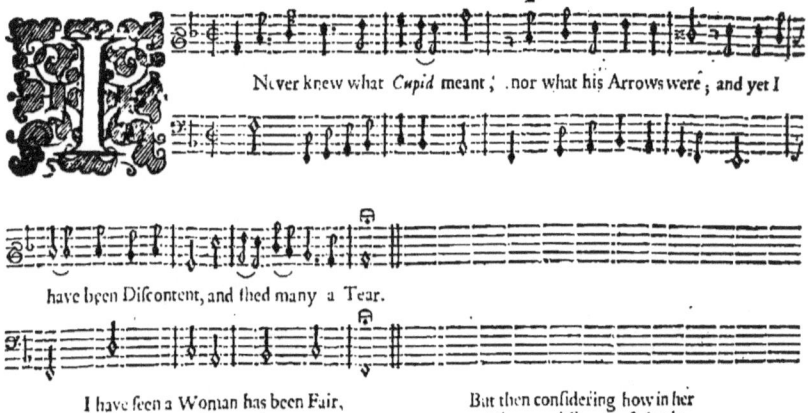

Never knew what *Cupid* meant, nor what his Arrows were; and yet I have been Discontent, and shed many a Tear.

I have seen a Woman has been Fair,
And yet could never be
Caught in the Net-work of her Hair,
Or Faces Pagentry.

I wondred that my stubborn Heart,
That hath so long held out,
Should, by the piercing of his Dart
Unseen, be brought about.

But then considering how in her
Virtue and Sweetness dwelt,
I wondred not at any stir,
That in my Heart I felt.

But *Cupid* with a reverend Knee
I worship now, like those
That rank him as a Deity;
And Thank him for my Blows.

On a Stolen Heart.

What conscience say is it in Thee, when I'ave a Heart but one to take away that Heart from me, and so to leave me none : For shame or pi-ty now encline to act a loving part, either to send me kindly Thine, or give me back my Heart : Covet not both : But if thou dost resolve to part with neither, why yet to shew that thou art Just, take Me take Me and Mine take Me and Mine together.

Tho. Blagrave.

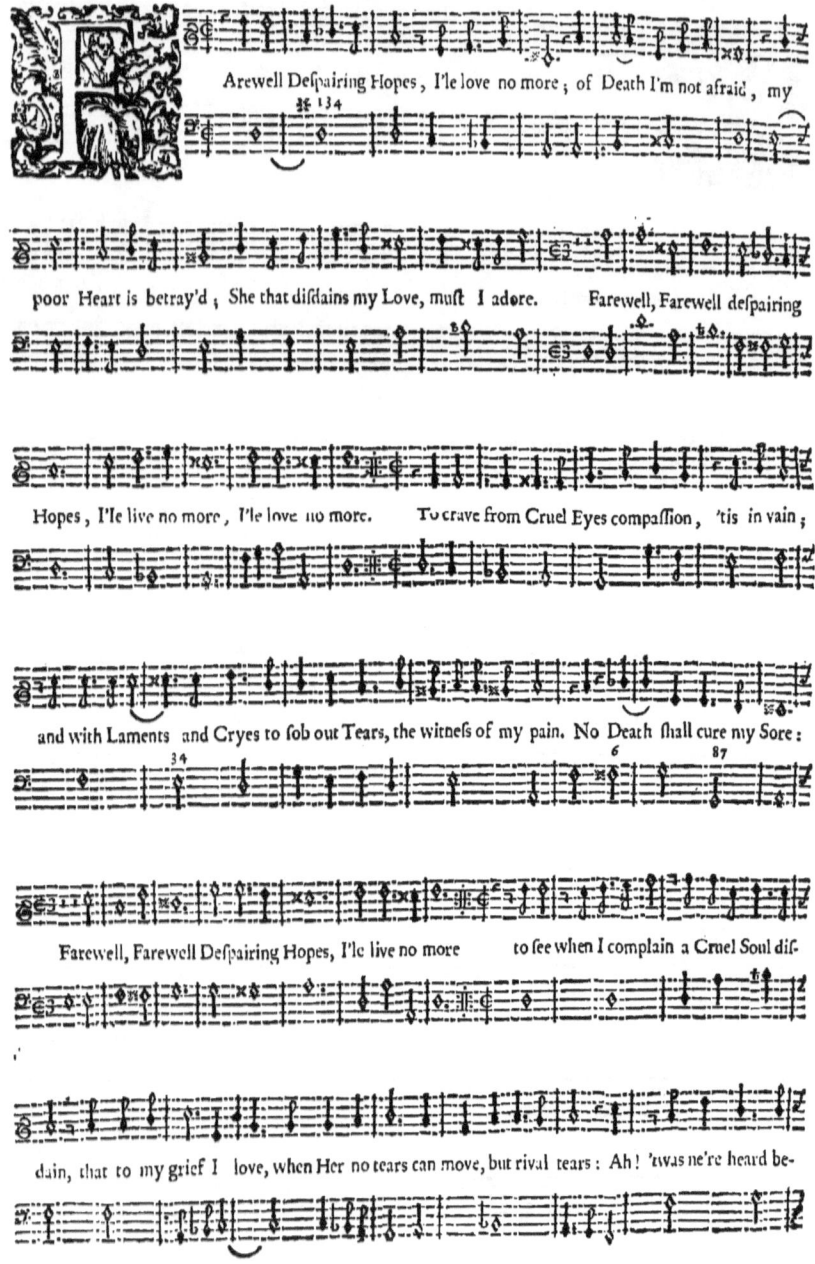

A Despairing Lover.

Farewell Despairing Hopes, I'le love no more; of Death I'm not afraid, my poor Heart is betray'd; She that disdains my Love, must I adore. Farewell, Farewell despairing Hopes, I'le live no more, I'le love no more. To crave from Cruel Eyes compassion, 'tis in vain; and with Laments and Cryes to sob out Tears, the witness of my pain. No Death shall cure my Sore: Farewell, Farewell Despairing Hopes, I'le live no more to see when I complain a Cruel Soul disdain, that to my grief I love, when Her no tears can move, but rival tears: Ah! 'twas ne're heard before. Farewell, Farewell Defpairing Hopes, I'le live no more: Ne're flatter more my fenfe with

fweet and courteous Breath, 'twixt outrage and offence I am condemn'd, I am condemn'd to Death.

No more on Joys I dote, but with a dole-ful Note my Life and Death deplore. Farewell,
8 6 5   3 4

Farewell Defpairing Hopes, I'le live no more, Ile live no more.

Mr. *Hen. Lawes.*

To his THEORA.

F ftill *Theora* you wear this difguife of Scorn up on your Eyes, and fuffer

not one fmile approve th'obedience of my Immortal Love: Two Hells at once my Soul muft try;

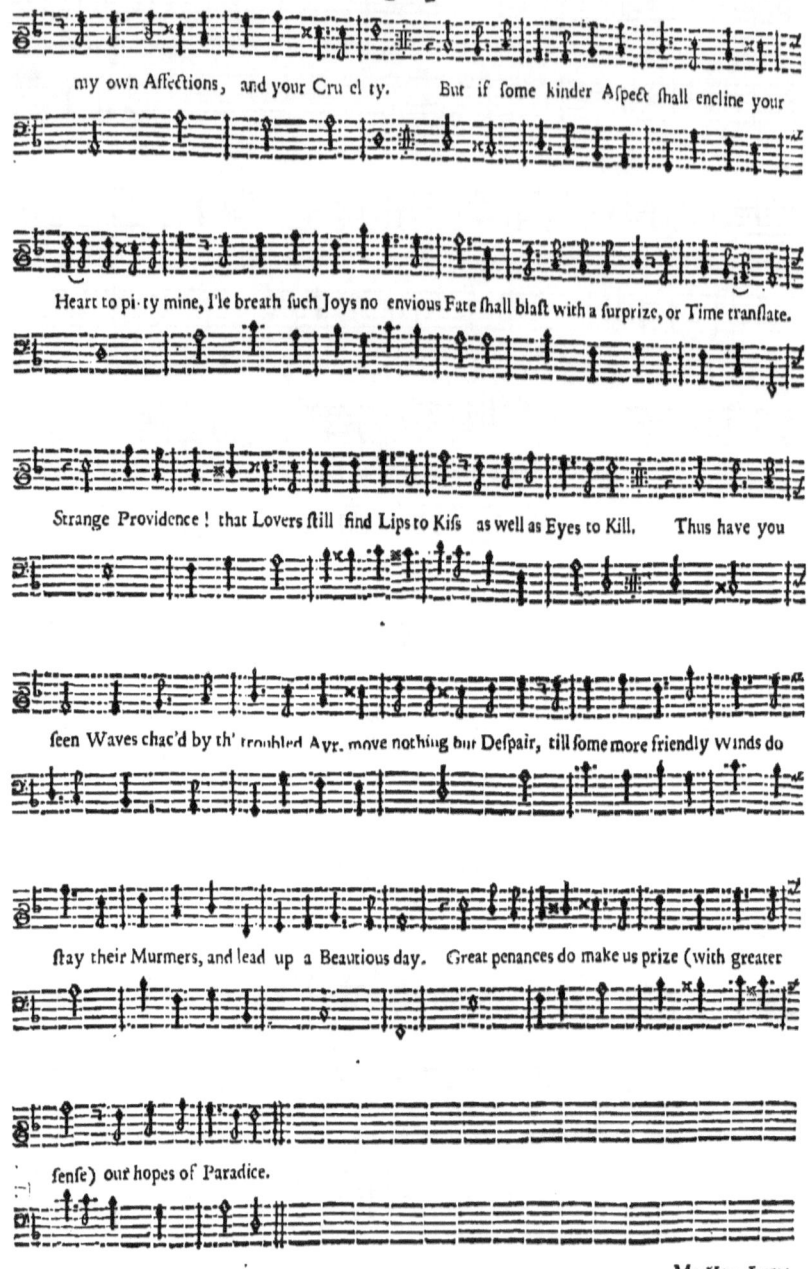

Mr *Hen.Laws.*

To a Stream.

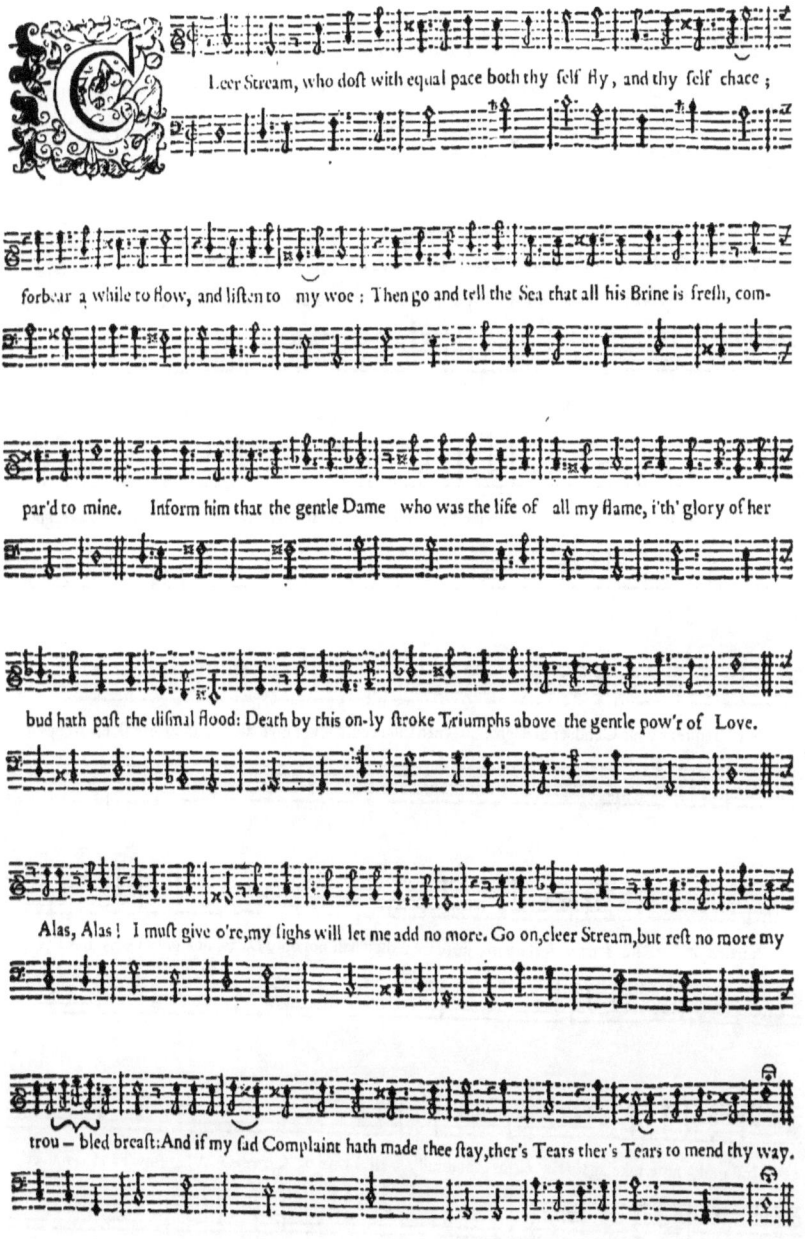

Cleer Stream, who dost with equal pace both thy self fly, and thy self chace; forbear a while to flow, and listen to my woe: Then go and tell the Sea that all his Brine is fresh, compar'd to mine. Inform him that the gentle Dame who was the life of all my flame, i'th' glory of her bud hath past the dismal flood: Death by this on-ly stroke Triumphs above the gentle pow'r of Love. Alas, Alas! I must give o're, my sighs will let me add no more. Go on, cleer Stream, but rest no more my trou-bled breast: And if my sad Complaint hath made thee stay, ther's Tears ther's Tears to mend thy way.

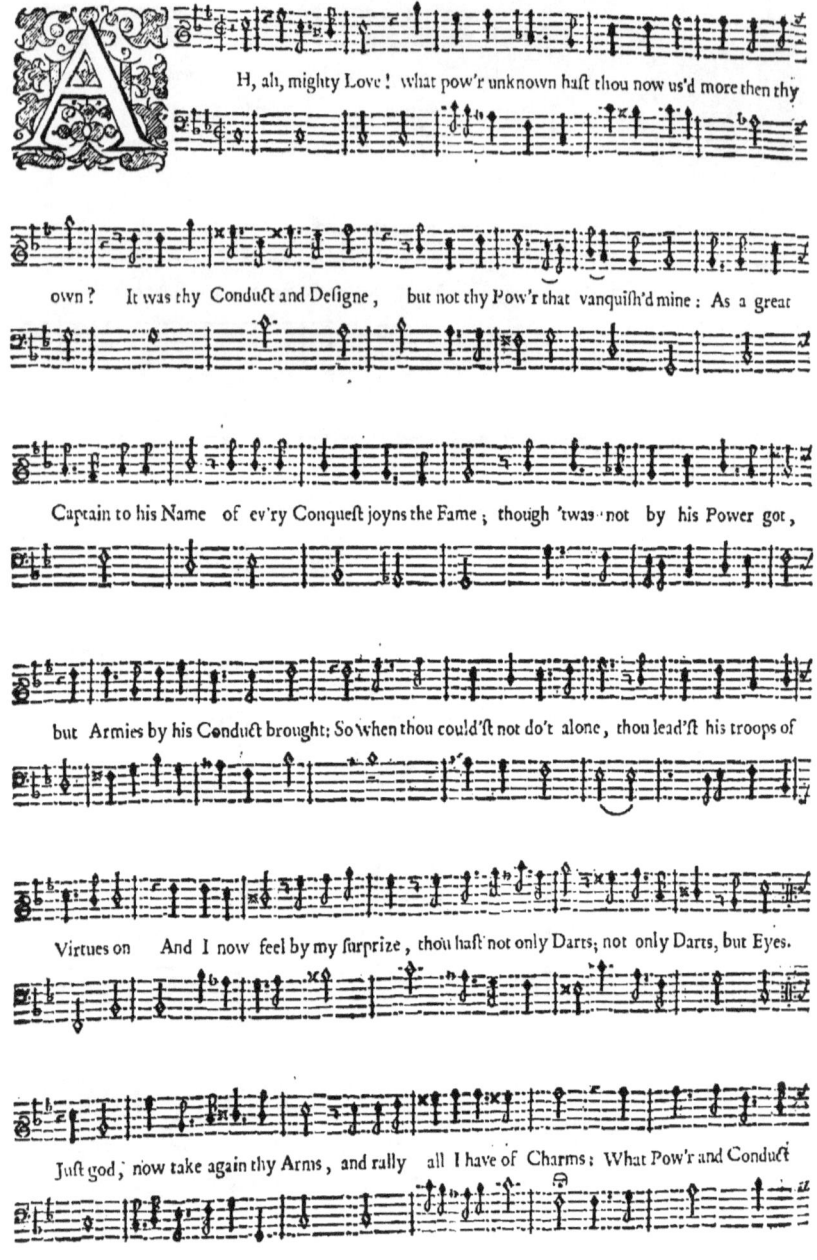

[83]

cannot doe, make his Belief contribute too: So when the Earth some promise shows that she does yet more Wealth enclose: Believing men search her rich Veins, and crown their hopes with unknown gains: May.he but at the first incline to Love, then by my Faith and Time, his Justice after the surprize shall be more fetter'd, shall be more set - - - - ter'd than his Eyes.

Mr. Hen. Lawes.

On the soft and gentle Motions of EUDORA.

Strike, Strike sweet *Licoris*, strike th' harmonious Lute; but with a stroke so gentle as may sute the si-lent gly–ding of the Hours, or the yet calmer growth of Flow'rs, th' ascending

[84]

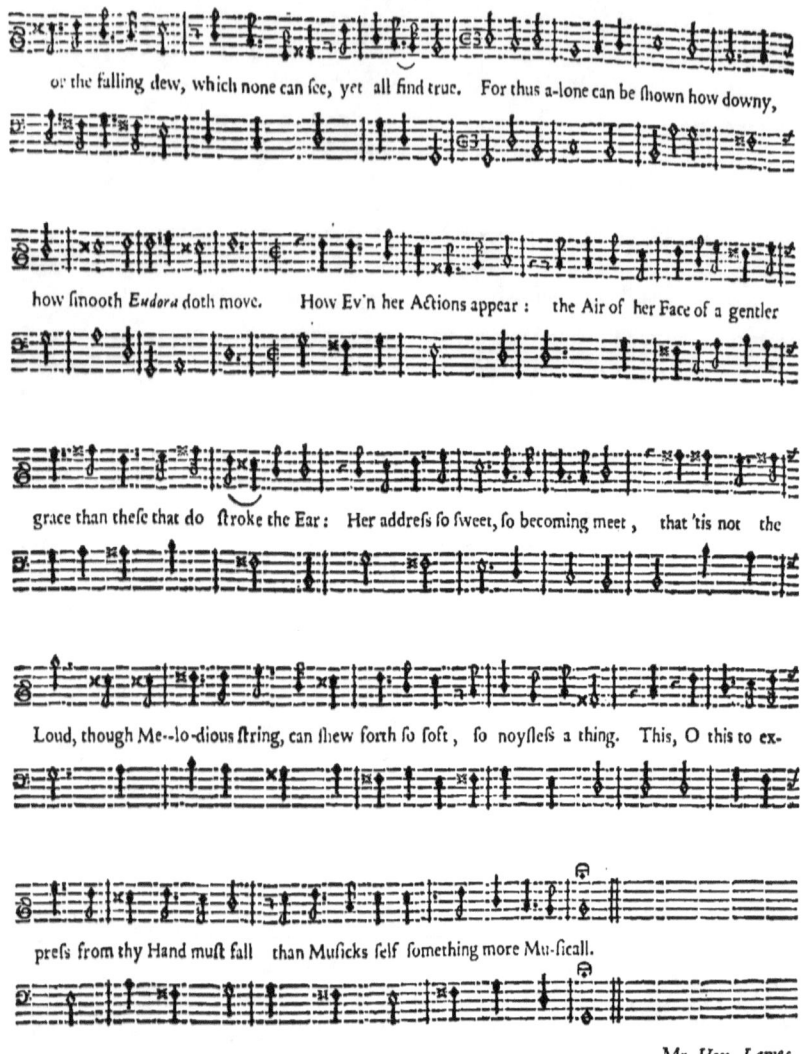

Mr. *Hen. Lawes.*

Amintor Distracted, Complains.

I Had a *Cloris* my Delight, hey down hey down, with Hair as brown as Berries;

her Cheeks like Roses red and white, her Lips more sweet than Cherries.

Mr. *Hen. Laws.*

II.

Though lovely Black dwelt in her Eyes,
  Hey down hey down,
Like brightest Day that shin'd;
And Hills of Snow upon her Breast,
  Made me and all men blinde.

III.

She was so sweet, so kind, so free,
  Hey down hey down,
To kiss, to sport, and play;
But all this was with none but Me,
  So Envy 't self will say.

IV.

She fed her flock on yonder Plane,
  Hey down hey down,
'Tis wither'd now and dry;
How can *Amintor* longer live
  When such things for her die?

V.

Her wandring Kids look in my face,
  Hey down hey down,
And with Dumb Tears Express
The want of *Cloris*, my True Love,
  And their kind Shepherdess.

VI.

She lov'd me without fraud or guile,
  Hey down hey down,
But not for flocks or treasure;
And I was happy all the while,
  But now woe worth all pleasure.

VII.

When she liv'd I went fine and gay,
  Hey down hey down,
With Flowers and Ribons deck'd;
But now I am (as Shepherds say)
  The Emblem of Neglect.

VIII.

Where are those pretty Garlands now
  Hey down hey down,
Of Ivy and of Bays,
Which *Cloris* platted on my Brow
  For Singing in her praise?

IX.

With naked Legs and Arms I go,
  Hey down hey down,
For why the Clothes I wore,
With Bonnets, Scarfs, and many mo,
  Upon her Grave lie tore.

X.

For woe is me I should be warm;
  Hey down hey down,
Or any Comfort have,
As long as my dear *Cloris* lies
  So cold within her Grave.

XI.

I'le gather sticks and make a fire,
  Hey down a down;
To warm her where she lies,
Of Mirtles, Cypress and Sweet-Bryer,
  And then perhaps she'l rise.

Union in Love.

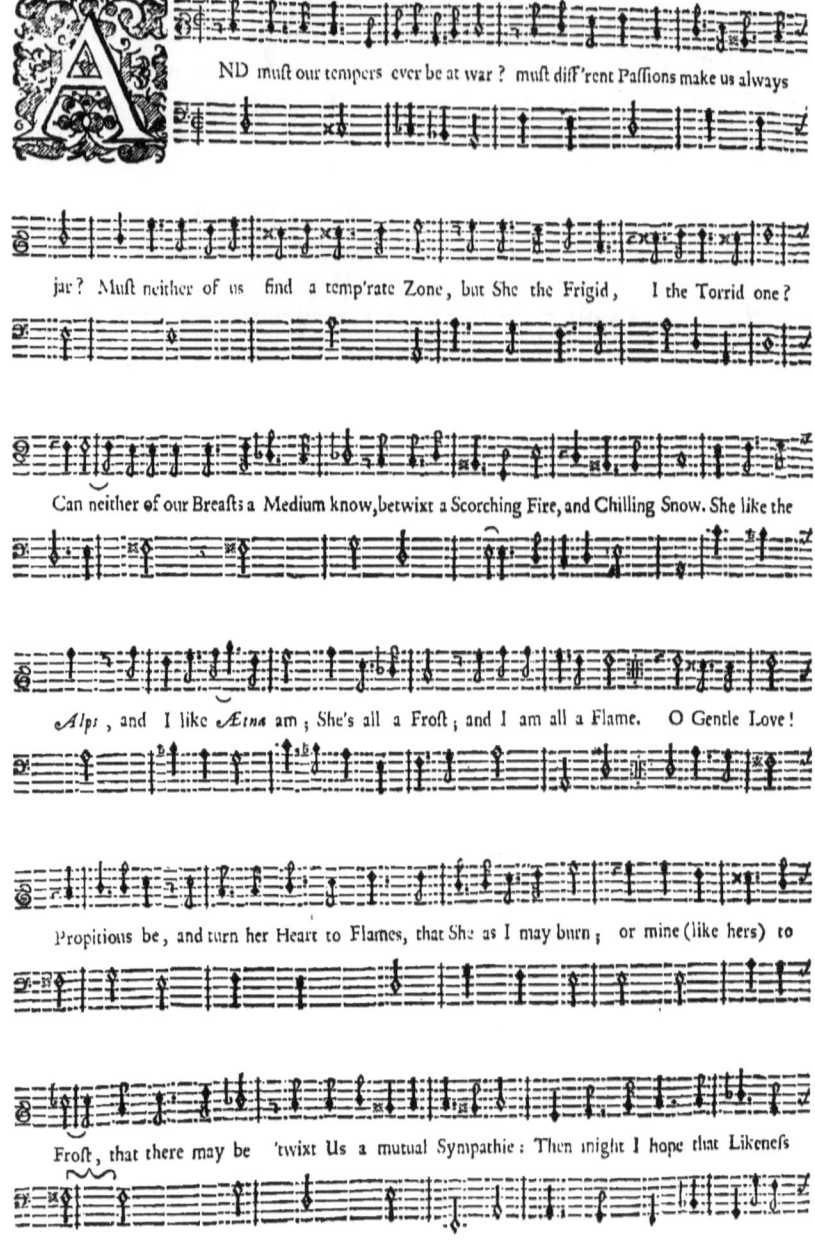

AND must our tempers ever be at war? must diff'rent Passions make us always jar? Must neither of us find a temp'rate Zone, but She the Frigid, I the Torrid one? Can neither of our Breasts a Medium know, betwixt a Scorching Fire, and Chilling Snow. She like the Alps, and I like Ætna am; She's all a Frost, and I am all a Flame. O Gentle Love! Propitious be, and turn her Heart to Flames, that She as I may burn; or mine (like hers) to Frost, that there may be 'twixt Us a mutual Sympathie: Then might I hope that Likeness

An old Knight to a young Lady.

Madam, your Beauty (I confess) may our young Gallants wound or bless; but cannot warm my frozen Heart, not capable of Joy or Smart; 'Cause neither Wit, nor Looks, nor Kindness can make Young a Super-annu-ated man.

Those sparks that every minute fly
From your bright Eyes, do falling die;
Not kindle flames, as heretofore,
Because old I can love no more:
Beauty on wither'd Hearts no Trophy gains;
For Tinder over us'd, no Fire retains.

If you'l indure to be admir'd
By an old Dotard new Inspir'd,
You may enjoy the Quintessence
Of my past Loves without Expence:
For I can wait, and prate, I thank my Fate,
I can do all, but no new Fire Create.

Cupid's Power.

Disdain not, Fair one, since we know your Heart's a Mark for Cupid's Bow: The Scorns you cast at Love will turn like Lightning back, and make you burn.

Let those whom Age hath set aside
To Court the Grave for their next Bride;
Or let the frigid Matron say
They will no god of Love obey.

But you who want nor Youth, nor Fire
To kindle Altars of Desire;
I doubt not but ere long you'l be
Loves Proselite as well as we.

To a Friend who desired no more then to admire the Mind, and the Beauty of SILVIA.

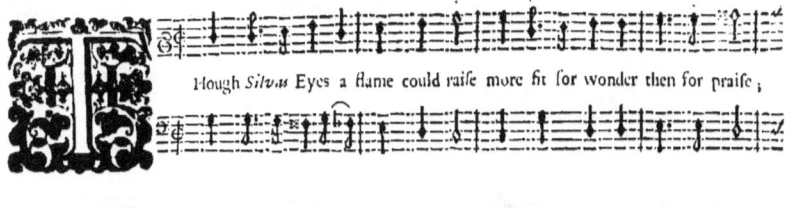

Hough *Silvas* Eyes a flame could raise more fit for wonder then for praise;

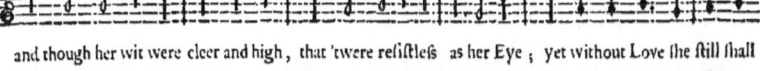

and though her wit were cleer and high, that 'twere resistless as her Eye; yet without Love she still shall

find I'm deaf to one, to the other blind.

Mr. *Hen. Lawes.*

II.
Those Fools that think Beauty can prove
A cause sufficient for their Love,
I wish they never may have more,
To try how Looks can cure their sore:
'Tis such the Sex so high have set,
They take it not for gift, but debt.

III.
If Love were unto Sight confin'd,
The god of it would not be blind;
Nor would the pleasure of it be
So often in obscuritie:
No, to know Joys each sense hath right,
Equal at least to that of Sight.

IV.
The gods, who knew the noblest part
In Love, sought not the Mind, but Heart;
And when hurt by the winged Boy,
What they admir'd, they did enjoy;
Knowing a Kindness Love could prove
The hope, reward, and cure of Love.

V.
I'le rather my Affections keep
For Nimphs only injoy'd in sleep,
Then cast away an houre of Care
On any, 'cause she's only fair:
Nay, Sleep more pleasing Dreams do move
Then are your waking ones of Love.

VI.
The Frensie's less love to endure,
Then after to decline the Cure;
Yet you do both, aiming no higher
Then for to see, and to admire,
An Idol you'l not only frame,
But you will too adore the same.

VII.
Had therein *Silvia* nothing shin'd
But the unseen charms of her Mind,
You would have had the like esteem
For her that I have still for them:
If flesh and blood your flame inspire,
Then make those only your desire.

VIII. And Friend, that you may cleerly prove
'Tis not her Mind alone you love;
Let her 'twixt us her self impart,
Give you her Mind, and me her Heart:
As little cause then you will find
As I do now, to love her Mind.

The Earl to the Countess of CARBERY.

You ask, my Dear, if I be well; feel thine own pulse, and that will tell:
Vain is all o--ther Art that beats the Temper of my Heart; if I may call that mine is so entire-ly thine.
Dearest, then tell me how I doe; for both my Health and Heart's in You.

Mr. *Hen. Lawes.*

When first I view'd thee, I did spy
Thy Soul stand beck'ning in thine Eye;
My Heart knew what it meant,
And at the very first Kiss went,
Two Balls of Wax so run
When melted into one:
Mix'd now with thine, my Heart now lies,
And much Loves Riddle as thy Prize.

For, since I can't pretend to have
That Heart, which I so freely gave;
Yet now 'tis Mine the more,
Because 'tis thine, then 'twas before:
Death will unriddle this;
For when thou 'rt call'd to bliss,
He needs not throw at me his Dart,
'Cause piercing thine; he kills my Heart.

Constancy in Love.

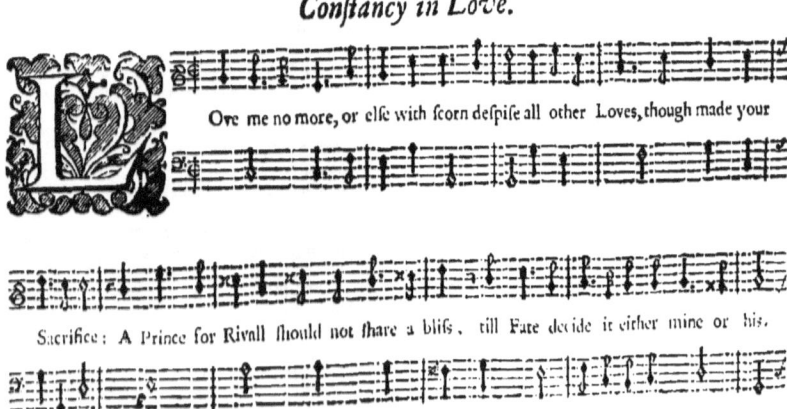

Love me no more, or else with scorn despise all other Loves, though made your
Sacrifice: A Prince for Rivall should not share a bliss, till Fate decide it either mine or his.

In Love and Courage, Titles has no Claim, Merit and Virtue give the highest Name.

Mr. Henry Lawes.

 Let then thy *Cupid* soar on Honours wings,
 Thy Constancy and Love appear like Twins;
 So shall thy Mind excell thy Shape much more
 Than thou all other Beauties didst before,
  Crowning with glory both thy self and me,
  And when thou dy'st be thought a Deitie.

Cupid *Discovered.*

*C*upid's no god, a wanton Childe, his Arts are weak, his Pow'rs are milde; no active heat or nobler fire feathers his Arrows with Desire: 'Tis not his Bow or Shaft, 'tis *Venus* Eye makes him ador'd, and crowns his De-i-tie.

Mr. Hen. Lawes.

 Each Amorous glance creates this Fire,
 As Coyns dulls and chills Desire;
 'Tis then the Face and Eyes we see,
 Not the fond Boys Artillerie:
 Tis the Consentive nimbler Sense creates
 Love's subtler piercing Fires, not the Fates.

Inconstancy in Love.

IF thou wilt know the reason why I hate thee now once held so Deer, upon thy Glass but cast thine Eye, and thou shalt find it written there; for as in that thou mayst survey thy fair, false Eyes, and lovely Face; so nothing in thy Glass will stay, when thou art parted from the place.

Mr. *Hen. Lawes.*

II.
So when my Love did first pretend,
Me thought I saw my self in thee;
And therefore chose thee for a Friend,
That ought Anothers self to be:
All Vows and Oaths I made to Love
Thou shouldst repeat when I had done,
And by a sweet reflection prove
We were (though seeming Two) but One.

III.
But when I absent was a while,
And others came to look in thee,
As they would laugh, so wouldst thou smile,
And no impression left of mee:
Now, though to have a Friend were best,
That might reflect thoughts as they pass,
My Mind shall rather go ill-drest
Than mind it self by such a Glass.

For a Bass.

When I taste my Goblet deep, all my Cares are rock'd a Sleep:
Then I'm Cræsus, Lord of th' Earth, Singing Odes of Wit and Mirth; and with I-vy Garlands crown'd, I can kick the Globe round, round. Others Fight, but let me Drink; Boy, my Goblet fill to th' brink; for when I lay down my head, better to be Drunk, better to be Drunk, Dead Drunk, than Dead.

Mr. *Hen. Lawes.*

[94]
The GREEK's Song.

[For a Bass.]

HE thirsty Earth sucks up the Rain, and drinks, and gapes for Drink again: The Plants suck in the Earth, and are with constant drinking fresh and fair: The Sea it self which one would think should have but little need to drink, drinks ten thousand Rivers up, so fill'd they over-flow - - - flow - - - - the Cup: The busie Sun, and one would guess by's drunken fiery Face no less, drinks up the Sea; and when that's done, the Moon and Stars drin - - - - - - - - - kes up the Sun.

Cælia's Complaint.

Poor Cælia once was very fair, a quick bewitching Eye she had; most neatly look'd her braided Hair, her dainty Cheek would make you mad; up-on her Lips did all the Gra-ces pla- - - - - -y and on her Breasts ten Thousand Thousand Cupids lay.

Mr. *Roger Hill*.

II.

Then many a doting Lover came
From Seventeen till Twenty one;
Each told her of his mighty flame,
But She, forsooth, affected none:
One was not Handsome, th' other was not Fine;
This of Tobacco smelt, and that of Wine.

III.

But t' other day it was my fate
To walk along that way alone;
I saw no Coach before her gate,
But at her dore I heard her moan:
She dropt a Tear, and sighing seem'd to say,
Young Ladies, Marry, Marry while you may.

Here Endeth the AYRES for One Voice to the Theorbo or Bass Viol.

[89]

Select *Italian* Ayrs for One or Two Voices to the Theorbo Lute.

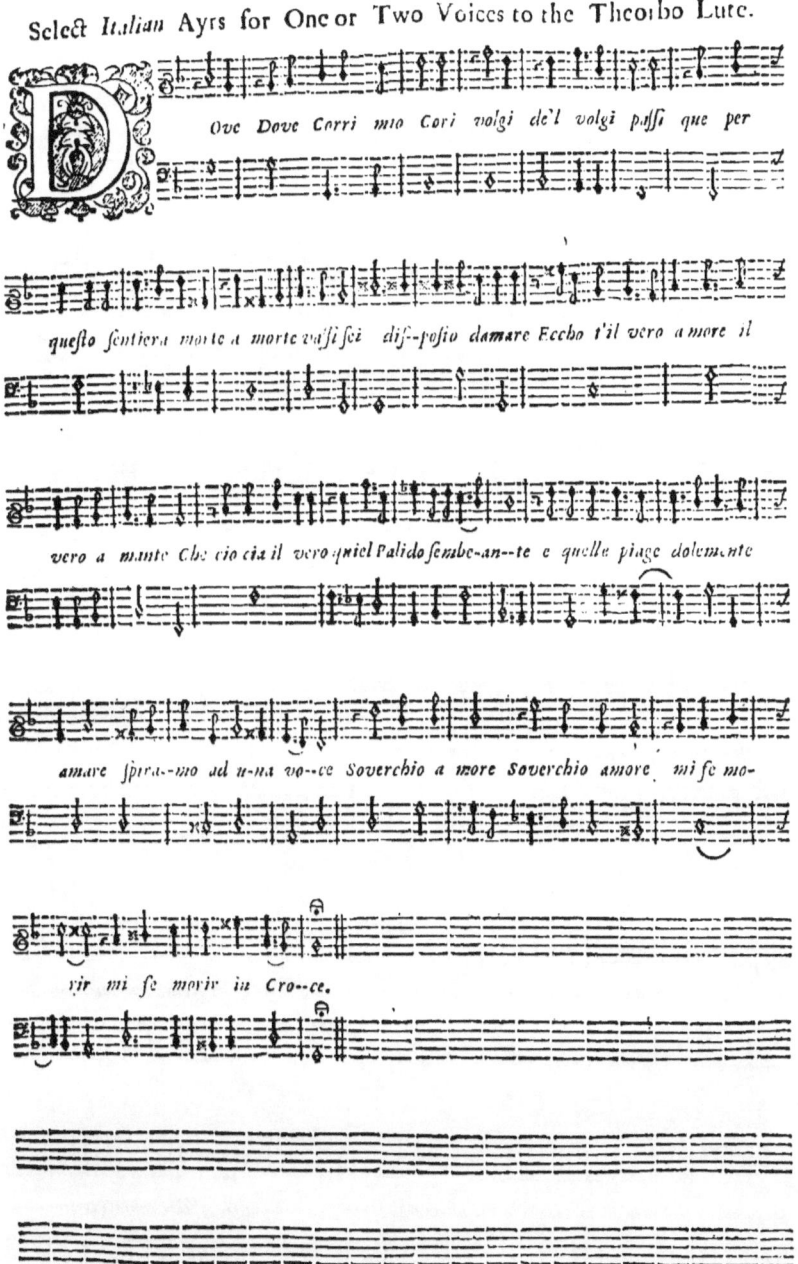

A a

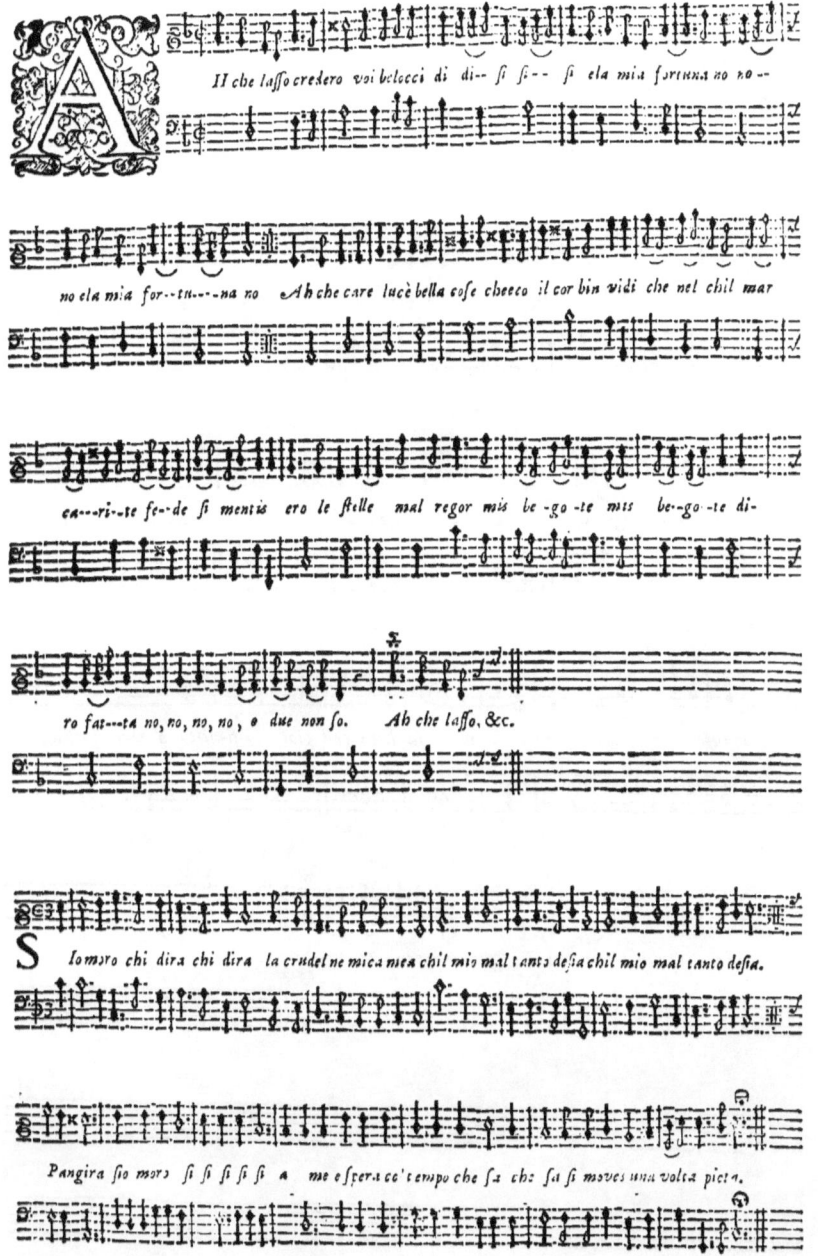

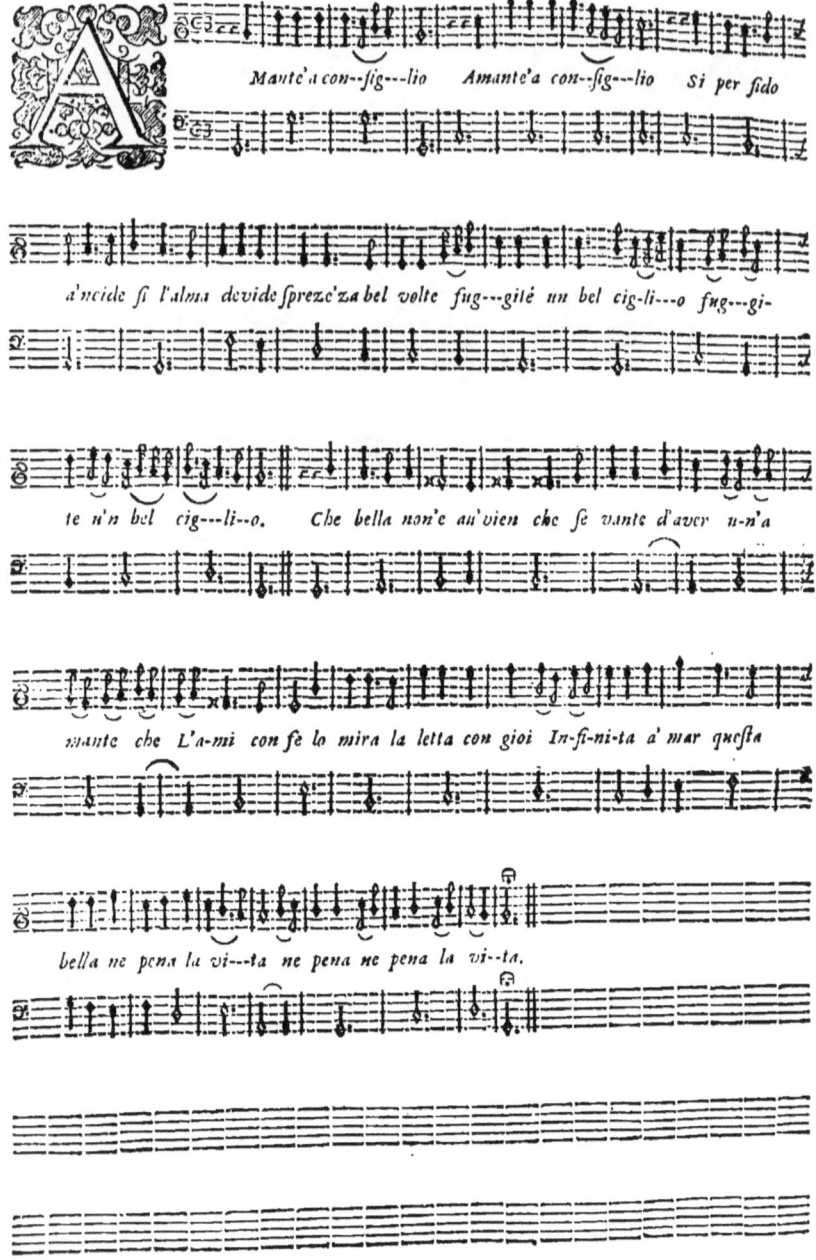

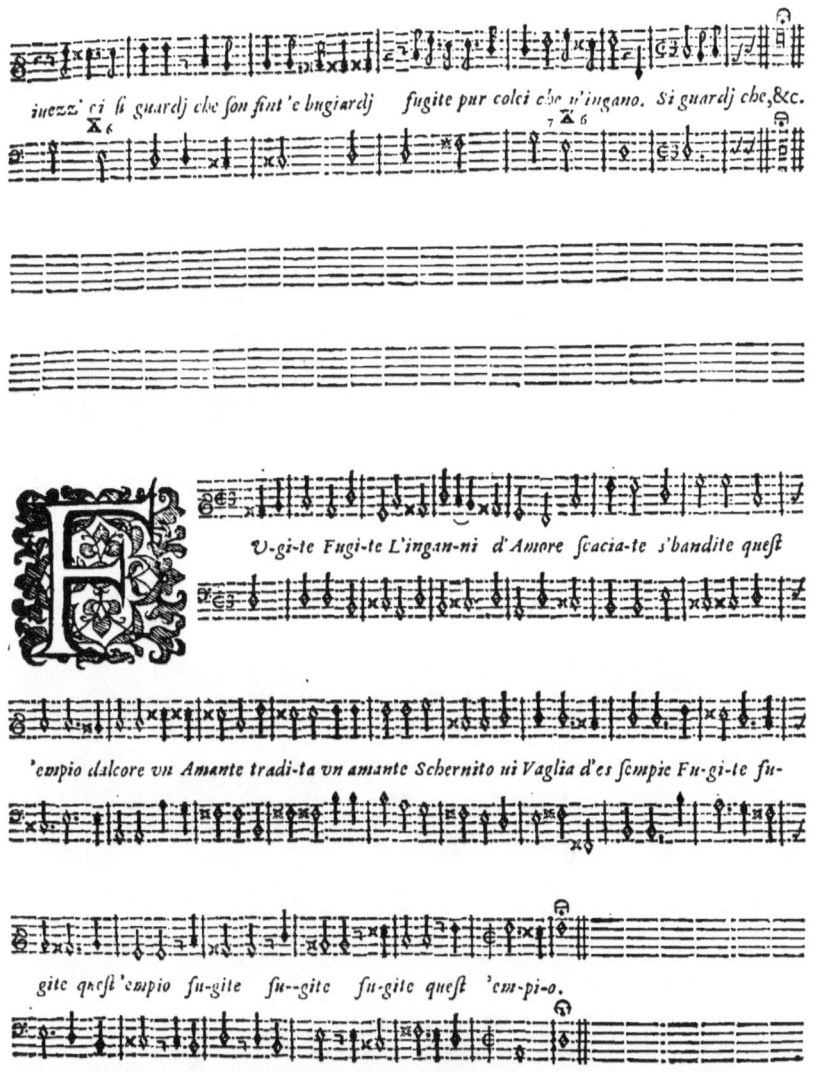

iuezzi ci si guardj che son finti e bugiardj   fugite pur colei che v'ingano. Si guardj che,&c.

V-gi-te Fugi-te L'ingan-ni d'Amore scacia-te s'bandite quest

'empio dalcore vn Amante tradi-ta vn amante Schernito ni Vaglia d'es sempie Fu-gi-te fu-

gite quest 'empio fu-gite   fu--gite   fu-gite quest 'em-pi-o.

Lusinga Col canto d'angelico viso
Ma subit impianto si Cangia quell viso
Questi fuimi Correnti questi lumi dolenti
Vi segno d' esempio fugite, &c.

Vi chiama Col guardo con occhio cheride
Pei scocca quel dardo che l'amim ancide
La mia grave ferita la mia doglia infinite
Vi vaglia d'essempio, &c.

D E quei begliocchi de quei begliocchi i guardi Amorosi digia sinclina il fiore E pian piano le gratie sen vano le gratie sen vano se fug--gi la bel-la sè muore lamore, deh Godiamo il giorno presente dimani retor-na ill sole Ca-den-te, dimani re-tor-na ill sole Candente Ma in vano in vano belezze perdute belezze perdute s'as pet-te-ra---no s'as pet---te----rano.

Mr Hen. Laws.

SELECT DIALOGUES
To Sing to the *LUTE* or *VIOL*.
A DIALOGUE. [Treble & Bass.]
Shepherd and Nimph.

Shepherd.
Sweet Lovely Nimph! whose Eyes do move me above all other Swains to

Nimph.
Love thee. Shepherd, you feign; and I know there is no flattering Swain like you.

Shepherd.
O fair one! do not wrong me so; for if ever Shepherd Lov'd, I doe.

Nimph.
May I believe thy

Shep:
Vows unfained. Or may I die by you disdained.

CHORUS.
Then let us Joy, then let us Joy each

Then let us Joy, then let us Joy each

others Love, and strive and strive who shall most Constant prove.

others Love, and strive and strive who shall most Constant prove.

Mr. *Hen: Lawes.*

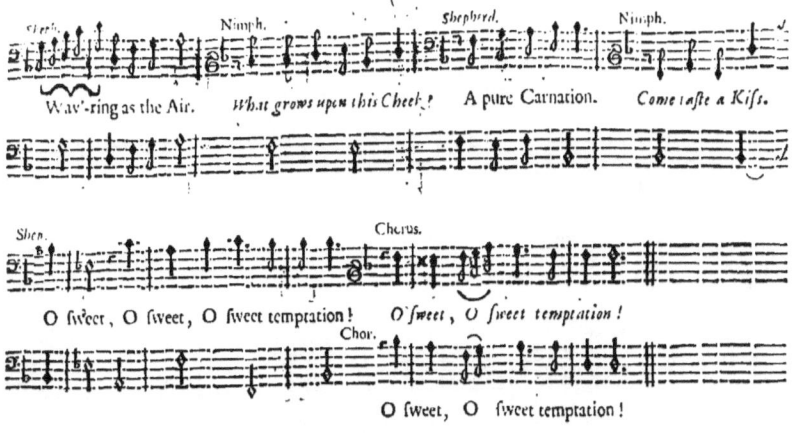

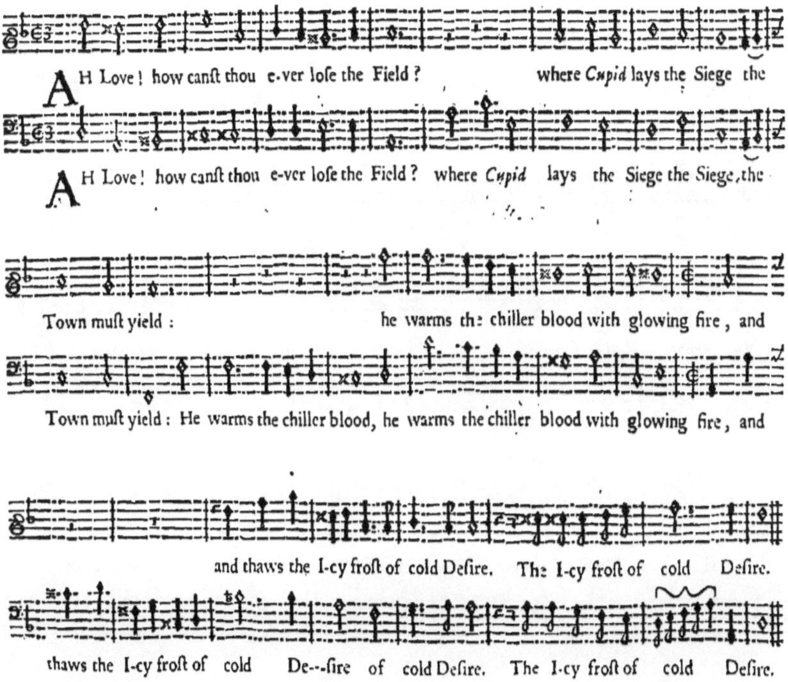

A DIALOGUE. [Treble & Bass.]
Nimph and Shepherd.

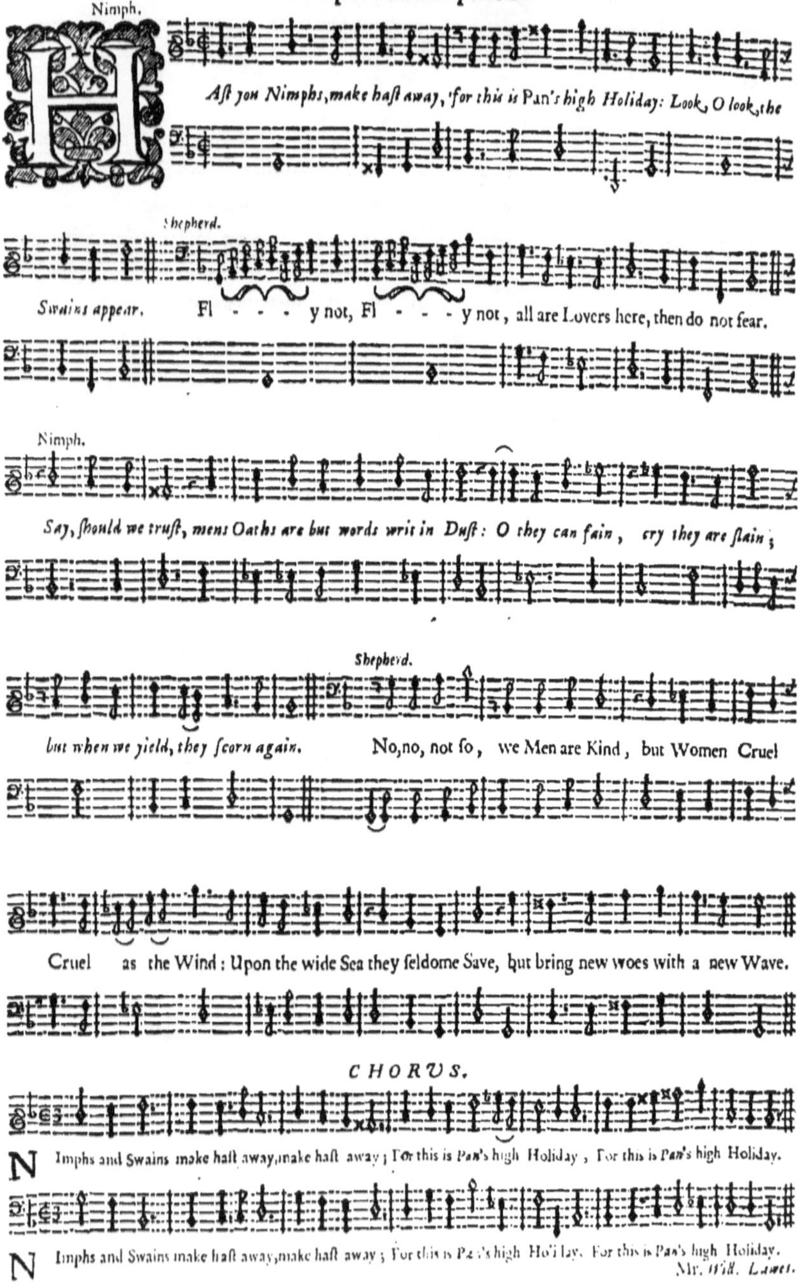

Nimph.

Ast you Nimphs, make hast away, for this is Pan's high Holiday: Look, O look, the Swains appear. Fly not, Fly not, all are Lovers here, then do not fear.

Nimph.

Say, should we trust, mens Oaths are but words writ in Dust: O they can fain, cry they are slain; but when we yield, they scorn again.

Shepherd.

No, no, not so, we Men are Kind, but Women Cruel Cruel as the Wind; Upon the wide Sea they seldome Save, but bring new woes with a new Wave.

CHORUS.

Nimphs and Swains make hast away, make hast away; For this is Pan's high Holiday, For this is Pan's high Holiday.

Nimphs and Swains make hast away, make hast away; For this is Pan's high Holiday, For this is Pan's high Holiday.

Mr. Will. Lawes.

A DIALOGUE. [Treble & Basi.]

Occasioned by the Death of the young Lord HASTINGS, *who dyed some few days before he was to have been Married to Sir* Theodore Meibern's *Daughter, in* June, 1649.

Charon and Eucosmia.

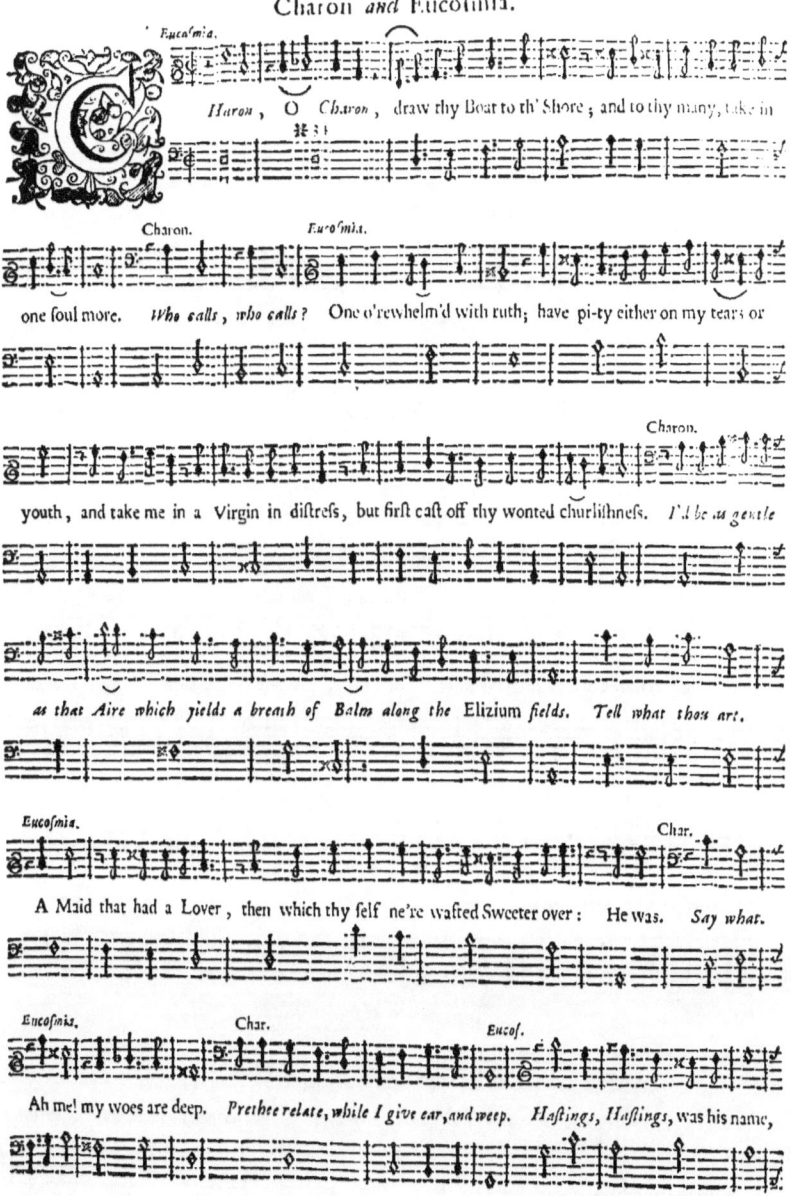

Charon, O Charon, draw thy Boat to th' Shore; and to thy many, take in one soul more. Who calls, who calls? One o'rewhelm'd with ruth; have pi-ty either on my tears or youth, and take me in a Virgin in distress, but first cast off thy wonted churlishness. I'd be as gentle as that Aire which yields a breath of Balm along the Elizium fields. Tell what thou art. A Maid that had a Lover, then which thy self ne're wasted Sweeter over: He was. Say what. Ah me! my woes are deep. Prethee relate, while I give ear, and weep. Hastings, Hastings, was his name,

Dd

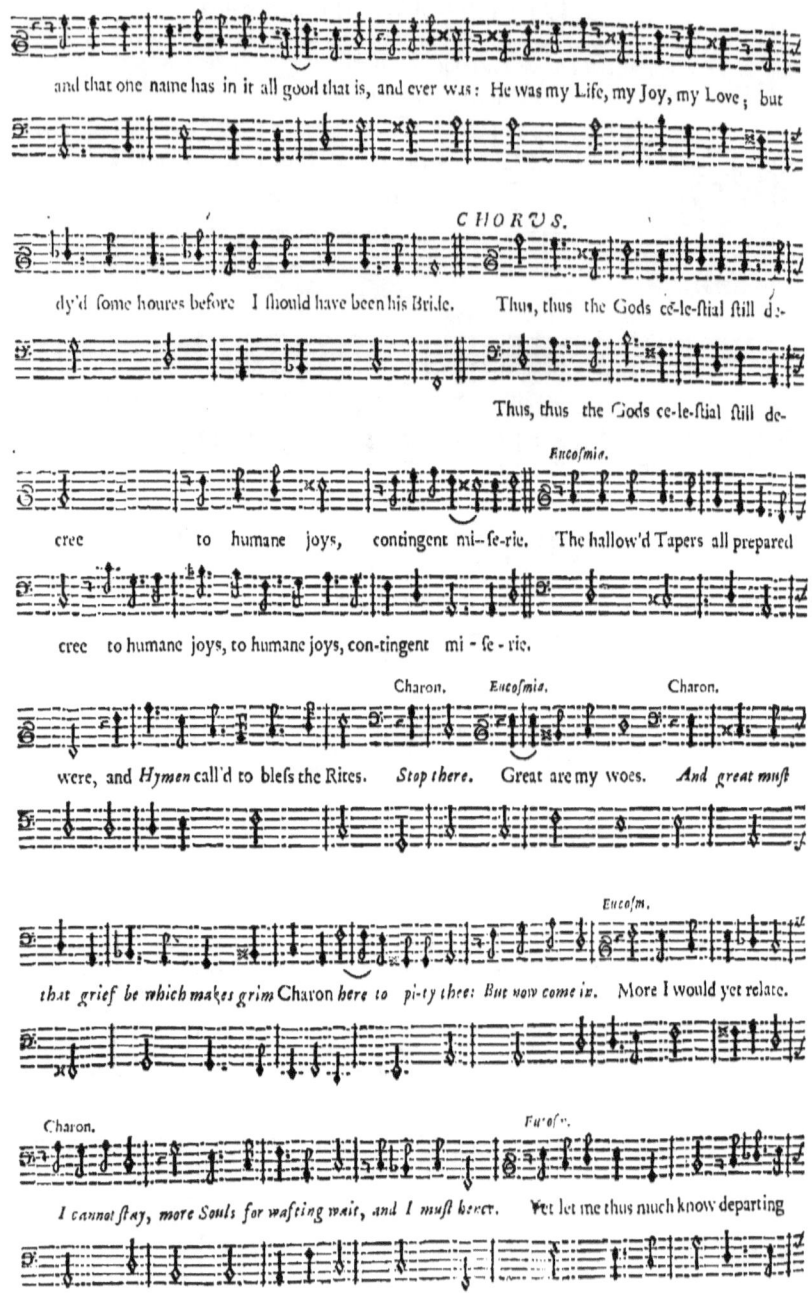

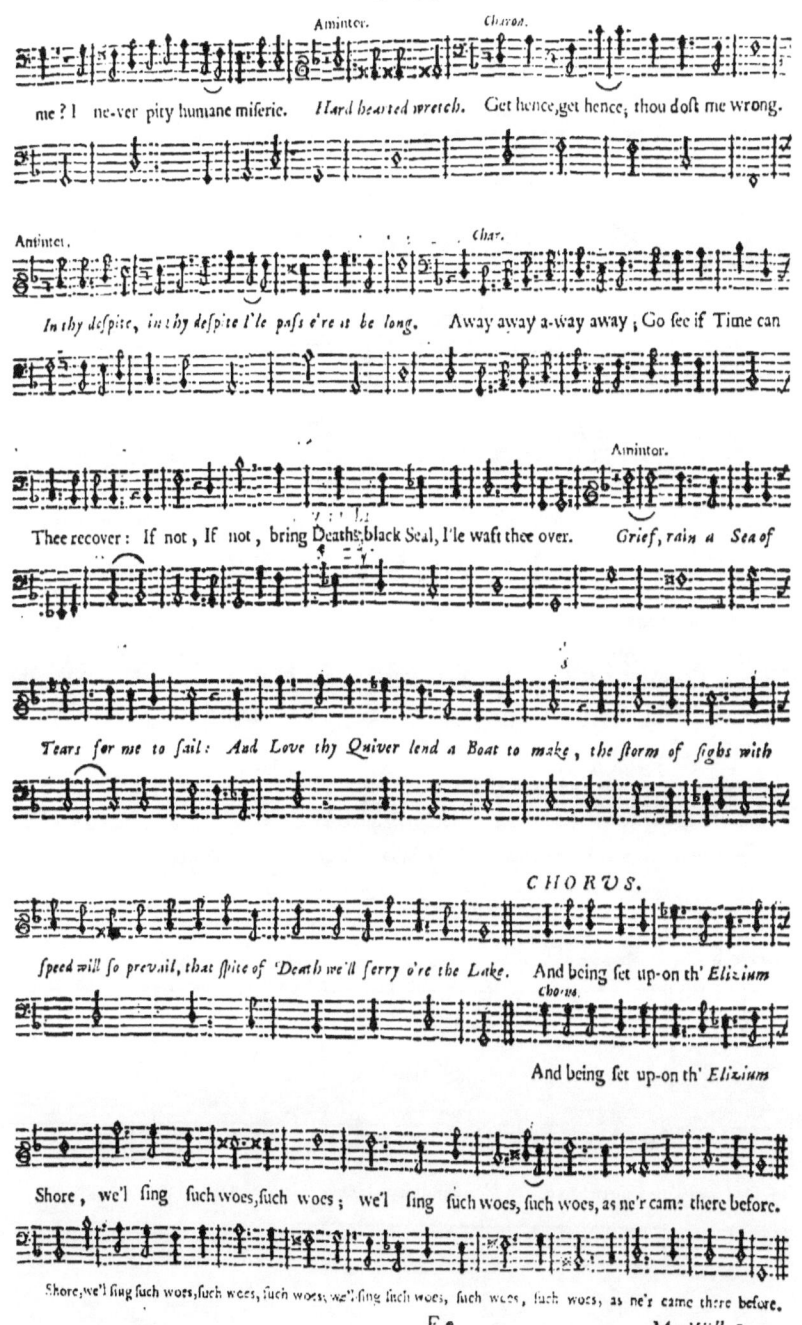

[114]

A DIALOGUE. [Two Trebles or Tenor s.]
Shepherd and Nimph.

Shepherd.

T His Mossy-Bank they prest.

Nimph.

That Aged Oke did canopy the happy Pair all

CHORUS.

Here let us fit and sing the words they spoke, when the Day breaking their Em-

Chorus

Night from the dark Air. Here let us sit and sing the words they spoke, when the Day breaking their Em-

Shepherd.

braces broke. See Love the blushes of the Morn appear, and now she hangs her pearly store

braces broke.

robb'd from the Eastern Shore, i'th Cowslips-bell and Roses ear: Sweet, I must stay no longer here.

[115]

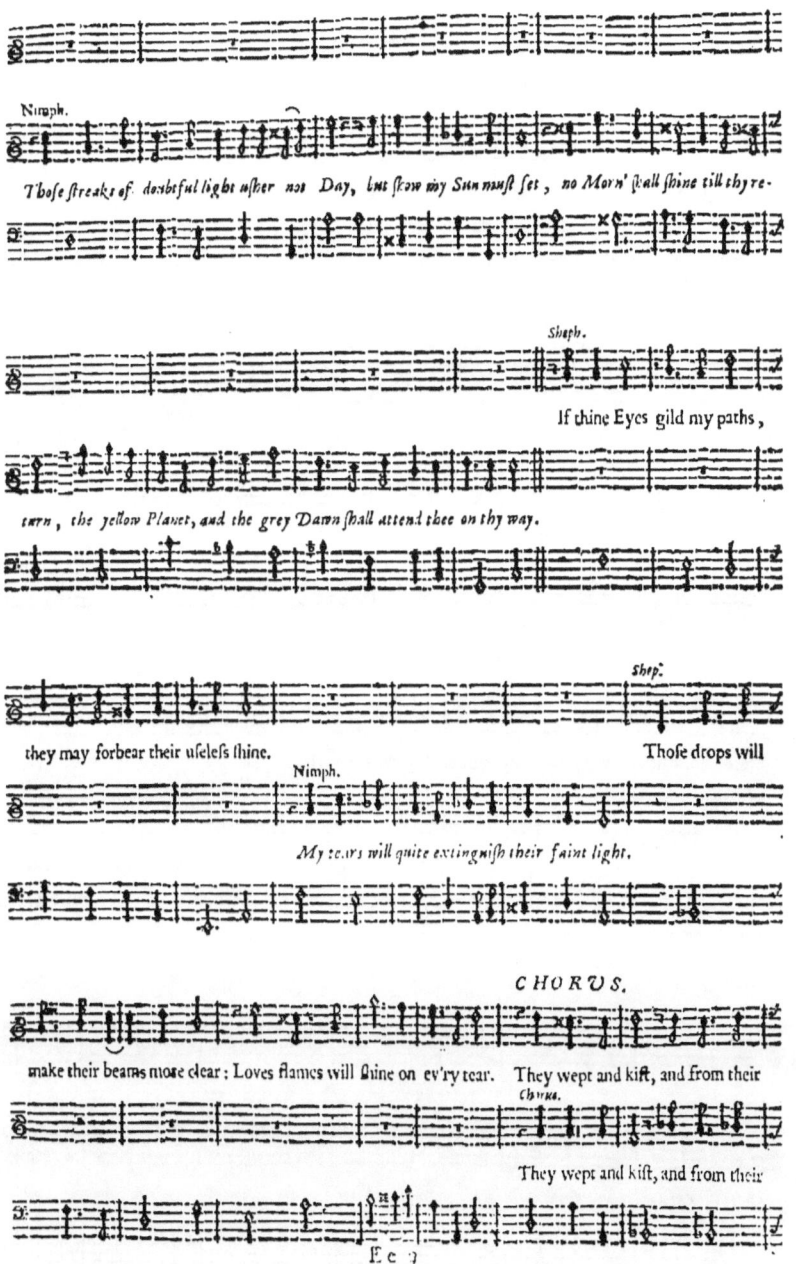

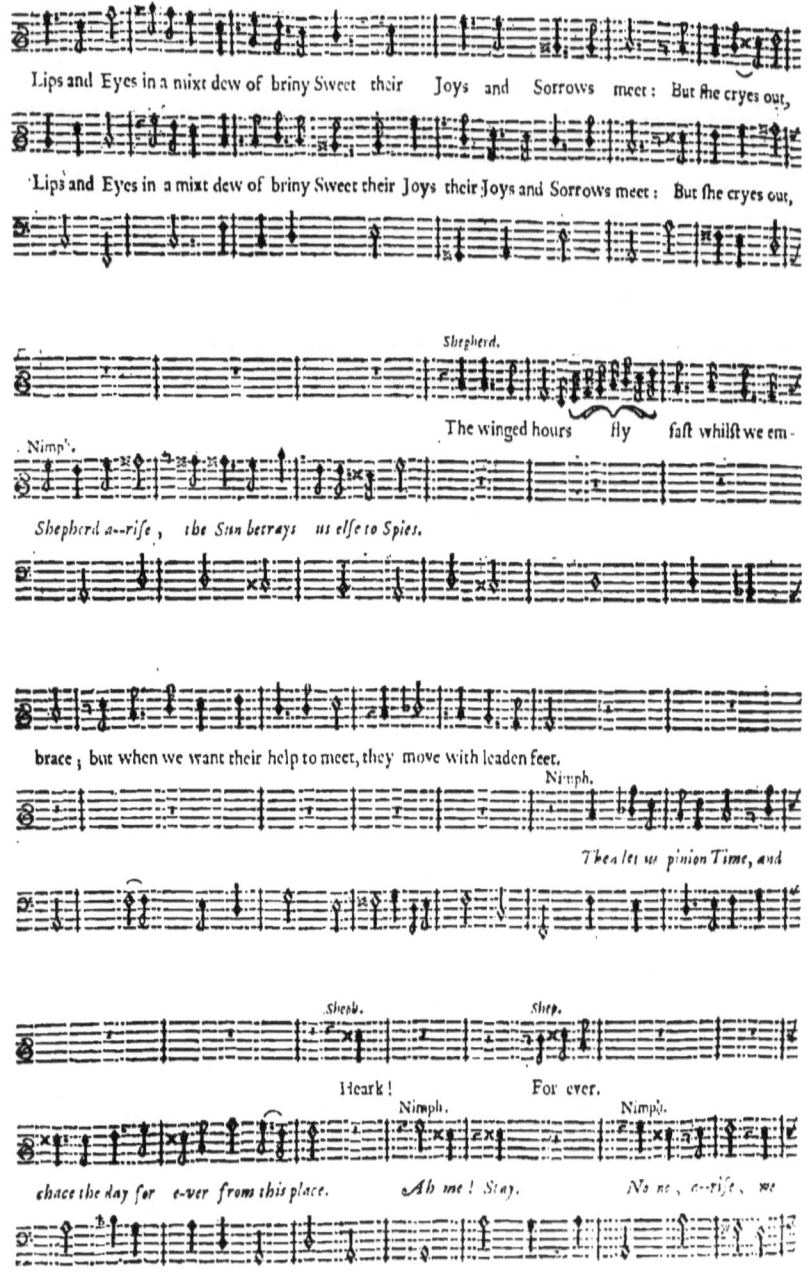

[117]

Mr. *Henry Lawes*:

A Dialogue.
Shepherd and Nimph. [Two Trebles or Teno s.]

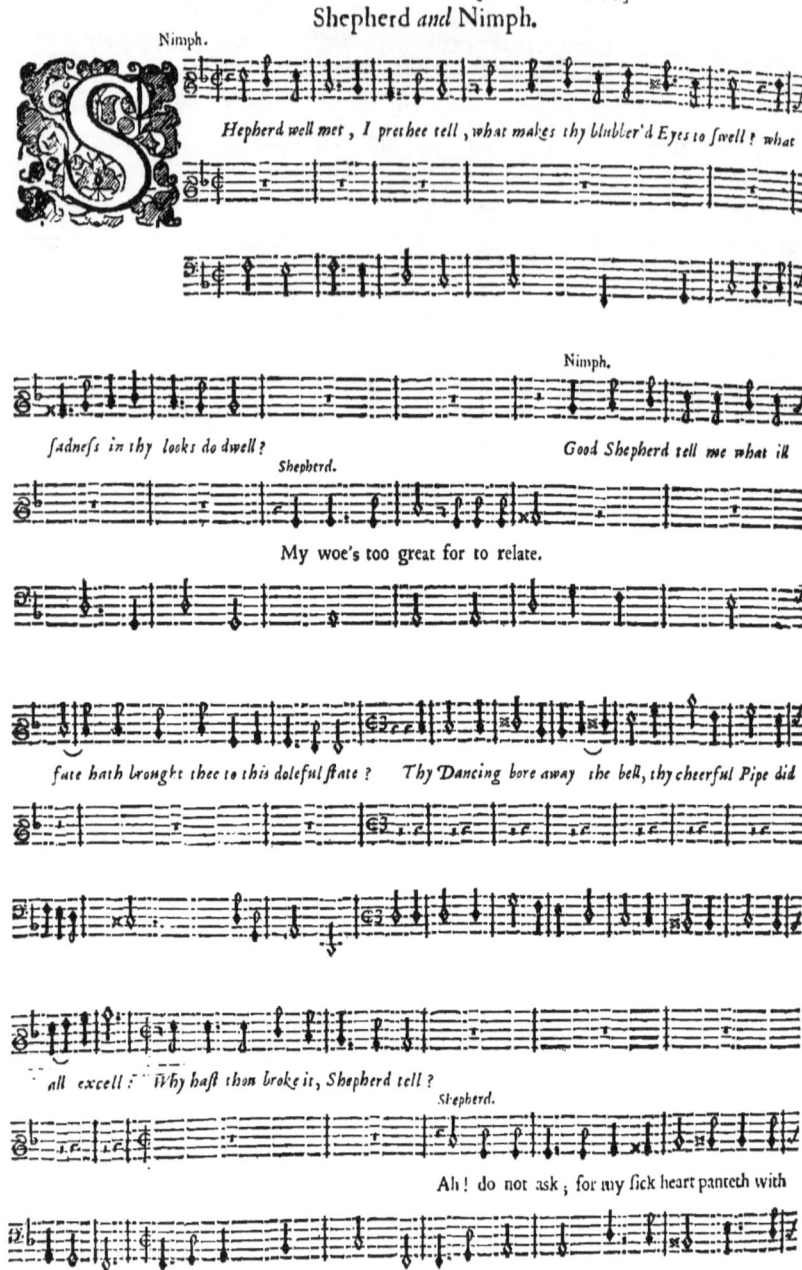

[119]

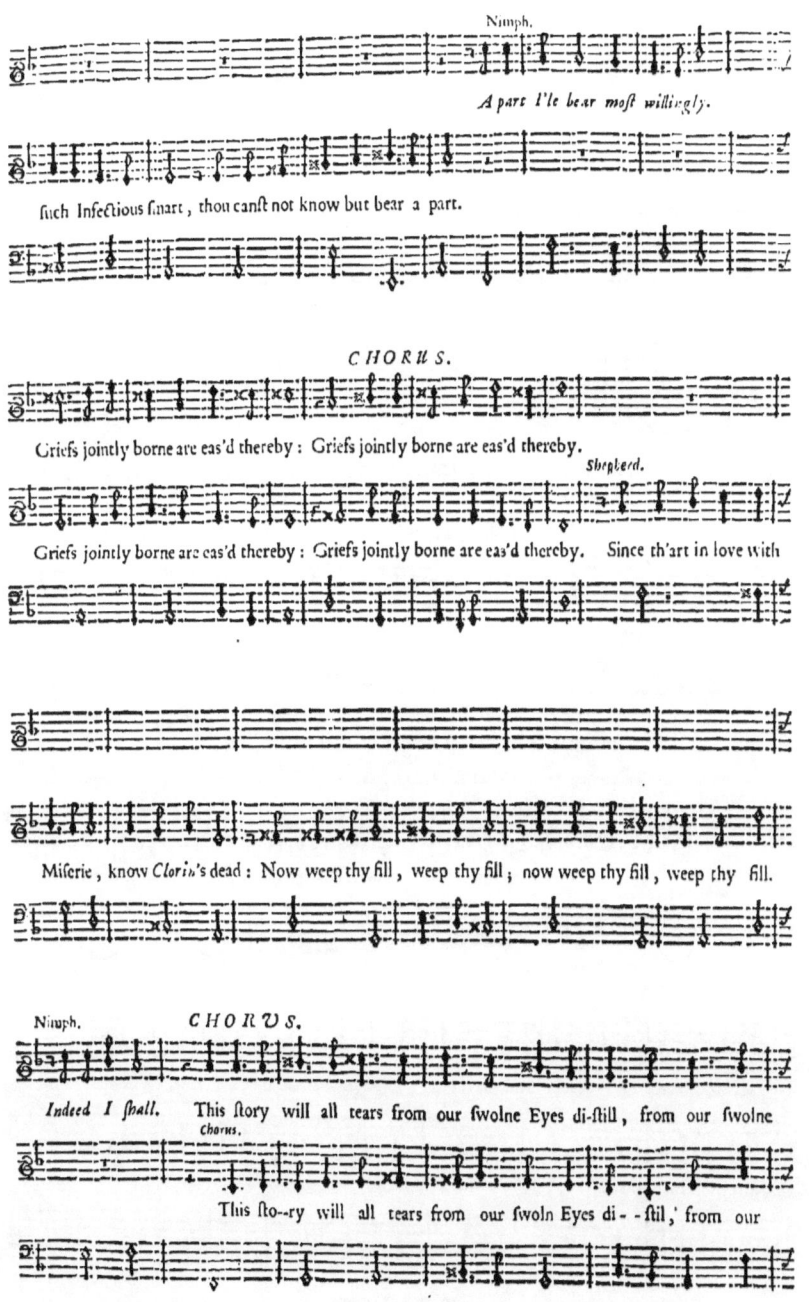

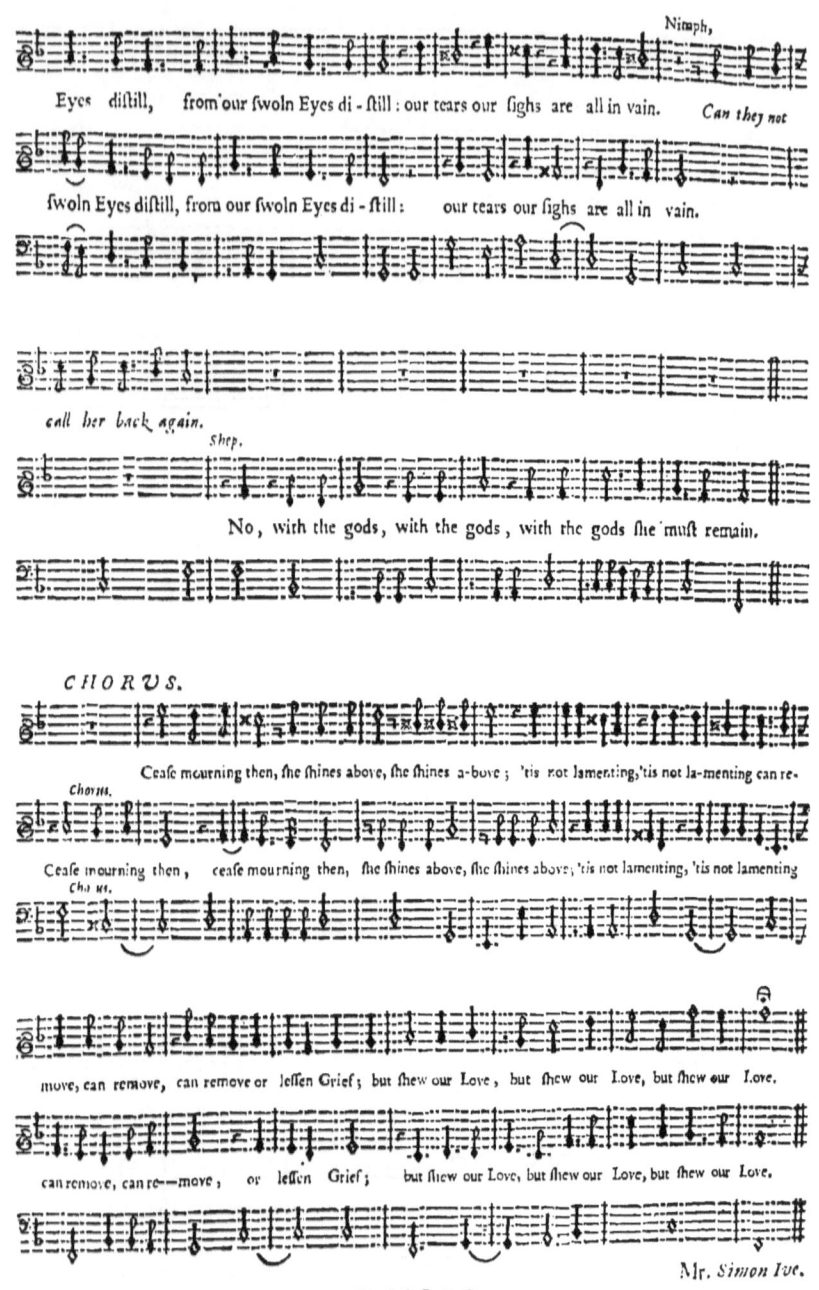

CHOICE
Ayres, Songs, & Dialogues

To SING to the

THEORBO-LUTE, or *BASS-VIOL.*

BEING

Moſt of the Neweſt *Ayres*, and *Songs*, Sung at *COURT*,
And at the Publick *THEATRES.*

Compoſed by ſeveral Gentlemen of His Majeſties Muſick, *and others.*

The SECOND EDITION *Corrected and Enlarged.*

LONDON,
Printed by *W.* Godbid, and are to be ſold by *John* Playford,
near the *Temple* Church, 1675.

CHOICE
Ayres, Songs, & Dialogues

To SING to the

THEORBO-LUTE, or *BASS-VIOL*.

BEING

Moſt of the Neweſt *Ayres*, and *Songs*, Sung at *COURT*,
And at the Publick *THEATRES*.

Compoſed by ſeveral Gentlemen of His Majeſties Muſick, *and others.*

The SECOND EDITION *Corrected and Enlarged.*

LONDON,
Printed by *W. Godbid*, and are to be ſold by *John Playford*,
near the *Temple* Church, 1675.

To the LOVERS of

MUSICK.

Gentlemen & Ladies,

MUSICK is of different effects, and admits of as much variety of Fancy to pleafe all Humours as any Science whatever. It moves the Affections fometimes into a fober Compofure, and other-times into an active Jollity. Thefe *Songs* and *Ayres* are fuch as were lately Compofed, and are very fuitable and acceptable to the *Genius* of thefe *Times*. Many of the Words have been already Publifhed, which gave but little content to divers Ingenious Perfons, who thought them as dead, unlefs they had the *Airy Tunes* to quicken them; to gratifie whom, was a great inducement to me for their Publication. Your kind acceptance and general good liking of the former Impreffion of this Book has both encouraged and obliged me to prefent you with a Second; wherein I have taken care to Correct thofe Errors that before efcaped in the *Mufick* untaken notice of; and have likewife added feveral *Stanza's* of Verfes to the *Songs* that then wanted them; as alfo Thirty five new *Ayres*, *Songs*, and *Dialogues*, never till now Printed; moft of which, (as well as thofe in the firft Edition) were Tranfcribed from the Original Copies of the *Authors*, and by them allowed to be made publick. By your approbation of this, you will engage to the publication of more of this kind,

Your Servant,

J. P.

An Alphabetical Table of the *Songs* and *Dialogues* in this Book.

Those that are added in this Edition have this mark *

A

A Lover I'm born and a Lover I'le be	14
After the pangs of a desperate Lover	4
And I'le go to my Love, where he lies in the deep	10
At the sight of my Phillis	24
Ah Coridon, in vain you boast	16
As I walk'd in the Woods, one evening of late	36
Ah, false Amintas, can that hour	42
Amintas led me to a Grove	50
* Amintas, that true hearted Swain	53
* Ah cruel Eyes that first enflam'd	56
* Away with the silly blind god	ibid.
* Ah Phillis, would the gods decree	62
* Ah fading Joy, how quickly art thou past	70
* Ah, what shall we do when our eyes are surrounded	74

B

Beneath a Myrtle shade	37
Be jolly my Friends, for the Mony we spend	40
Beauty no more shall suffer eclips	49

C

Cheer up my Mates the wind doth fairly blow	2
Calm was the Ev'ning and clear was the Sky	8
Can Luciamira so mistake	18
Come lay by your care, and hang up your sorrow	40
* Come away, to ther Glass, he's a temperate Ass	76

F

Farewel fair Armida, my joy and my grief	9
Fill round the Health good natur'd and free	39
Forth from the dark and dismal cell	75
For my Love sleeps now in a watry Grave	10
* Fye Cloris, 'tis silly to sigh thus in vain	64
* Forgive me Jove	55

G

Give o're foolish heart, and make hast to despair	28
* God Cupid for certain as foolish as blind	45

H

Hark, hark, the Storm grows loud	1
How strangely severe and unjust are we grown	22
How severe is forgetful old age	30
How unhappy a lover am I	32
How pleasant is mutual love, if 'tis true	38
How bonny an I brisk, ah how pleasant and sweet	42
* How oft have I bid defiance in vain	59

I

I pass all my hours in a shady old Grove	11
I'le have no more dealing fond Cupid with thee	21
I languish all night, and sigh all the day	26
* I am no subject unto fate	44
* Insult not too much on thy fading success	45
* I languish for one that ne're thinks of me	57
* If languishing Eyes without language can move	74

L

Let Fortune and Phillis frown if they please	27
Let's Drink dear Friends lets Drink	38
Long betwixt hope and fear, Phillis tormented	50
Lo behind a Sceau of Seas	52
* Long since fair Clorinda my passion did move	62

M

Mine own Sabina come along	15

My Youth I kept free from all sorts of care	25
Me thinks the poor Town has been troubled too long	41

N

Now affairs of the State are already decreed	30
Nay let me alone, I protest I'le be gone	54

O

O Love! if e're thou't ease a heart	1
Of all the brisk Dames, Misselina for me	12
On the bank of a Brook, as I sat Fishing	30
* Oh name not the day, left my senses reprove	4
Oh the time that is past, when she held me so fast	5
* Of all the gay Ladies that walk the brisk town	6
Oh how I abhor the tumult and smoak	6

P

Phillis, for shame let us improve	3
Phillis, the time is come that we must sever	2
* Phillis, Oh turn that face away	4

R

Run to Loves Lottery, ynn Maids and rejoyce	

S

Since we poor slavish Women know our men	1
Some happy soul come down and tell	1
* Since Phillis we find we grow so inclin'd	7

T

Thus Cupid commences his Rapes and Vagaries	
Thus all our life long we frolick and gay	1
Too justly, alass, and yet so much in vain	1
The Nymph that undoes me is fair and unkind	3
* To what modest grief is a Lover confin'd	4
The day you wish'd arriv'd at last	7
* 'Tis the Grape that discovers the passionate Lovers	7

W

When Coridon a slave did lie	
When Aurelia first I courted	1
Whilst Alexis lay prest in her arms	2
What fancies of pleasure doth love all alone	2
Where ever I am, and what ever I do	2
Why Phillis to me so untrue and unkind	3
Why should a foolish Marriage Vow	3
* When Thirsis did the splended Eye	4
* Why, O Cupid, so long hast thou stunn'd me	4
* When a woman that's buxom	5
* What madness it is to give over our drinking	5
When first my free heart was surpriz'd by desire	6
* Were Cælia but as chast as fair	6
* When first I saw fair Cælia's face	6
* Wrong not your lovely eyes my fair	7
* What sighs and groans now fills my breast	7
* When I shall leave this clod of clay	7

Dialogues.

A Heart in Loves Empire	Two Shepherdesses. 6
* O Sorrow, Sorrow,	Nature and Sorrow. 7
* Celadon on Delias Singing	A Pastoral. 8
* When death shall part us	Thirsis and Dorinda. 8
* I charge thee Neptune	Apollo and Neptune 8

The Storm. [1]

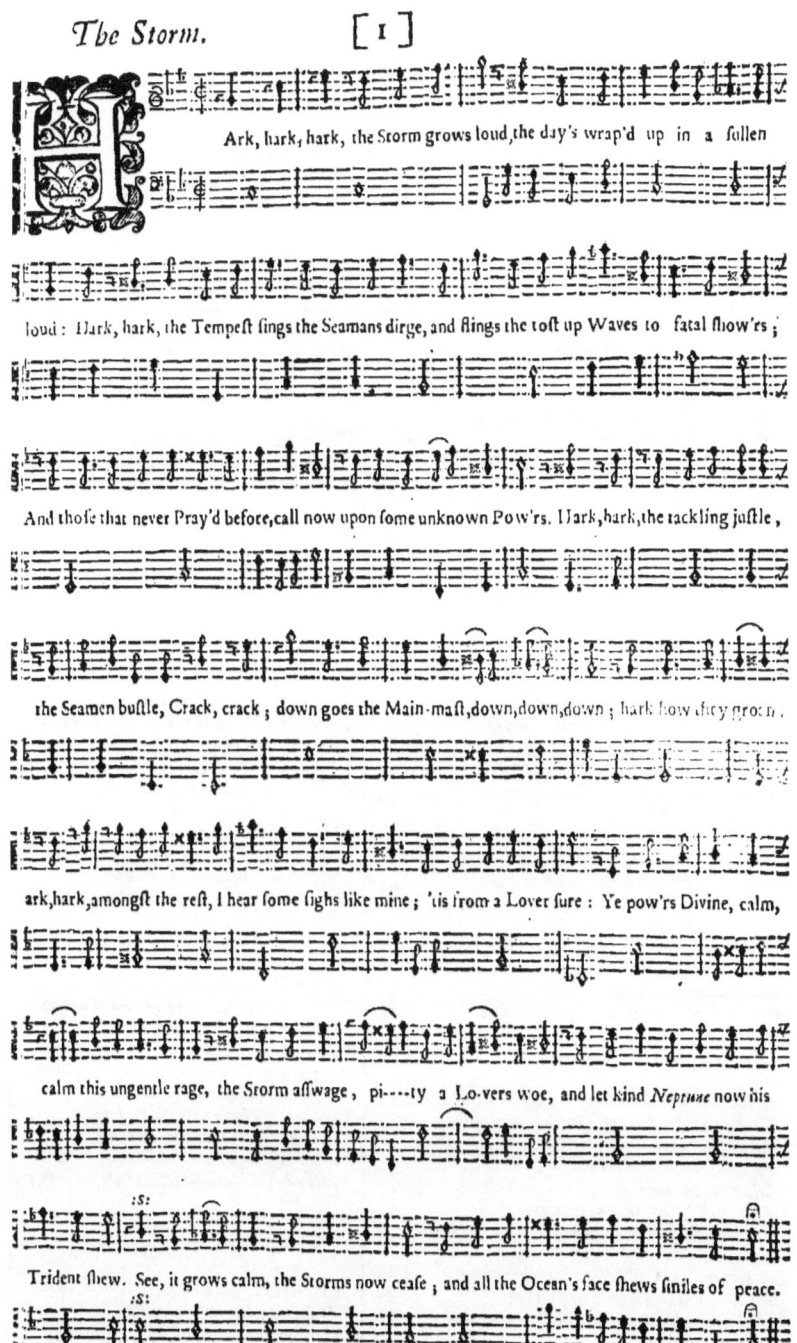

Ark, hark, hark, the Storm grows loud, the day's wrap'd up in a sullen loud : Hark, hark, the Tempest sings the Seamans dirge, and flings the tost up Waves to fatal show'rs ; And those that never Pray'd before, call now upon some unknown Pow'rs. Hark, hark, the tackling justle, the Seamen bustle, Crack, crack ; down goes the Main-mast, down, down, down ; hark how they groan. ark, hark, amongst the rest, I hear some sighs like mine ; 'tis from a Lover sure : Ye pow'rs Divine, calm, calm this ungentle rage, the Storm asswage, pi----ty a Lovers woe, and let kind *Neptune* now his Trident shew. See, it grows calm, the Storms now cease ; and all the Ocean's face shews smiles of peace.

An Alphabetical Table of the *Songs* and *Dialogues* in this B[ook]

Those that are added in this Edition have this mark *

A

A Lover I'm born and a Lover I'le be	14
After the pangs of a desperate Lover	4
And I'le go to my Love, where he lies in the deep	10
At the sight of my Phillis	24
Ah Coridon, in vain you boast	16
As I walk'd in the Woods, one evening of late	36
Ah, false Amintas, can that hour	42
Amintas led me to a Grove	50
* Amintas, that true hearted Swain	53
* Ah cruel Eyes that first enflam'd	56
* Away with the silly blind god	ibid.
* Ah Phillis, would the gods decree	62
* Ah fading Joy, how quickly art thou past	70
* Ah, what shall we do when our eyes are surrounded	74

B

Beneath a Myrtle shade	37
Be jolly my Friends, for the Mony we spend	40
Beauty no more shall suffer eclips	49

C

Cheer up my Mates the wind doth fairly blow	2
Calm was the Ev'ning and clear was the Sky	8
Can Luciamira so mistake	18
Come lay by your care, and hang up your sorrow	40
* Come away, to'ther Glass, he's a temperate Ass	76

F

Farewel fair Armida, my joy and my grief	9
Fill round the Health good natur'd and free	39
Forth from the dark and dismal cell	75
For my Love sleeps now in a watry Grave	10
* Fye Cloris, 'tis silly to sigh thus in vain	64
* Forgive me Jove	55

G

Give o're foolish heart, and make hast to despair	28
* God Cupid for certain as foolish as b'ind	45

H

Hark, hark, the Storm grows loud	1
How strangely severe and unjust are we grown	22
How severe is forgetful old age	30
How unhappy a lover am I	32
How pleasant is mutual love, if 'tis true	38
How bonny and brisk, ah how pleasant and sweet	42
* How oft have I bid defiance in vain	59

I

I pass all my hours in a shady old Grove	11
I'le have no more dealing fond Cupid with thee	21
I languish all night, and sigh all the day	26
* I am no subject unto fate	44
* Insult not too much on thy fading success	45
* I languish for one that ne're thinks of me	57
* If languishing Eyes without language can move	74

L

Let Fortune and Phillis frown if they please	27
Let's Drink dear Friends lets Drink	38
Long betwixt hope and fear, Phillis tormented	50
Lo behind a Scean of Seas	52
* Long since fair Clorinda my passion did move	62

M

Mine own Sabina come along	15
My Youth I kept free from all sorts of care	
Me-thinks the poor Town has been troubled too l[ong]	

N

Now affairs of the State are already decreed	
Nay let me alone, I protest I'le be gone	

O

O Love! if e're thou'lt ease a heart	
Of all the brisk Dames, Misselina for me	
On the bank of a Brook, as I sat Fishing	
Oh name not the day, lest my senses reprove	
Oh the time that is past, when she held me so fast	
* Of all the gay Ladies that walk the brisk tow[n]	
Oh how I abhor the tumult and smoak	

P

Phillis, for shame let us improve	
Phillis, the time is come that we must sever	
* Phillis, Oh turn that face away	

R

Run to Loves Lottery, run Maids and rejoyce	

S

Since we poor slavish Women know our men	
Some happy soul come down and tell	
* Since Phillis we find we grow so inclin'd	

T

Thus Cupid commences his Rapes and Vagari[es]	
Thus all our life long we frolick and gay	
Too justly, alass, and yet so much in vain	
The Nymph that undoes me is fair and unkind	
* To what modest grief is a Lover confin'd	
The day you wish'd arriv'd at last	
* 'Tis the Grape that discovers the passionate L[over]	

W

When Coridon a slave did lie	
When Aurelia first I courted	
Whilst Alexis lay prest in her arms	
What fancies of pleasure doth love all alone	
Where ever I am, and what ever I do	
Why Phillis to me so untrue and unkind	
Why should a foolish Marriage Vow	
* When Thirsis did the splended Eye	
* Why, O Cupid, so long hast thou shunn'd me	
* When a woman that's buxom	
* What madness it is to give our our drinking	
When first my free heart was surpriz'd by desire	
* Were Cælia but as chast as fair	
* When first I saw fair Cælia's face	
* Wrong not your lovely eyes my fair	
* What sighs and groans now fills my breast	
* When I shall leave this clod of clay	

Dialogues

A Heart in Loves Empire	Two Shepherd[s]
* O Sorrow, Sorrow,	Nature and Sorro[w]
* Celadon on Delia Singing	A Pastora[l]
* When death shall part us	Thirsis and Dorin[da]
* I charge thee Neptune	Apollo and Neptu[ne]

The Storm.

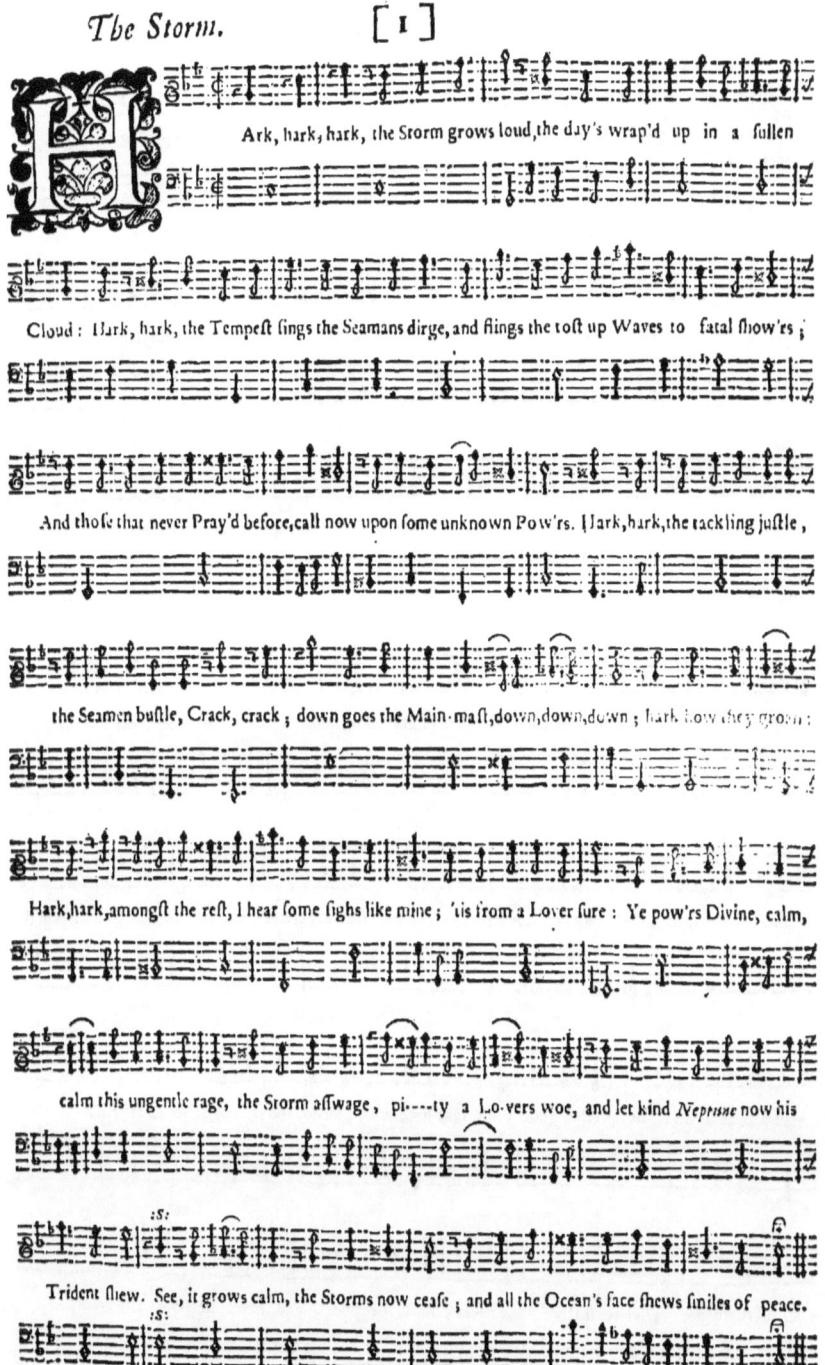

Ark, hark, hark, the Storm grows loud, the day's wrap'd up in a sullen Cloud: Hark, hark, the Tempest sings the Seamans dirge, and flings the tost up Waves to fatal show'rs; And those that never Pray'd before, call now upon some unknown Pow'rs. Hark, hark, the tackling justle, the Seamen bustle, Crack, crack; down goes the Main-mast, down, down, down; hark how they groan: Hark, hark, amongst the rest, I hear some sighs like mine; 'tis from a Lover sure: Ye pow'rs Divine, calm, calm this ungentle rage, the Storm asswage, pi----ty a Lovers woe, and let kind *Neptune* now his Trident shew. See, it grows calm, the Storms now cease; and all the Ocean's face shews smiles of peace.

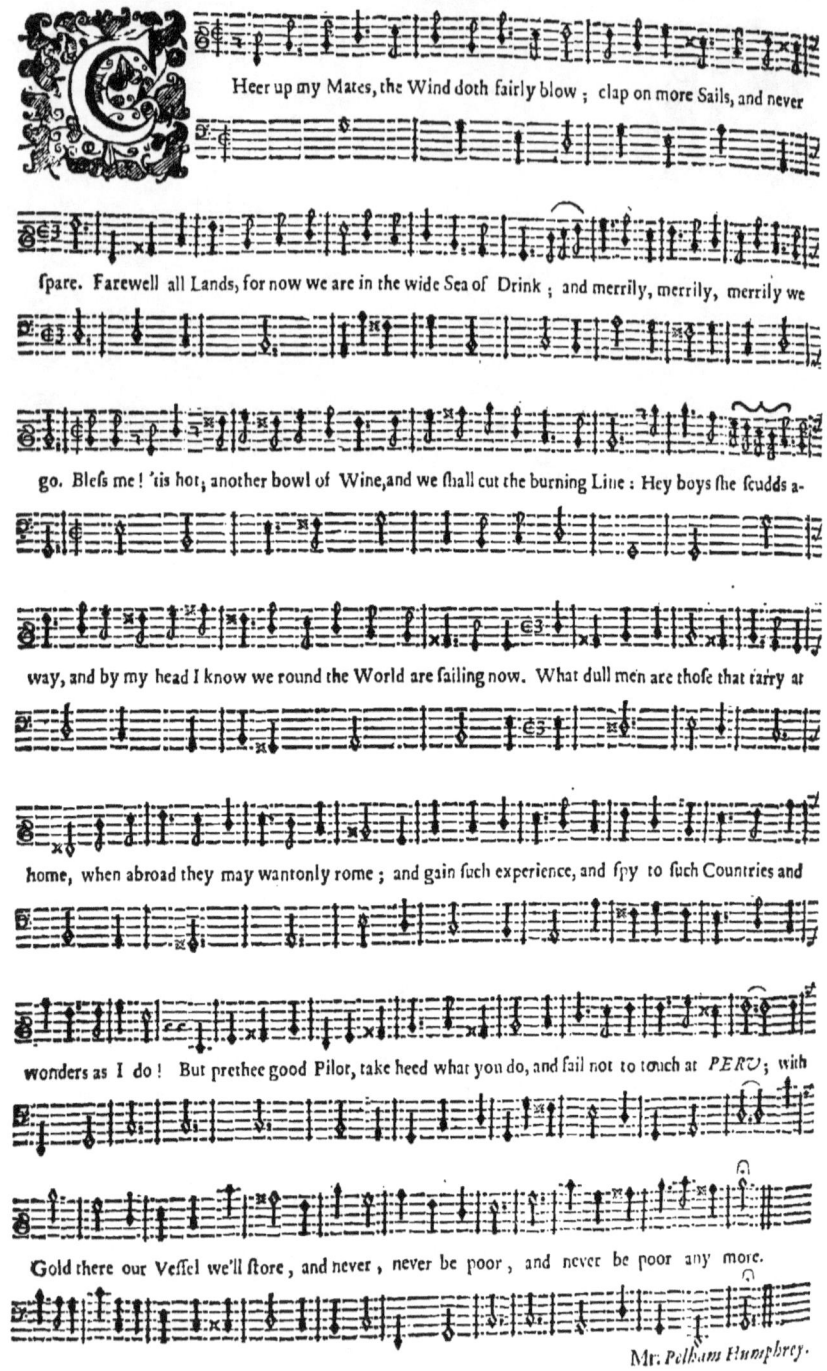

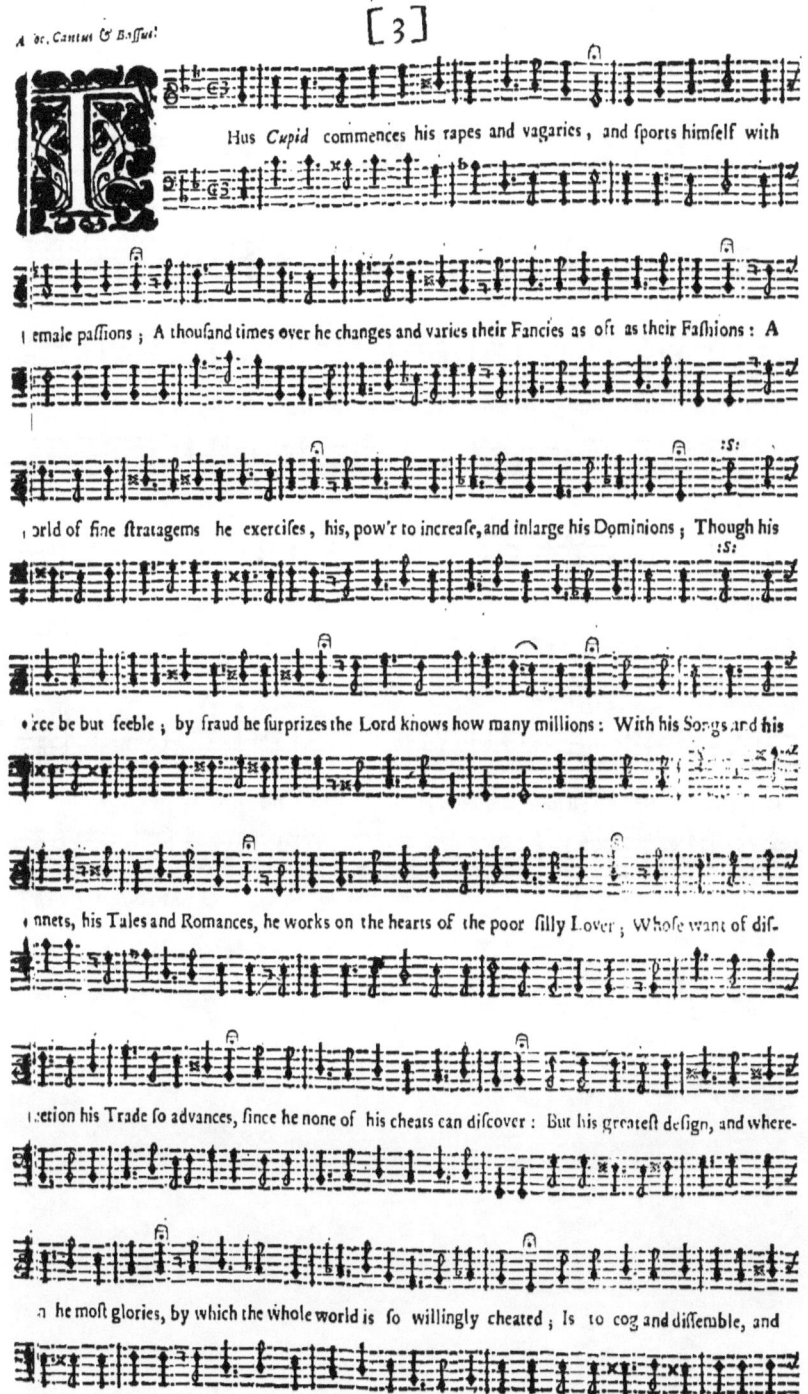

go. Bless me! 'tis hot, another bowl of Wine, and we shall cut the burning Line : Hey boys she scudds a way, and by my head I know we round the World are sailing now. What dull men are those that tarry a home, when abroad they may wantonly rome ; and gain such experience, and spy to such Countries and wonders as I do! But prethee good Pilor, take heed what you do, and fail not to touch at *PERU*; wi Gold there our Vessel we'll store, and never, never be poor, and never be poor any more.

Mr. *Pelham Humphr*

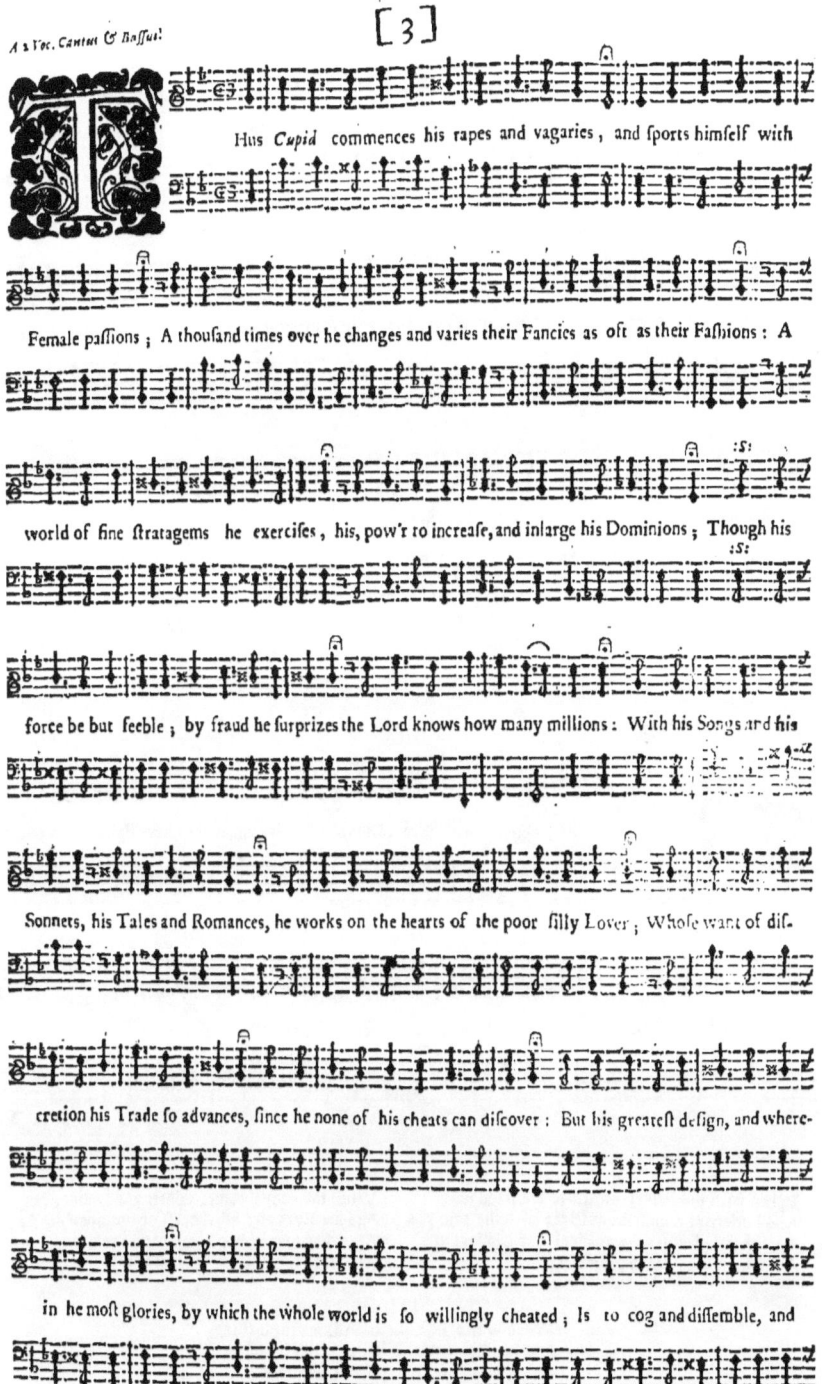

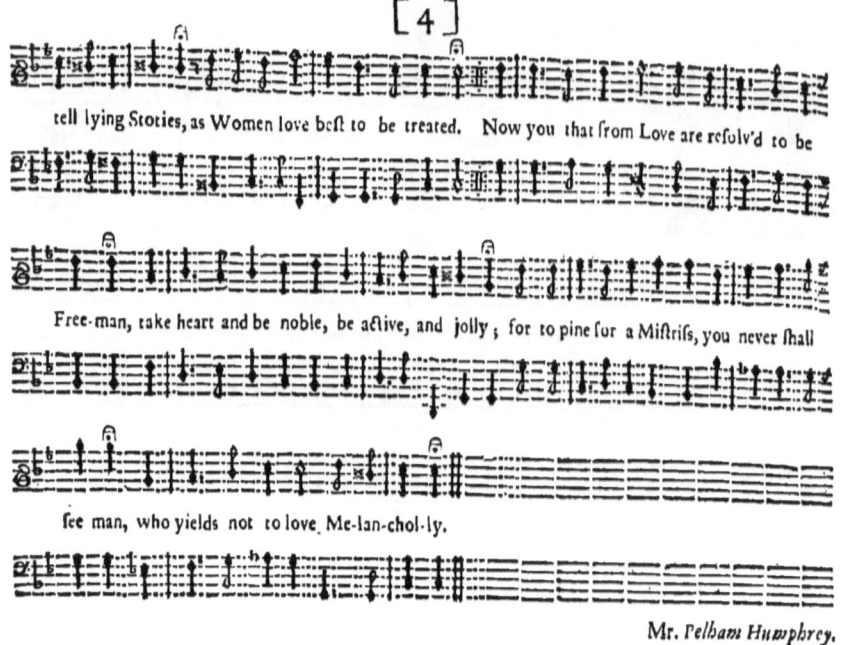

Mr. *Pelham Humphrey*.

A 2 Voc. Cantus & Bassus.

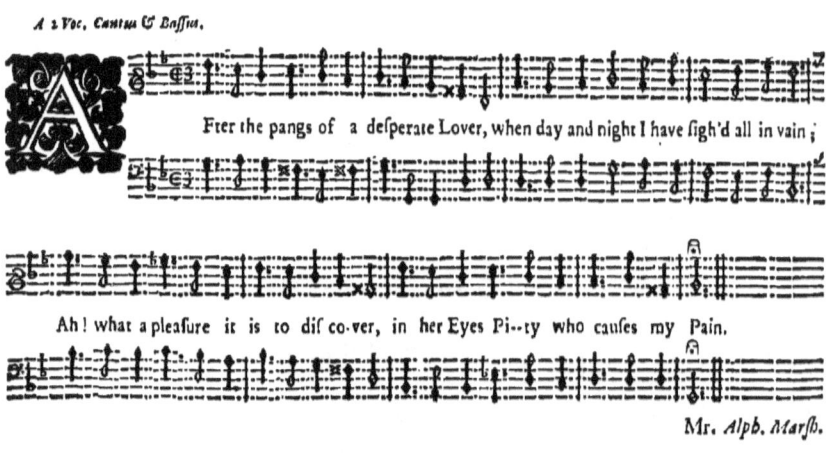

Mr. *Alph. Marsh*.

I.
When with unkindness our Love at a stand is,
And both have punish'd our selves with the pain;
Ah, what a pleasure the touch of her hand is!
Ah, what a pleasure to press it again!

II.
When the denyal comes fainter and fainter,
And her Eyes give what her Tongue does deny;
Ah, what a trembling I feel when I venture!
Ah, what a trembling does usher my Joy!

III.
When with a sigh, she accords me the blessing,
And her Eyes twinkle 'twixt pleasure and pain:
Ah, what a Joy 'tis beyond all expressing!
Ah! what a Joy to hear, Shall we again?

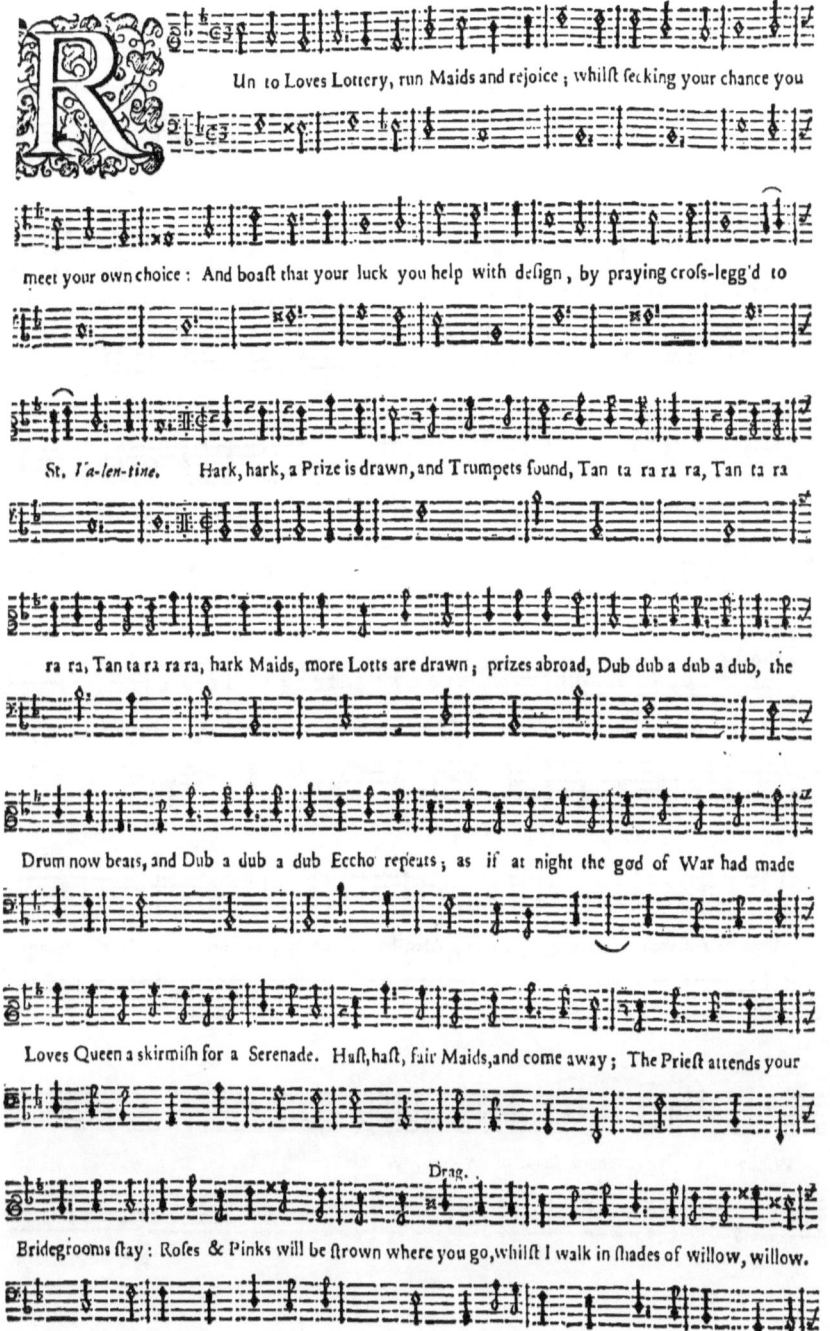

[6]

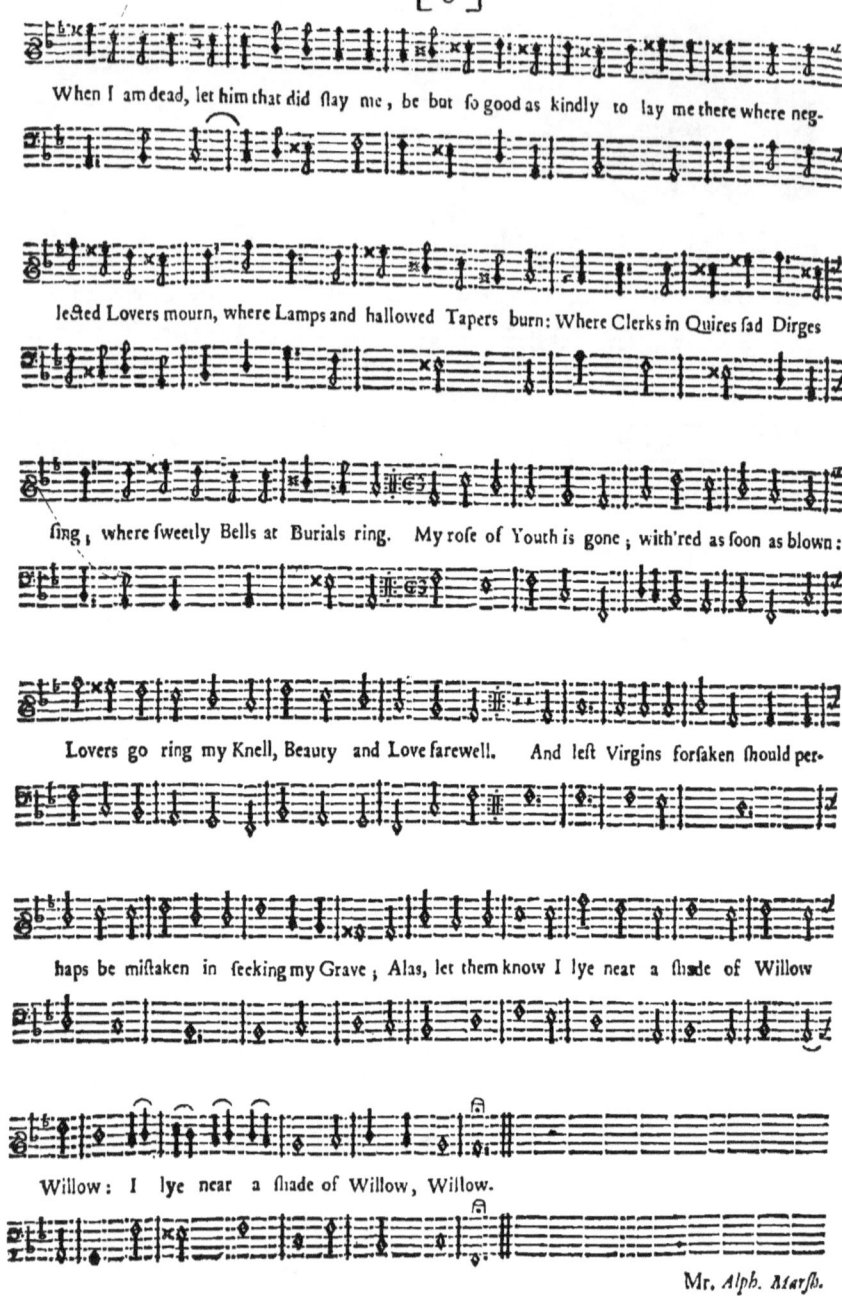

When I am dead, let him that did slay me, be but so good as kindly to lay me there where neg-

lected Lovers mourn, where Lamps and hallowed Tapers burn: Where Clerks in Quires sad Dirges

sing, where sweetly Bells at Burials ring. My rose of Youth is gone; wither'd as soon as blown:

Lovers go ring my Knell, Beauty and Love farewell. And left Virgins forsaken should per-

haps be mistaken in seeking my Grave; Alas, let them know I lye near a shade of Willow

Willow: I lye near a shade of Willow, Willow.

Mr. *Alph. Marsh.*

[7]

hen Co-ri-don, a slave, did lye entangled in his Phillis Eye, how did he sigh, how did he groan, how melancholly was his tone! He told his story to the Woods; and wept his passion by the Floods: Yet Phillis, cruel Phillis, too to blame, regarded not his suff'rings, nor his Flame. Then Co-ri-don re---solv'd no more his Mi-stress mer---cy to im-plore; How did he laugh, how did he sing, how did he make the Forrest ring! He told his Conquest to the Woods; And drown his passion in the Floods: Then Phillis, cru-el

Mr. Alph. Marsh.

II.
He blush'd to himself, and laid still for a while,
   His modesty curb'd his desire;
But strait I convinc'd all his fears with a smile,
   And added new flames to his fire:
Ah, *Silvia*! said he, you are cruel,
   To keep your poor Lover in awe;
Then once more he prest with his hand to my breast,
   But was dash'd with a Ha ha ha ha ha, &c.

III.
I knew 'twas his Passion that caused his fear,
   And therefore I pitty'd his case;
I whisper'd him softly, there's no body near,
   And laid my Cheek close to his Face:
But as we grew bolder and bolder,
   A Shepherd came by us and saw:
And strait as our bliss, we began with a kiss,
   He laught out with a Ha ha ha ha ha, &c.

Arewel fair Ar--mi--da, my Joy and my Grief, in vain I have
.ov'd you, and hope no relief: Undone by your Virtue too strict and se-vere; Your Eyes gave me
Love, and you gave me despair. Now call'd by my Honour, I seek with content, the Fate which in
pi--ty you would not prevent: To Languish in Love, were to find by de---lay a
Death that's more welcome the speedier way.

Mr. *Robert Smith.*

II.

On Seas and in Battles, 'mongst Bullets and Fire,
The danger is less than in hopeless desire:
My Deaths wound you gave me though far off I bear,
My Fate from your sight not to cost you a Tear.
But if the kind Floods on a Wave would convey,
And under your Window my Body should lay:
The Wound on my Breast, when you happen to see,
You'l say with a sigh, it was given by me.

D

Mr. *Alph. M*[...]

II.

He blush'd to himself, and laid still for a while,
    His modesty curb'd his desire;
But strait I convinc'd all his fears with a smile,
    And added new flames to his fire:
Ah, *Silvia*! said he, you are cruel,
    To keep your poor Lover in awe;
Then once more he prest with his hand to my breast,
    But was dash'd with a Ha ha ha ha ha, *&c.*

III.

I knew 'twas his Passion that caused his fear,
    And therefore I pitty'd his case;
I whisper'd him softly, there's no body near,
    And laid my Cheek close to his Face:
But as we grew bolder and bolder,
    A Shepherd came by us and saw:
And strait as our bliss, we began with a kiss,
    He laught out with a Ha ha ha ha ha, *&c.*

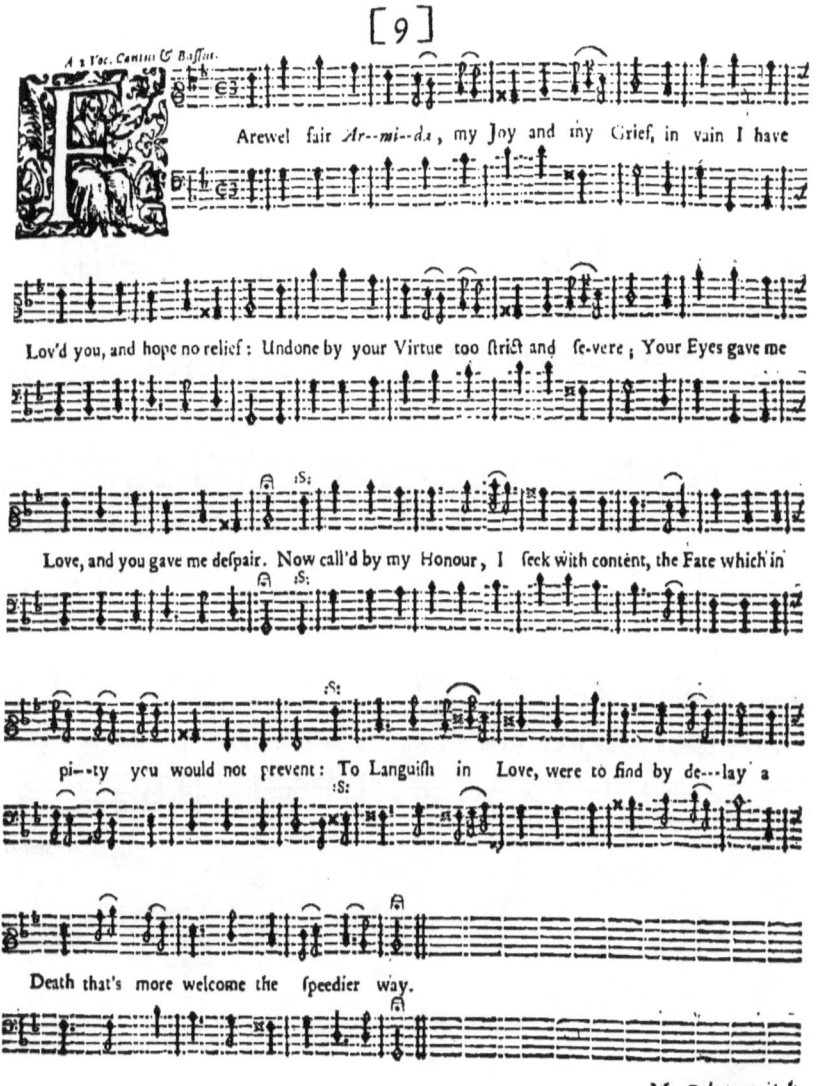

Farewel fair *Armida*, my Joy and my Grief, in vain I have Lov'd you, and hope no relief: Undone by your Virtue too strict and severe; Your Eyes gave me Love, and you gave me despair. Now call'd by my Honour, I seek with content, the Fate which in pity you would not prevent: To Languish in Love, were to find by delay a Death that's more welcome the speedier way.

Mr. *Robert Smith.*

II.
On Seas and in Battles, 'mongst Bullets and Fire,
The danger is less than in hopeless desire:
My Deaths wound you gave me though far off I bear,
My Fate from your sight not to cost you a Tear.
But if the kind Floods on a Wave would convey,
And under your Window my Body should lay:
The Wound on my Breast, when you happen to see,
You'l say with a sigh, it was given by me.

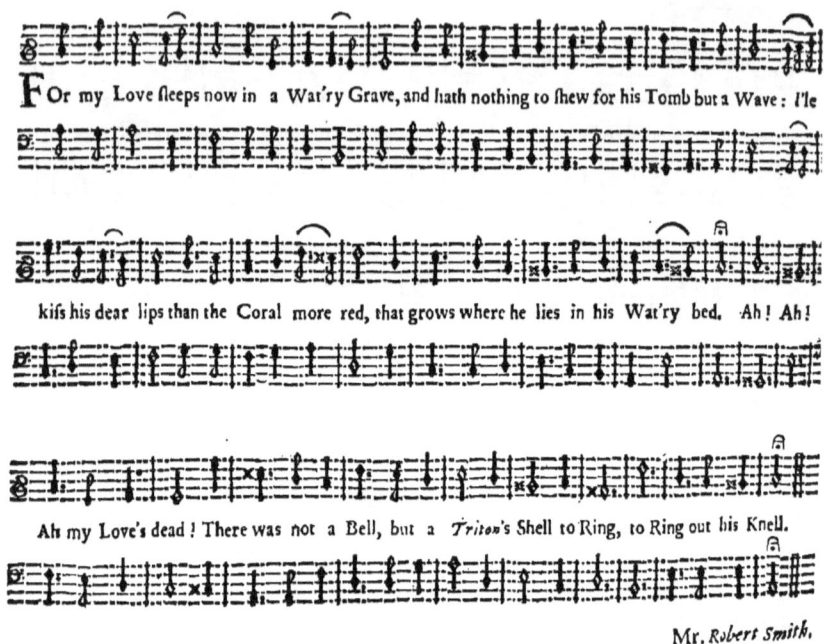

Mr. *Robert Smith.*

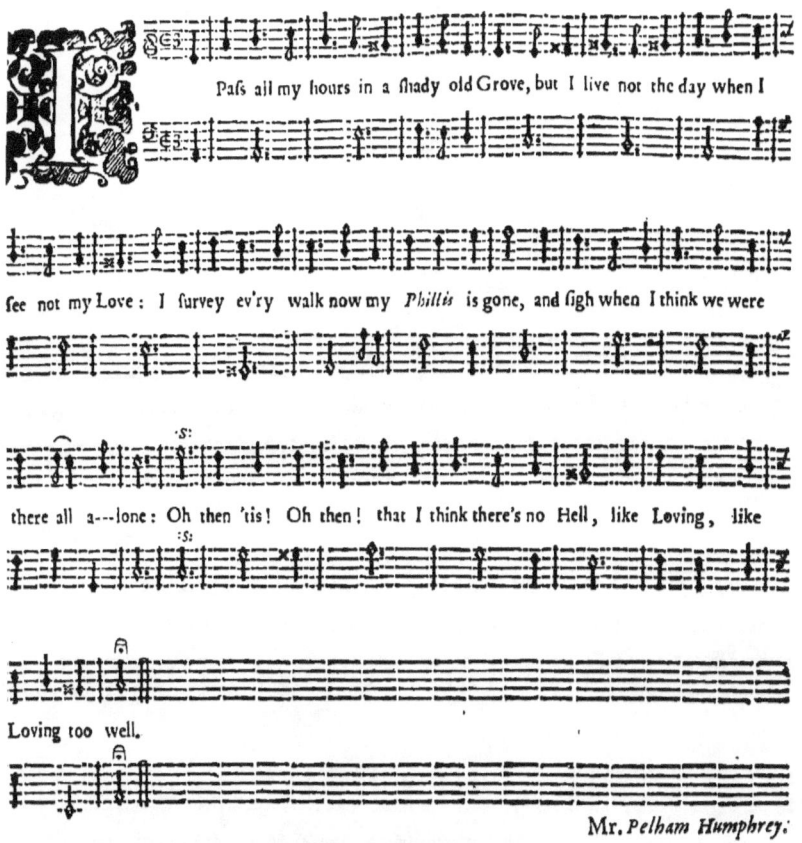

I Pass all my hours in a shady old Grove, but I live not the day when I see not my Love: I survey ev'ry walk now my *Phillis* is gone, and sigh when I think we were there all a---lone: Oh then 'tis! Oh then! that I think there's no Hell, like Loving, like Loving too well.

Mr. *Pelham Humphrey.*

II. But each Shade and each conscious Bow'r, when I find
Where I once have been happy, and She has been kind:
When I see the print left of her shape in the Green,
And imagin the pleasure may yet come agen:
    Oh then 'tis! Oh then 'tis, I think no Joys above
    Like the pleasures, the pleasures of Love.

III. While alone to my self I repeat all her Charms,
She I love may be lockt in another mans arms;
She may laugh at my Cares, and so false she may be,
To say all the kind things she before said to me:
    Oh then 'tis! Oh then 'tis, that I think there's no Hell
    Like Loving, like Loving too well.

IV. But when I consider the truth of her heart,
Such an innocent Passion, so kind without Art;
I fear I have wrong'd her, and hope she may be
So full of true love to be Jealous of me:
    And then 'tis, and then 'tis I think no Joys above
    Like the pleasures, the pleasures of Love.

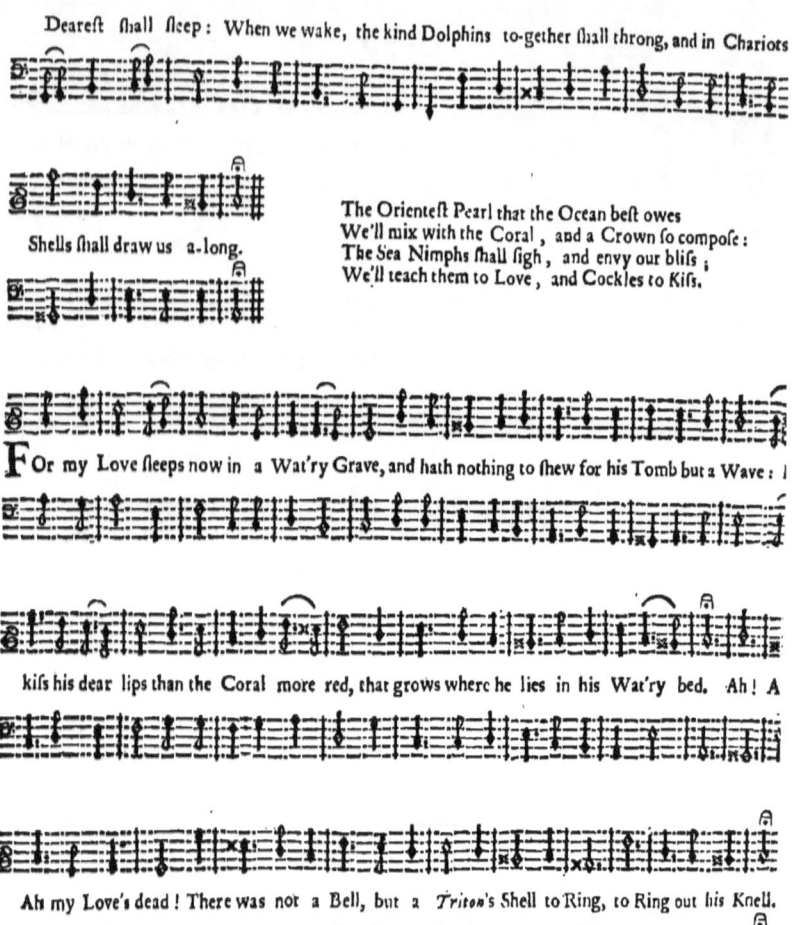

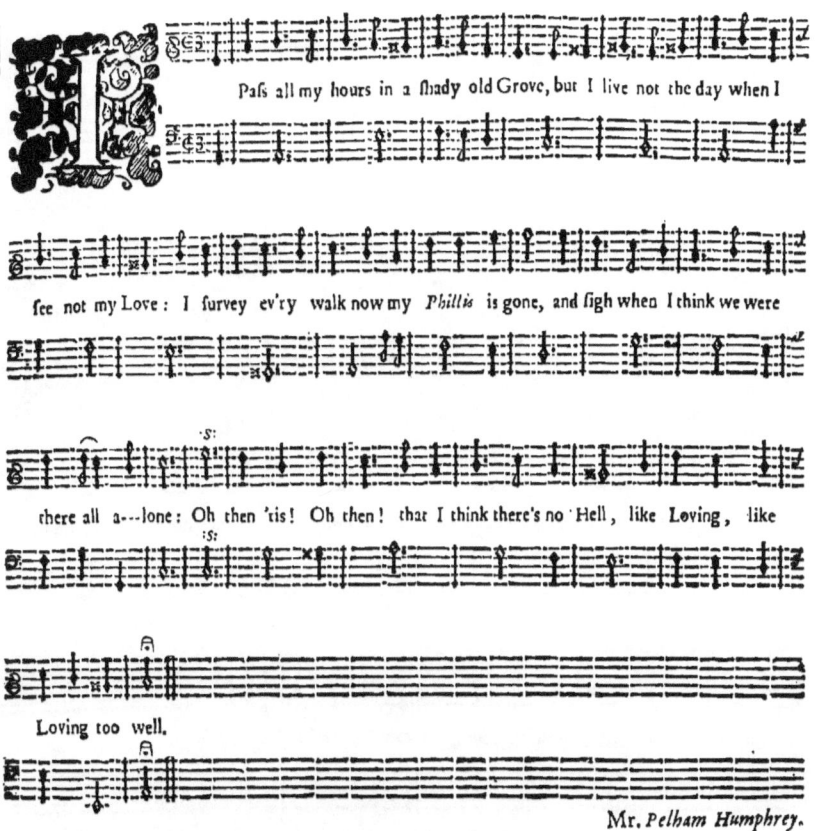

I Pass all my hours in a shady old Grove, but I live not the day when I see not my Love: I survey ev'ry walk now my *Phillis* is gone, and sigh when I think we were there all a---lone: Oh then 'tis! Oh then! that I think there's no Hell, like Loving, like Loving too well.

Mr. *Pelham Humphrey.*

II. But each Shade and each conscious Bow'r, when I find
Where I once have been happy, and She has been kind:
When I see the print left of her shape in the Green,
And imagin the pleasure may yet come agen:
   Oh then 'tis! Oh then 'tis, I think no Joys above
   Like the pleasures, the pleasures of Love.

III. While alone to my self I repeat all her Charms,
She I love may be lockt in another mans arms;
She may laugh at my Cares, and so false she may be,
To say all the kind things she before said to me:
   Oh then 'tis! Oh then 'tis, that I think there's no Hell
   Like Loving, like Loving too well.

IV. But when I consider the truth of her heart,
Such an innocent Passion, so kind without Art;
I fear I have wrong'd her, and hope she may be
So full of true love to be Jealous of me:
   And then 'tis, and then 'tis I think no Joys above
   Like the pleasures, the pleasures of Love.

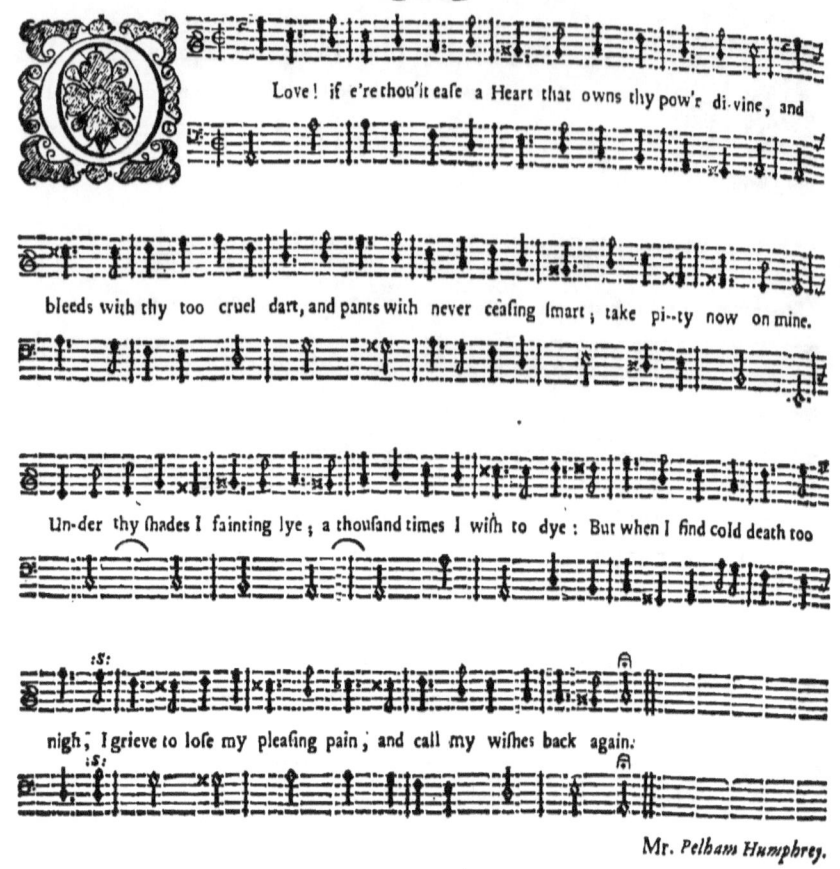

Mr. *Pelham Humphrey.*

II.
But thus, as I sat all alone
In th' shady Mirtle Grove,
When to each gentle Sigh and Moan,
Some neighb'ring Eccho gave a Groan,
 Came by the Man I lov'd:
Oh, how I strove my Grief to hide!
I Panted, Blush'd, and almost Dy'd,
And did each tatling Eccho chide,
 For fear some breath of moving Air
Should to his Ears my sorrows bear.

III.
And, oh ye Pow'rs! I'de dye to gain
 But one poor parting Kiss;
And yet I'le suffer wracks of pain,
E're I'de one thought or wish retain
 That Honour thinks amiss:
Thus are poor Maids unkindly us'd,
By Love and Nature both abus'd;
Our tender Hearts all ease refus'd:
 And when we burn with secret flame,
Most bear the grief, or dye with shame.

Hus all our lives long we're frolick and gay; and instead of Court Revels, we mer-ri-ly play at Trap and at Kettles, at Barly-break run, at Goff and at Stool-ball; and when we have done these in-no-cent Sports, we laugh and lie down, and to each pretty Lass we give a green Gown.

Mr. *John Banister*.

II.
We teach our little Dogs to fetch and to carry,
The Partridge, Hare, the Phesant our Quarry;
The nimble Squirrels with cudgel we chase,
And the little pretty Lark betray with a glass.
   And when we have done, &c.

III.
About the May-pole we dance all a round,
And with Garlands of Pinks and Roses are crown'd;
Our little kind tribute we merrily pay
To the gay Lad, and the bright Lady o'th' May.
   And when we have done, &c.

IV.
With our delicate Nimphs we kiss and we toy,
What others but dream of we daily enjoy;
With our Sweet-hearts we dally so long till we find
Their pretty Eyes say their Hearts are gown kind:
   And when we have done we laugh and lye down,
   And to each pretty Lass we give a green Gown.

II.

But thus, as I fat all alone
  In th' fhady Mirtle Grove,
When to each gentle Sigh and Moan,
Some neighb'ring Eccho gave a Groan,
  Came by the Man I lov'd:
Oh, how I ftrove my Grief to hide!
I Panted, Blufh'd, and almoft Dy'd,
And did each tatling Eccho chide,
    For fear fome breath of moving Air
    Should to his Ears my forrows bear.

III.

And, oh ye Pow'rs! I'de dye to gain
  But one poor parting Kifs;
And yet I'le fuffer wracks of pain,
E're I'de one thought or wifh retain
  That Honour thinks amifs:
Thus are poor Maids unkindly us'd,
By Love and Nature both abus'd;
Our tender Hearts all eafe refus'd:
    And when we burn with fecret flame,
    Moft bear the grief, or dye with fhame.

[musical notation]

Thus all our lives long we're frolick and gay; and instead of Court Revels, we merrily play at Trap and at Kettles, at Barly-break run, at Goff and at Stool-ball; and when we have done these in-no-cent Sports, we laugh and lie down, and to each pretty Lass we give a green Gown.

Mr. *John Banister.*

II.
We teach our little Dogs to fetch and to carry,
The Partridge, Hare, the Phesant our Quarry;
The nimble Squirrels with cudgel we chase,
And the little pretty Lark betray with a glass
    And when we have done, &c.

III.
About the May-pole we dance all a round,
And with Garlands of Pinks and Roses are crown'd;
Our little kind tribute we merrily pay
To the gay Lad, and the bright Lady o'th' May.
    And when we have done, &c.

IV.
With our delicate Nimphs we kiss and we toy,
What others but dream of we daily enjoy;
With our Sweet-hearts we dally so long till we find
Their pretty Eyes say their Hearts are gown kind:
    And when we have done we laugh and lye down,
    And to each pretty Lass we give a green Gown.

E

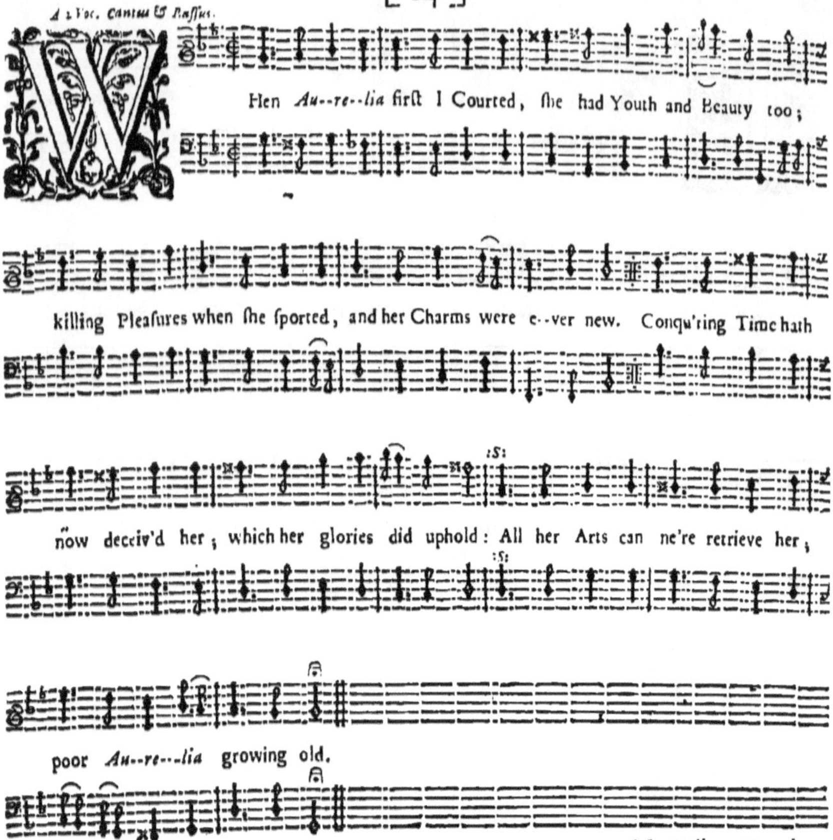

[14]

A 2 Voc. Cantus & Bassus.

WHEN *Au--re--lia* first I Courted, she had Youth and Beauty too; killing Pleasures when she sported, and her Charms were e--ver new. Conqu'ring Time hath now deceiv'd her; which her glories did uphold: All her Arts can ne're retrieve her, poor *Au--re--lia* growing old.

Mr. *Pelham Humphrey*.

Those Airy Spirits which invited,
Are return'd, and now no more;
And her Eyes are now benighted,
Which were Comets heretofore.
Want of these abates her merits;
Yet I have passion for her Name:
Only kind and amorous Spirits,
Kindle, and maintain the Flame.

A Lover I'm Born, and a Lover I'le be; and hope from my Love I shall

[15]

ne--ver be free. Let wisdom abound in the grave Woman-hater; yet ne--ver to love is a sign of ill Nature: But he who loves well, and whose Passion is strong, can ne-ver be wretched, but e--ver be Young.

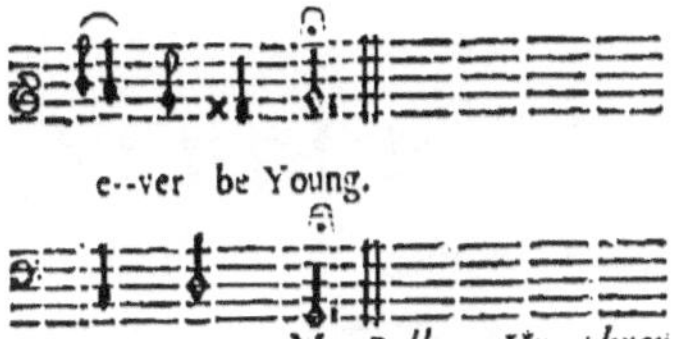

Mr. *Pelham Humphrey.*

II.
With hopes and with fears, like a Ship in the Ocean,
Our Hearts are kept dancing, and ever in motion:
When our Passion is pall'd, and our Fancy would fail,
Some little quarrel supplyes a fresh Gale:
But when the doubt's clear'd, and the jealousies gone,
How we Kiss and Embrace, and can never have done.

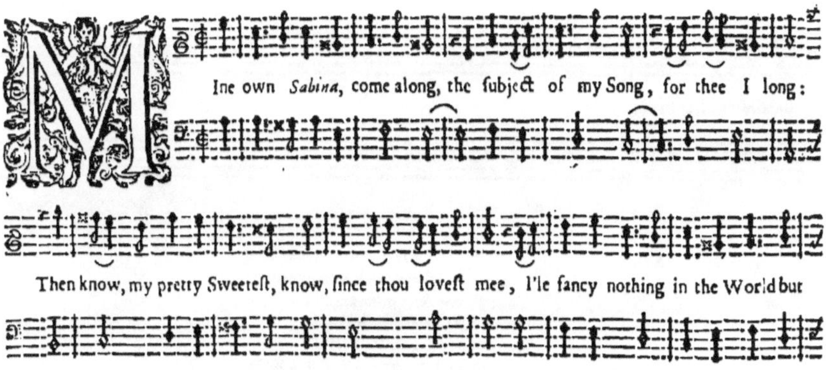

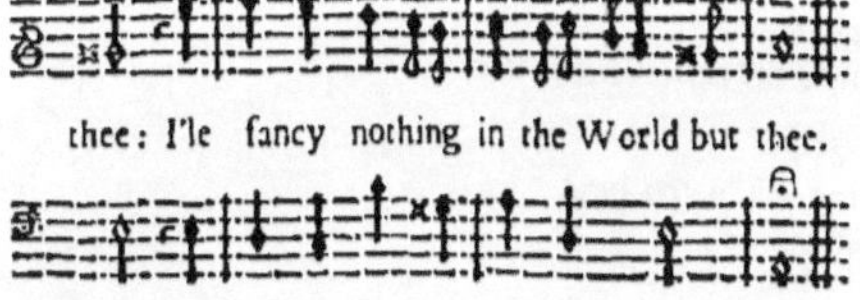

Mine own *Sabina*, come along, the subject of my Song, for thee I long: Then know, my pretty Sweetest, know, since thou lovest mee, I'le fancy nothing in the World but thee: I'le fancy nothing in the World but thee.

II.
Unvail those Damask Cheeks of thine,
Where ev'ry beautious line
is so Divine;
That were I to receive my Death by thy fair Eye,
I'de court it in the pits to buried lye.

III.
Display thine Arms, thy Wealth unfold,
Then like to Jove of old,
in liquid Gold;
And we'll carouse it in Loves bowls to such a bliss,
Our Souls shall mingle, while our Bodies Kiss.

IV.
Thus will we Live, thus will we Love;
When as the gods above
shall envious prove;
And after death, we'll toy as they; 'till that appear,
We'll have *Elizium* here, as they have there.

[16]

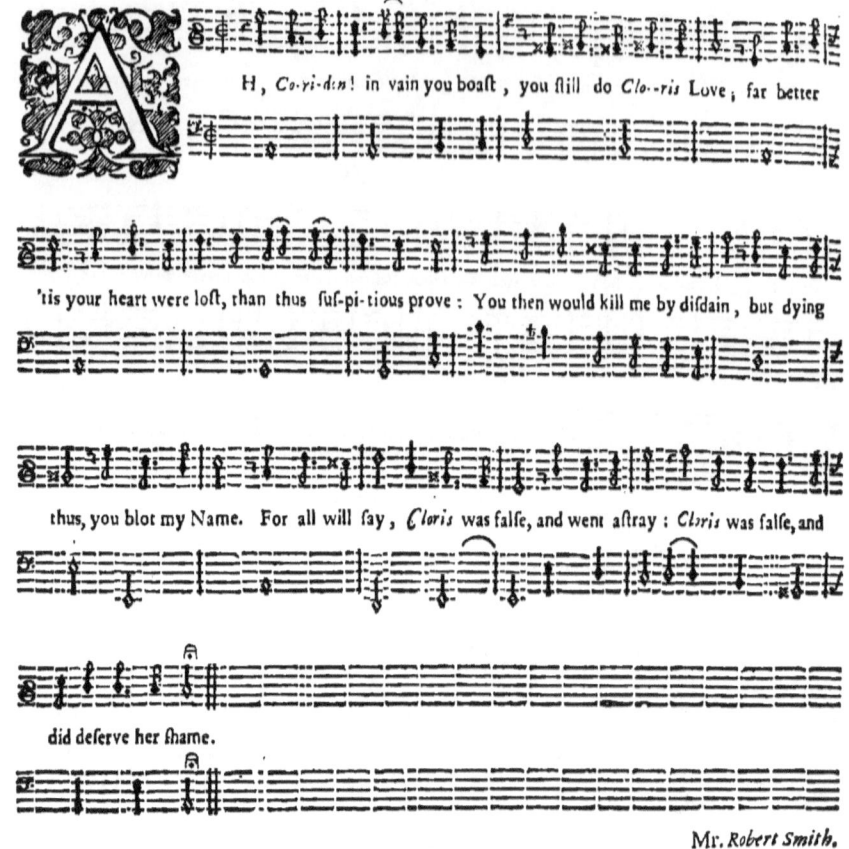

AH, Co-ri-don! in vain you boast, you still do Clo-ris Love, far better 'tis your heart were lost, than thus suf-pi-tious prove: You then would kill me by disdain, but dying thus, you blot my Name. For all will say, Cloris was false, and went astray: Cloris was false, and did deserve her shame.

Mr. *Robert Smith*.

II.
For happy Shepherd, well you know
Your Flame does mine excell;
All generous *Coridon* doth know,
But none my Tale will tell:
Cloris, though true, must lose her name;
But *Coridon* will keep his fame:
For all will say, *Cloris* was false,
And went astray:
Cloris was false, and did deserve her shame.

III.
But cruel Shepherd, when you hear
That I am dead indeed;
I do believe you'll shed one Tear,
Though now you have decreed,
That *Cloris* true, must lose her Name,
For *Coridon* to keep his Fame.
For then you'll say, *Cloris* was true,
And ne're did stray:
Cloris was true, and I deserve the shame.

Too justly, alas! and yet so much in vain, of a fate too severe, may the Lover complain; whose soul is di-vi-ded, and tort'red like mine, when his Duty forbids what his Love does injoyn. Then patience in vain, doth a passion withstand; for we cannot obey, when we cannot command.

Mr. *James Hart.*

II.
Sure Nature design'd us a blesseder state;
There's no other Creature but chuses a Mate:
And the Turtles in pairs, through an Amorous grove,
Do Love where they like, and injoy where they Love.
  What Tyrants are those who do seek to destroy
  The liberty we do by Nature enjoy.

III.
Yet since 'tis a blessing the Gods have ordain'd,
That our wills should be free, though our pow'r be restrain'd:
We'll Love while we live, for the constant at last
Do the perfectest Joys of *Elixium* taste:
  O there, O there, we may Love out our fill,
  When to do and enjoy is the same as to will.

F

[18]

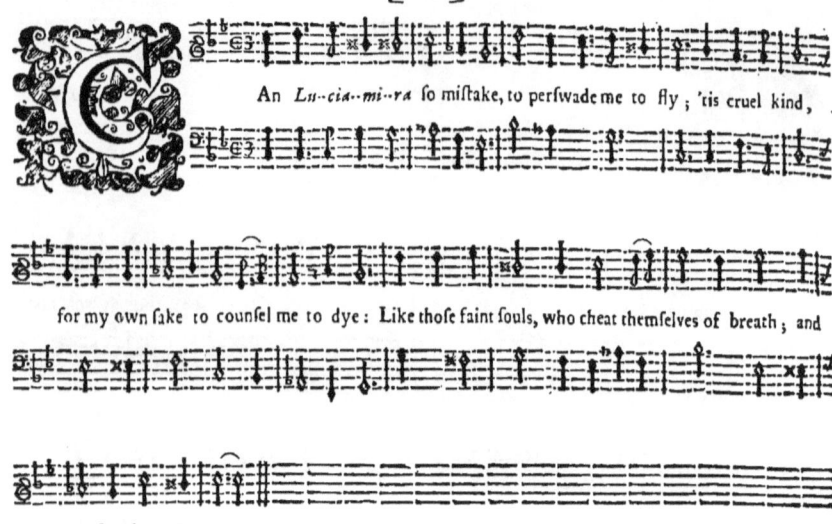

An Lu-cia-mi-ra so mistake, to perswade me to fly; 'tis cruel kind, for my own sake to counsel me to dye: Like those faint souls, who cheat themselves of breath; and dye, for fear of death.

Mr. *John Banister.*

II.
Since Love's the principle of Life,
And you the object Lov'd;
Let's, *Luciamira,* end this strife,
I cease to be remov'd:
We know not what they do are gone from hence;
But here we Love by sense.

III.
If the Platonicks, who would prove
Souls without Bodies Love;
Had with respect, well understood
The Passions of the Blood:
They'd suffer Mortals to have had their part;
And seated Love i'th' Heart.

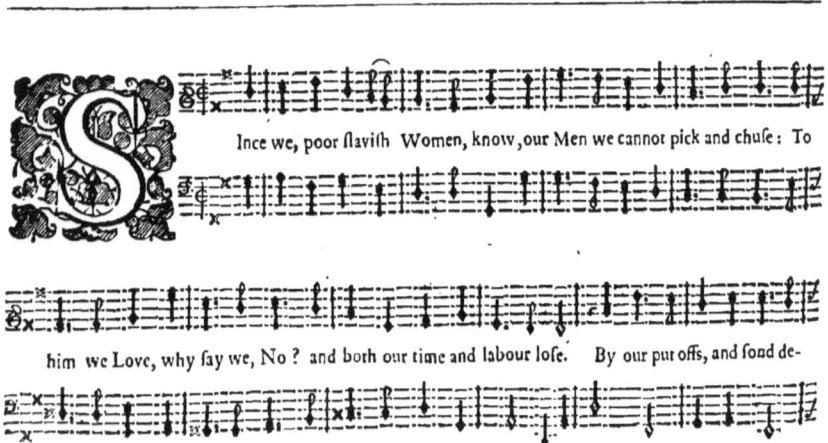

Since we, poor slavish Women, know, our Men we cannot pick and chuse: To him we Love, why say we, No? and both our time and labour lose. By our put offs, and fond de-

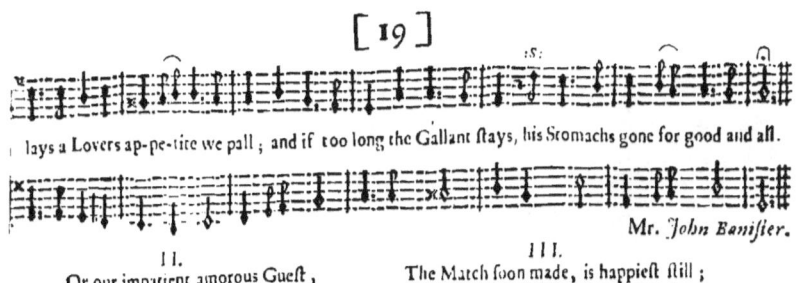

lays a Lovers ap-pe-tite we pall; and if too long the Gallant stays, his Stomachs gone for good and all.

Mr. *John Banister.*

II.
Or our impatient amorous Guest,
Unknown to us, away may steal;
And rather than stay for a feast,
Take up with some course ready meal.
When opportunity is kind,
Let prudent Women be so to;
And if the Man be to her mind,
Be sure she do not let him go.

III.
The Match soon made, is happiest still;
For Love has only there to do:
Let no one Marry 'gainst her will,
But stand off, when her Parents woo:
And to the Suitor be not coy;
For they whom Joynture can obtain,
To let a Fop her Bed enjoy,
Is but a lawful Wench for gain.

Some happy soul come down and tell what Joys are those with you do dwell: If it be happiness like ours below, which from our want of ills does only flow: Then, then 'tis plain, that mighty theam of Im--mor--ta--li--ty is but a Dream.

Mr. *Robert Smith.*

II.
'Tis Love, 'tis Love! For nothing can
Give real happiness to man:
But Joys like those Lovers souls enjoy,
Which here on Earth there's nothing can destroy.
 Ay, ay, 'tis Love can only be
 The happy souls felicitie.

III.
Are your delights in what you see,
Of wonderful varietie?
Or can your Joys arise from pleasant things;
Your taft, or smelling, to your fancy brings?
 No, no, 'tis plain, if it were so,
 Eternity by gradual steps must go.

[18]

An Luciamira so mistake, to perswade me to fly; 'tis cruel kin-

for my own sake to counsel me to dye: Like those faint souls, who cheat themselves of breath,

dye, for fear of death.

Mr. *John Ba*

II.
Since Love's the principle of Life,
And you the object Lov'd,
Let's, *Luciamira*, end this strife,
I cease to be remov'd :
We know not what they do are gone from hence,
But here we Love by sense.

III.
If the Platonicks, who would prove
Souls without Bodies Love,
Had with respect, well understood
The Passions of the Blood:
They'd suffer Mortals to have had their part
And seated Love i'th' Heart.

Since we, poor slavish Women, know, our Men we cannot pick and chuse

him we Love, why say we, No ? and both our time and labour lose. By our put offs, and fond

lays a Lovers ap-pe-tite we pall; and if too long the Gallant stays, his Stomachs gone for good and all.

Mr. *John Bamster*.

II.
Or our impatient amorous Guest,
Unknown to us, away may steal;
And rather than stay for a feast,
Take up with some course ready meal.
When opportunity is kind,
Let prudent Women be so to;
And if the Man be to her mind,
Be sure she do not let him go.

III.
The Match soon made, is happiest still;
For Love has only there to do:
Let no one Marry 'gainst her will,
But stand off, when her Parents woo:
And to the Sutor be not coy;
For they whom Joynture can obtain,
To let a Fop her Bed enjoy,
Is but a lawful Wench for gain.

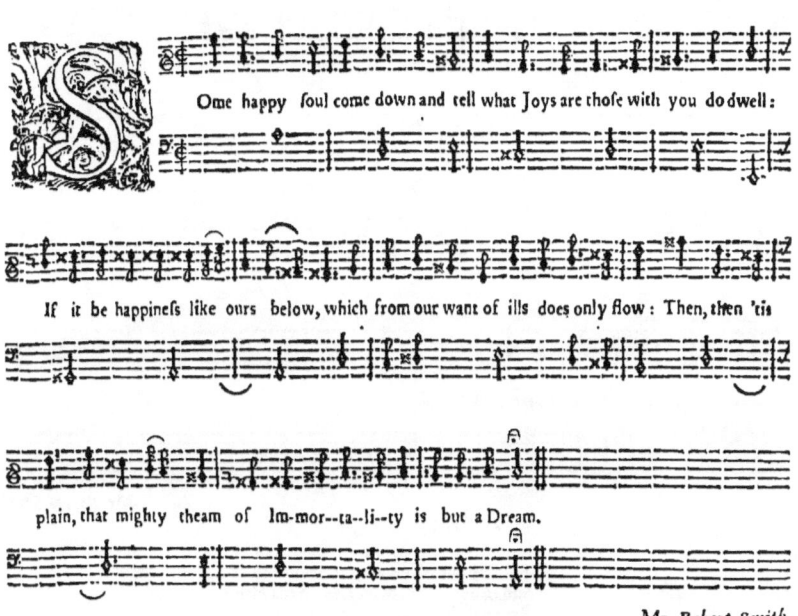

Some happy soul come down and tell what Joys are those with you do dwell: If it be happiness like ours below, which from our want of ills does only flow: Then, then 'tis plain, that mighty theam of Im-mor-ta-li-ty is but a Dream.

Mr. *Robert Smith*.

II.
'Tis Love, 'tis Love! For nothing can
Give real happiness to man:
But Joys like those that Lovers souls enjoy,
Which here on Earth there's nothing can destroy.
   Ay, ay, 'tis Love can only be
   The happy souls felicitie.

III.
Are your delights in what you see,
Of wonderful varietie?
Or can your Joys arise from pleasant things;
Your tast, or smelling, to your fancy brings?
   No, no, 'tis plain, it it were so,
   Eternity by gradual steps must go.

PHillis, the time is come that we must sever; long have we linger'd 'twixt kindness and strife: And though we promis'd our selves to love ever, there is a fate in Love, as well as Life. So many jealousies daily we try, sometimes we freez, and then sometimes we fry; that Love in Colds, or in Feavers will dye.

Mr. *Robert Smith*

II.
Both by our selves, and others tormented,
Still in suspence betwixt Heaven and Hell:
Ever desiring, and never contented;
Either not Loving, or Loving too well.
Parting we still are in each others pow'rs;
Our Lov's a weather of Sun-shine, and show'rs:
Its dayes are bitter, though sweet are its hours.

III.
Why should we Fate any longer importune,
Since to each other unhappy we prove:
Like losing Gamesters, we tempt our ill Fortune;
Both might be luckier in a new Love.
This were the way our reason bear sway;
But when we so pleasing a Passion destroy,
We may be more happy, but less should enjoy.

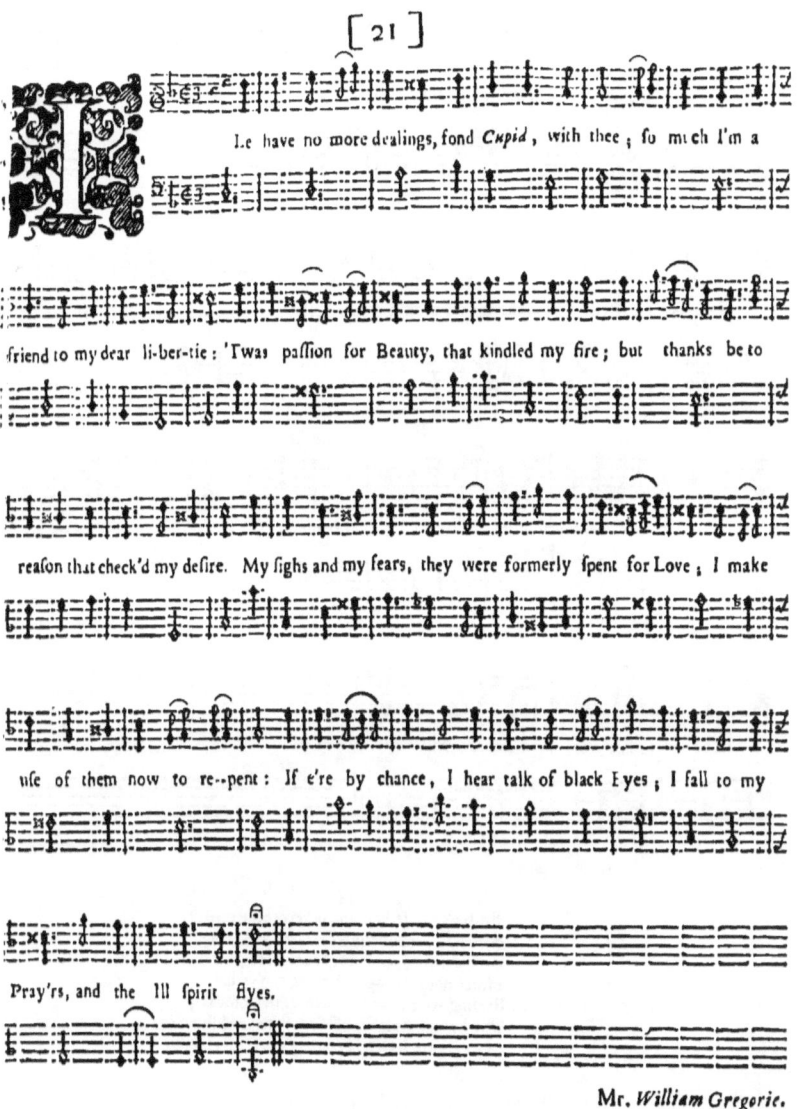

I'le have no more dealings, fond *Cupid*, with thee; so much I'm a friend to my dear li-ber-tie: 'Twas passion for Beauty, that kindled my fire; but thanks be to reason that check'd my desire. My sighs and my fears, they were formerly spent for Love; I make use of them now to re--pent: If e're by chance, I hear talk of black Eyes; I fall to my Pray'rs, and the Ill spirit flyes.

Mr. *William Gregorie.*

II.
There's none in the world madder than he,
That loves his own dangers, and will not be free:
I'le ne're be confin'd to the Devils black Rod,
For serving in Love a fantastical God.
Experience hath taught me the infallible Art,
Of curbing my Eye-sight, to preserve my Heart:
Where e're I encounter a Beautious face,
I bless my self! turn aside, and mend my pace.

Phillis, the time is come that we must sever; long have we linger'd kindness and strife: And though we promis'd our selves to love ever, there is a fate in Love well as Life. So many jealousies daily we try, sometimes we freez, and then sometimes we fry Love in Colds, or in Feavers will dye.

Mr. *Robert*

II.
Both by our selves, and others tormented,
Still in suspence betwixt Heaven and Hell:
Ever desiring, and never contented;
Either not Loving, or Loving too well.
Parting we still are in each others pow'rs;
Our Lov's a weather of Sun-shine, and show'rs:
Its dayes are bitter, though sweet are its hours.

III.
Why should we Fate any longer importune,
Since to each other unhappy we prove:
Like losing Gamesters, we tempt our ill Fortune;
Both might be luckier in a new Love.
This were the way our reason bear sway;
But when we so pleasing a Passion destroy,
We may be more happy, but less should enjoy.

Mr. *William Gregorie.*

II.

There's none in the world madder than he,
That loves his own dangers, and will not be free:
I'le ne're be confin'd to the Devils black Rod,
For serving in Love a fantastical God.
Experience hath taught me the infallible Art,
Of curbing my Eye-sight, to preserve my Heart:
Where e're I encounter a Beautious face,
I bless my self! turn aside, and mend my pace.

[22]

A 2. Voc. Cantus & Bassus.

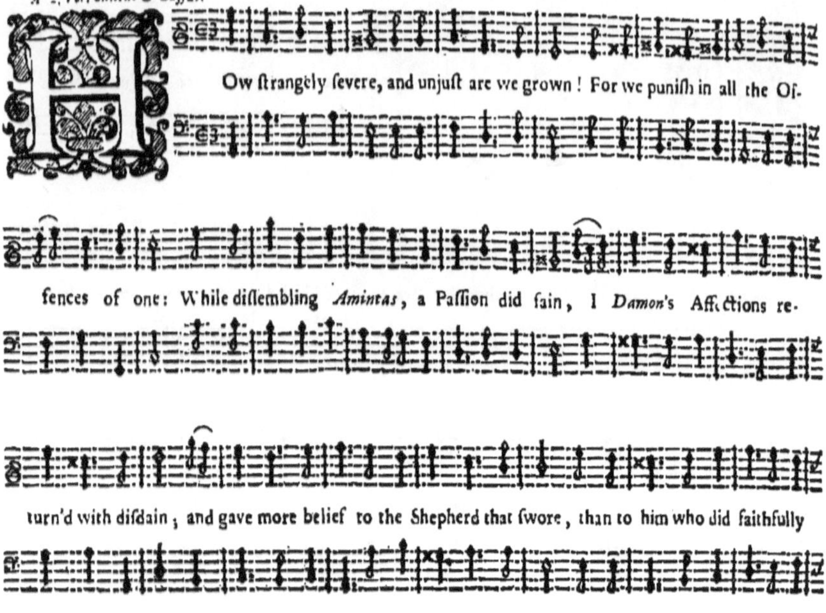

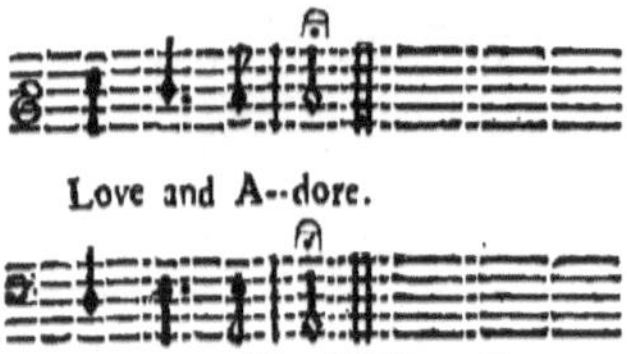

How strangely severe, and unjust are we grown! For we punish in all the Offences of one: While dissembling *Amintas*, a Passion did fain, I *Damon*'s Affections return'd with disdain; and gave more belief to the Shepherd that swore, than to him who did faithfully Love and A--dore.

Mr. *William Turner.*

II.
Then how is it Just, O ye Powers divine!
That *Damon* should dye, when the error was mine:
Yet pardon me once, and if ever again
I'm deaf to the Voice of a Lover in pain;
Then let me not prosper in what I've begun,
But dye in despair, as my *Damon* has done.

A. 2. Voc. Cantus & Bassus.

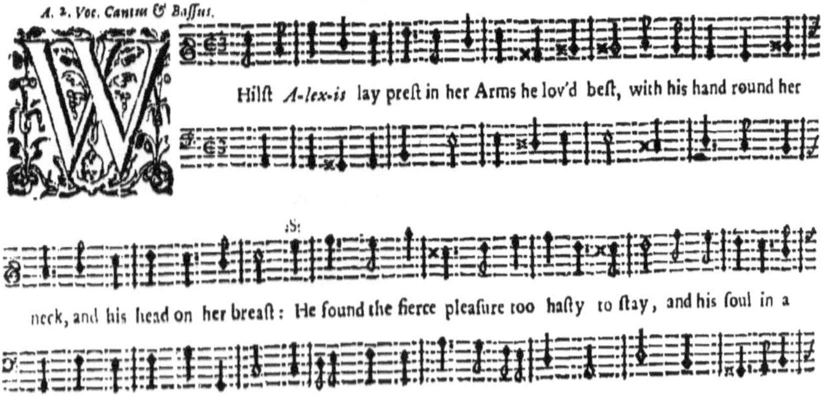

Whilst *A-lex-is* lay prest in her Arms he lov'd best, with his hand round her neck, and his head on her breast: He found the fierce pleasure too hasty to stay, and his soul in a

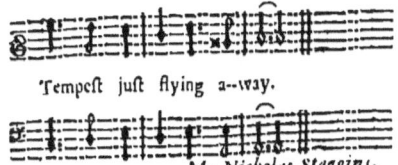

'Tempest just flying a-way.

Mr. *Nicholas Staggins*.

II.
When *Celia* saw this, with a Sigh and a Kiss,
She cry'd, O my Dear! I'm robb'd of my bliss:
'Tis unkind to your Love, and unfaithfully done,
To leave me behind you, and dye all alone.

III.
The Youth, though in haste, and breathing his last,
In pity dy'd slowly, whil'st she dy'd more fast;
'Till at length she cry'd, now, my Dear, now
Let's go; Now dye, my *Alexis*, and I will dye too.

IV.
Thus intranc'd she did lye, while *Alexis* did try
To recover new breath, that again he might dye:
Then often they dy'd; but the more they did so,
The nymph di'd more quick, and the shepherd more slow

Fall the brisk Dames, *Misselina* for me; for I love not a woman un-less she be free. The Affection that I to my Mistress do pay, grows weary, unless she does meet it half way. There can be no pleasure 'till humours do hit; and jumping's as good in Affection as Wit.

Mr. *Pelham Humphrey*.

II.
No sooner I came, but she lik'd me as soon;
No sooner I askt, but she granted my boon:
And without a Preamble, a Portion, or Joynture,
She promis'd to meet me, where e're I'de appoint her.
So we struck up a match, and embraced each other,
Without the consent of Father or Mother.

III.
Then away with a Lady that's Modest and coy;
Let her ends be the pleasures that we do enjoy:
Let her tickle her fancy with secret delight,
And refuse all the day, what she longs for at night.
I believe my *Selina*, who shews they'r all mad
To feed on dry bones, when flesh may be had.

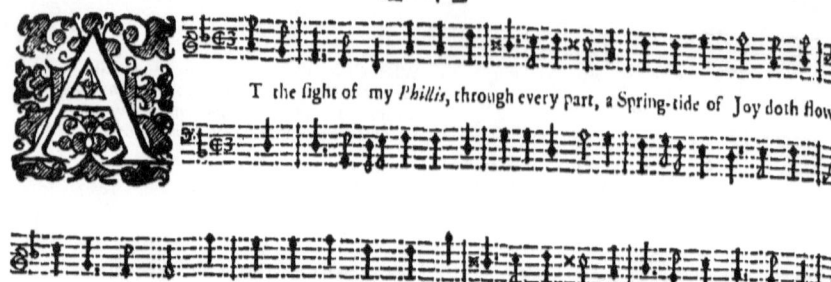

AT the sight of my *Phillis*, through every part, a Spring-tide of Joy doth flow up to my Heart, which quickens each Pulse, and swells e-ve-ry Vein, yet all my Delights are still

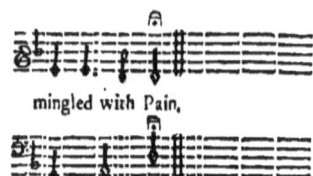

mingled with Pain.

So strong a Distemper, sure Love cannot bring;
To my Knowledge, Love was a quieter thing:
So gentle and tame, that he never was known
So much as to wake me, when I lay alone.

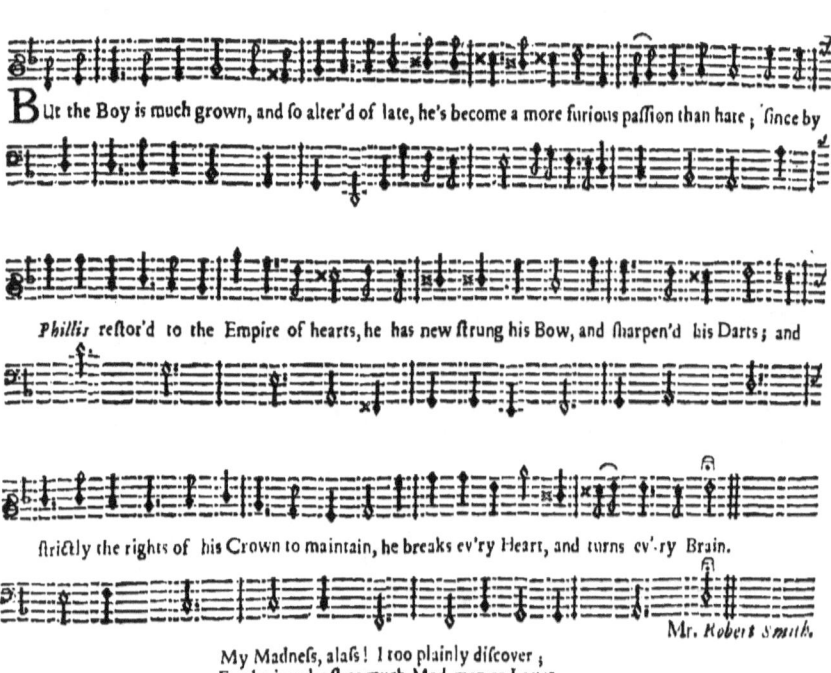

But the Boy is much grown, and so alter'd of late, he's become a more furious passion than hate; since by *Phillis* restor'd to the Empire of hearts, he has new strung his Bow, and sharpen'd his Darts; and strictly the rights of his Crown to maintain, he breaks ev'ry Heart, and turns ev'ry Brain.

Mr. Robert Smith.

My Madness, alass! I too plainly discover;
For he is at least as much Mad-man as Lover,
Who for one cruel Beauty, is ready to quit
All the Nymphs of the Stage, and those of the Pit:
The Joys of *Hide-park*, and the *Mall's* dear delight,
To be Sober all day, and Chast all the Night.

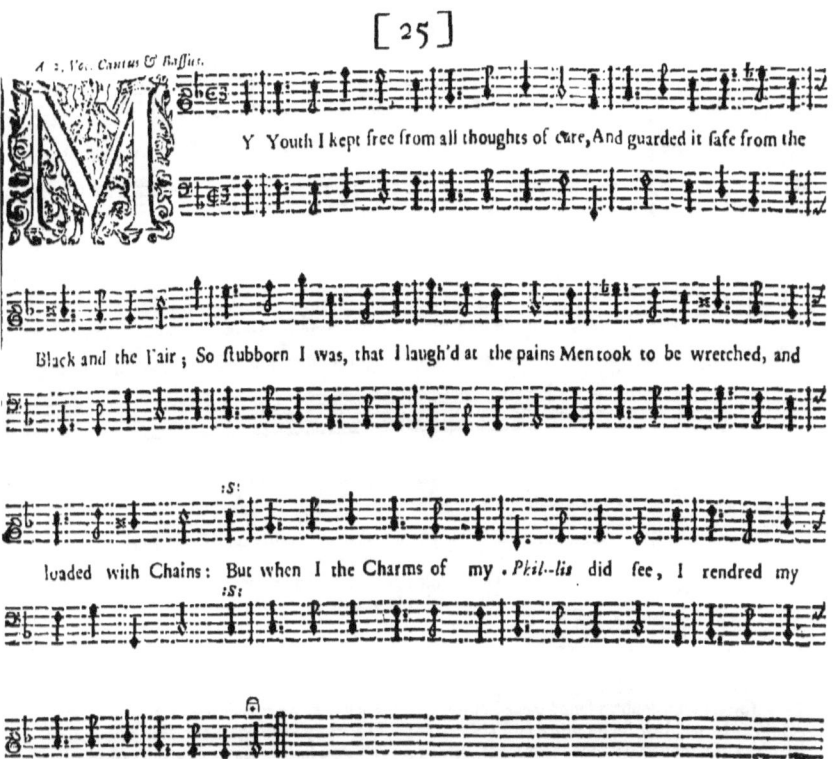

Mr. *Alph. Marsh*, Junior.

II.

I Lov'd with a Zeal and Passion so strong,
Forgot she was woman, and could not love long:
I never consider'd the tricks and the arts
She us'd to entangle and captivate hearts:
   At length I discover'd, and plainly I knew
   My *Phillis* was fickle, and could not be true.

III.

I curst my hard fate that kindled my flame;
I oft'ner my self than my *Phillis* did blame:
Yet I bore such respect unto her, that I thought
Want of merit in me, this humour had wrought.
   And then I resolv'd I never would be
   So bold as to Love, but would always be free.

[26]

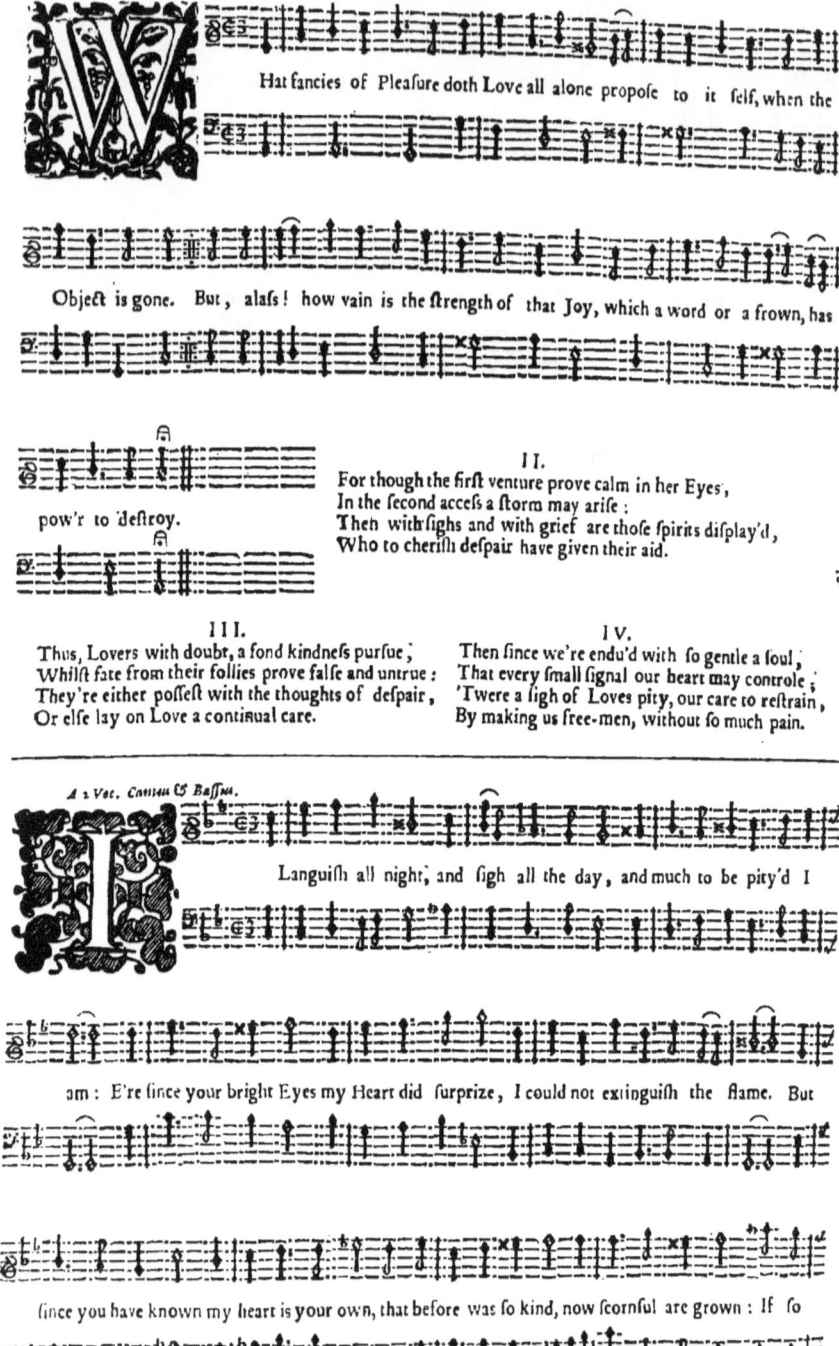

What fancies of Pleasure doth Love all alone propose to it self, when the Object is gone. But, alass! how vain is the strength of that Joy, which a word or a frown, has pow'r to destroy.

II.
For though the first venture prove calm in her Eyes,
In the second acces a storm may arise:
Then with sighs and with grief are those spirits display'd,
Who to cherish despair have given their aid.

III.
Thus, Lovers with doubt, a fond kindness pursue,
Whilst fate from their follies prove false and untrue:
They're either possest with the thoughts of despair,
Or else lay on Love a continual care.

IV.
Then since we're endu'd with so gentle a soul,
That every small signal our heart may controle;
'Twere a sigh of Loves pity, our care to restrain,
By making us free-men, without so much pain.

A 2 Voc. Cantus & Bassus.

I Languish all night, and sigh all the day, and much to be pity'd I am: E're since your bright Eyes my Heart did surprize, I could not extinguish the flame. But since you have known my heart is your own, that before was so kind, now scornful are grown: If so

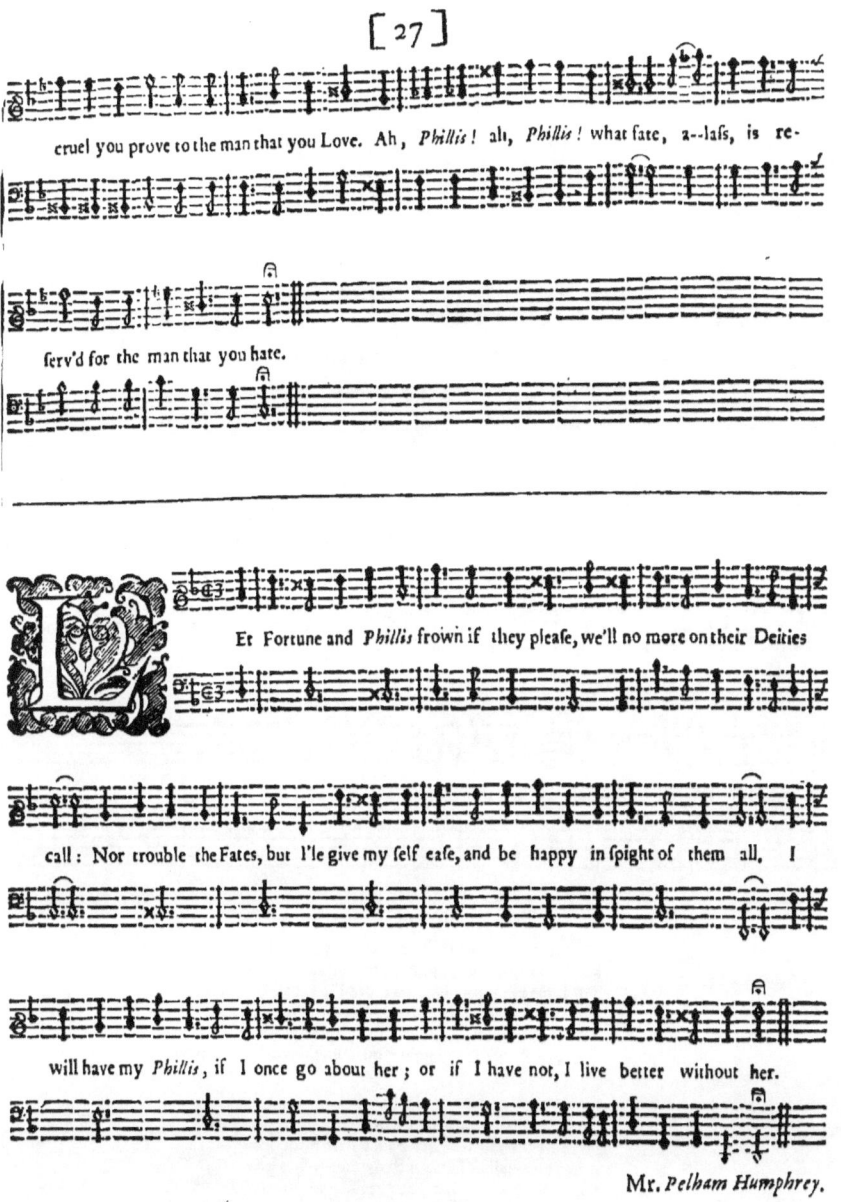

cruel you prove to the man that you Love. Ah, *Phillis!* ah, *Phillis!* what fate, a--lafs, is re-

ferv'd for the man that you hate.

Et Fortune and *Phillis* frown if they pleafe, we'll no more on their Deities call: Nor trouble the Fates, but I'le give my felf eafe, and be happy in fpight of them all. I will have my *Phillis,* if I once go about her ; or if I have not, I live better without her.

Mr. *Pelham Humphrey.*

II.
But If fhe prove Virtuous, Obliging, and Kind ,
  Perhaps I'le vouchfafe to love her :
But if Pride or Inconftancy in her, I find ,
  I'de have her to know I'm above her.
For at length I have learn'd, now my Fetters are gone ,
  To Love, if I pleafe, or to let it alone.

Give o're foolish heart, and make haft to despair, For *Daphne* regards not thy Vows nor thy Pray'r: When I plead for thy passion, thy pains to prolong: She courts her Gittar, and replyes with a Song. No more shall true Lovers such beauties adore: Were the gods so severe, men would worship no more.

Mr. *Alph. Marsh.*

II.

No more will I wait, like a Slave at your Dore,
I'le spend the cold Night at your Window no more:
My Lungs in long sighs, no more I'le exhale,
Since your Pride is to make me grow sullen and pale.
   No more shall *Amintas* your pity implore,
   Were the gods so ingrate, men would worship no more.

III.

No more shall your frowns, or free humour perswade
To court the fair Idol my Fancy hath made:
When your saint's so neglected, your follies give o're,
Your Deity's lost, and your beauties no more.
   No more shall true Lovers such Beautie's adore,
   Were the gods so severe, men would worship no more.

IV.

How weak are the Vows of a Lover in pain,
When flatter'd with hope, or opprest with disdain:
No sooner my *Daphne*'s bright eyes I review,
But all is forgot, and I vow all a new.
   No more, fairest Nymph, I will murmur no more;
   Did the gods seem so fair, men would ever adore.

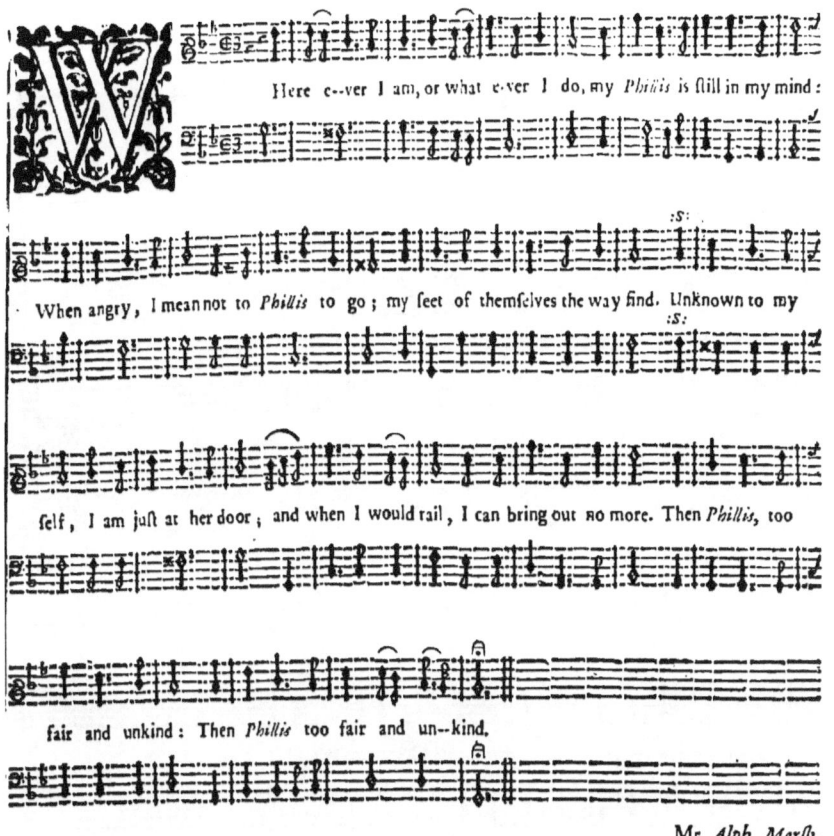

Mr. *Alph. Marsh.*

II.

When *Phillis* I see, my heart burns in my breast,
And the Love I would stifle is show'n:
But asleep or awake, I am never at rest,
When from mine eyes *Phillis* is gone.
Sometimes a sweet dream doth delude my sad mind;
But alass! when I wake, and no *Phillis* I find,
Then I sigh to my self all alone!
Then I sigh to my self all alone!

III.

Should a King be my rival in her I adore,
He should offer his treasure in vain:
O let me alone to be happy and poor,
And give me my *Phillis* again.
Let *Phillis* be mine, and ever be kind,
I could to a Desart with her be confin'd,
And envy no Monarch his reign:
And envy no Monarch his reign.

IV.

Alas! I discover too much of my Love,
And she too well knows her own pow'r:
She makes me each day a new Martyrdom prove,
And makes me grow jealous each hour.
But let her each minute torment my poor mind,
I had rather love *Phillis*, both false and unkind,
Then ever be freed from her pow'r:
Then ever be freed from her pow'r.

[31]

ᴵe ; and there he counts ev'ry Hey ho ! hey ho !

Mr. *Pelham Humphrey.*

II.
How shall I this *Argus* blind ?
And so put an end to my wo ;
For whilst I beguile
His Frowns with a Smile ;
I betray my self with a Hey ho ! hey ho !

III.
My restraint, then alass ! must endure ;
So that since my sad doom I know :
I'le pine for my Love
Like the Turtle-Dove ;
And breath out my Life in Hey ho ! hey ho !

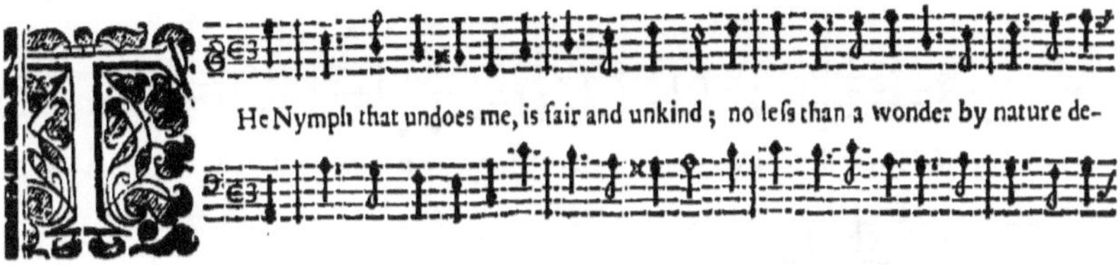

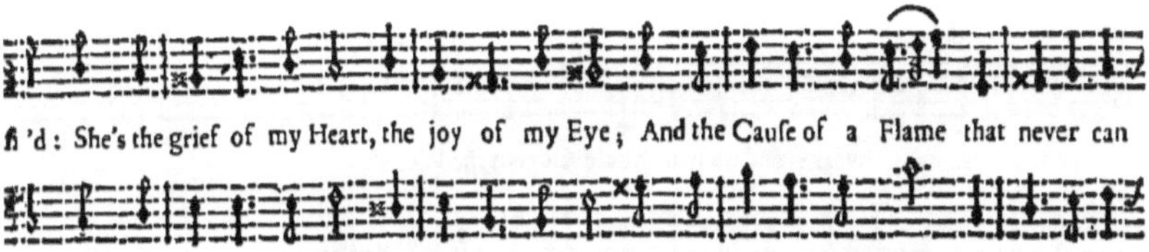

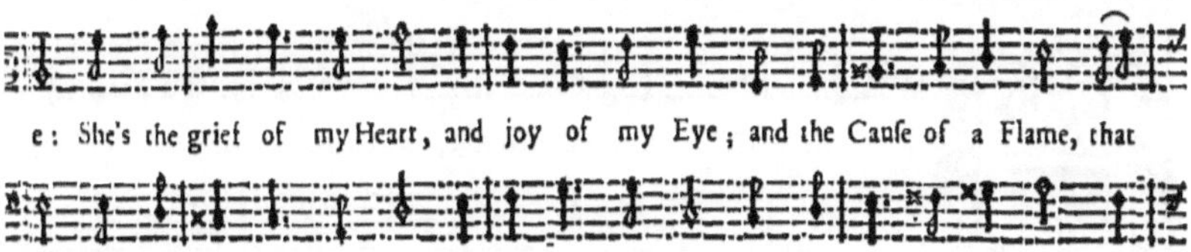

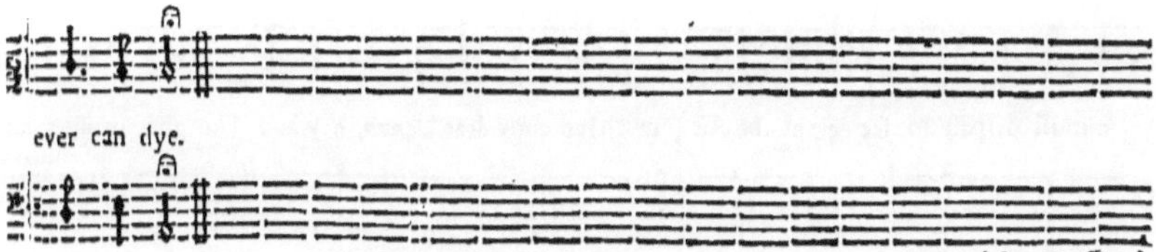

THe Nymph that undoes me, is fair and unkind ; no less than a wonder by nature defi'd : She's the grief of my Heart, the joy of my Eye ; And the Cause of a Flame that never can e : She's the grief of my Heart, and joy of my Eye ; and the Cause of a Flame, that ever can dye.

Mr. *Stafford.*

II.
Her Lips, from whence Wit obligingly flows,
Have the colour of Cheries, and smell of the Rose:
Fate and Destiny both attends on her Will ;
She saves with a Smile, with a Frown she can Kill.

III.
The desparate Lover can hope no Redress ;
Where Beauty and Rigour are both in excess :
In *Cælia* they meet, so unhappy am I ;
Who sees her must Love, who Loves her must dye.

I 2

[31]

me; and there he counts ev'ry Hey ho! hey ho!

Mr. *Pelham Humphrey.*

II.
How shall I this *Argus* blind?
And so put an end to my wo;
For whilst I beguile
His Frowns with a Smile;
I betray my self with a Hey ho! hey ho!

III.
My restraint, then alas! must endure,
So that since my sad doom I know:
I'le pine for my Love
Like the Turtle-Dove;
And breath out my Life in Hey ho! hey ho!

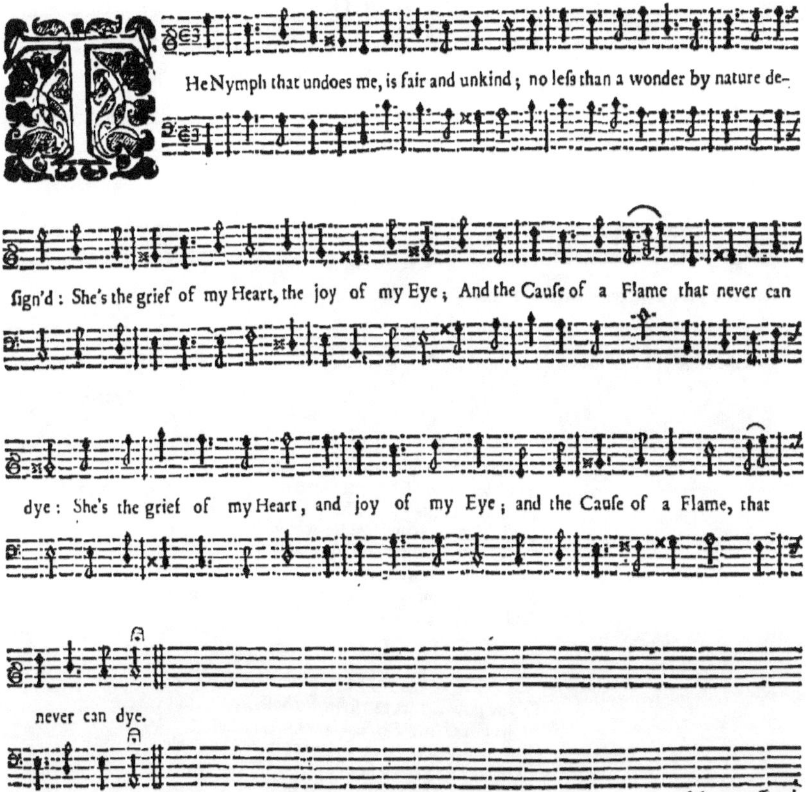

He Nymph that undoes me, is fair and unkind; no less than a wonder by nature designd: She's the grief of my Heart, the joy of my Eye; And the Cause of a Flame that never can dye: She's the grief of my Heart, and joy of my Eye; and the Cause of a Flame, that never can dye.

Mr. *Stafford.*

II.
Her Lips, from whence Wit obligingly flows,
Has the colour of Cheries, and smell of the Rose:
Love and Destiny both attends on her Will;
She Saves with a Smile, with a Frown she can Kill.

III.
The desparate Lover can hope no Redress,
Where Beauty and Rigour are both in excess:
In *Cælia* they meet, so unhappy am I;
Who sees her must Love, who Loves her must dye.

I 2

How unhappy a Lover am I, whilst I sigh for my *Phillis* in vain: All my hopes of delight are a-nother man's right; who is happy, whilst I am in pain. Since her honour affords no re--lief, but to pi-ty the pains which you bear: 'Tis the best of your fate in a hopeless e-state, to give o're, and betimes to de--spair.

Mr. *Nicholas Staggins.*

II.

I have try'd the false Medicine in vain;
Yet I wish what I hope not to win:
From without my desire has no food to its fire,
But it burns and consumes me within.
Yet at least, 'tis a comfort to know
That you are not unhappy alone:
For the Nymph you adore is as wretched or more,
And accounts all your suff'rings her own.

III.

O you pow'rs! let me suffer for both,
At the feet of my *Phillis* I'le lye:
I'le resign up my breath, and take pleasure in death,
To be pity'd by her when I dye.
What her honour deny'd you in life,
In her death she will give to her love:
Such a flame as is true, after fate will renew,
When the souls do meet closer above.

Why *Phillis*, to me, so untrue and unkind? Remember the Vow which you made; Though Love cannot see, let not Honour be blind, whereon is the other betray'd.

Though, Sir, to your Bed, true Alleg'ance I vow'd: I am not oblig'd by that Oath: No longer than you keep both constant and true: The same Vow ob--li--geth us both.

II.

Man.
Fair Nymph, did you feel
But those Passions I bear,
My Love you would never suspect:
An Heart made of steel
Sure must needs love the fair,
And what we love cannot neglect.
Woman.
Then since we love both,
Let us both be agreed;
Man.
And seal both our Loves with a Kiss:
Woman.
From breaking our Oath
We shall both then be freed;
Man.
And Princes will envy our bliss.

How unhappy a Lover am I, whilst I sigh for my *Phillis* in vain: All hopes of delight are a-nother man's right; who is happy, whilst I am in pain. Since her honour fords no re--lief, but to pi-ty the pains which you bear: 'Tis the best of your fate in a hopeless state, to give o're, and betimes to de--spair.

Mr. *Nicholas Stag*

II.
I have try'd the false Medicine in vain;
Yet I wish what I hope not to win:
From without my desire has no food to its fire,
But it burns and consumes me within.
Yet at least, 'tis a comfort to know
That you are not unhappy alone:
For the *Nymph* you adore is as wretched or more,
And accounts all your suff'rings her own.

III.
O you pow'rs! let me suffer for both;
At the feet of my *Phillis* I'le lye:
I'le resign up my breath, and take pleasure in death,
To be pity'd by her when I dye.
What her honour deny'd you in life,
In her death she will give to her love:
Such a flame as is true, after fate will renew,
When the souls do meet closer above.

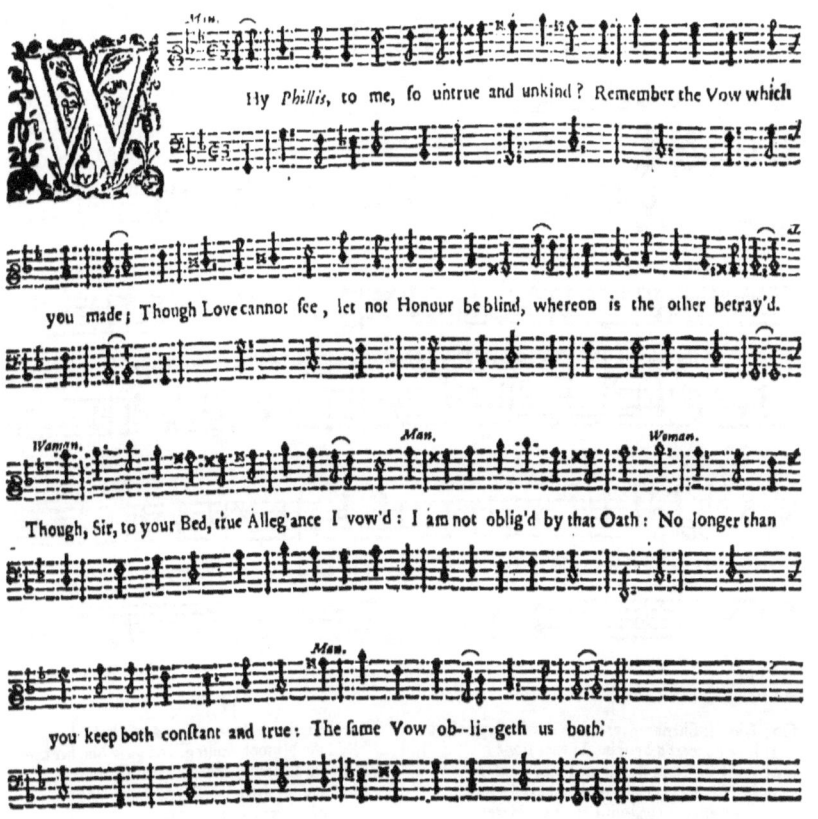

Hy *Phillis*, to me, so untrue and unkind? Remember the Vow which you made; Though Love cannot see, let not Honour be blind, whereon is the other betray'd.

Though, Sir, to your Bed, true Alleg'ance I vow'd: I am not oblig'd by that Oath: No longer than you keep both constant and true: The same Vow ob--li--geth us both.

II.

Man.
Fair Nymph, did you feel
But those Passions I bear,
My Love you would never suspect:
An Heart made of steel
Sure must needs love the fair,
And what we love cannot neglect.
Woman.
Then since we love both,
Let us both be agreed;
Man.
And seal both our Loves with a Kiss:
Woman.
From breaking our Oath
We shall both then be freed;
Man.
And Princes will envy our bliss.

K

[34]

O N the bank of a Brook as I sat fishing; hid in the Osiers that grew on the side; I over-heard a Nymph and Shepherd wishing, no time or fortune their Love might devide: To *Cupid* and *Venus* each offred a Vow, to Love e--ver as they love now.

Mr. *John Banister.*

II.
Oh! said the Shepherd, and sigh'd, what a pleasure
Is love conceal'd betwixt Lovers alone?
Love must be secret kept, like Fairy treasure,
When 'tis discover'd, 'twill quickly be gone:
And envy or jealousie if it could stay,
Will too soon, alas! make it decay.

III.
Then let us leave the world and care behind us,
Said the Nymph smiling, and gave him her hand;
All alone, all alone, where none shall finds us,
In some far desart we'll seek a new land:
And there live from envy or jealousie free,
And a world to each other we'll be.

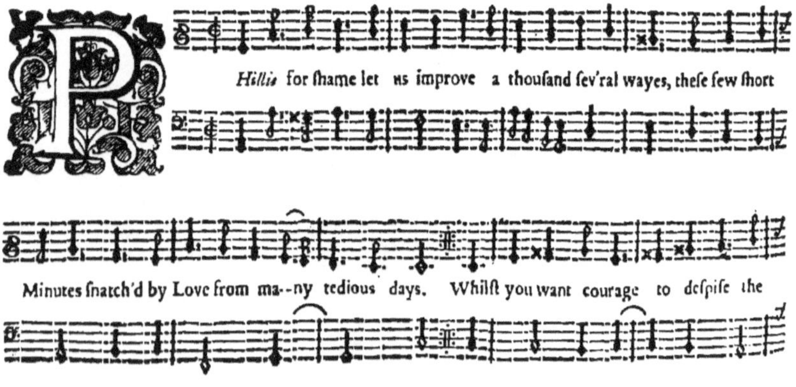

P*Hillis* for shame let us improve a thousand sev'ral wayes, these few short Minutes snatch'd by Love from ma--ny tedious days. Whilst you want courage to despise the censures of the Grave; for all the tyrant in your eyes, your heart is but a slave.

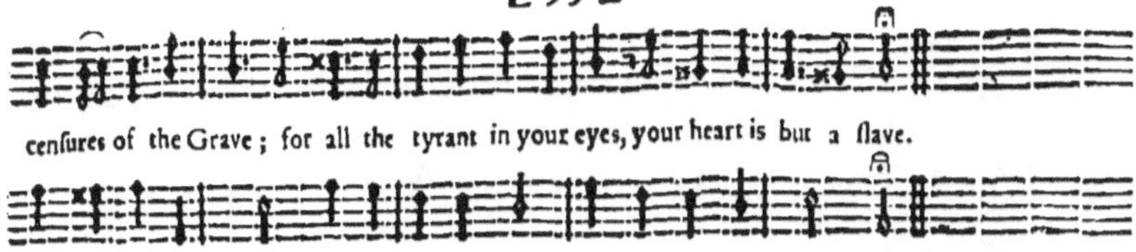

Mr. *Pelham Humphrey*.

II.	III.	IV.
My Love is full of noble pride, And never shall submit, To let that Fop discretion ride In triumph over wit.	False friends I have as well as you, Who daily counsel me, Fame and ambition to pursue, And leave of loving you.	When I the least belief bestow On what such fools advise: May I be dull enough to grow Most miserably wise.

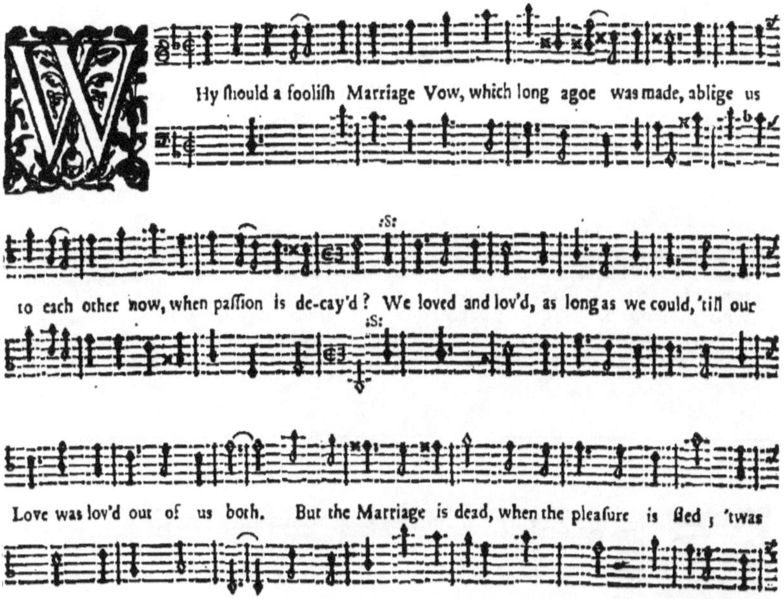

WHy should a foolish Marriage Vow, which long agoe was made, ablige us to each other now, when passion is de-cay'd? We loved and lov'd, as long as we could, 'till our Love was lov'd out of us both. But the Marriage is dead, when the pleasure is fled, 'twas pleasure first made it an Oath.

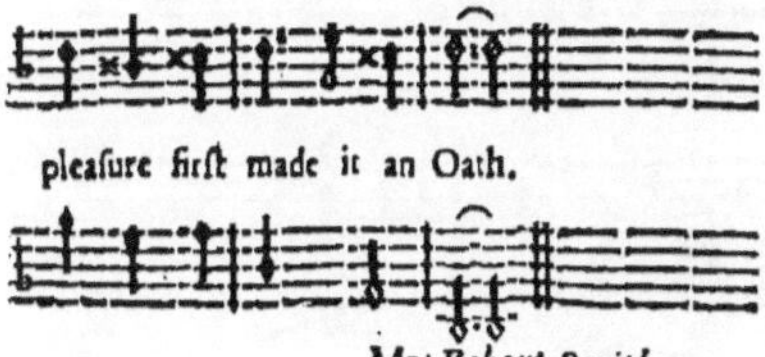

Mr. *Robert Smith*.

II.
If I have pleasure for a friend,
And further joy in store,
What wrong has he whose joys did end,
And who could give no more?
It's a madness that he
Should be jealous of me,
Or that I should bar him of another;
When all we can gain
Is to give our selves pain,
And neither can hinder the other.

Mr. *John Banist*

II.
Oh! said the Shepherd, and sigh'd, what a pleasure
Is love conceal'd betwixt Lovers alone?
Love must be secret kept, like Fairy treasure,
When 'tis discover'd, 'twill quickly be gone:
And envy or jealousie if it could stay,
Will too soon, alass! make it decay.

III.
Then let us leave the world and care behind us,
Said the Nymph smiling, and gave him her hand
All alone, all alone, where none shall finds us,
In some far desart we'll seek a new land:
And there live from envy or jealousie free,
And a world to each other we'll be.

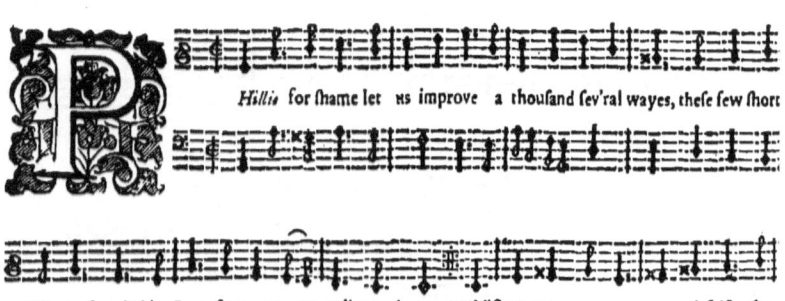

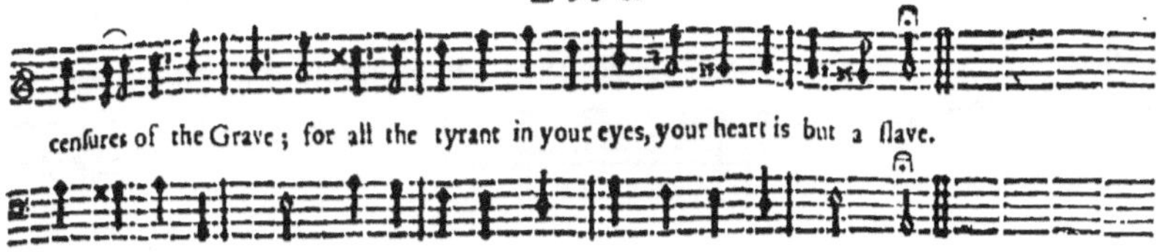

censures of the Grave; for all the tyrant in your eyes, your heart is but a slave.

Mr. *Pelham Humphrey*.

II.
My Love is full of noble pride,
And never shall submit,
To let that Fop discretion ride
In triumph over wit.

III.
False friends I have as well as you,
Who daily counsel me,
Fame and ambition to pursue,
And leave of loving you.

IV.
When I the least belief bestow
On what such fools advise:
May I be dull enough to grow
Most miserably wife.

Hy should a foolish Marriage Vow, which long agoe was made, ablige us to each other now, when passion is de-cay'd? We loved and lov'd, as long as we could, 'till our Love was lov'd out of us both. But the Marriage is dead, when the pleasure is fled; 'twas pleasure first made it an Oath.

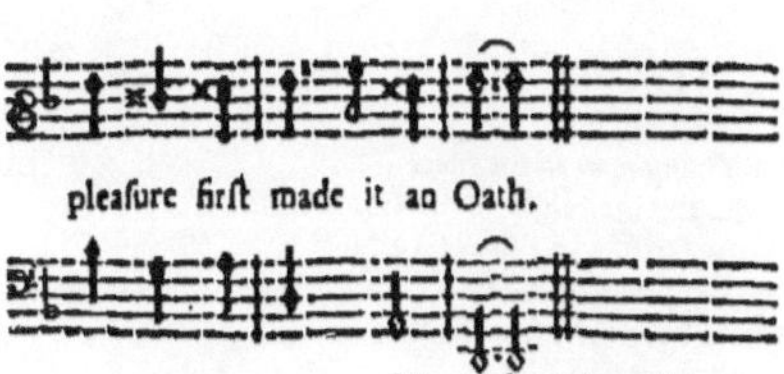

Mr. *Robert Smith*.

II.
If I have pleasure for a friend,
And further joy in store,
What wrong has he whose joys did end,
And who could give no more?
It's a madness that he
Should be jealous of me,
Or that I should bar him of another;
When all we can gain
Is to give our selves pain,
And neither can hinder the other.

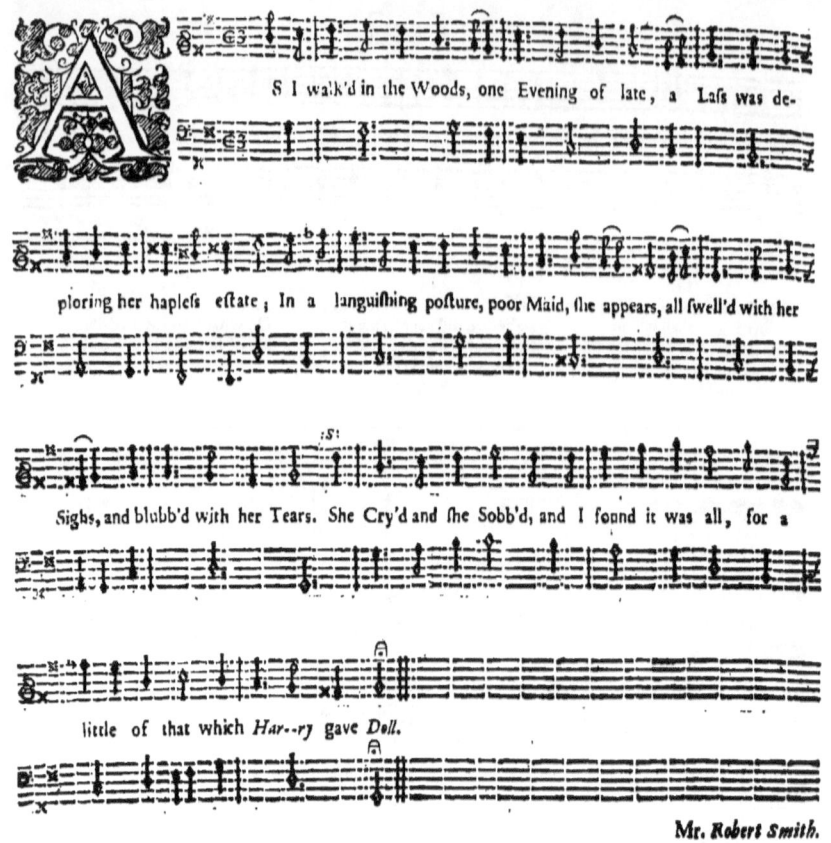

Mr. *Robert Smith*.

II.

At laſt ſhe broke out, Wretched, ſhe ſaid,
Will no Youth come ſuccour a languiſhing Maid;
With what he with éaſe and with pleaſure may give,
Without which, alaſs, poor I cannot live!
Shall I never leave ſighing, and crying, and call,
For a little of that, &c.

III.

At firſt when I ſaw a Young man in the place,
My colour would fade, and then fluſh in my face;
My breath would grow ſhort, and I ſhiver'd all o're,
My Breaſt never popp'd up and down ſo before:
I ſcarce knew for what, but now I find it was all
For a little of that, &c.

Beneath a Mirtle shade, which Love for none but happy Lovers made;
I slept, and streight my Love before me brought, *Phillis*, the Object of my waking thought:
Undrest she comes, my flames to meet; whilst Love straw'd flow'rs beneath her Feet, so prest by
her, became, became more sweet.

Mr. *John Banister*.

II
From the bright Visions head,
A careless vail of Lawn was loosly spread;
From her white Temples fell her shaded Hair,
Like cloudy Sun-shine, not too brown or fair:
Her Hands, her Lips, did Love inspire,
Her ev'ry Grace my Heart did fire;
But most her Eyes, that languish'd with desire.

III.
Ah, charming Fair, said I,
How long can you my bliss and yours deny:
By Nature and by Love this lovely shade
Was for revenge of suff'ring Lovers made.
Silence and shades with Love agree,
Both shelter you, and favour me;
You cannot Blush, because I cannot see.

IV.
No, let me dye, she said,
Rather than lose the spotless name of Maid:
Faintly she spoke, me-thought, for all the while
She bid me not believe her with a smile.
Then dye, said I, she still deny'd;
And is it thus? thus, thus, she cry'd,
You use a harmless maid? and so she dy'd.

V.
I wak't, and straight I knew
I Lov'd so well, it made my Dream prove true:
Fancy the kinder Mistress of the two,
Fancy had done what *Phillis* would not do.
Ah, cruel Nymph, cease your disdain,
While I can dream you scorn in vain,
Asleep, or waking, you must ease my pain.

L

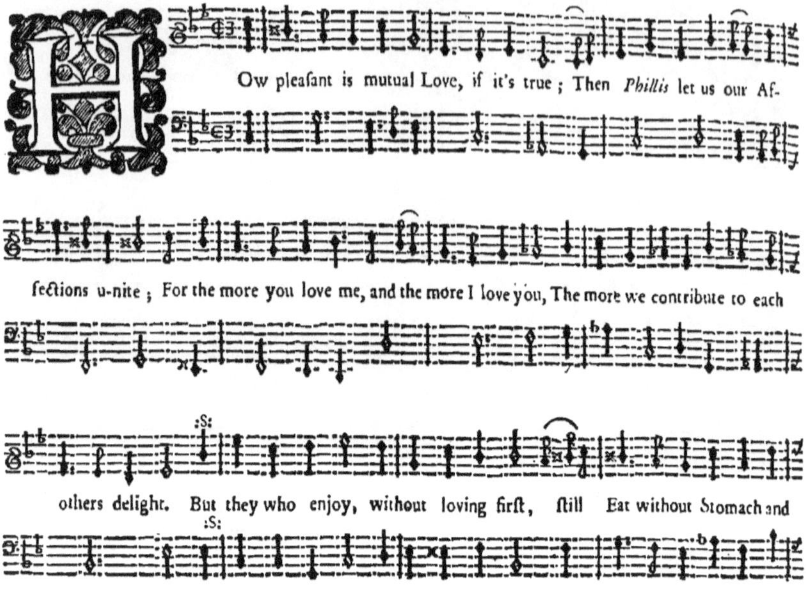

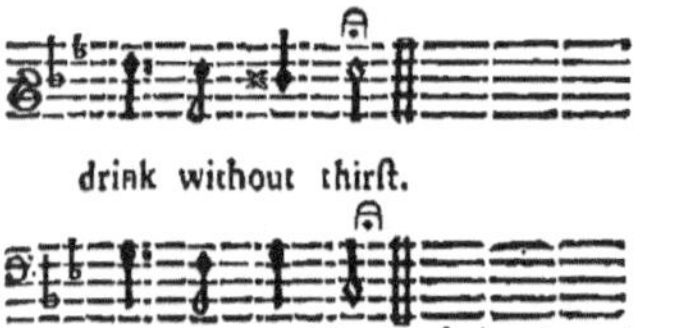

How pleasant is mutual Love, if it's true; Then *Phillis* let us our Affections u-nite; For the more you love me, and the more I love you, The more we contribute to each others delight. But they who enjoy, without loving first, still Eat without Stomach and drink without thirst.

II.
Such is the poor Fool, who loves upon duty,
Because a Canonick a Coxcomb hath made him:
He ne're tasts the sweets of Love and of Beauty;
But drudges, because a dull Priest hath betray'd him.
But who in enjoyment from love take their measure,
Are wrapt with delights, and still ravish'd with pleasure.

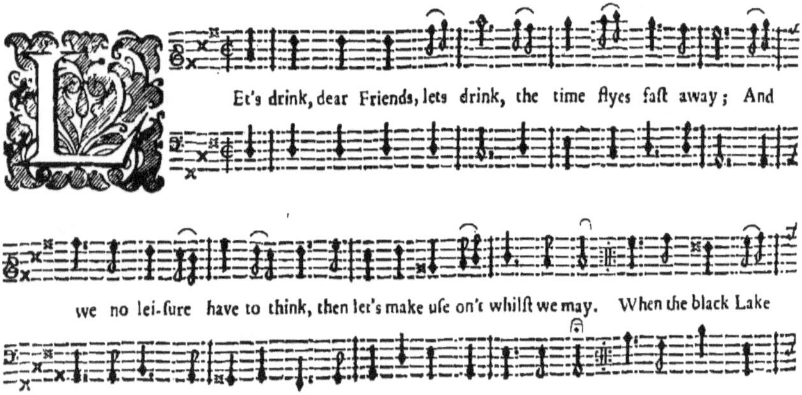

Mr. *Nicholas Staggins*.

Let's drink, dear Friends, lets drink, the time flyes fast away; And we no lei-sure have to think, then let's make use on't whilst we may. When the black Lake

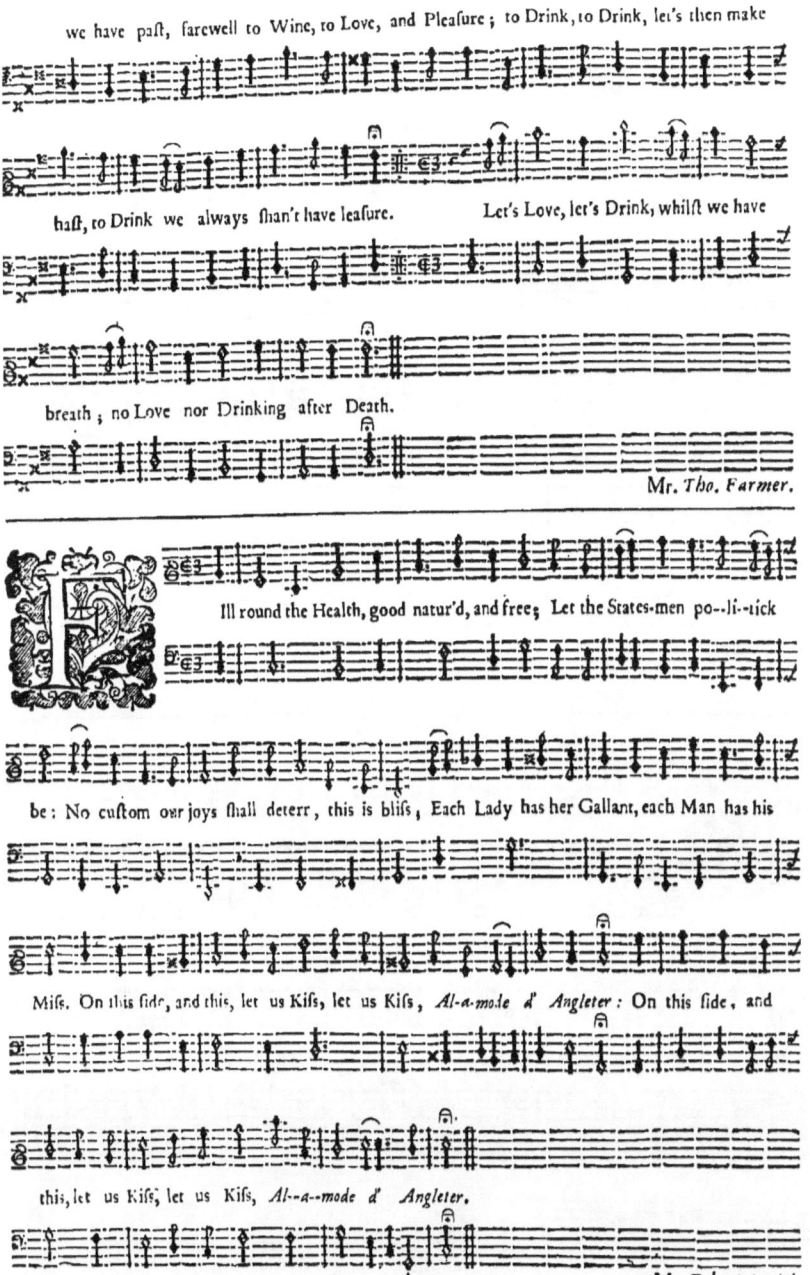

[40]

A. 2. Voc. Cantus & Bassus.

Come lay by your Cares, and hang up your Sorrow, drink on he's a Sot, that e're thinks of to Morrow: Great store of good Clarret supplys ev'ry thing; and the man that is Drunk is as great as a King.

II.
Let none at Misfortunes or Losses repine,
But take a full dose of the Juice of the Vine:
Diseases and troubles are ne're to be found,
But in the damn'd place where the glass goes not round.

Mr. *Robert Smith.*

A. 2. Voc. Cantus & Bassus.

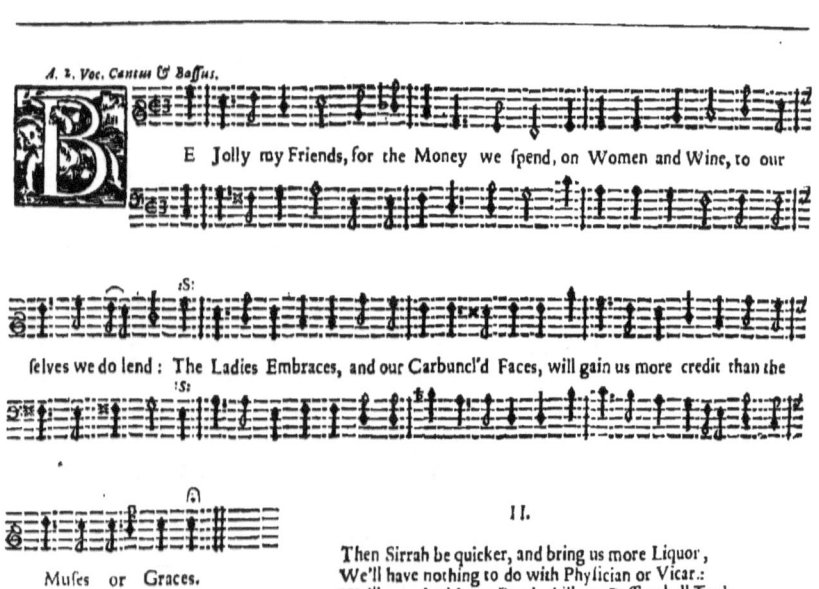

Be Jolly my Friends, for the Money we spend, on Women and Wine, to our selves we do lend: The Ladies Embraces, and our Carbuncl'd Faces, will gain us more credit than the Muses or Graces.

II.
Then Sirrah be quicker, and bring us more Liquor,
We'll have nothing to do with Phylician or Vicar.:
We'll round with our Bowls, 'till our Passing-bell Touls,
And trust no such Quacks with our Bodies or Souls.

Mr. *Robert Smith.*

M-thinks the poor Town has been troubled too long, with *Phillis* and

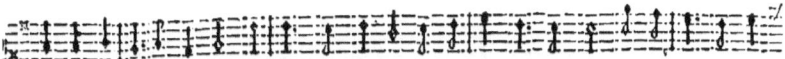

Clo-ris in e-ve-ry Song: By Fools, who at once can both Love and despair; And will never leave

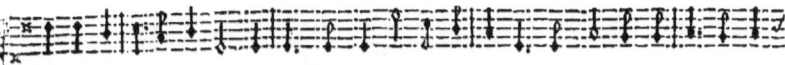

calling them Cruel and Fair. Which justly provokes me in Rhime to express, The truth that I

know of bonny Black *Bess*.

John Playford.

II.
This *Bess* of my Heart, this *Bess* of my Soul,
Has a Skin white as milk, but Hair black as a coal;
She's plump, yet with ease you may span round her Wast,
But her round swelling Thighs can scarce be embrac'd:
Her Belly is soft, not a word of the rest,
But I know what I mean, when I drink to the best.

III.
The Plow-man and Squire, the erranter Clown,
At home she subdu'd in her Paragon gown;
But now she adorns the Boxes and Pit,
And the proudest Town Gallants are forc'd to submit:
All Hearts fall a leaping where-ever she comes,
And beat day and night, like my Lord ———'s Drums.

IV.
But to those who have had my dear *Bess* in their Arms,
She's gentle, and knows how to soften her Charms;
And to every Beauty can add a new grace,
Having learn'd how to lispe, and trip in her pace:
And with head on one side, and a languishing Eye,
To Kill us with looking as if she would dye.

M

[40]

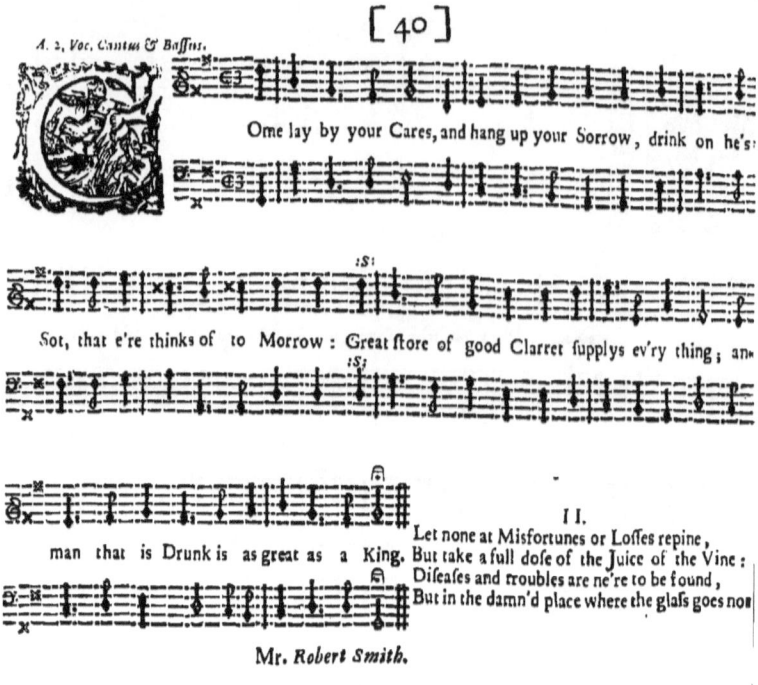

Ome lay by your Cares, and hang up your Sorrow, drink on he's
Sot, that e're thinks of to Morrow: Great store of good Claret supplys ev'ry thing, an
man that is Drunk is as great as a King.

II.
Let none at Misfortunes or Losses repine,
But take a full dose of the Juice of the Vine:
Diseases and troubles are ne're to be found,
But in the damn'd place where the glass goes not

Mr. Robert Smith.

E Jolly my Friends, for the Money we spend, on Women and Wine, to
selves we do lend: The Ladies Embraces, and our Carbuncl'd Faces, will gain us more credit than
Muses or Graces.

II.
Then Sirrah be quicker, and bring us more Liquor,
We'll have nothing to do with Physician or Vicar:
We'll round with our Bowls, 'till our Passing-bell Touls,
And trust no such Quacks with our Bodies or Souls.

Mr. Robert Smith.

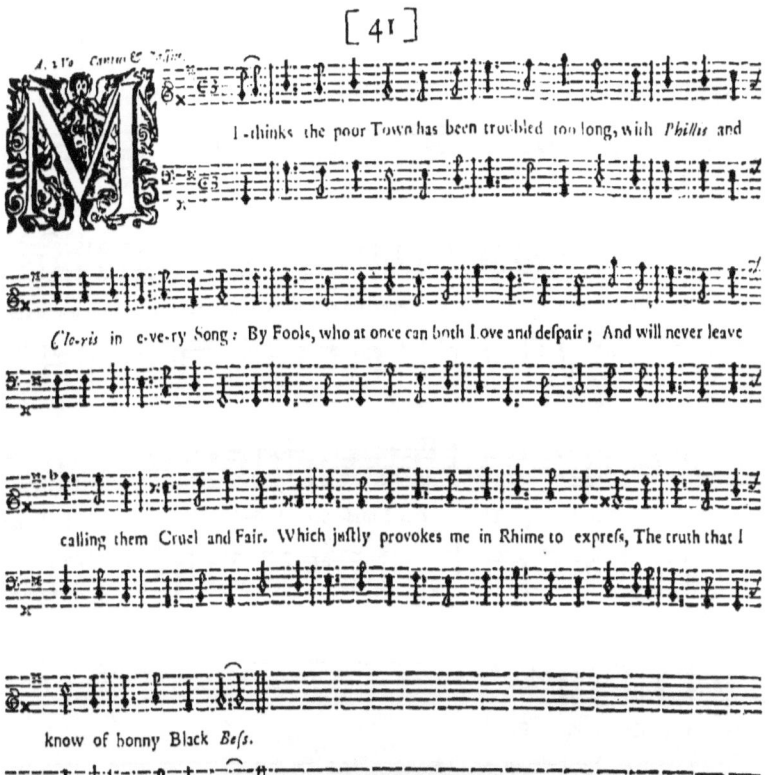

Methinks the poor Town has been troubled too long, with *Phillis* and *Cloris* in e-ve-ry Song: By Fools, who at once can both Love and despair; And will never leave calling them Cruel and Fair. Which justly provokes me in Rhime to express, The truth that I know of bonny Black *Bess*.

John Playford.

II.
This *Bess* of my Heart, this *Bess* of my Soul,
Has a Skin white as milk, but Hair black as a coal;
She's plump, yet with ease you may span round her Wast,
But her round swelling Thighs can scarce be embrac'd:
Her Belly is soft, not a word of the rest,
But I know what I mean, when I drink to the best.

III.
The Plow-man and Squire, the erranter Clown,
At home she subdu'd in her Paragon gown;
But now she adorns the Boxes and Pit,
And the proudest Town Gallants are forc'd to submit:
All Hearts fall a leaping where-ever she comes,
And beat day and night, like my Lord ———'s Drums.

IV.
But to those who have had my dear *Bess* in their Arms,
She's gentle, and knows how to soften her Charms;
And to every Beauty can add a new grace,
Having learn'd how to lispe, and trip in her pace:
And with head on one side, and a languishing Eye,
To Kill us with looking as if she would dye.

M

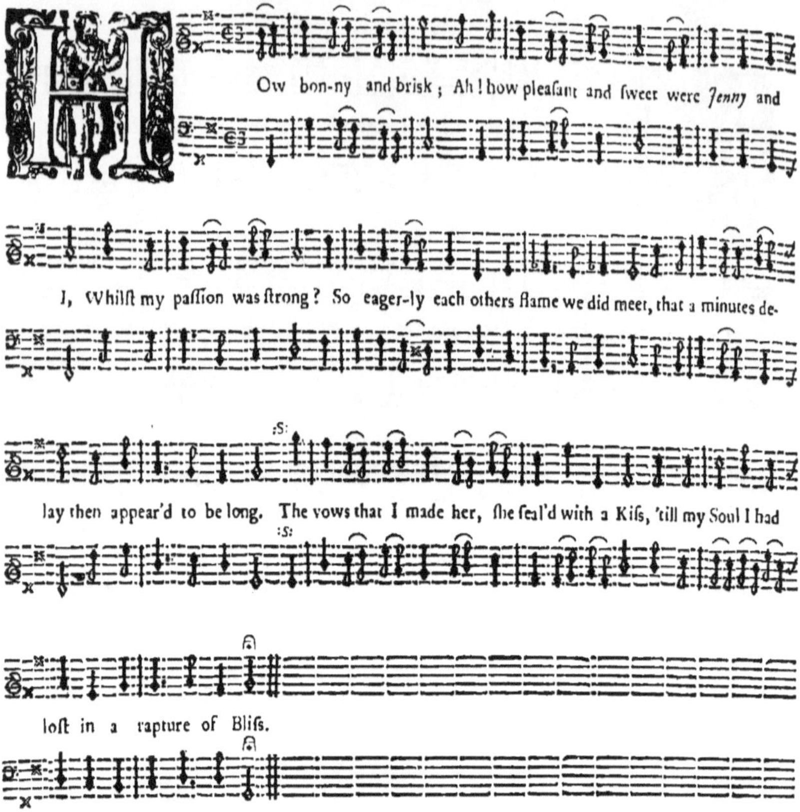

How bonny and brisk; Ah! how pleasant and sweet were *Jenny* and I, Whilst my passion was strong? So eagerly each others flame we did meet, that a minutes delay then appear'd to be long. The vows that I made her, she seal'd with a Kiss, 'till my Soul I had lost in a rapture of Bliss.

Mr. *Robert Smith*.

II.
I Vow'd, and I thought I could ever have Lov'd,
Where Beauty and Kindness together I found;
So sweetly she lookt, and so sweetly she mov'd,
That I fancy'd my strength with my joyes to abound:
For the pleasure I gave, she did doubly requite,
By finding out ever new ways to delight.

III.
At last, when enjoyment had put out my Fire,
My Strength was decay'd, and my Passion was done;
So pall'd was my Fancy, so tame my Desire,
That I from the Nymph, very fain would have gone:
Ah *Jenny*! said I, we adore thee in vain;
For Beauty enjoy'd does but burn to disdain.

Ah, false *Amintas*, can that hour so soon forgotten be, when first I

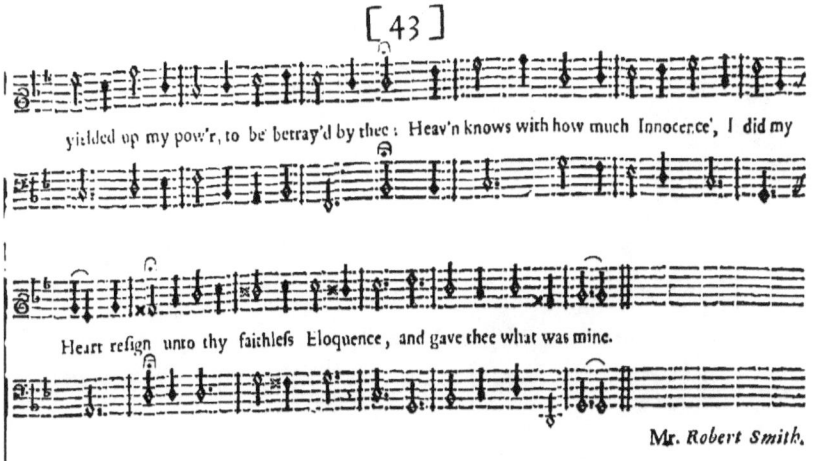

yielded up my pow'r, to be betray'd by thee; Heav'n knows with how much Innocence, I did my Heart resign unto thy faithless Eloquence, and gave thee what was mine.

Mr. *Robert Smith*.

II.

I had not one Reserve in store,
But at thy feet I lay'd
Those Arms that conquer'd heretofore,
Though now thy Trophies made:
Thy Eyes in silence told their Tale
Of Love in such a way,
That 'twas as easie to prevail,
As after to betray.

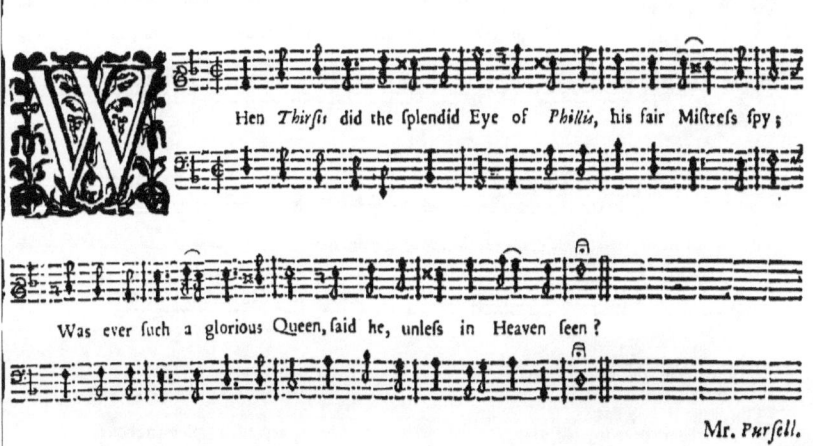

Hen *Thirsis* did the splendid Eye of *Phillis*, his fair Mistress spy; Was ever such a glorious Queen, said he, unless in Heaven seen?

Mr. *Purfell*.

II.
Fair *Phillis*, with a blushing Air,
Hearing these words, became more Fair:
Away, said he, you need not take
Fresh Beauty, you more fair to make.

III.
Then with a winning smile and look
His candid flatteries she took:
O stay, said he, 'tis done I vow,
Thirsis is Captivated now.

[44]

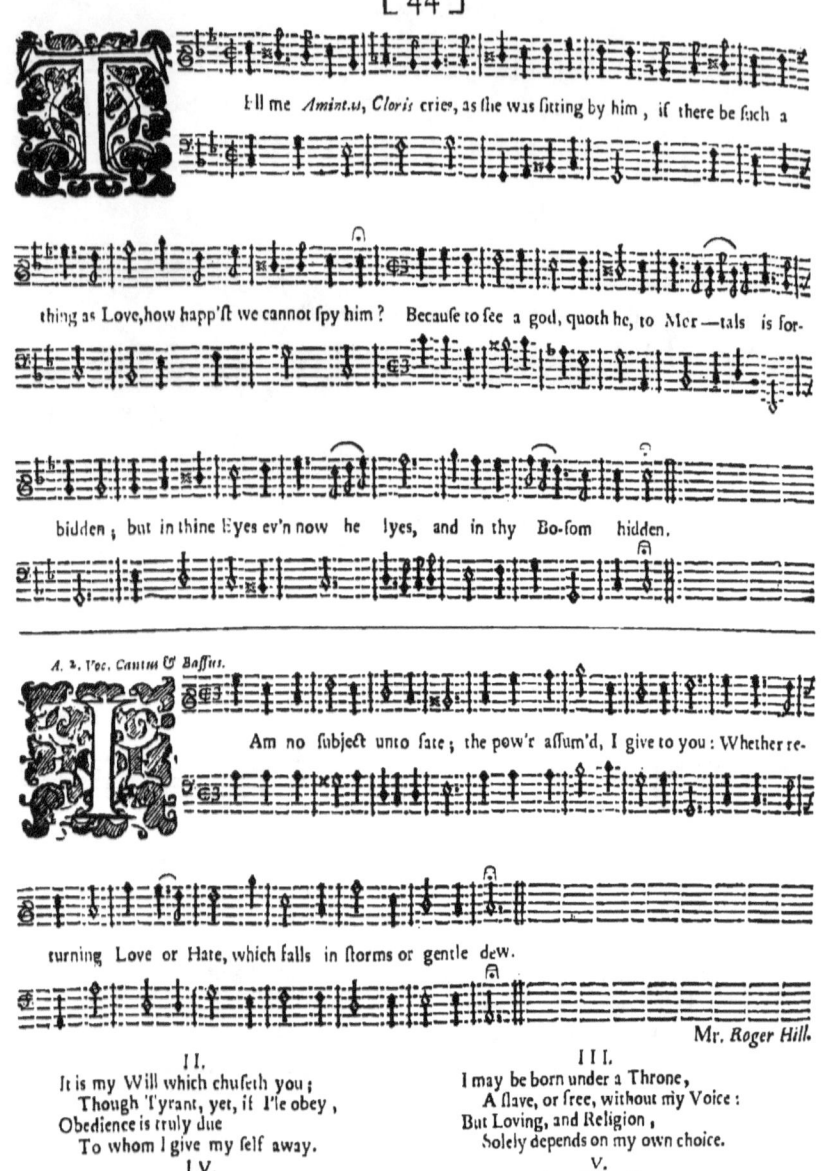

Tell me *Amintas*, *Cloris* cries, as she was sitting by him, if there be such a thing as Love, how happ'st we cannot spy him? Because to see a god, quoth he, to Mer—tals is forbidden; but in thine Eyes ev'n now he lyes, and in thy Bosom hidden.

A. 2. Voc. Cantus & Bassus.

I Am no subject unto fate; the pow'r assum'd, I give to you: Whether returning Love or Hate, which falls in storms or gentle dew.

Mr. *Roger Hill.*

II.
It is my Will which chuseth you;
 Though Tyrant, yet, if I'le obey,
Obedience is truly due
 To whom I give my self away.

IV.
The Worlds dimensions are wide;
 My mind not Heaven can confine:
That outward worship is bely'd,
 Who inward bows to other Shrine.

VI.
Thus fettered, I freely Love;
 My choice doth make the conquest shine:
And 'twill thy power best improve,
 That to thy Subject thou incline.

III.
I may be born under a Throne,
 A slave, or free, without my Voice:
But Loving, and Religion,
 Solely depends on my own choice.

V.
Force may be called Victory;
 Yet only those are overcome,
Who yield unto an Enemy,
 That is their certain fate and doom.

VII.
Who wisely Rules, deserves Command;
 Then keep thee Loyal next thy Heart:
Elective Monarchs cannot stand,
 Nor Loves without an equal dart.

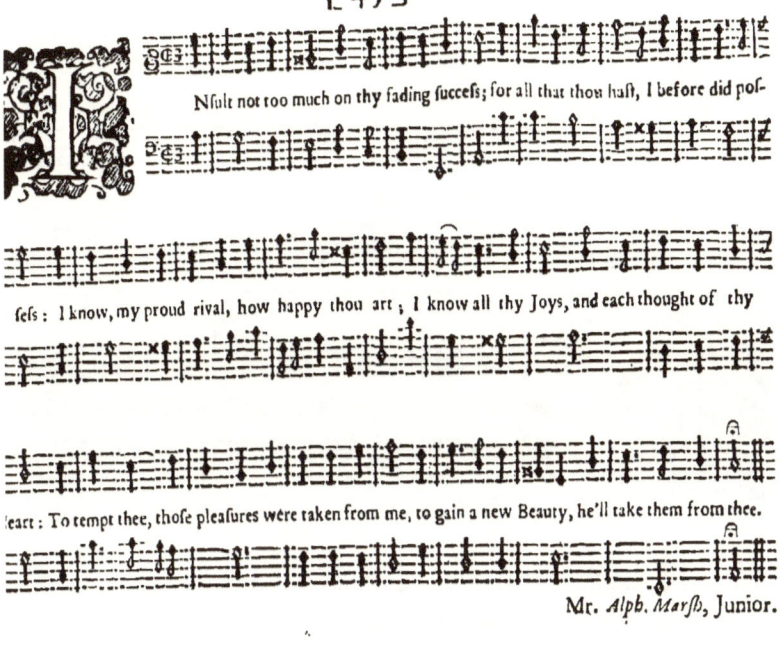

Insult not too much on thy fading success; for all that thou hast, I before did possess: I know, my proud rival, how happy thou art; I know all thy Joys, and each thought of thy heart: To tempt thee, those pleasures were taken from me, to gain a new Beauty, he'll take them from thee.

Mr. *Alph. Marsh*, Junior.

A. 2. Voc. Cantus & Bassus.

God *Cupid* for certain, as foolish as blind, to settle his heart upon people unkind; his punishment's just, for not having regard to the gentle Complyer, but ungrateful and hard: And you'l find it for ever like Oracle true, Love will fly the pursuer, the flyer pursue.

John Playford.

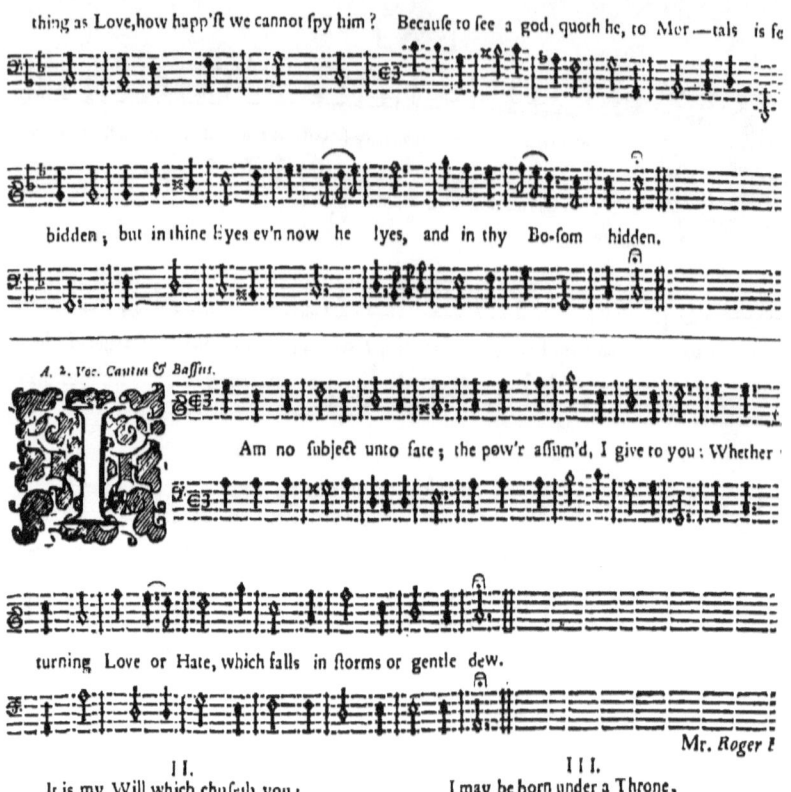

thing as Love, how happ'ft we cannot fpy him? Becaufe to fee a god, quoth he, to Mor—tals is fe bidden; but in thine Eyes ev'n now he lyes, and in thy Bo-fom hidden.

A. 2. Voc. Cantus & Baffus.

I Am no fubject unto fate; the pow'r affum'd, I give to you: Whether turning Love or Hate, which falls in ftorms or gentle dew.

Mr. *Roger*

II.
It is my Will which chufeth you;
   Though Tyrant, yet, it I'le obey,
Obedience is truly due
   To whom I give my felf away.

IV.
The Worlds dimenfions are wide;
   My mind not Heaven can confine:
That outward worfhip is bely'd,
   Who inward bows to other Shrine.

VI.
Thus fettered, I freely Love;
   My choice doth make the conqueft fhine:
And 'twill thy power beft improve,
   That to thy Subject thou incline.

III.
I may be born under a Throne,
   A flave, or free, without my Voice:
But Loving, and Religion,
   Solely depends on my own choice.

V.
Force may be called Victory;
   Yet only thofe are overcome,
Who yield unto an Enemy,
   That is their certain fate and doom.

VII.
Who wifely Rules, deferves Command;
   Then keep thee Loyal next thy Heart:
Elective Monarchs cannot ftand,
   Nor Loves without an equal dart.

Nsult not too much on thy fading succefs; for all that thou haft, I before did pof-

fefs: I know, my proud rival, how happy thou art; I know all thy Joys, and each thought of thy

Heart: To tempt thee, thofe pleafures were taken from me, to gain a new Beauty, he'll take them from thee.

Mr. *Alph. Marſh*, Junior.

A. 2. Voc. Cantus & Baſſus.

Od *Cupid* for certain, as foolifh as blind, to fettle his heart upon people un-

kind; his punifhment's juft, for not having regard to the gentle Complyer, but ungrateful and hard:

And you'l find it for e-ver like O-ra-cle true, Love will fly the purfuer, the flyer purfue.

John Playford.

[46]

O H! name not the day, least my Senses re-prove, and curse my kind Heart from the Knowledge of Love: Ah, the ignorant Fate of a fearful young Lover, when a sign is return'd, not t' have Wit to discover. To delay a kind Nymph from her hour of design, is to digg for a Treasure, and sink in the Mine.

II.
The effect of a smile in a vein of discourse,
'Twixt fear and good will, ought to make a Divorse:
Such Items deserves to be well understood,
Like a Vizardess, that peeps under her Hood.
Had I known but the minute her joys were upon her,
She had bid me good-night, and adieu to her honour.

III.
I knew not, alass! the Intrigue of her Art;
I thought she design'd to make sport with my Heart:
It panted with fear, and leapt so with joy,
Yet I thought to attempt all my hopes would destroy:
But since, I'm resolv'd, e're I prove such a sot,
The Nymph I'le enjoy, though I dye on the spot.

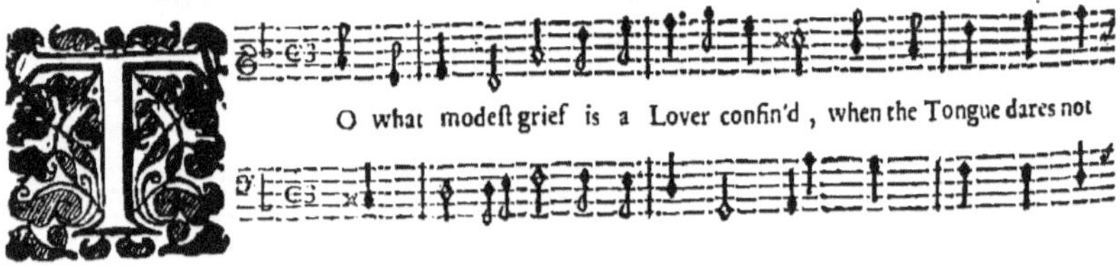

T O what modest grief is a Lover confin'd, when the Tongue dares not

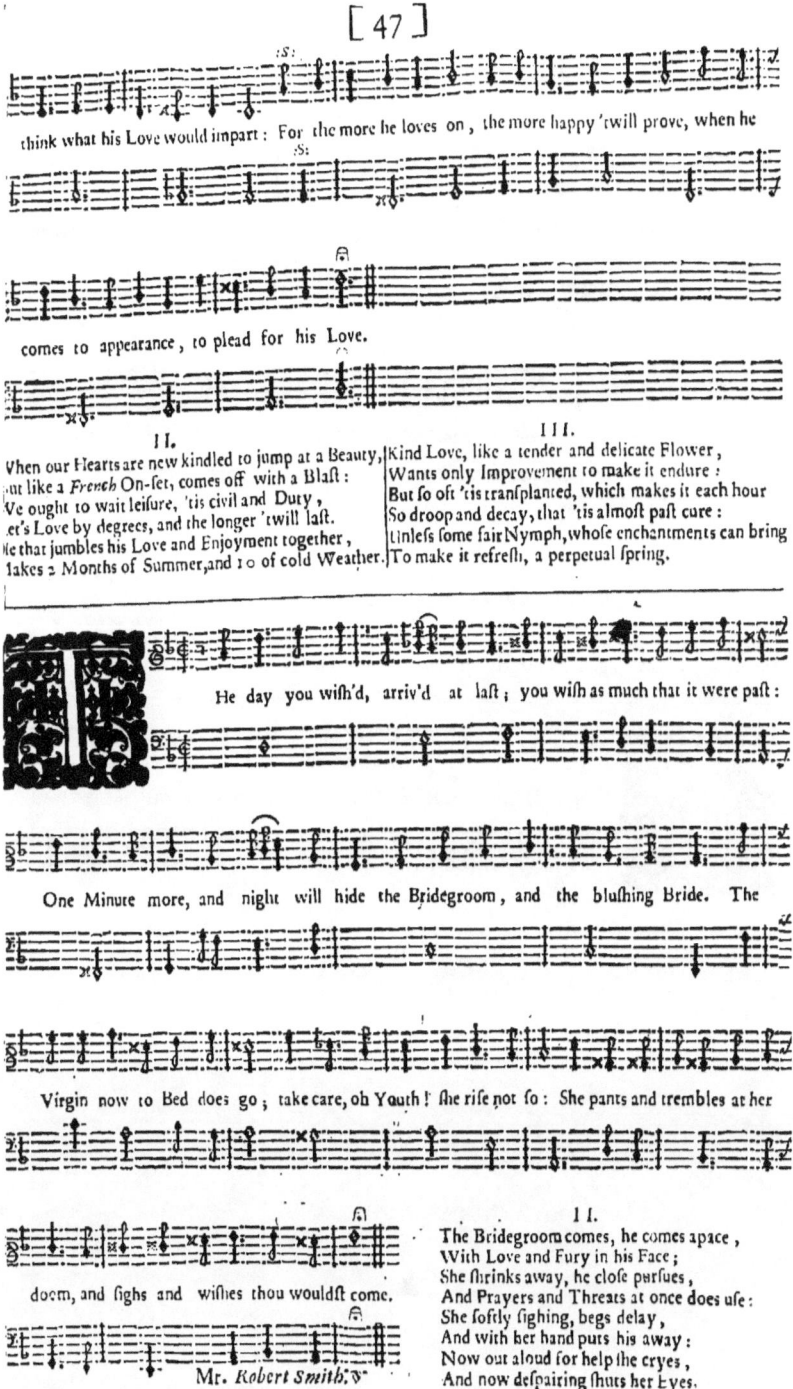

think what his Love would impart: For the more he loves on, the more happy 'twill prove, when he comes to appearance, to plead for his Love.

II.
When our Hearts are new kindled to jump at a Beauty,
But like a *French* On-set, comes off with a Blast:
We ought to wait leisure, 'tis civil and Duty,
Let's Love by degrees, and the longer 'twill last.
He that jumbles his Love and Enjoyment together,
Takes 2 Months of Summer, and 10 of cold Weather.

III.
Kind Love, like a tender and delicate Flower,
Wants only Improvement to make it endure:
But so oft 'tis transplanted, which makes it each hour
So droop and decay, that 'tis almost past cure:
Unless some fair Nymph, whose enchantments can bring
To make it refresh, a perpetual spring.

The day you wish'd, arriv'd at last; you wish as much that it were past: One Minute more, and night will hide the Bridegroom, and the blushing Bride. The Virgin now to Bed does go; take care, oh Youth! she rise not so: She pants and trembles at her doom, and sighs and wishes thou wouldst come.

Mr. *Robert Smith.*

II.
The Bridegroom comes, he comes apace,
With Love and Fury in his Face;
She shrinks away, he close pursues,
And Prayers and Threats at once does use:
She softly sighing, begs delay,
And with her hand puts his away:
Now out aloud for help she cryes,
And now despairing shuts her Eyes.

Heart from the Knowledge of Love: Ah, the ignorant Fate of a fearful young Lover, when

sign is return'd, not t'have Wit to discover. To delay a kind Nymph from her hour of desi[gn]

is to digg for a Treasure, and sink in the Mine.

II.
The effect of a smile in a vein of discourse,
'Twixt fear and good will, ought to make a Divorse:
Such Items deserves to be well understood,
Like a Vizardess, that peeps under her Hood.
Had I known but the minute her joys were upon her,
She had bid me good-night, and adieu to her honour.

III.
I knew not, alass! the Intrigue of her Art;
I thought she design'd to make sport with my Heart,
It panted with fear, and leapt so with joy,
Yet I thought to attempt all my hopes would destr[oy]
But since, I'm resolv'd, e're I prove such a sot,
The Nymph I'le enjoy, though I dye on the spot.

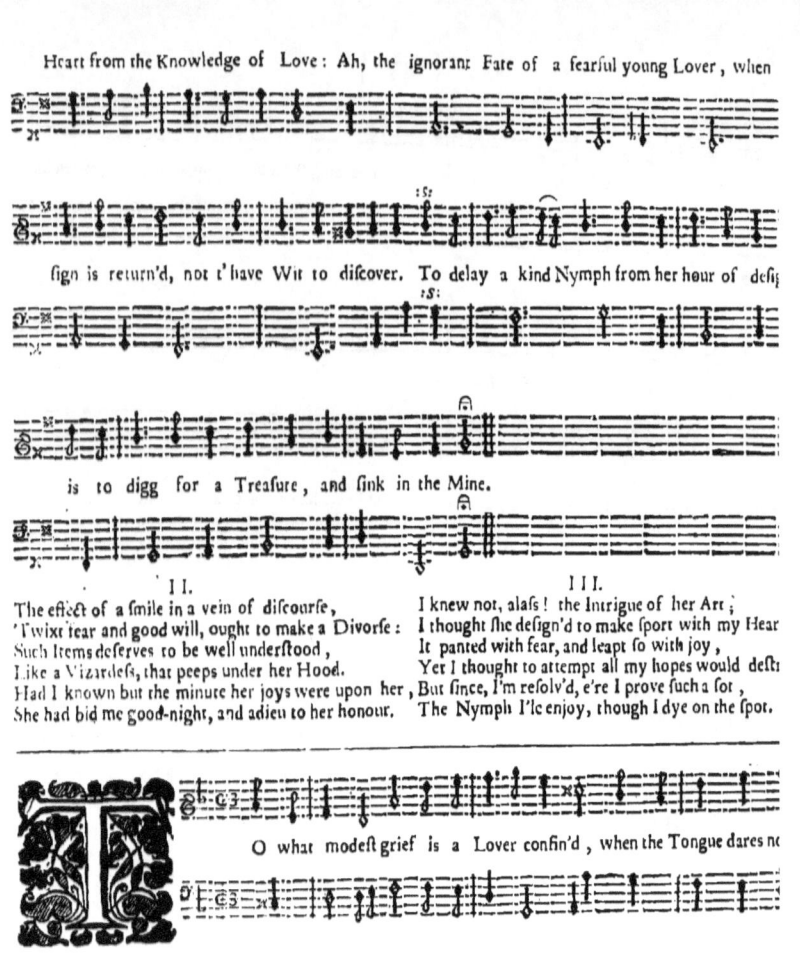

TO what modest grief is a Lover confin'd, when the Tongue dares n[ot]

[47]

think what his Love would impart: For the more he loves on, the more happy 'twill prove, when he comes to appearance, to plead for his Love.

II.
When our Hearts are new kindled to jump at a Beauty,
But like a *French* On-set, comes off with a Blast:
We ought to wait leisure, 'tis civil and Duty,
Let's Love by degrees, and the longer 'twill last.
He that jumbles his Love and Enjoyment together,
Makes 2 Months of Summer, and 10 of cold Weather.

III.
Kind Love, like a tender and delicate Flower,
Wants only Improvement to make it endure:
But so oft 'tis transplanted, which makes it each hour
So droop and decay, that 'tis almost past cure:
Unless some fair Nymph, whose enchantments can bring
To make it refresh, a perpetual spring.

The day you wish'd, arriv'd at last; you wish as much that it were past: One Minute more, and night will hide the Bridegroom, and the blushing Bride. The Virgin now to Bed does go; take care, oh Youth! she rise not so: She pants and trembles at her doom, and sighs and wishes thou wouldst come.

Mr. *Robert Smith.*

II.
The Bridegroom comes, he comes apace,
With Love and Fury in his Face;
She shrinks away, he close pursues,
And Prayers and Threats at once does use:
She softly sighing, begs delay,
And with her hand puts his away:
Now out aloud for help she cryes,
And now despairing shuts her Eyes.

PHillis, oh! turn that Face away, whose splendor but benights my day:
Sad Eyes like mine, and wounded Hearts, shun the bright rayes which Beau-ty darts. Unwelcome is that Sun, which pries into those shades where Sor-row lies.

II.
Go shine on happy things, to me
That Blessing is a Miserie ;
Whom thy fierce Sun not warms, but burns ;
Like that the sooty *Indian* turns :
I'le serve your night, and there confin'd,
Wish thee, less fair, or else, more kind.

Mr. *Jo. Jackson.*

WHy, O *Cupid!* so long hast thou shun'd me ? my disdains, alass, have undone me :
Since you've left me to choose at my Pleasure, I have robb'd my poor heart of it Treasure. And

Beauty no more shall suffer Eclips, nor jealousie dare to confine the pow'r of those Eyes, or use of those Lips, which nothing but kindness design. Our Ladies shall be as frolick as we; nor shall Husband or Father repine: Our Ladies shall be as frollick as we; nor shall Husband or Father repine.

Mr. *Robert Smith*.

II.
We'll banish the stratagems us'd by the State,
To keep the poor Lover in awe;
Henceforth they themselves shall rule their own fate,
And desire shall be to them Law:
Thus they being free from Padlock and Key,
May with their Reformers withdraw.

III.
Where in private we'll teach them the Mysteries of love
And practice that Lecture over;
'Till we the fond scruple of honour remove,
And the end of our passion discover.
No Maid shall complain, or Wife sigh in vain,
For each may be eas'd by her Lover.

IV.
Away with all things that sound like to Laws,
In this our New Reformation;
Let the Formalist prate the Good old Cause,
'Tis a general Tolleration:
From this time we're free from Vile Heresie,
And a vizard Excommunication.

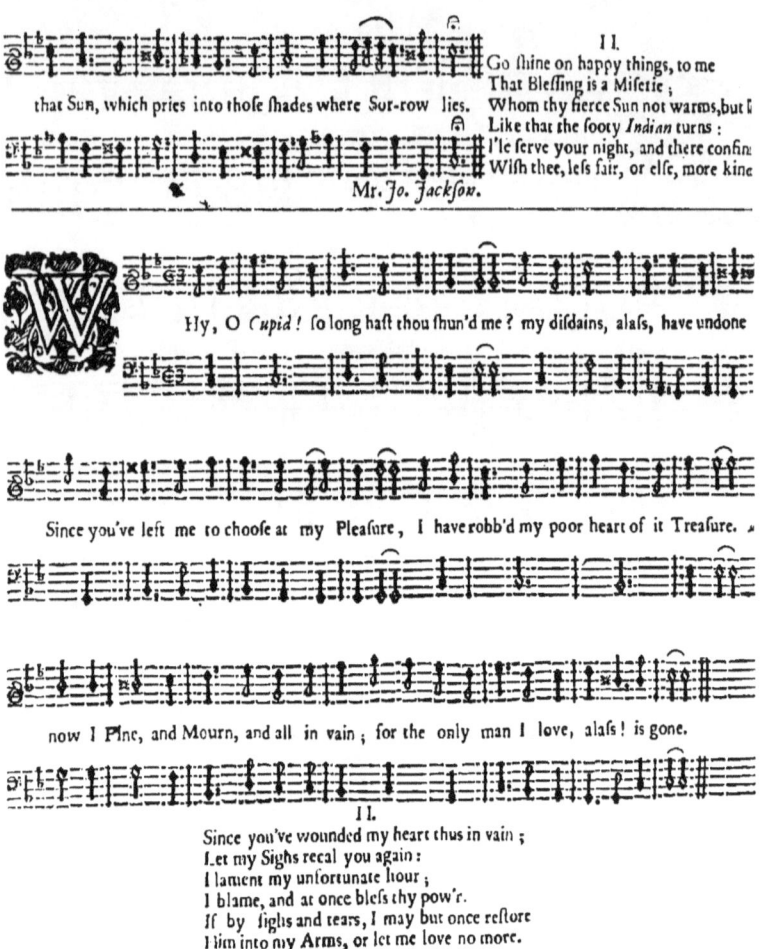

that Sun, which pries into those shades where Sor-row lies.

II.
Go shine on happy things, to me
That Blessing is a Miserie;
Whom thy fierce Sun not warms, but b[urns]
Like that the sooty *Indian* turns:
I'le serve your night, and there confin[e]
With thee, less fair, or else, more kin[d.]

Mr. *Jo. Jackson.*

Hy, O *Cupid!* so long hast thou shun'd me? my disdains, alass, have undone

Since you've left me to choose at my Pleasure, I have robb'd my poor heart of it Treasure.

now I Pine, and Mourn, and all in vain; for the only man I love, alass! is gone.

II.
Since you've wounded my heart thus in vain;
Let my Sighs recal you again:
I lament my unfortunate hour;
I blame, and at once bless thy pow'r.
If by sighs and tears, I may but once restore
Him into my Arms, or let me love no more.

Mr. *Robert Smith*.

II.
We'll banish the stratagems us'd by the State,
 To keep the poor Lover in awe;
Henceforth they themselves shall rule their own fate,
 And desire shall be to them Law:
Thus they being free from Padlock and Key,
 May with their Reformers withdraw.

III.
Where in private we'll teach them the Mysteries of love
 And practice that Lecture over;
'Till we the fond scruple of honour remove,
 And the end of our passion discover.
No Maid shall complain, or Wife sigh in vain,
 For each may be eas'd by her Lover.

IV.
Away with all things that sound like to Laws,
 In this our New Reformation;
Let the Formalist prate the Good old Cause,
 'Tis a general Tolleration:
From this time we're free from Vile Heresie,
 And a vizard Excommunication.

Mr. *Robert Smith*

II.

Now cold as Ice I am, now hot as Fire;
I dare not tell my self my own defire:
But let day fly away, and bid night haft her;
    Grant ye kind pow'rs above
    Slow hours to parting Love:
But when to blifs we move, let them fly fafter.

III.

How fweet is it to Love, when I difcover
Thofe flames that burn my Soul, warming my Lover
'Tis pity Love fo true, fhould be miftaken;
    If that this night he be
    Falfe, or unkind to me:
Let me dye, e're I fee, That I'm forfaken.

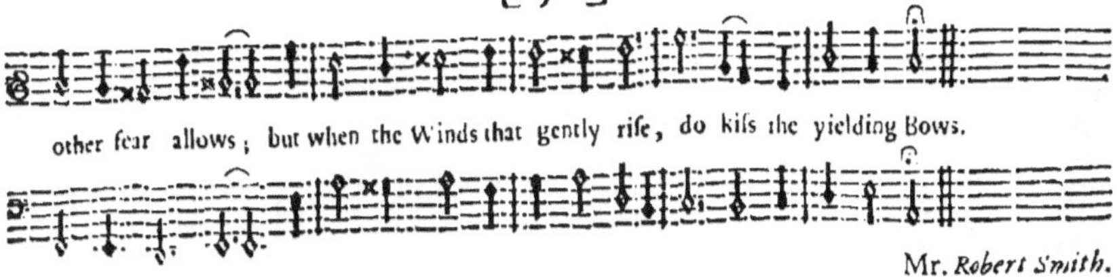

other fear allows; but when the Winds that gently rise, do kiss the yielding Bows.

Mr. *Robert Smith.*

II.
Down there we sat upon the Moss,
And did begin to play
A thousand wanton Tricks, to pass
The heat of all the day:
A-many Kisses he did give,
And I return'd the same;
Which made me willing to receive
That which I dare not name.

III.
His charming Eyes no aid requir'd
To tell his amorous Tale,
On her that was already fir'd,
'Twas easie to prevail:
He did but Kiss, and clasp me round,
Whilst those his thoughts exprest;
And laid me softly on the ground:
Oh, who can guess the rest!

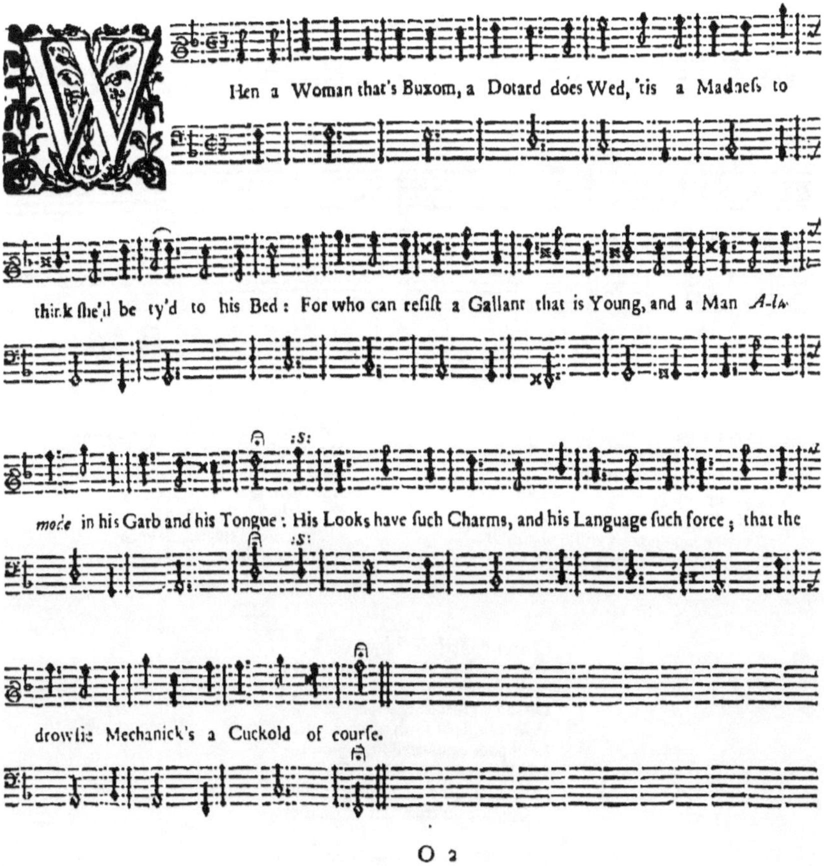

When a Woman that's Buxom, a Dotard does Wed, 'tis a Madness to think she'd be ty'd to his Bed: For who can resist a Gallant that is Young, and a Man A-la-mode in his Garb and his Tongue: His Looks have such Charms, and his Language such force; that the drowsie Mechanick's a Cuckold of course.

Mr. *John Banister.*

II.
Her poor Heart had no defence,
But its Maiden innocence;
In each sweet retyring eye,
You might easily decry
Troops of yielding beauties fly,
Leaving rare ungarded treasure
To the Conquerors will and pleasure.
   And now she cryes, &c.

III.
Now and then, a straggling frown,
(Through the shade slips up and down)
Shooting such a piercing dart,
As would make the Tyrant smart,
And preserve her Lips and Heart:
But, alas, her Empires gone,
Throne, and Temples, all undone.
   And now she cryes, &c.

IV.
Charm aloft, those stormy winds,
That may keep these Golden Mines;
And let *Spaniards* Love be tore
On some cruel Rocky shore,
Where he'll put forth to Sea no more:
Least poor conquered Beauty cry,
Oh, I'm wounded! Oh, I dye!
   And then, there is no pow'r above
   Can save me from this Tyrant Love.

[53]

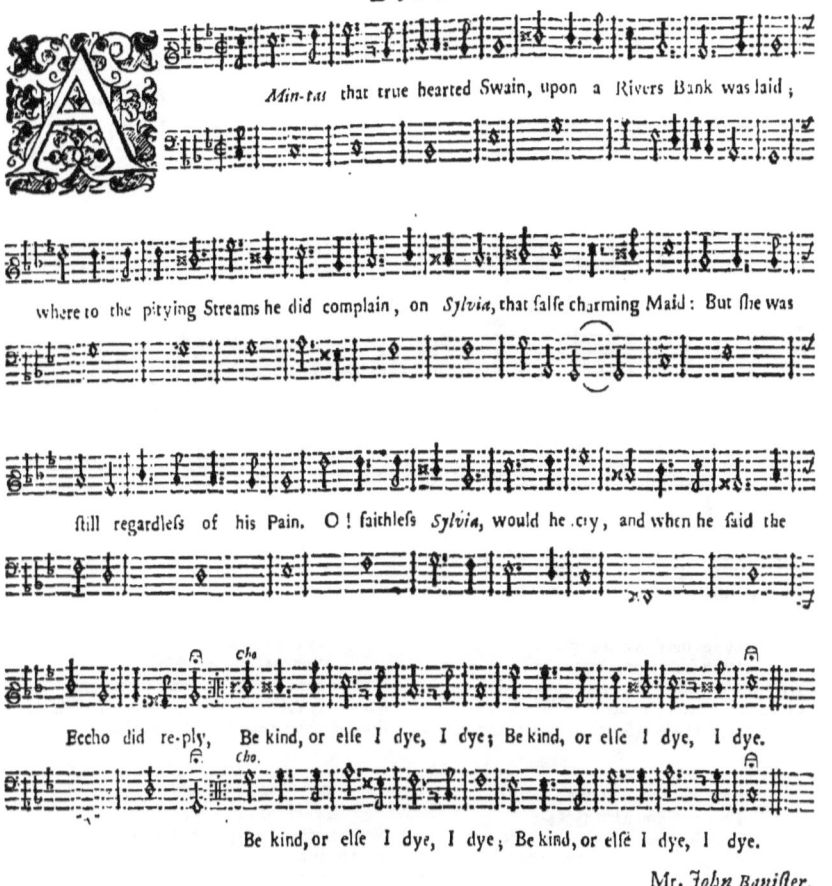

A Min-tas that true hearted Swain, upon a Rivers Bank was laid; where to the pitying Streams he did complain, on *Sylvia*, that false charming Maid: But she was still regardless of his Pain. O! faithless *Sylvia*, would he cry, and when he said the Eccho did re-ply, Be kind, or else I dye, I dye; Be kind, or else I dye, I dye.

Be kind, or else I dye, I dye; Be kind, or else I dye, I dye.

Mr. John Banister.

II.

A show'r of Tears his Eyes let fall,
  Which in the River made impress;
Then Sigh'd, and *Sylvia* false would call,
  O cruel, faithless Shepherdess!
Is Love, with you, become a Criminal?
  Ah! lay aside this needless scorn,
Allow your poor Admirer some return:
  Consider how I burn, I burn: Consider, &c.

III.

Those Smiles and Kisses which you give,
  Remember, *Sylvia*, are my due;
And all the Joys my Rival does receive,
  He ravishes from me, not you:
Ah! *Sylvia*, can I live, and this believe,
  Insensible are taught to see
My Languishments, and seems to pity me;
  Which I demand of thee, of thee: Which I demand, &c.

A. 2. Voc. Cantus & Bassus.

[54]

The time that is past, when she held me so fast; And declar'd that her

Honour no longer could last: When no light, but her languishing Eyes did appear, to pre-

vent all excuses of Blushes and Fear.

II.
When she sigh'd and unlac'd,
With such trembling and hast,
As if she had long'd to be closer imbrac'd:
My Lips the sweet pleasure of Kisses enjoy'd
While my mind was in search of hid treasure imploy'd

III.
My heart set on fire
With the flames of desire,
I boldly pursu'd what she seem'd to enquire:
But she cry'd, For pi-ty-sake, change your ill mind;
Pray *Amintas*, be civil, or I'le be unkind.

IV.
Dear *Amintas*, she cryes,
Then casts down her eyes;
And in Kisses she gives, what in words she denys:
Too sure of my Conquest, I purpose to stay,
'Till her freer consent had more sweetned the pray.

V.
But too late I begun,
For her passion was done;
Now *Amintas*, she crys, I will never be won:
Your tears and your courtship no pity can move,
For you've slighted the critical minute of Love.

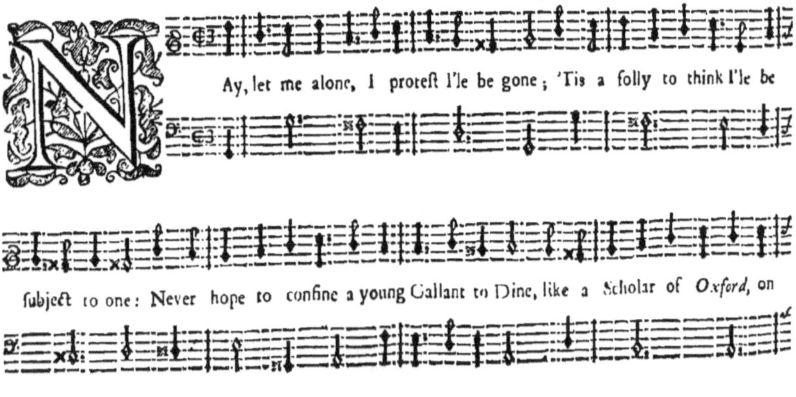

Ay, let me alone, I protest I'le be gone; 'Tis a folly to think I'le be

subject to one: Never hope to confine a young Gallant to Dine, like a Scholar of *Oxford*, on

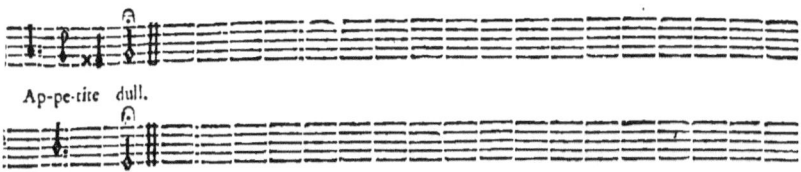

Ap-pe-tite dull.

Mr. *Pelham Humphrey.*

II.

y your wantoning Art, of a Sigh and a Start,
ou endeavour in vain, to inveagle my Heart;
or the pretty disguise of your languishing Eyes,
ill never prevail with my Sinews to rise:
And 'twas never the Mode, in an Amorous Treat,
When a Lover has Din'd, to perswade him to Eat.

III.

Then, *Betty,* the Jest is almost at the best,
'Tis only variety makes up the Feast:
For when we've enjoy'd, and with pleasures are cloy'd,
The Vows that we made, to Love ever, are void.
And you know pretty Nymph, it was ever unfit
That a Meal should be made of a Relishing bit.

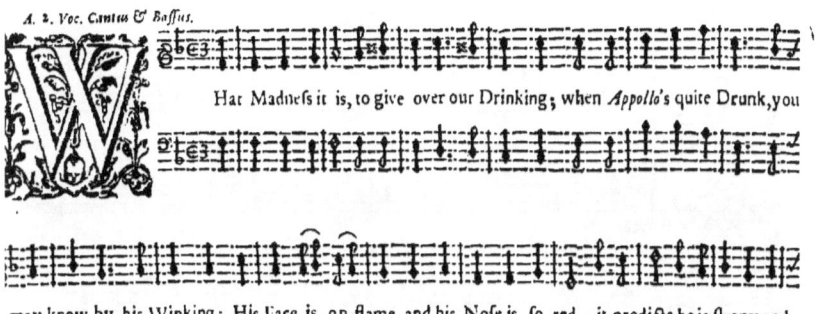

A. 2. *Voc. Cantus & Bassus.*

What Madness it is, to give over our Drinking; when *Appollo's* quite Drunk, you may know by his Winking: His Face is on flame, and his Nose is so red, it predicts he is sleepy and

vent all excuses of Blushes and Fear.

II.
When she sigh'd and unlac'd,
With such trembling and haft,
As if she had long'd to be closer imbrac'd :
My Lips the sweet pleasure of Kisses enjoy'd
While my mind was in search of hid treasure imploy'd

III.
My heart set on fire
With the flames of desire,
I boldly pursu'd what she seem'd to enquire :
But she cry'd, For pi-ty-sake, change your ill
Pray *Amintas*, be civil, or I'le be unkind.

IV.
Dear *Amintas*, she cryes,
Then casts down her eyes ;
And in Kisses she gives, what in words she denys :
Too sure of my Conquest, I purpose to stay,
'Till her freer consent had more sweetned the pray.

V.
But too late I begun,
For her passion was done ;
Now *Amintas*, she crys, I will never be won :
Your tears and your courtship no pity can mov
For you've slighted the critical minute of Love.

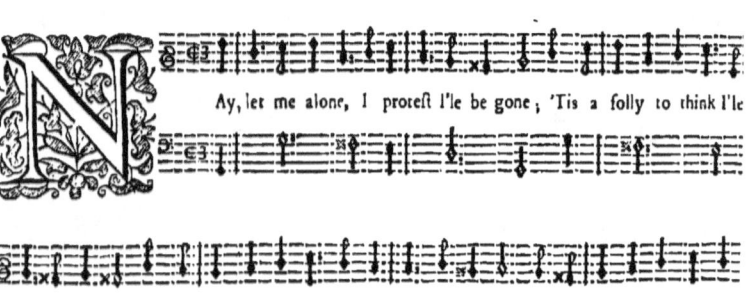

Ay, let me alone, I protest I'le be gone, 'Tis a folly to think I'le subject to one: Never hope to confine a young Gallant to Dine, like a Scholar of *Oxford*,

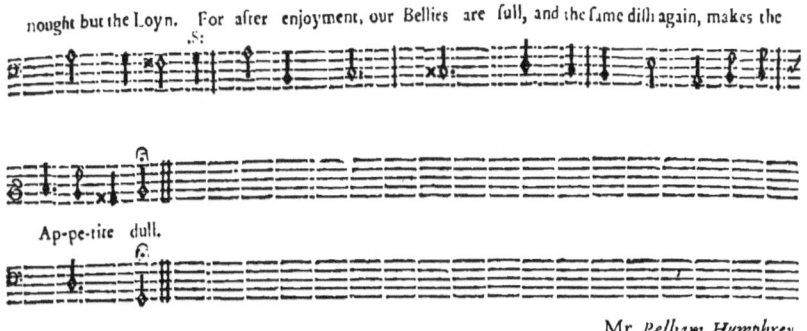

nought but the Loyn. For after enjoyment, our Bellies are full, and the same dish again, makes the Ap-pe-tite dull.

Mr. *Pelham Humphrey*.

II.

By your wantoning Art, of a Sigh and a Start,
You endeavour in vain, to inveagle my Heart;
For the pretty disguise of your languishing Eyes,
Will never prevail with my Sinews to rise:
And 'twas never the Mode, in an Amorous Treat,
When a Lover has Din'd, to perswade him to Eat.

III.

Then, *Betty*, the Jest is almost at the best,
'Tis only variety makes up the Feast:
For when we've enjoy'd, and with pleasures are cloy'd,
The Vows that we made, to Love ever, are void.
And you know pretty Nymph, it was ever unfit
That a Meal should be made of a Relishing bit.

A. 2. Voc. Cantus & Bassus.

What Madness it is, to give over our Drinking; when *Appollo*'s quite Drunk, you may know by his Winking: His Face is on flame, and his Nose is so red, it predicts he is sleepy and goes Drunk to Bed. Let him Sleep to grow Sober, while we tarry hear, and Drink 'till the morning appear.

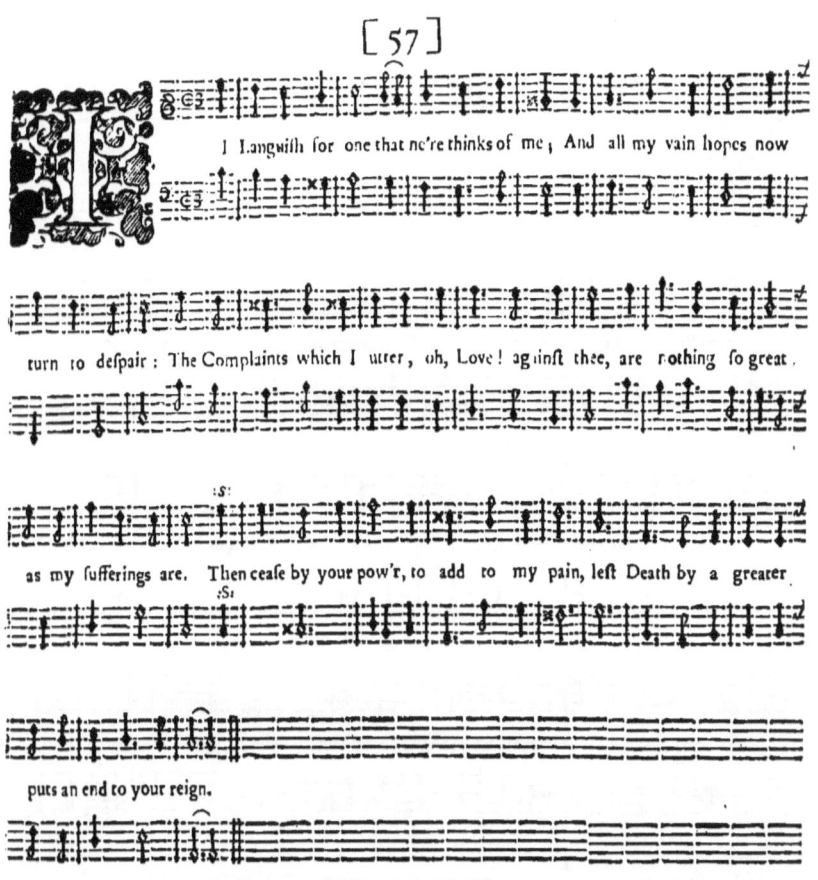

I Languish for one that ne're thinks of me, And all my vain hopes now turn to despair: The Complaints which I utter, oh, Love! against thee, are nothing so great as my sufferings are. Then cease by your pow'r, to add to my pain, lest Death by a greater puts an end to your reign.

Mr. *John Banister.*

II.

My Sighs and my Tears so privately I
Do give to a Passion, I ne're will impart;
That though I am vanquish'd, and conquer'd dye,
No one can e're say, that I first lost my Heart:
Since the torments I feel, I will not discover,
It ne're shall be said, There dyes a poor Lover.

III.

How strangely severe is fate, since I find
That with all my resistance, I cannot get free
From a slavery, by which I see I'm design'd,
My dearest *Philander*, thy Martyr to be:
O fate! so unkind, to make me esteem
My death to be welcome, cause given by thee.

Q

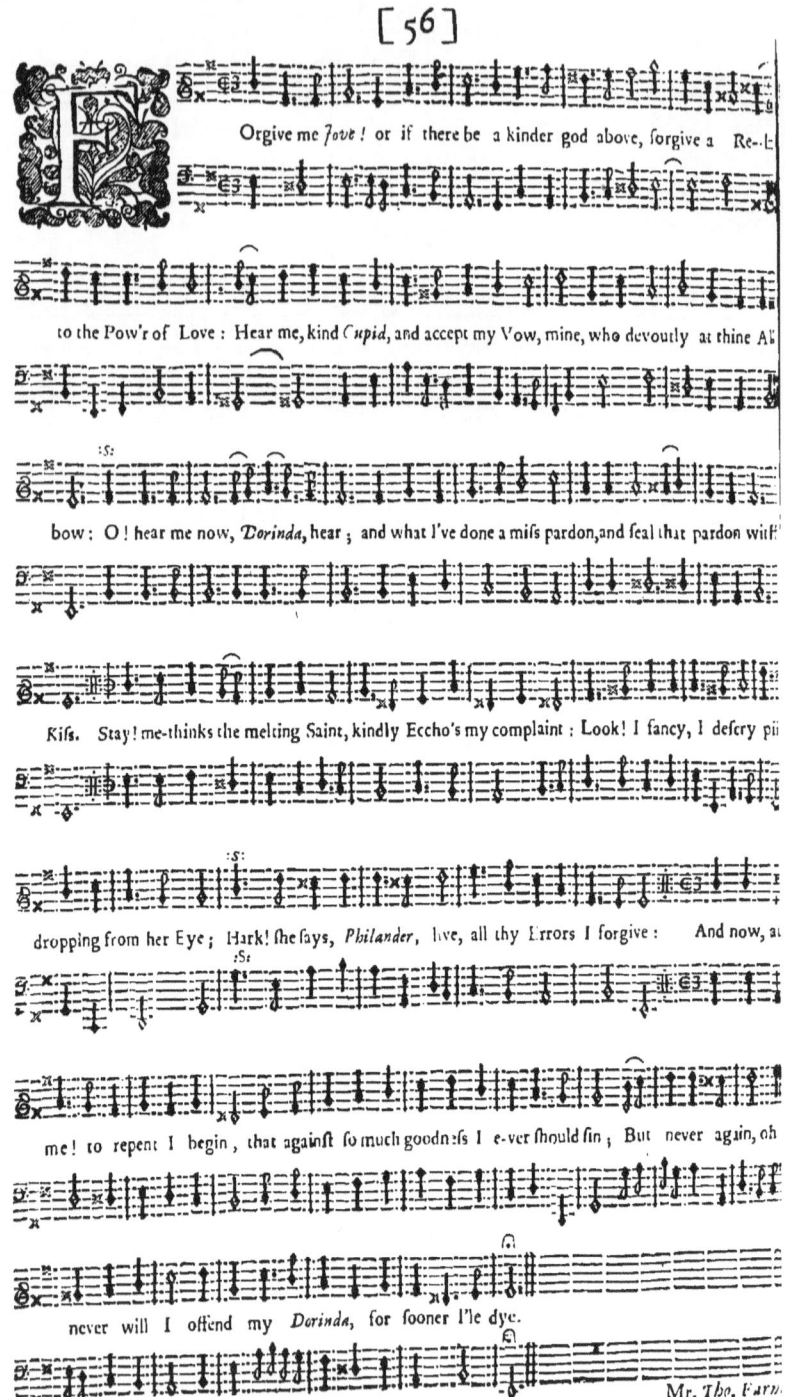

Mr. Tho. Farm.

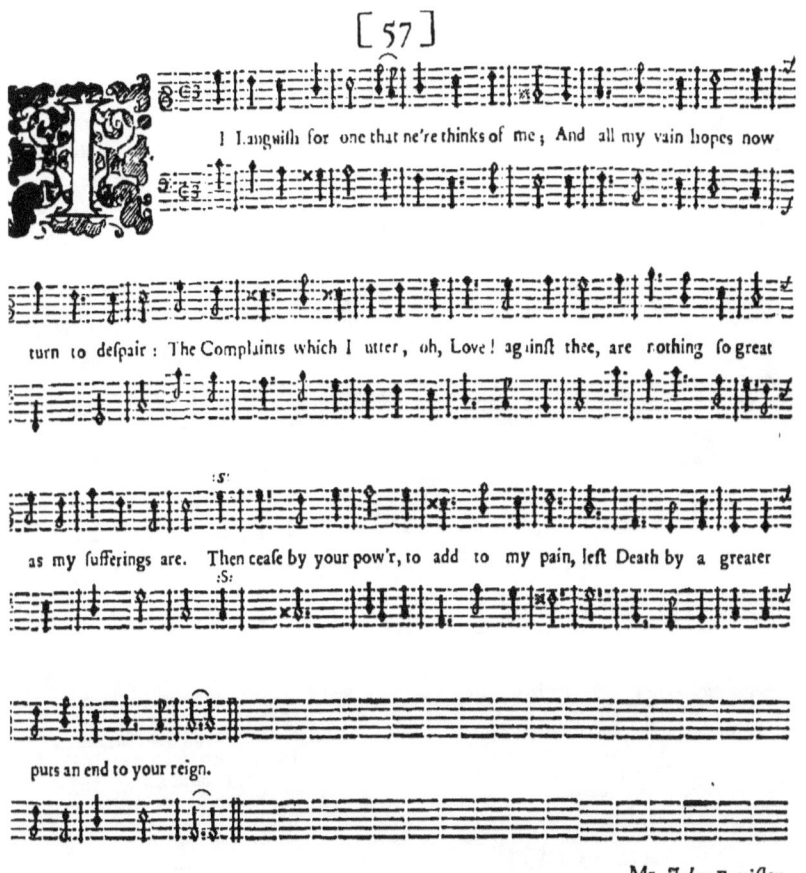

Mr. *John Banister.*

II.

My Sighs and my Tears so privately I
Do give to a Passion, I ne're will impart;
That though I am vanquish'd, and conquer'd dye,
No one can e're say, that I first lost my Heart:
Since the torments I feel, I will not discover,
It ne're shall be said, There dyes a poor Lover.

III.

How strangely severe is fate, since I find
That with all my resistance, I cannot get free
From a slavery, by which I see I'm design'd,
My dearest *Philander*, thy Martyr to be:
O fate! so unkind, to make me esteem
My death to be welcome, cause given by thee.

A. 2. Voc. Cantus & Bassus.

AH, cruel Eyes! that first enflam'd my poor resistless heart; that when I would my thoughts have blam'd, they still increase the smart: What pow'r above creates such Love to languish with desire? May some disdain encrease my pain, or may the flame expire.

II.
And yet I dye to think how soon
My wishes may return,
If slighted, and my hope once gone,
I must in silence mourn:
Then Tyranness,
Do but express,
The Mystery of your pow'r;
'Tis as soon said,
You'l Love and Wed,
As studying for't an hour.

III.
I yield to fate, though your fair Eyes
Have made the pow'r your own;
'Twas they did first, my heart surprize,
Dear Nymph! 'twas they alone:
For Honours sake,
Your heart awake;
And let your pity move:
Least in despair
Of one so fair,
I bid adieu to Love.

AWay with the silly blind god, and his Darts, who makes such a bustle, and noise in the Town, with Wounding, Surprizing, and Breaking of Hearts; from the proud

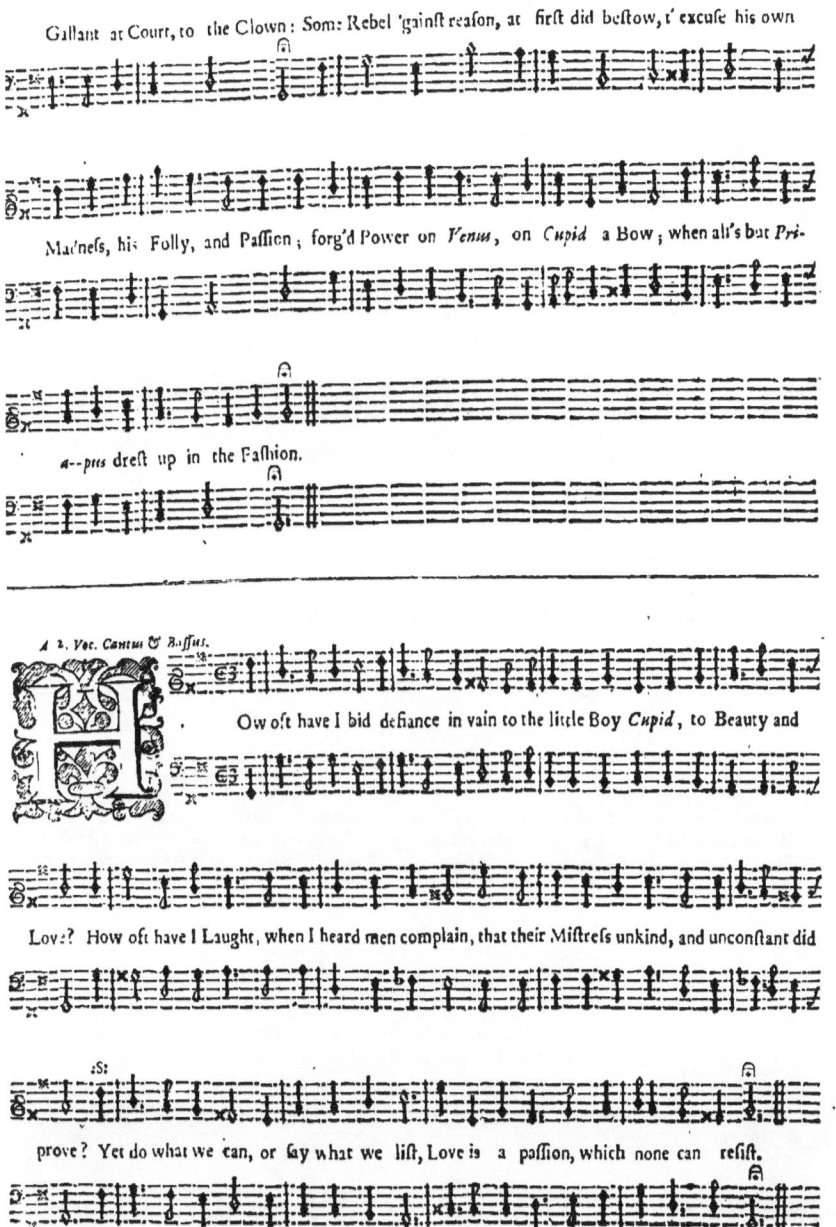

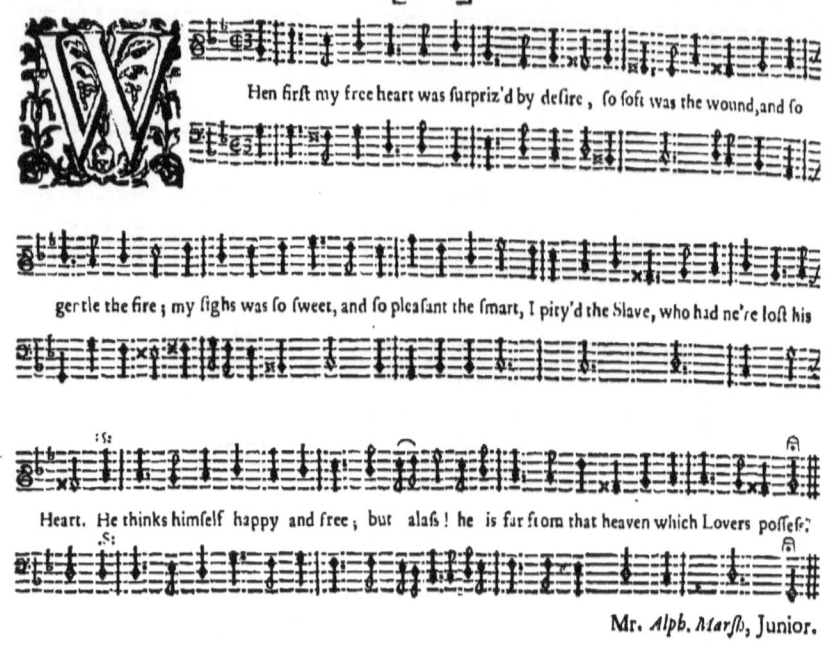

Hen first my free heart was surpriz'd by desire, so soft was the wound, and so gentle the fire; my sighs was so sweet, and so pleasant the smart, I pity'd the Slave, who had ne're lost his Heart. He thinks himself happy and free; but alas! he is far from that heaven which Lovers possess.

Mr. *Alph. Marsh*, Junior.

II.
In Nature was nothing I found to compare
With the Beauty of *Phillis*, I thought her so fair:
A Wit so divine all her sayings did fill;
A Goddess she seem'd, and I thought on her still:
  With a zeal more inflam'd, and a passion more true
  Than a Martyr in flames for Religion, can shew.

III.
More Virtues and Graces I find in her Mind,
Then the Schools can invent, or gods e're design:
She seem'd to be mine, by each glance of her Eye,
If Mortals may aim at a blessing so high.
  Each day, with new favours, new hopes she did give;
  But, alas! what we wish, we too soon do believe.

IV.
With awful respect while I lov'd and admir'd,
But fear'd to attempt what I so much desir'd;
In a moment the life of my hopes was destroy'd,
For a Shepherd, more daring, fell on, and enjoy'd.
  But in spite of my fate, and the pains I endure,
  I will try her again in a second Amour.

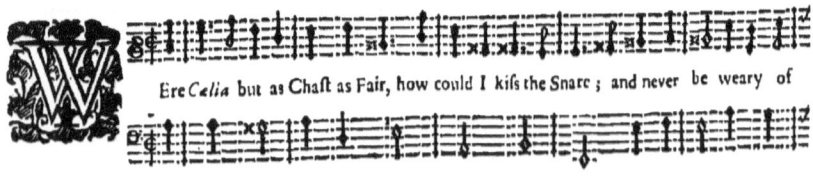

Ere *Celia* but as Chast as Fair, how could I kiss the Snare; and never be weary of

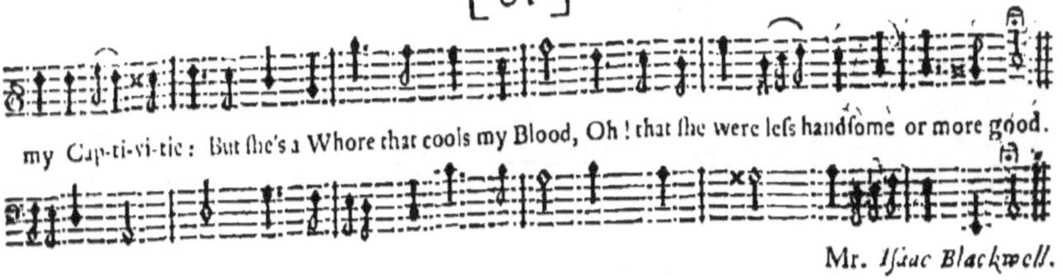

[61]

my Cap-ti-vi-tie: But she's a Whore that cools my Blood, Oh! that she were less handsome or more good.

Mr. *Isaac Blackwell*.

II.
Would you believe that there can rest
Deceit within that Breast;
Or that those Eyes,
Which look like Friends, are only spies:
But she's a Whore; yet sure I lye;
May there not be, degrees of Chastity?

III.
No, no, what means that wanton Smile,
But only to beguile;
Thus did the first
Of Women, make all Men accurst:
I, for their sakes, give Women o're;
The first was false, the fairest was a Whore.

F all the gay Ladies that walk the brisk Town, my *Sylvia* for Beauty has got the Renown; Her carriage, where ever she comes do surprize, she wounds with her Wit and she kills with her Eyes: So Jaunty, so pretty, so full of Delight, she laughs all the day, and loves all the night.

R

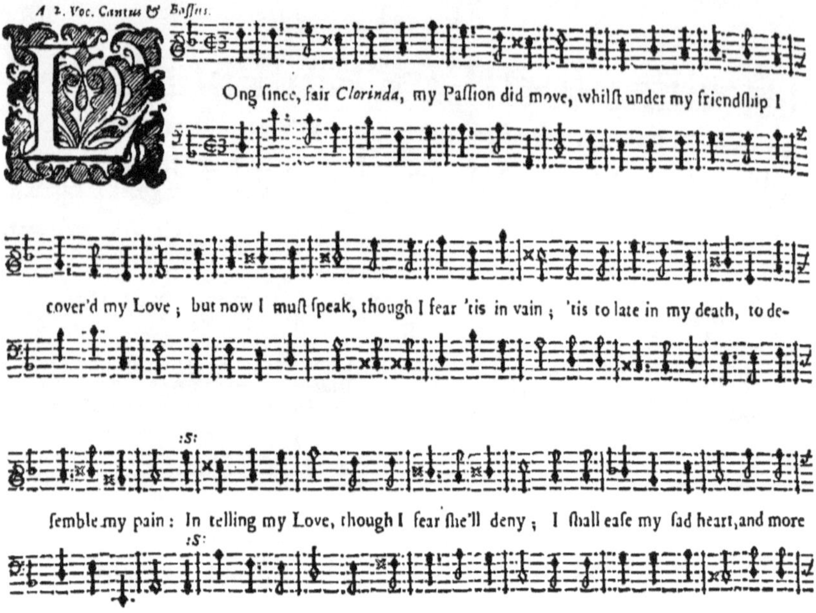

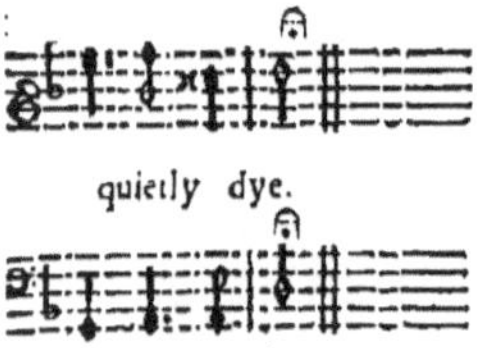

A 2. Voc. Cantus & Bassus.

Long since, fair *Clorinda*, my Passion did move, whilst under my friendship I cover'd my Love; but now I must speak, though I fear 'tis in vain; 'tis to late in my death, to desemble my pain: In telling my Love, though I fear she'll deny; I shall ease my sad heart, and more quietly dye.

Mr. *Tho. Farmer.*

II.
My Thoughts are so tender, my Tongue cannot tell
What bliss would be yours, could you Love half so well:
Let the thing with a title our property prove,
Let him have the show, and let me have the Love.
I've lov'd you so long, that if now you delay,
You'l owe me so much as you never can pay.

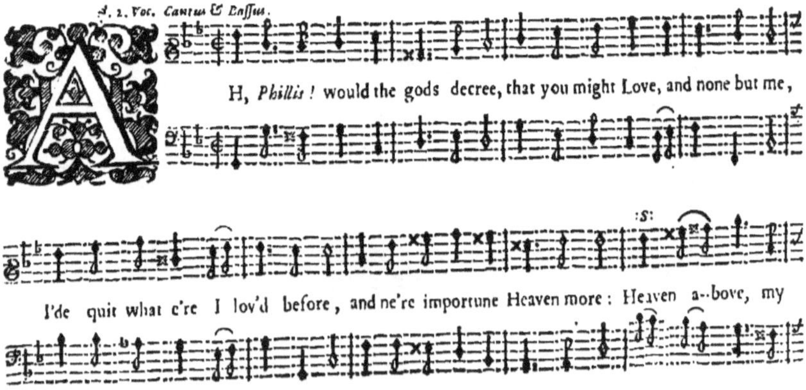

A 2. Voc. Cantus & Bassus.

AH, *Phillis!* would the gods decree, that you might Love, and none but me, I'de quit what e're I lov'd before, and ne're importune Heaven more: Heaven a--bove, my hopes would be, to be belov'd again by thee.

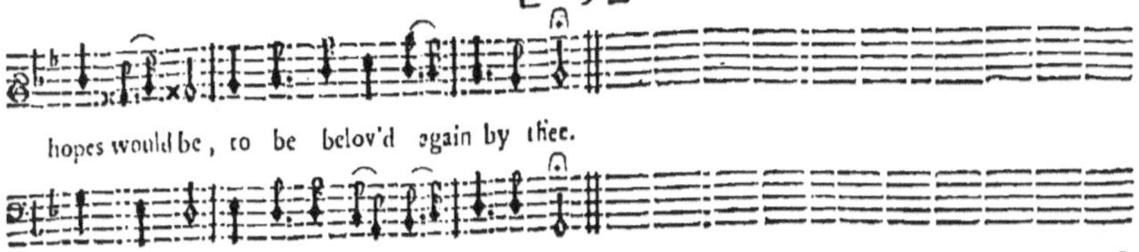

Mr. *Twist.*

II

Ah! should my *Phillis* cruel prove,
And with disdain receive my Love;
Though all my hopes were then in vain,
I'de look on you, and hope again;
And Martyr-like, charm'd with your cause,
Glory to suffer by your laws.

A 2. Vec. Cantus & Bassus

When first I saw fair *Cælia's* Face, so full of Majesty and Grace, As potent Armies do attaque the place, which can't resistance make: So she by pow'r has made her way unto my heart, and there does stay, receiving homage, which I pay.

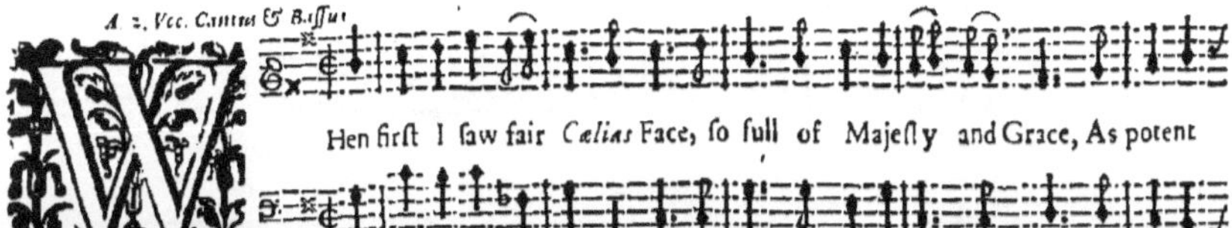

Mr. *James Hart.*

II.
The force of Love, who can withstand;
It is in vain to countermand,
What envious, *Cupid*, has decreed;
Then my poor heart must ever bleed,
'Till you, fair Nymph, by pity mov'd,
My Passion having once approv'd,
Can Love, as now you are belov'd.

III.
It would be gallantry in Love,
If *Cælia* would the act approve;
Where she so long has caus'd a smart,
There to bestow, at length, her heart.
In doing this, fair Saint, you may,
From your blest name, derive a day,
When Lovers unto you shall pray.

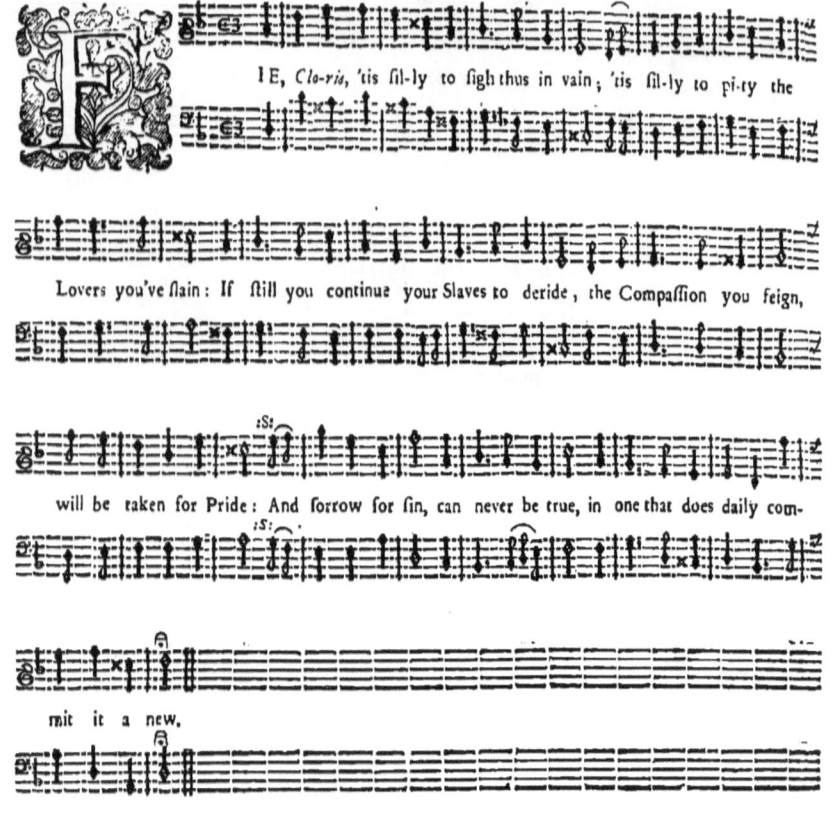

FIE, *Cloris*, 'tis silly to sigh thus in vain, 'tis silly to pity the Lovers you've slain: If still you continue your Slaves to deride, the Compassion you feign, will be taken for Pride: And sorrow for sin, can never be true, in one that does daily commit it anew.

II.

If, while you are Fair, you resolve to be coy,
You may hourly repent, as you hourly destroy;
Yet none will believe you, protest what you will,
That you grieve for the dead, if you daily do kill.
And where are our hopes, when we zealously wooe,
If you vow to abhor what you constantly doe.

III.

Then, *Cloris*, be kinder, and tell me my fate,
For the worst I can suffer's to dy by your hate:
If this you design, never fancy in vain
By your Sighs and your tears, to recal me again:
Nor weep at my Grave, for, I swear, if you do,
As you now laugh at me, I will then laugh at you.

[65]

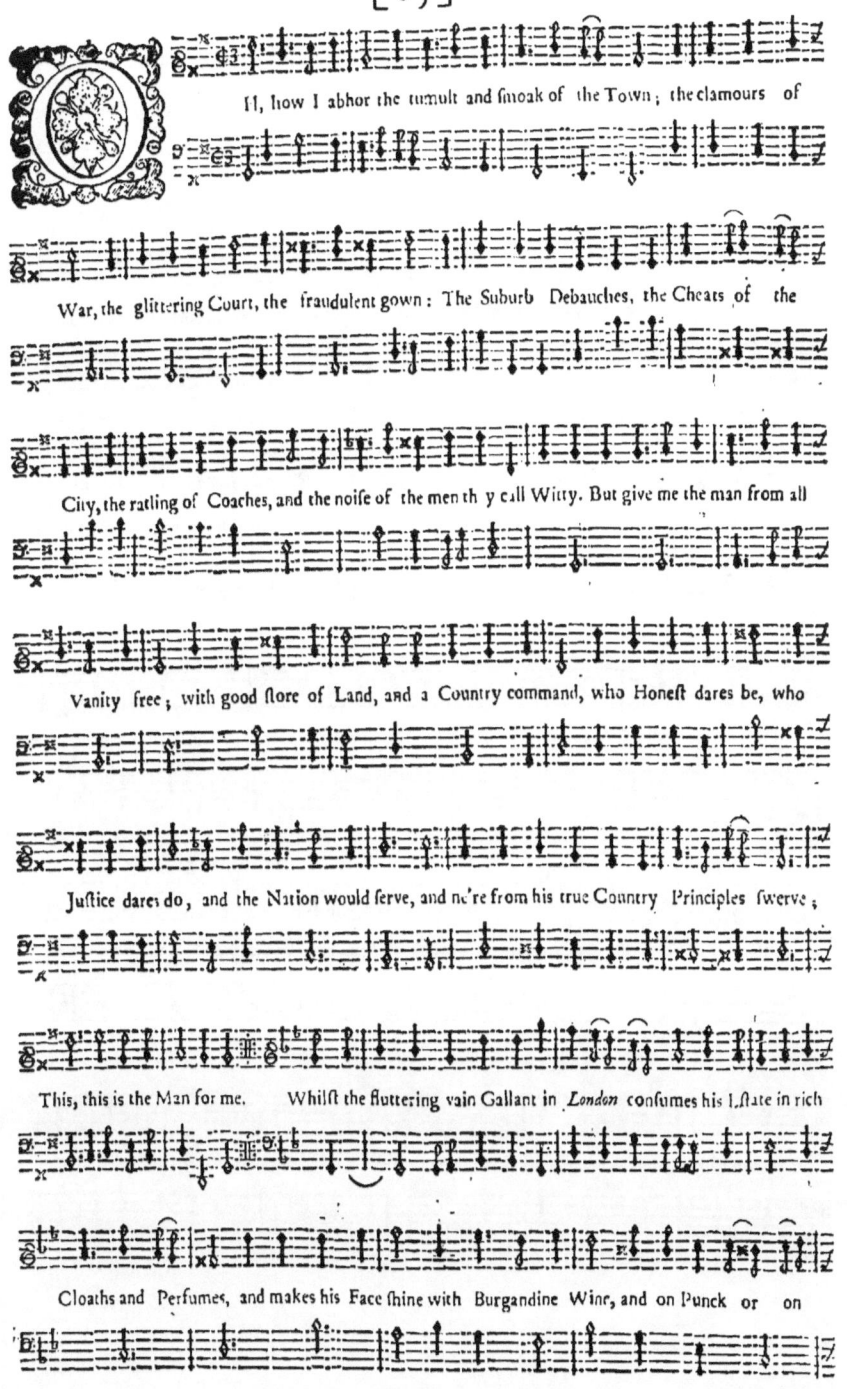

O, how I abhor the tumult and smoak of the Town; the clamours of War, the glittering Court, the fraudulent gown: The Suburb Debauches, the Cheats of the City, the ratling of Coaches, and the noise of the men th y call Witty. But give me the man from all Vanity free, with good store of Land, and a Country command, who Honest dares be, who Justice dares do, and the Nation would serve, and ne're from his true Country Principles swerve; This, this is the Man for me. Whilst the fluttering vain Gallant in *London* consumes his Estate in rich Cloaths and Perfumes, and makes his Face shine with Burgandine Wine, and on Punck or on

Mr. Robert Smith.

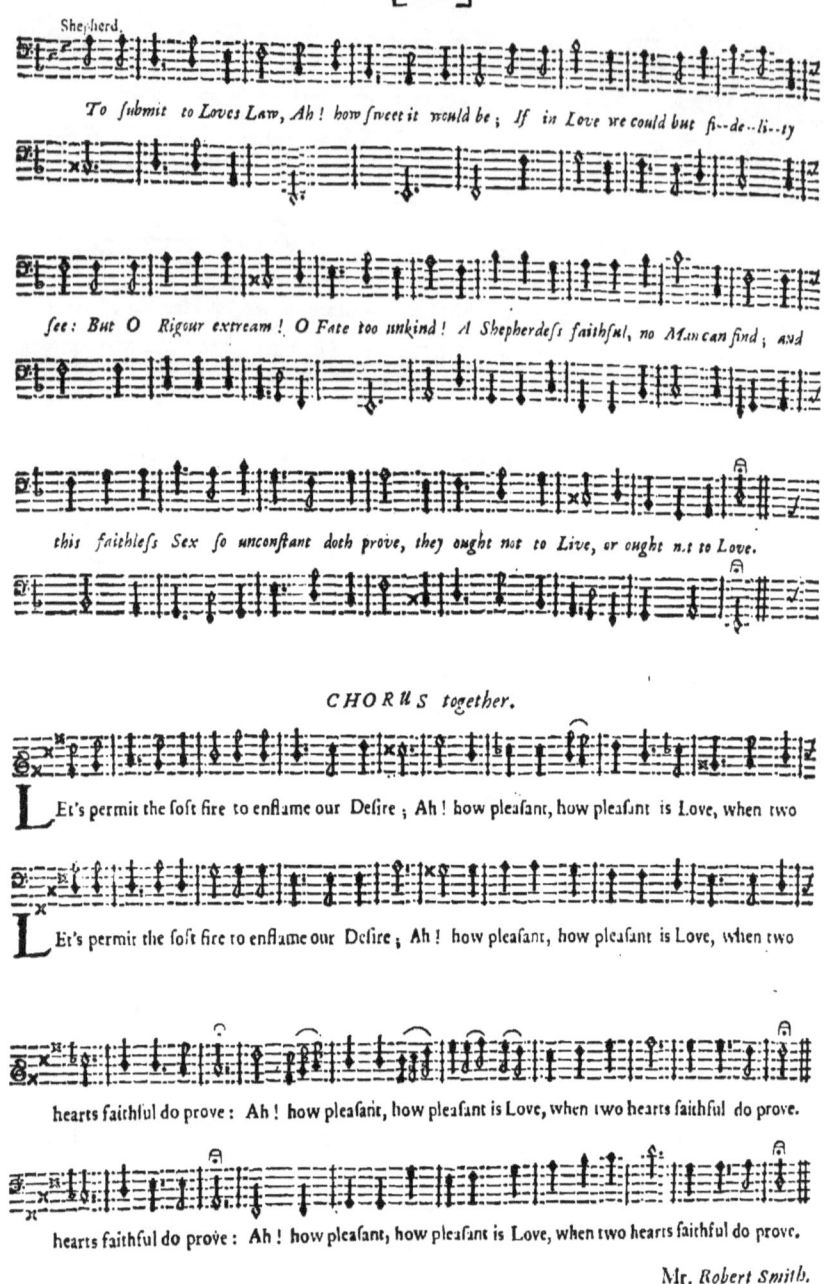

[69]

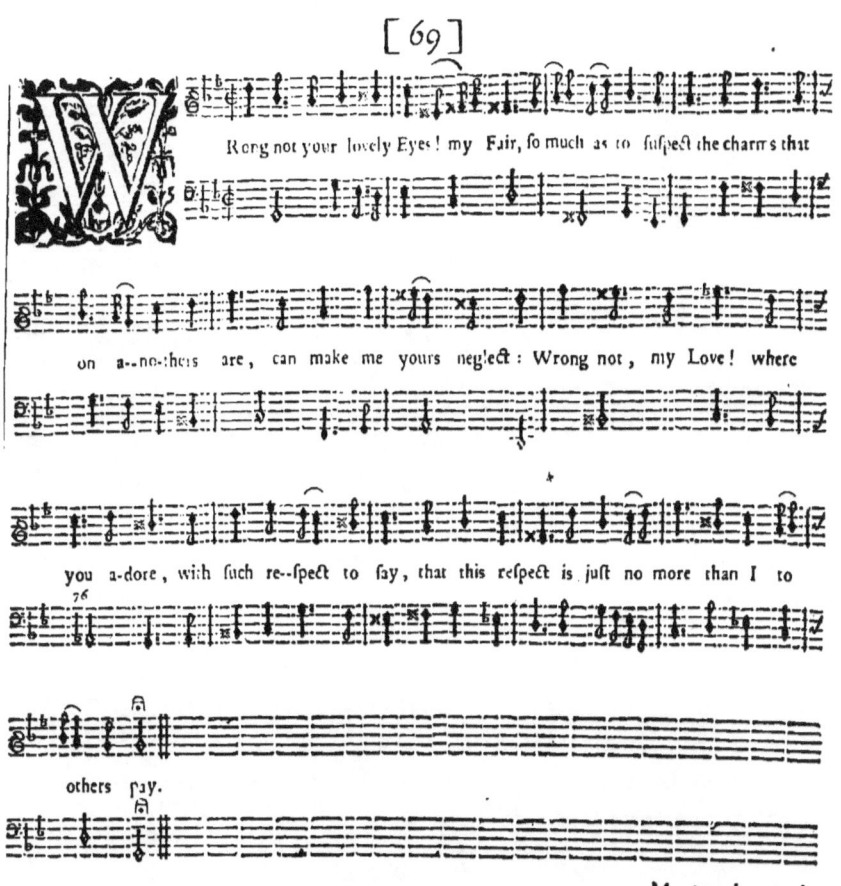

Wrong not your lovely Eyes! my Fair, so much as to suspect the charms that on a--no--thers are, can make me yours neglect: Wrong not, my Love! where you a-dore, with such re--spect to say, that this respect is just no more than I to others pay.

Mr. *Matthew Locke.*

II.
A general desire to please,
  Dwells in all Humane kind;
Such, I am sure, would you confess,
  In your own Heart you find:
And if the light of others Eyes,
  To follow, I appear,
'Tis that to yours a Sacrifice
  More worthy I may bear.

III.
Your Beauty thus, more triumph gains,
  I nothing from it take;
But only of your glorious Chains,
  My self more worthy make:
Then is this fear of yours but vain,
  You cannot be betray'd;
Whatever Trophies I can gain,
  Must at your feet be laid.

IV.
Let other Beauties apprehend
  To lose their Lovers Heart;
But you have charms, that may pretend
  To scorn Loves utmost art:
To others therefore, you, the show
  Of Love may well endure;
Since only yours my heart, you know,
  In your own Eyes secure.

T

AH, fading Joy! how quickly art thou past, yet we thy ruin hast? And what too soon would dye, help to destroy; as if the cares of Humane life were free, we seek out new, And follow Fate, which will too fast pursue. In vain does Natures bounteous hand supply what pevish Mortals to themselves deny. See how, on ev'ry bough the Birds ex-press in their wild Notes, their happiness: Not anxious, how to get or spare, they on their Mother Nature lay their care. Why then should Man, the Lord of all below, such troubles chuse to know, as none of all his subjects undergo?

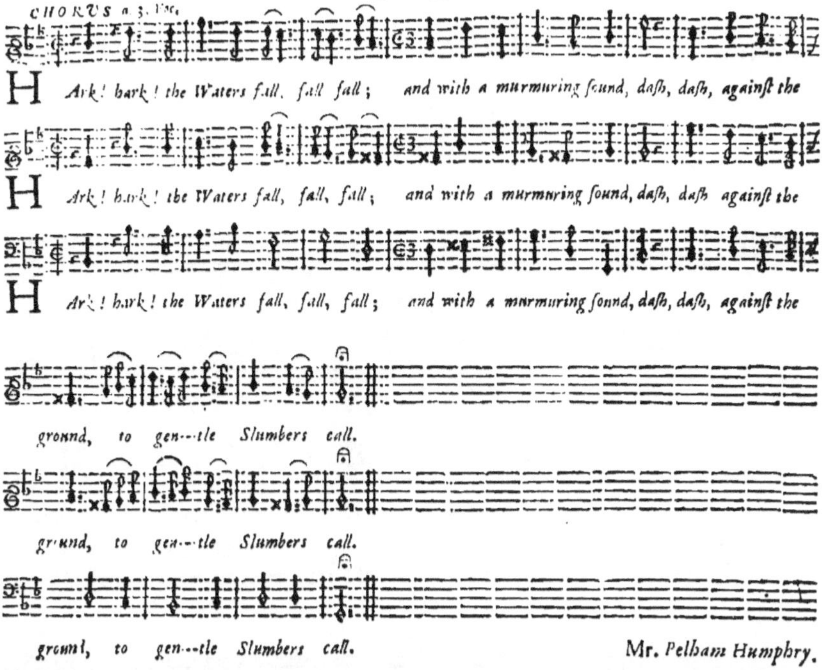

[71]

CHORUS a 3 Voc.

Hark! hark! the Waters fall, fall fall; and with a murmuring sound, dash, dash, against the

Hark! hark! the Waters fall, fall, fall; and with a murmuring sound, dash, dash against the

Hark! hark! the Waters fall, fall, fall; and with a murmuring sound, dash, dash, against the

ground, to gen--tle Slumbers call.

ground, to gen--tle Slumbers call.

ground, to gen--tle Slumbers call.

Mr. *Pelham Humphry.*

What Sighs and Groans now fills my breast, and suff.rs me to take no rest

for my *Carmelia*? Oh! she's gone, and left me here to Mourn alone; But, is she dead? then I'le go

see, if in her Grave there's room for mee.

Mr. *Robert Smith.*

II. O cruel Fate! that so design'd
To take her, but leave me be behind:
And you, O Death! whose quick Alarms
Hath snatch'd her rudely from my Arms,
Could you not find a way for mee
To my *Carmelia's* Breast to flee.

III. Dye, then *Anselmo*! why should'st stay,
Since 'tis *Carmelia* show'd the way?
O Dye, more faster, do not live
That dearest Nymph for to survive!
O now, dear soul, I come, I flye,
Always to live with you, I dye.

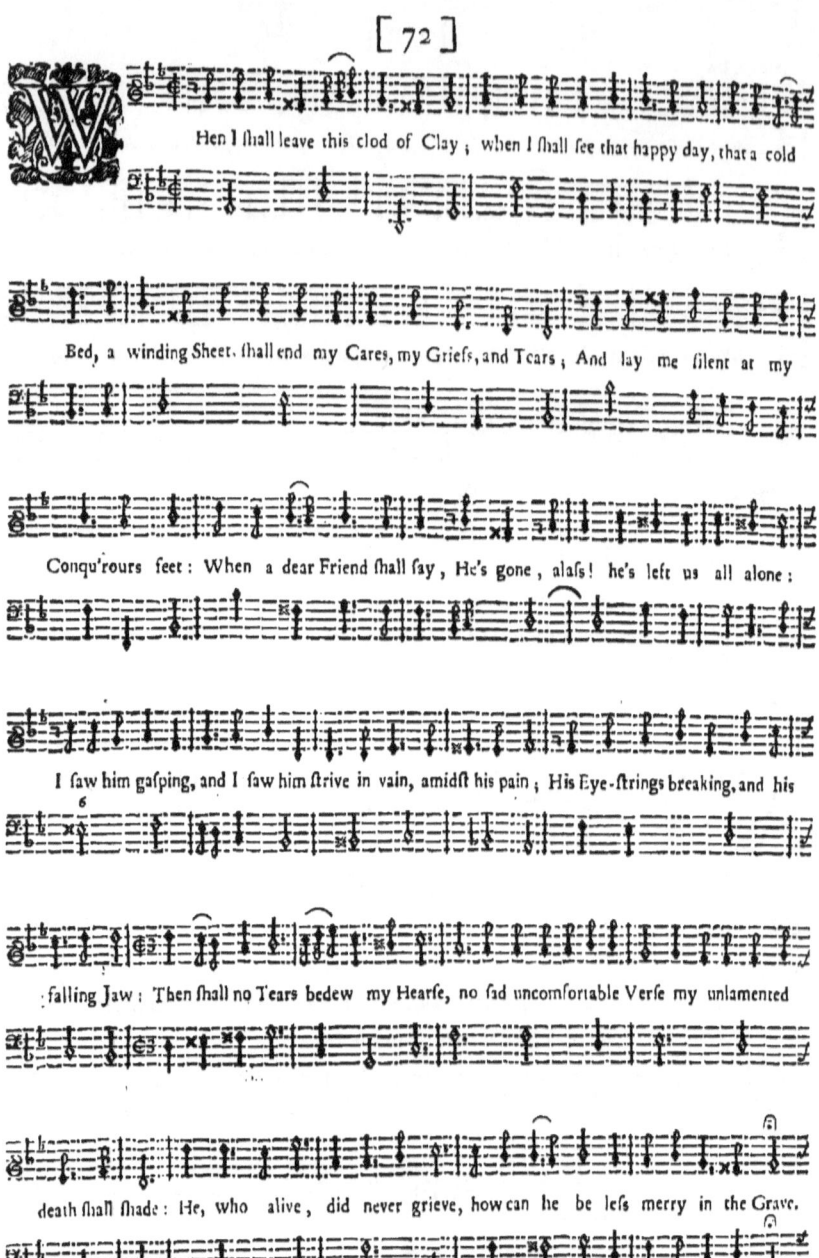

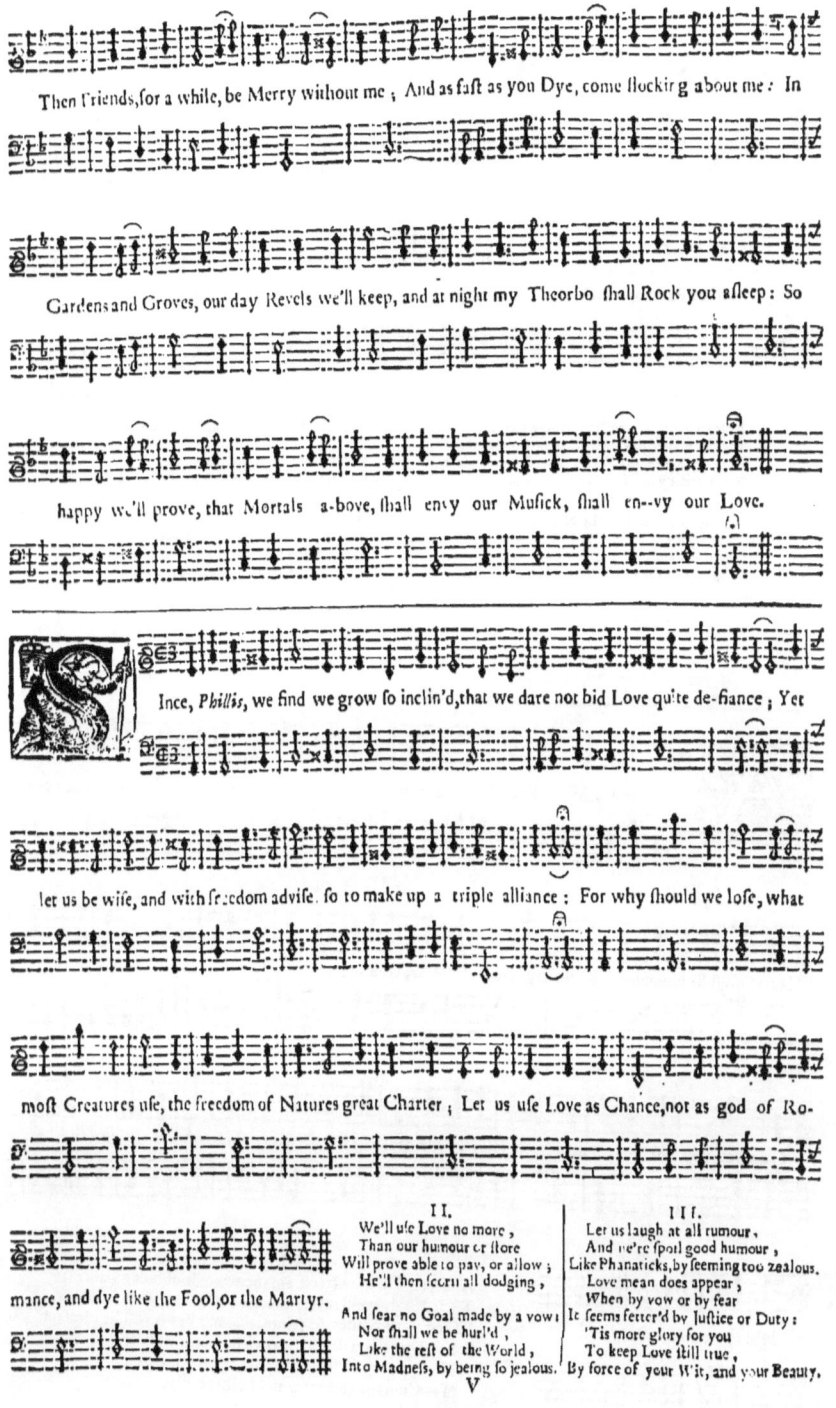

Then Friends, for a while, be Merry without me ; And as fast as you Dye, come flocking about me: In

Gardens and Groves, our day Revels we'll keep, and at night my Theorbo shall Rock you asleep: So

happy we'll prove, that Mortals a-bove, shall envy our Musick, shall en--vy our Love.

Ince, *Phillis*, we find we grow so inclin'd, that we dare not bid Love quite de-fiance ; Yet

let us be wise, and with freedom advise. so to make up a triple alliance : For why should we lose, what

most Creatures use, the freedom of Natures great Charter ; Let us use Love as Chance, not as god of Ro-

mance, and dye like the Fool, or the Martyr.

II.
We'll use Love no more ,
Than our humour or store
Will prove able to pay, or allow ;
He'll then scorn all dodging ,
And fear no Goal made by a vow;
Nor shall we be hurl'd ,
Like the rest of the World ,
Into Madness, by being so jealous.

III.
Let us laugh at all rumour ,
And we're spoil good humour ,
Like Phanaticks, by seeming too zealous.
Love mean does appear ,
When by vow or by fear
It seems fetter'd by Justice or Duty :
'Tis more glory for you
To keep Love still true ,
By force of your Wit, and your Beauty.

[74]

IF languishing! yes, without language can move, I have long told my *Phillis*, I dye for her Love: Ah, pity that Passion, which words cannot speak! could I tell what I feel, my poor heart would not break.

Mr. *Isaac Blackwell*.

II.
I plead not desert, for the Beauty I serve;
But 'tis nobler to give what none can deserve:
In the croud of my Rival's, who sigh and adore,
None merit you less, or can value you more.

III.
To purchase a Smile, or a glance from your Eyes,
Both my Fortune and Life were too little a prize:
But if to desert you can only be kind,
Like Heaven, you must to your self be confin'd.

IV.
All joys are so order'd by Natures great doom,
That what e're we possess from another must come:
Then, *Phillis*, what pleasure with me may you prove,
What s wanting in worth, is supply'd by my Love.

V.
Our life is uneasie, and sullen our state,
Ev'ry Minute is angry, and full of debate:
But kind was the power, who, our quiet to keep,
Sent Love to relieve us, and lay us asleep.

VI.
In Oceans of Care, though against Tide we Sail,
Yet our Love from behind us supplies a fresh gale:
The passage is pleasant, but, ah! 'tis too short;
Let us live while we may, we must part at the port.

AH! what shall we do, when our Eyes are surrounded with Beauties, like you! our Hearts must be wounded: If we flye from the War, your darts do o're-take us; and if we stay there, your Captives you make us. Engaging or Flying, we are sure to be slain; then who is so mad such a Fight to maintain?

II.
And yet, Oh how sweet are the wounds of your glances!
Then Nobly we'll meet, though we fall by your Lances:
When your Smiles do evince, that our death will be pleasant,
Better Dye like a Prince, than Live like a Peasant.
If engaging or flying, we are certain to Dye,
'Tis Courage to Fight, and Folly to Fly.

TOM of Bedlam.   *For a Bass alone.*

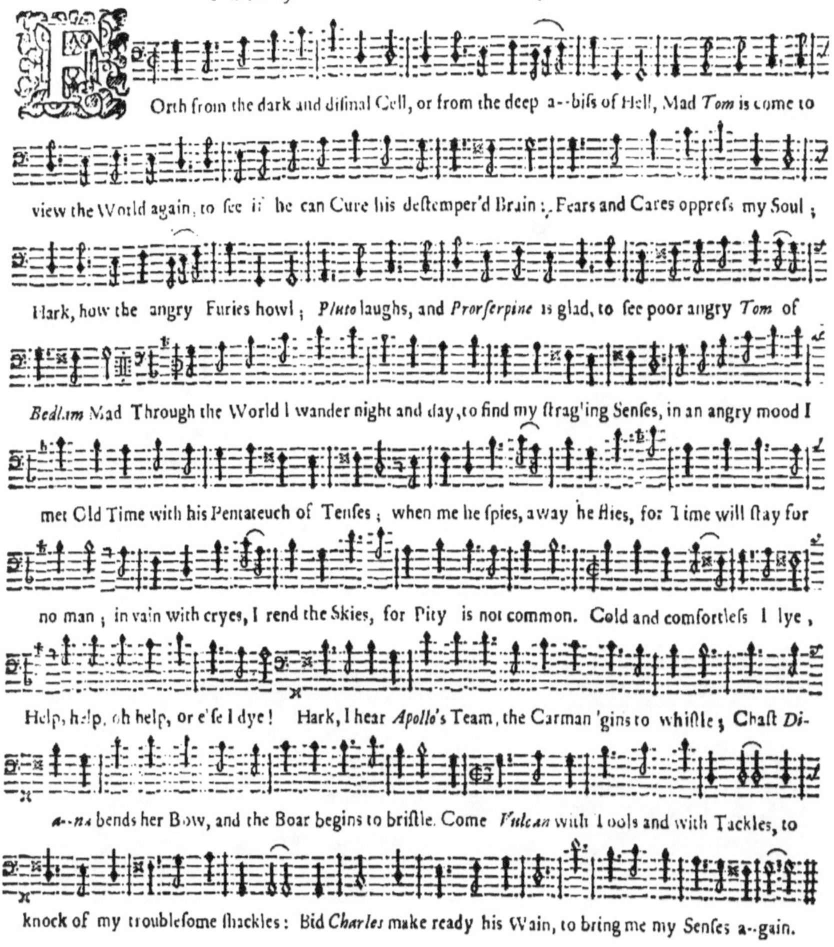

Forth from the dark and dismal Cell, or from the deep a-biss of Hell, Mad *Tom* is come to view the World again, to see if he can Cure his destemper'd Brain: Fears and Cares oppress my Soul; Hark, how the angry Furies howl; *Pluto* laughs, and *Proserpine* is glad, to see poor angry *Tom* of Bedlam Mad Through the World I wander night and day, to find my strag'ling Senses, in an angry mood I met Old Time with his Pentateuch of Tenses; when me he spies, away he flies, for Time will stay for no man; in vain with cryes, I rend the Skies, for Pity is not common. Cold and comfortless I lye, Help, help, oh help, or e'se I dye! Hark, I hear *Apollo's* Team, the Carman 'gins to whistle; Chast Di-a-na bends her Bow, and the Boar begins to bristle. Come *Vulcan* with Tools and with Tackles, to knock of my troublesome shackles: Bid *Charles* make ready his Wain, to bring me my Senses a-gain.

II.

Last Night I heard the Dog-star bark,
  Mars met *Venus* in the Dark;
Lymping *Vulcan* heat an Iron Bar,
  And furiously made at the great God of War.
Mars with his Weapon laid about,
  Lymping *Vulcan* had got the Gout;
His broad Horns did hang so in his light,
  That he could not see to aim his blows aright,
Mercury the nimble Post of Heaven
  Stood still to see the Quarrel;
Gorrel-belly'd *Bacchus*, Gyant-like,
  Bestrid a Strong-beer Barrel:
To me he Drank, I did him thank,

But I could drink no Sider;
He drank whole Butts, 'till he burst his Guts,
  But mine was ne're the wider.
Poor *Tom* is very Dry;
  A little Drink, for Charity:
Hark! I hear *Acteon's* Hounds,
  The Hunts-man Hoops and Hollows;
Ringwood, Rockwood, Jowler, Bowman,
  All the Chace doth follow.
The Man in the Moon drinks Clarret,
  Eats Powder'd-Beef, Turnep, and Carret·
But a Cup of Malligo Sack
  Will fire the Bush at his Back.

A. 2. Voci Canini & Bassus.

Come away, to'th'r Glass, he's a temperate Ass, that refuses his brimmer of Rhenish; while our Bottles go round, a new way we have found, both our Heads, and our Veins to replenish: We'll be witty and brave, when our Noddles are full, whilst the Sober young Fop is but prudently dull.

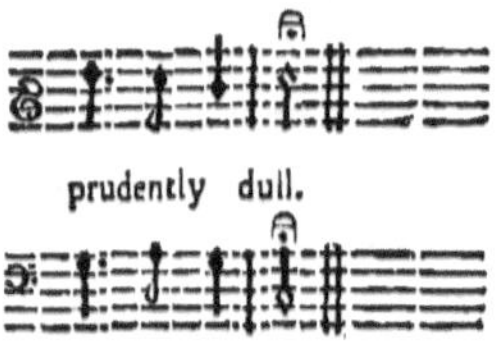

II.
Thus with Wenches and Wine
Our Hearts we'll refine
From the Dross of the Melancholly City;
We care not a Louse
For the dull Coffee-house,
'Tis the Tavern that makes a Man Witty:
Then in spight of misfortunes,
Thus happy we are,
In a Jolly brave Soul,
That's a stranger to care.

Tis the Grape that dis-covers the Passionate Lovers, and makes the coy Miss to resign: To the *Rose* then repair, to *Canary*, to cheer our Souls, and our Spirits refine.

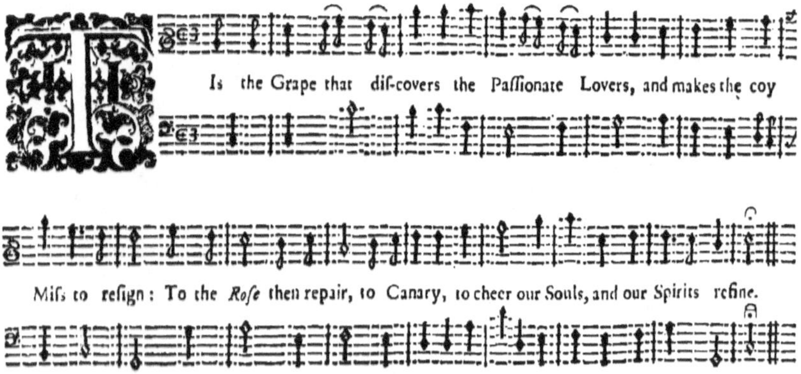

Mr. *Robert Smith*.

[77]

A DIALOGUE between NATURE and SORROW.

Mr. *Robert Smith*.

CELADON on DELIA's Singing: A Pastoral.

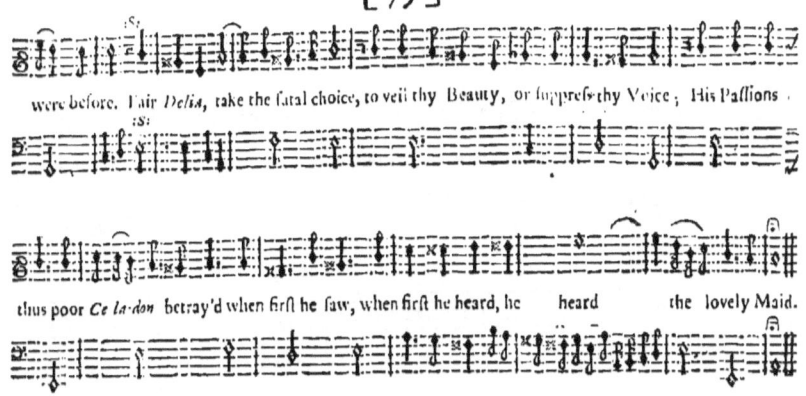

CHORUS.

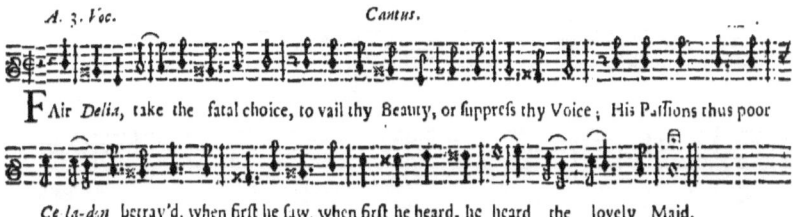

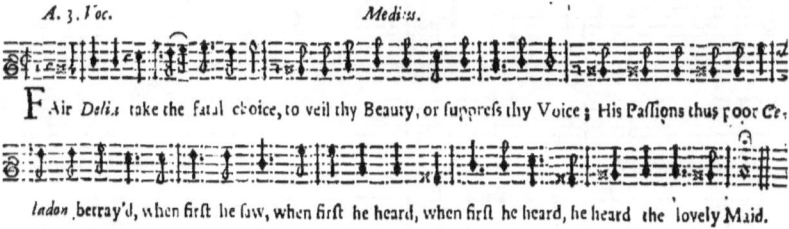

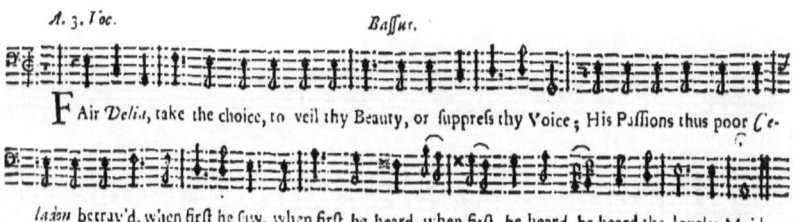

Mr. *William Gregorie.*

[80]

A DIALOGUE between THIRSIS and DORINDA.

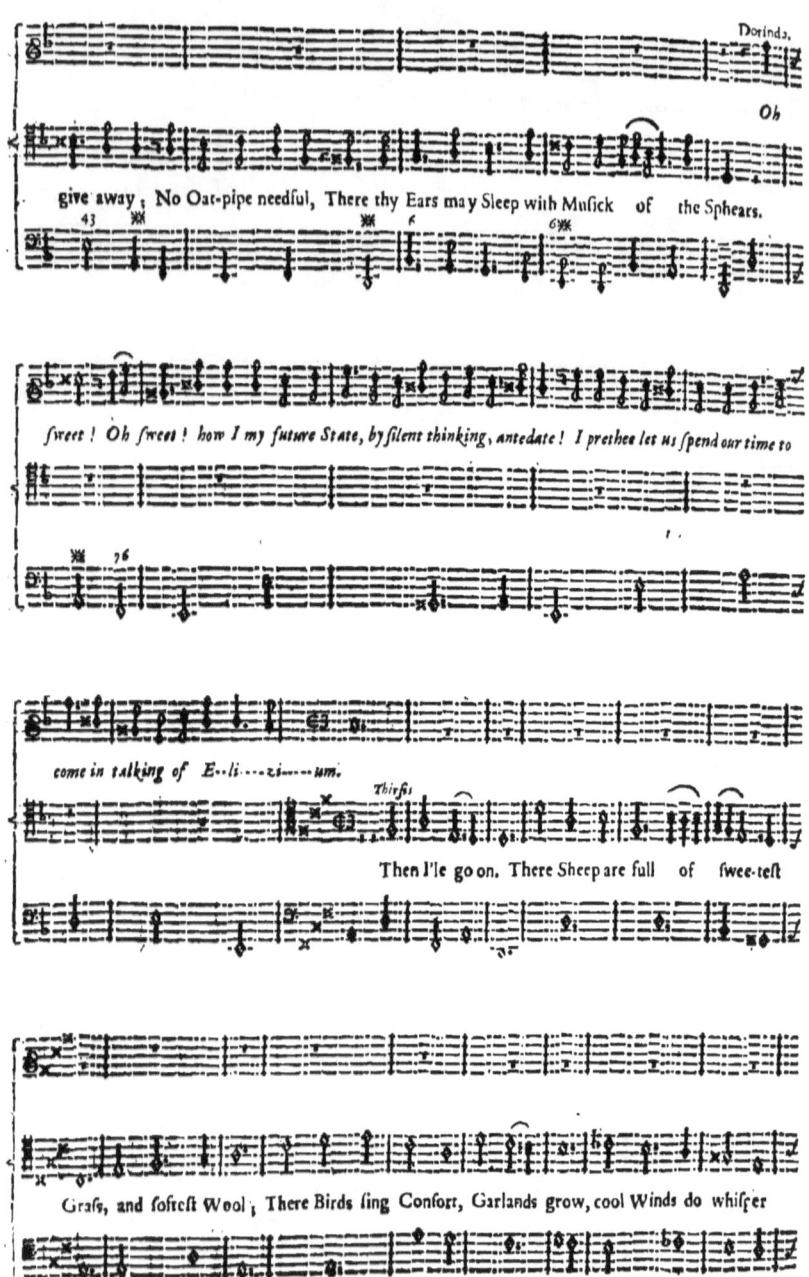

[85]

A DIALOGUE between APOLLO and NEPTUNE:
Occasioned by the unfortunate Death of the Right Honourable
EDWARD, Earl of Sandwich.

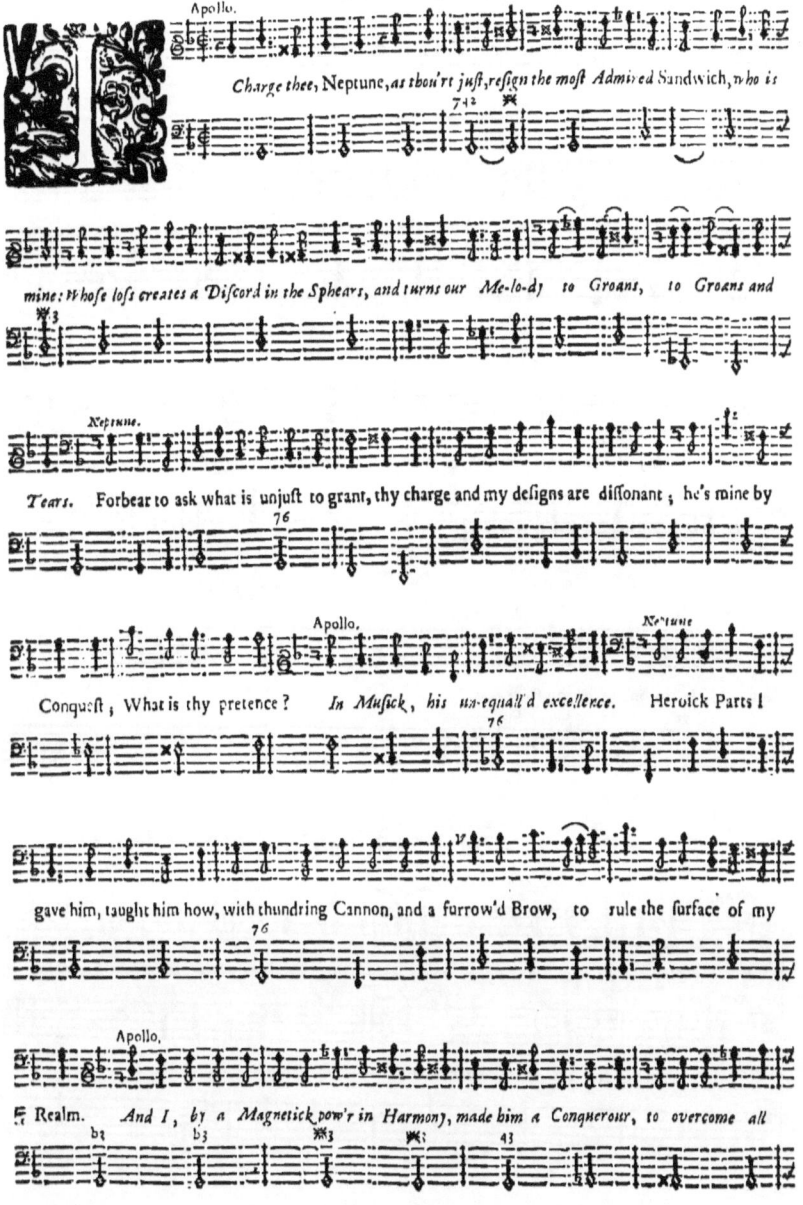

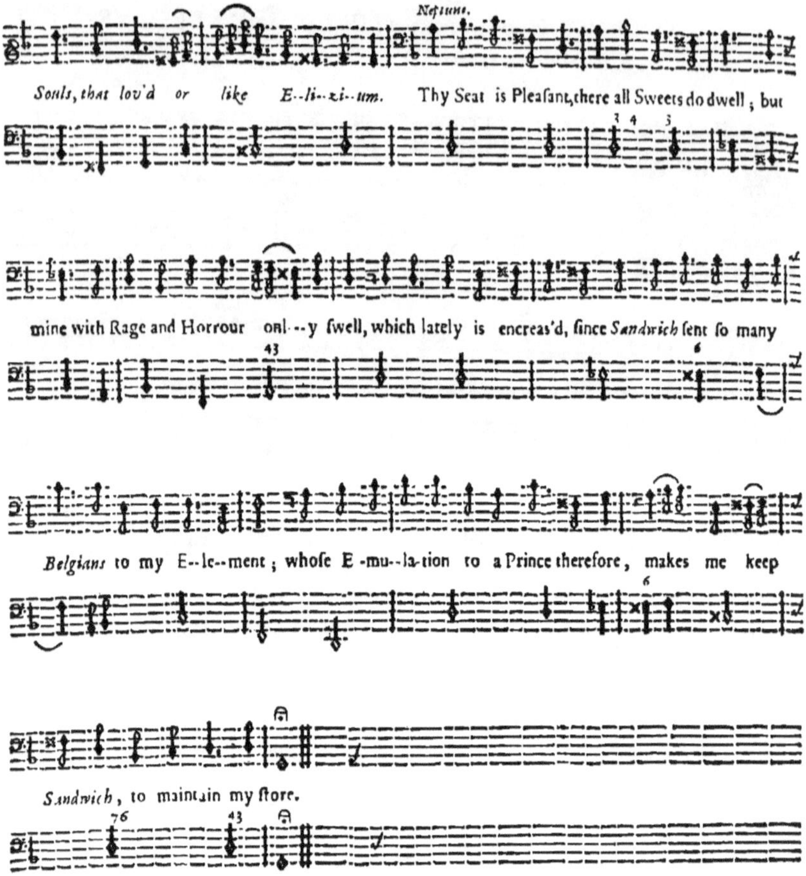

[86]

Neptune.

Souls, that lov'd or like E--li--zi--um. Thy Seat is Pleasant, there all Sweets do dwell; but mine with Rage and Horrour onl--y swell, which lately is encreas'd, since *Sandwich* sent so many *Belgians* to my E--le--ment; whose E--mu--la--tion to a Prince therefore, makes me keep *Sandwich*, to maintain my store.

CHORUS *together.*

Apollo.
WE'll Sing his Re--qui--em by some murm'------ring Brook, on which, as th' emblem of our

Neptune.
WE'll Sing his Re--qui--em by some murm'------ring Brook, on which,

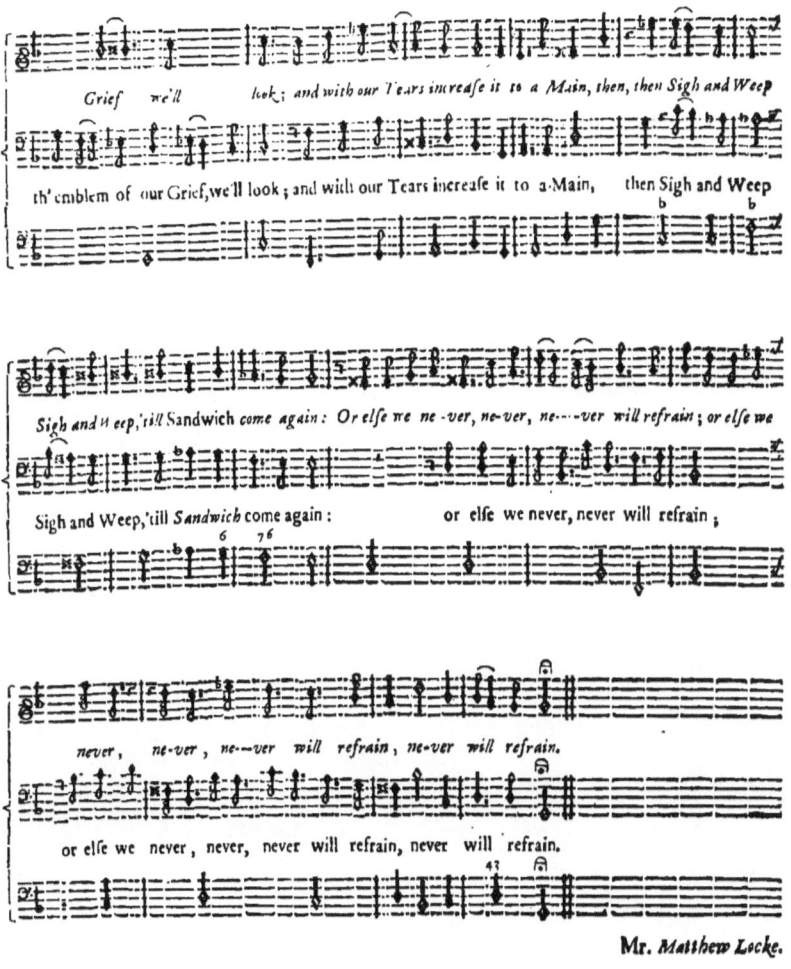

FINIS.

www.ingramcontent.com/pod-product-compliance
Lightning Source LLC
Chambersburg PA
CBHW020311240426
43673CB00039B/770